Hard at Play

THE UNIVERSITY OF MASSACHUSETTS PRESS, AMHERST

& THE STRONG MUSEUM, ROCHESTER, NEW YORK

# Hard at Play

## Leisure in America, 1840–1940

**Edited by Kathryn Grover**

Copyright © 1992 by The Strong Museum

All rights reserved

Printed in the United States of America

LC 91–39908

ISBN 0–87023–792–6 (cloth); 793–4 (pbk.)

Designed by Edith Kearney

Set in Adobe Minion by Keystone Typesetting, Inc.

Printed and bound by Thomson-Shore

Library of Congress Cataloging-in-Publication Data

Hard at play : leisure in America, 1840–1940 / edited by Kathryn Grover.

    p.  cm.

  "This collection of essays originated from the Symposium "American Play, 1820–1900" which took place at the Strong Museum on November 6 and 7, 1987"—Introduction.

  Includes index.

  ISBN 0–87023–792–6 (alk. paper). — ISBN 0–87023–793–4 (pbk. : alk. paper)

  1. Leisure—United States—History—Congresses.   2. Leisure—Social aspects—United States—History—Congresses.   3. Recreation—United States—History—Congresses.   4. Recreation—Social aspects—United States—History—Congresses.   I. Grover, Kathryn, 1953–   .   II. Symposium "American Play, 1820–1900" (1987 : Strong Museum)

  GV53.H28   1992

  790'.01'350973—dc20    91–39908   CIP

British Library Cataloguing in Publication data are available.

Unless otherwise indicated, the illustrations in this book are from the Strong Museum collections.

Frontispiece: "Snap the Whip" (reversed), by Winslow Homer, *Harper's Weekly*, 20 September 1873.

# Contents

Hard at Play

# Introduction

## Are We Having Fun Yet?

KATHERINE C. GRIER

This collection of essays originated from the symposium "American Play: 1820–1900," which took place at the Strong Museum on November 6 and 7, 1987. The symposium, part of an ongoing series of scholarly meetings the museum has organized since 1984, differed from its predecessors in that it was not associated with the opening of a new exhibition on a related topic. Rather, "American Play" grew out of a perceived need on the part of a number of staff members, including me, who were interested in furthering the museum's interpretation of the history of leisure pursuits and children's play. Previous exhibitions at the Strong, particularly *Fit for America* and *Century of Childhood, 1820–1920*, had already begun this interpretive project. Organized as an informal work group, we proposed a series of four exhibits on topics in the history of play in the United States. Harvey Green, then head of the museum's interpretation department, agreed that sponsoring a symposium on the topic, with an open call for papers, would aid the exhibit research. Because the history of organized sport is well covered by the North American Society for Sport History and because the Strong's own collections and the proposed exhibitions emphasized forms of leisure other than organized sport, the call for papers specifically excluded this enormous subject matter.

Our request for proposals eventually generated almost eighty responses, representing a wide variety of subject concerns and approaches. This collection of essays reflects that variety and results from the revision for publication of ten of the twelve symposium presentations. The wide range of topics suggests, in truth, that the concepts of "leisure" and "play" themselves elude simple definition. In this society, "leisure" is essentially defined negatively; it is opposed to the business of earning a living. We commonly think of the term as connoting adult activity that is voluntary and takes place during "free time." Children do not have "leisure time" until they also "go to work"—that is, until they attend school. Some activities taken up as leisure are income-producing work for others, particularly certain handcrafts or hobbies—gardening or weekend farming, making furniture, or fixing up an old car, for example. And the activities that people undertake as acceptable leisure are heavily mediated by such considerations as social class (investment bankers may tinker with old cars as a hobby, but they lose social status when they take up auto repair as a second career). "Play" is a more encompassing concept, seemingly less age specific and connoting everything from participation in an organized game to the childhood activity of "pretending." In his book-length essay *Homo Ludens* (1950), European historian Johan Huizinga questioned the notion that "play" and "work" were always in opposition. He suggested that "play" was a condition rather than an activity, a state of mind that can find joy and refreshment in challenging activities as well as relaxing ones, in work as well as in leisure.

The complexities of simply defining "leisure" and "play" indicate that the scholarly study of leisure and play is serious stuff indeed. It requires mastery of interdisciplinary methods, as Bernard Mergen notes in his essay "Children's Play in American Autobiographies, 1820–1914." "The inner history of childhood—history from the diaper up—requires the methods of the literary critic and the ethnographer, as well as those of the historian," he asserts. Mergen's research also confronts the problem of gathering information about a stage in the life cycle where most surviving accounts are secondhand, filtered through the eyes of an observing adult, or are recounted firsthand after a considerable amount of time has passed. Other essays in this volume demonstrate the complex relationship of leisure to work, and how the constraints of social class, gender, and ethnicity affected how many—perhaps most—individuals participated in both folk play and the "leisure revolution" in the late nineteenth and twentieth centuries. All of the contributions suggest that the student of leisure in America contends with subject matter that crisscrosses the turf of the history of the American family and changes in the typical life courses of its individual members; the development of modern consumer society; and even the history of American religion.

Dwight Hoover's essay "Roller-skating toward Industrialism," which wins my vote for the best title in this collection, demonstrates

how leisure history, the history of business and industry, and the study of American consumer society are bound together. The manufacture of roller skates in the early 1880s, Hoover argues, was a prototype for modern industrial practice in Muncie, Indiana. Businessmen raised capital from outside the community, they assembled the skates from parts manufactured elsewhere, and they sold the finished product in faraway places. The roller-skating craze in the community also illustrates that, while technology and other material circumstances may have created the necessary preconditions for a new form of leisure, the social and cultural phenomenon of the "fad" actually powered the small economic boom the roller skate instigated.

Hoover's essay demonstrates how small things are at the root of great historical change as individuals and communities experience it. It reinforces the insights of Neil McKendrick, John Brewer, and J. H. Plumb on the character of the consumer revolution. *The Birth of a Consumer Society* (1982) analyzes late eighteenth-century England, arguably the first true consumer society. The authors remind us that "profits—even small fortunes" were made from "very modest artefacts indeed" and that "the first industries to blossom in the Industrial Revolution were more characteristically to be found in the consumer sector . . . pins and nails, buttons and forks, knobs and knockers, pots and pans, hats and coats, gloves and shoes." In this instance, the Muncie Roller Skate contributed to the consumer revolution and its companion revolution in commercialized leisure.

Glenn Uminowicz and David Gerber also tie the history of leisure to established arenas of historical inquiry—the histories of American religion and ethnic groups and the chronicling of the formation and evolution of the American middle classes.

Gerber's " 'The Germans Take Care of Our Celebrations' " well describes the shape of middle-class life before the Civil War, including the long work hours (perhaps unusually long in the commercial port of Buffalo, New

York), the lack of public amenities in the urban centers that the new world of business created, and the moral universe that constrained the development of a rich and varied recreational life among the classes most benefiting materially from commercial and industrial development. The middle-class "condemnation of excessive stimulation," both mental and physical, insisted that rationality be applied to amusements as it was to the serious world of work. Further, domesticity isolated women and children from public life by proclaiming the necessary purity of women as both gatekeepers of the innocence of children and against the outside world.

Gerber recounts the impact of the new German immigrants, refugees from the political turmoil of the 1840s, on Buffalo's cultural life: they created a vibrant local music scene, introduced German ideas about physical training through *Turner* societies, and organized *feste*, which introduced new ideas about family entertainment in public places and even offered an alternative view of the consumption of alcohol—moderate consumption of lager beer. Buffalo's middle-class citizens not only accepted but participated eagerly in these new activities. Gerber attributes this acceptance to a number of factors, including the skill of educated German immigrants at "impression management." Fundamentally, however, he sees it as a reflection of a crisis in the culture that middle-class Americans had strived so hard to create, a sense that the obsession with commerce led to "a cultural barrenness that flattened and . . . 'disenchanted' the world." If so, this sense of malaise and receptivity to a leisure "cure" is contemporaneous with, and related to, the concern with physical well-being and health reform in antebellum America.

Uminowicz's essay, "Recreation in a Christian America: Ocean Grove and Asbury Park, New Jersey, 1869–1914," continues the saga of middle-class culture and leisure. It recounts the rise of two of the most important "respectable resorts" of the late nineteenth century, tying their appearance and viability to one of the dynamic tensions in middle-class Protestant culture. Such resorts—and there were many scattered across the United States—were a creative response to perceived needs for recreation on the part of genteel, middle-class Americans. The Protestant establishment of ministers which they supported agreed with doctors and advice authors that leisure pursuits were necessary to personal moral and physical development (part of the legacy of perfectionism) while it also encouraged one's constant vigilance against individual dissipation resulting from contact with immoral pastimes and entertainment. How could the requirements of personal relaxation and constant moral vigilance be met? The respectable resort, where leisure pursuits were already edited for family consumption, resolved the paradox.

Eventually the middle-class quest for suitable leisure consisted of two points of view, with resorts to match. Liberal Protestantism de-emphasized the overtly religious and embraced selectively the mass culture of commercial resorts and popular theatrical and printed media. The secularized impulses that underlay the creation of "family resorts" such as Asbury Park (and the appearance of self-consciously "decent" popular theater such as vaudeville) still operate in the self-conscious realm of "decent family entertainment" today. This sector of the leisure industry includes such resorts as Disney World and media such as cable "family channels." On the consumer side of the equation, one finds the self-appointed watchdog groups that monitor "decency" in the movies and in popular music lyrics.

According to Uminowicz, the Methodist resort of Ocean Grove represented the conservative Protestant quest for a "Christian America," with forms of leisure appropriate to it. A place for adherents of the holiness movement to "recreate" spiritually as well as physically, Ocean Grove was governed by an association that insisted on strict observation of the Sabbath and forbade such forms of leisure as card-playing at home, social dancing, and all forms of the popular theater. The quest for

Christian recreation also continues. Fundamentalism and Pentecostalism have demonstrated renewed vigor in the late twentieth century, and some of the more ingenious and entrepreneurial conservative Protestant leaders have offered extended critiques of American popular culture (such as Pentecostalist minister Jimmy Swaggart's attack on rock 'n' roll) and, occasionally, alternative forms of popular amusement such as Heritage U.S.A., the religious theme park constructed in North Carolina by the P.T.L. ministry.

"Recreation in a Christian America" reminds us that late Victorian culture was still largely shaped by the Protestantism that helped articulate it in the 1820s and 1830s, and that middle-class participation was essential to the creation of a "truly mass leisure industry." The framework of thought that linked spiritual health with physical health is part of the broadly deterministic cast of mind that also hoped to shape moral family life through proper domestic architecture and interior decor. The essay's treatment of the public architecture and spaces of the two resorts demonstrates that, like in utopian communities, the architecture and space planning in resorts could be used to articulate a vision of the ideal world or to provide a model for modern working cities, as Asbury Park's pioneering incorporation of water and sewerage systems did. Again, this vision of the resort as model city recalls the commercial utopianism of the Disney enterprise.

While Hoover, Gerber, and Uminowicz treat the history of leisure in communities, Bernard Mergen and Andrew Gulliford direct our attention to the informal, personal play of childhood. Mergen's sensitive essay offers a sampler of children's playful interactions with each other, with the environment around them, and with favorite books, toys, and even imaginary friends. Mergen also discusses the place of adults in these memoirs of childhood play. In the seventy-eight autobiographies of his sample, adults figured as powerful but "easily avoided" figures, rarely as actual playmates or companions and never as the principals of or-

ganized recreation for children. In the second half of the nineteenth century, childhood was widely recognized as a special stage of life, yet organized activities for children (at least middle-class children) seem to have impinged little on the freedom to play. At the risk of waxing nostalgic, one is tempted to see these decades as a golden age of middle-class childhood.

Gulliford's "Fox and Geese in the School Yard" offers additional detail on the character of free play among children in the late nineteenth and early twentieth centuries. Many of the folk games mentioned in Mergen's autobiographies of childhood appear again in the space of the rural school yard. Gulliford's paper is especially valuable for its documentation of the traditional games of immigrant children and for its discussion of the role of school-yard play in encouraging voluntary assimilation as children tried to bridge language gaps so that they might join in games together. He also reminds us of the place of the rural school in rural adult recreation. The historical role of schools, both rural and in urban neighborhoods, as facilitators of community-wide leisure is worth further examination.

Further, Gulliford's discussion of dangerous or "deep" play introduces another level to our contemporary understanding of the serious character of children's play. Mergen too mentions a variety of dangerous activities undertaken as play—in one instance, competitive diving for pennies led to one boy's drowning. It is clear (although parents try not to acknowledge it) that deep play remains an important part of group socialization among children. Today deep play is more likely to take the form of skateboard dares than of catching and killing rattlesnakes in the school yard. Gulliford's essay raises the question whether both boys and girls engaged in dangerous school-yard play in the past, or was it then, as it appears to be now, largely part of the informal socialization of boys by other boys into the culturally prescribed characteristics of masculinity?

The work of Gulliford and Mergen raises

questions about the study of play in the American past that have particular bearing upon those of us engaged in collecting and interpreting American material culture. For the fact of the matter is that much significant play took place without objects at all, or with objects that were improvised from materials at hand and discarded when the game was over. Like more formal "historical performance" (dances, parlor musicales, or even professional theatrical performances), informal play involves action in space and time. Recovering such forms of play and interpreting them to public audiences is difficult for museums, and the traditional exhibition is probably inappropriate for such purposes. Programs or videotapes that reconstruct documented performances of children's folk games are more suitable and lively media for presenting past forms of American play. Further, it behooves scholars of play to preserve current forms of folk play on videotape or film.

Is children's play a type of leisure per se, or is it more accurately characterized as the work of children? In his essay, Mergen suggests that children quickly learned to define their activities with the same dichotomy that characterizes adult thought about leisure or play. "As a child grows in self-awareness," he writes, "so does his appreciation of the nature of play. He learns that play—purposeless, frivolous, and limited in time—is opposed by work—purposeful, serious, and ongoing. Yet play is tolerated, even demanded by parents and other adults."

This fundamental cultural distinction, which did not acknowledge the possibility of "play" embedded in the work process, was the object of considerable elaboration by a group of psychologists, sociologists, and educators in the late nineteenth and twentieth centuries. Their thought about the nature of play and its place in human development forms the subject of Donald J. Mrozek's "The Natural Limits of Unstructured Play, 1880–1914." These theorists conceived play as "natural," the survival of human instinct in the artificial, "mechanistic" world of human society and work. The

"recapitulation theory" of human development, articulated first by psychologist G. Stanley Hall, found encapsulated in children's play all the stages of human evolution—not just development, but progress that required increasing amounts of supervision. Adolescence, the age for organized sport, was particularly needful of professional supervision. Yet, according to Mrozek, the writing of some play theorists represented "the desperate desire to preserve the vital, wild, animal side of the human being." In this regard, Luther Gulick, Hall, and others are a link between the older conception of the Victorian "duty to play" as a way to preserve vitality (which Uminowicz describes) and the anti-formalist, modern culture of personality identified by Warren Susman and others.

The theory of play articulated by this new kind of professional also contained a theory of gender based on a belief in the instinctual basis of male and female behavior. Mrozek suggests, however, that this conceptualization of gender-appropriate play was less restrictive (and was approved by women professionals) than it seems on the face of things. The role of gender in the history of American play is complex, and several of these papers address it from more than one direction.

Madelyn Moeller's "Ladies of Leisure: Domestic Photography in the Nineteenth Century" examines a group of dedicated women photographers, all women in comfortable financial situations whose work was accomplished, even prize-winning. However, with the exception of Catharine Weed Barnes, who became an editor of the *American Amateur Photographer,* all considered themselves amateurs and their photography as recreation. With social class as a given rather than a main focus of her analysis, Moeller sets these women and their work in two contexts, the commercialization of photography as a form of leisure and the limits placed on their photographic practice by the Victorian conception of domesticity and female gender roles.

While the technology and chemistry of photography represented a significant break with previous female "hearth crafts," the gender definition of amateur photographic practice took several forms. Men who were also dedicated amateurs tried to limit the access of their female contemporaries to networks of information, support, and recognition by refusing them membership in clubs and competitions. However, the more pervasive and important types of gender definition in amateur photography were associated with subject matter, aesthetics, and the decorum of photography in public. While Moeller suggests that some women ignored advice literature that suggested domestic interiors as more appropriate subject matter than city street scenes, some of the amateur photographers she describes limited their subject matter to domestic subjects and genre scenes that resembled women's amateur paintings and drawings.

By contrast, Colleen Sheehy's "American Angling" is primarily about men of the middle and upper classes, masculine leisure and conceptions of masculine identity forming the contexts of her analysis. Sheehy's discussion of the developing concept of the "sportsman" reveals one of the dynamics involved when an activity that once permitted subsistence becomes a form of leisure. Recreational angling was defined partly by social class, because expensive equipment and blocks of leisure time in faraway places were required for its pursuit. The categorization of prey according to combat worthiness rather than ease of capture or even edibility was another facet of this process, where artificial standards of difficulty were used to establish prowess.

Further, Sheehy's discussion of the sentimentalized image of the "barefoot boy" tells us something about how men conceived the process of becoming men. Lazy summertime fishing, accomplished with improvised equipment and live bait, became the epitome of the golden days of innocent boyhood. Ironically, serious amateur fly-fishermen ridiculed other grown (lower-class) men who continued to practice fishing in such lowly fashion. Manly sport fishing, even as it was a form of escape from the stress of business, needed to be made challenging in order to be worthwhile.

Russell S. Gilmore's " 'Another Branch of Manly Sport': American Rifle Games, 1840–1900" documents many of the same processes at work in the history of another predominantly male form of sport. The contribution of German immigration to American leisure, in the form of the *Schützenbünde*, appears again. For a second time, we learn how a deadly serious pursuit, a necessary component of pioneer subsistence, was converted into a form of commercialized leisure through the creation of rules and other artificial difficulties and the use of special and increasingly expensive equipment. Again, the concept of the "sportsman"—a device of social exclusion—was elaborated. However, riflery always smacked of the arts of war and nationalistic fervor in a way that fly fishing never could, and Gilmore explores the metaphorical connotations of what he terms the perfect "Calvinist sport," a pursuit which no one seems ever to have described as "fun." Among elite practitioners, rifle sports were a metaphor for the economic "hunt" in the Gilded Age's new business civilization. Finally, the nationalistic rhetoric of the sport's supporters during international competition more than one hundred years ago has a ring very much like the editorializing surrounding modern Olympic competition.

One essay uses small artifacts—stereoscopes and stereographs—as its interpretive focus, and the way the author uses evidence is instructive in the use of material culture as another point of access to social and cultural history. Shirley Wajda, like a number of historians working today, is interested in the transition from Victorian to "modernist" culture. How did domestic pastimes function as mediators of this sea change? Wajda ingeniously uses a small artifact of leisure, the stereograph, to trace large cultural shifts in "A Room with a Viewer: The Parlor Stereoscope, Comic Stereographs, and the Psychic Role of Play in Victorian America." In her choice of artifacts, Wajda follows the lead of a group of scholars affiliated with the Visual Studies Workshop in

Rochester, New York, whose exhibit catalog *Points of View: The Stereograph in America—A Cultural History* (1979) suggested that stereographs were particularly rich sources for reconstructing cultural meaning. Wajda's essay employs sophisticated visual analysis of a wide range of images in the Comic Series, a set sold through the Sears, Roebuck catalog in 1905. As a set, the images in the Comic Series addressed a wide range of domestic concerns and commonplaces through the medium of humor. The lengthy captions on the back of each image, Wajda argues, could have played a role in guiding the way the photographs on the front were received. To make her case for the importance of the Comic Series as an articulator of middle-class cultural transition at the level of popular culture, Wajda also addresses availability and sales, the social use of stereograph viewing, and even the character of Victorian visual literacy. "A Room with a Viewer" is a useful example of the kind of interdisciplinary scholarship that the study of material culture requires.

Most of these essays address the issue of recreation and play as the culturally mandated cure for bodily and psychological stress. Advocates of leisure with very different cultural goals—from millennial salvation to more effective performance in the workplace—were uniformly concerned about the effects of what we now call "stress" in American life. In some instances, as the case study of rifle games suggests, the symbolic baggage borne by a single leisure pursuit is almost beyond rational comprehension. Under such circumstances, leisure was a serious matter indeed, and the episodes in the history of leisure collected here suggest just how hard some Americans worked at defining what was fun and then, presumably, having it. They worked so hard at play that one is reminded of the anecdote of a disastrous family vacation where, at one of those critical moments (perhaps waiting in a block-long line for a chocolate custard) of collective misery, the youngest child asked, plaintively, "Are we having fun yet?" The essays collected here suggest that those of us involved in reconstructing and interpreting American play are notable examples of *homo ludens,* finding pleasure in the pursuit of American play as a viable and peculiarly revealing subject matter in American social and cultural history. I hope readers find as much pleasure in these essays as their authors seem to have found in their quests to understand American play.

# Recreation in a Christian America

## Ocean Grove and Asbury Park, New Jersey, 1869–1914

GLENN UMINOWICZ

In 1903 a reprint of an article from *Leslie's Weekly* appeared in an Asbury Park newspaper under the headline, "It Pays to Be Decent." The author took issue with what he felt was an increasingly prevalent formula for success in the American leisure industry.

> It has been argued too often that facilities for drinking and gambling, and other things that cater to vicious and depraved tastes, are necessary to secure the patronage of the American public. . . . [This] miserable fallacy . . . has been constantly employed to justify the existence of lewd plays and other immoral and degrading shows and exhibitions, including, we may add, the vileness seen on the "midways" of some of our recent great expositions. The assumption in all these cases is that unless some features like these are included . . . the crowds will not come, business will languish, and profits cease.

The author found this conclusion to be false and baseless. The majority of the American people, he argued, preferred "clean amusements and recreations for their children, pure literature, decent theaters, and reputable surroundings for their homes." Only a minority were attracted to "vile amusements." In short,

he concluded, "decency pays with the American public as a matter of business policy."[1]

As examples of this successful business policy, the article listed five resorts—Chautauqua and Lake Mohonk in New York; Old Orchard Beach, Maine; and Ocean Grove and Asbury Park, New Jersey (fig. 1). These places were among the respectable resorts that attracted vacationers in the late nineteenth and early twentieth centuries. They were vacation spots where middle-class notions about morality and propriety merged with the belief that leisure played a positive role in helping individuals adjust to life in an urban-industrial nation.

By the 1890s there were hundreds of respectable resorts throughout the country, although their greatest concentration was in the Midwest and the East. They fell into three general categories. First, Old Orchard Beach was part of the nationwide network of camp-meeting sites for which Ocean Grove served as a centerpiece. A second category of respectable resort included Chautauqua, New York, and its imitators. Originally founded as a training ground for Sunday school teachers, Chautau-

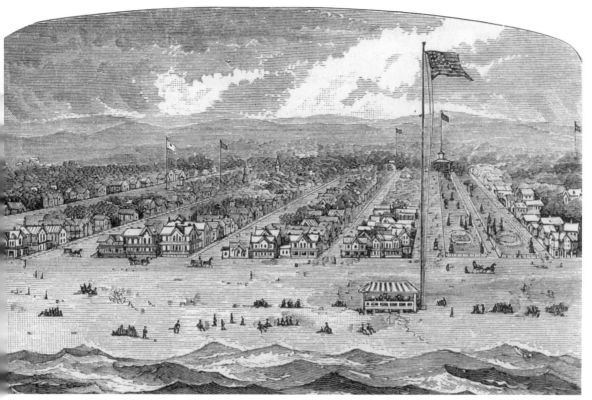

Fig. 1   A 1903 article titled "It Pays to Be Decent" praised Ocean Grove as a business that proved "decency pays with the American public as a matter of business policy." Ocean Grove from the sea, photograph in the *Ocean Grove Annual Report* (1889).

qua branched out into an interest in popular education generally. In a resort atmosphere, Chautauquans pursued culture influenced by religion and combined with wholesome recreation. Their "assembly" was not a camp meeting since evangelistic services and revival meetings were consciously omitted from the program. Finally, some resort developers emphasized high moral standards and wholesome amusements without formally organizing Chautauquas or camp-meeting grounds. Asbury Park and Lake Mohonk were resorts of this type.[2]

Respectable resorts are a relatively little-explored aspect of America's "leisure revolution," an explosion in the number and types of leisure pursuits available to Americans in the late nineteenth and early twentieth centuries.[3] As a means through which the largely Protestant middle class became willing participants in that revolution, these vacation spots are

significant. They were places where an ever-changing array of amusements was made available and offer insights into the leisure preferences of Americans in the period. They also reveal the truth of the axiom that a revolution, even one identified with play, must first occur in the minds of its participants.

Beginning in the 1850s increasing numbers of ministers, physicians, and intellectuals argued that play was crucial to the moral and physical development of individuals. By extension, it was important to the health of American society as a whole. Respectable resorts revealed how the leisure revolution could be integrated within a vision of a Christian nation widely shared by American Protestants. Perhaps nowhere was that effort more evident than at the so-called twin cities—Ocean Grove and Asbury Park. "The Grove" was dedicated to the search for Christian perfection. Asbury Park was founded by a reformer who intended to build a model city, combining modern technology with high standards of public morality.

The vision that shaped the development of the twin cities was a commitment to what Robert Handy has called the quest for a "Christian America." Despite denominational differences, American Protestants agreed that religion and civilization were intimately connected. By "religion" they really meant Protestantism. "Civilization" was never precisely defined, but it was generally conceived as a moral and orderly society based on a broadly Christian set of values and code of behavior. Observance of the so-called American Sabbath and a commitment to temperance, for example, were public affirmations that Christian civilization was still recognized within American culture.[4]

In the case of Ocean Grove, the commitment to the creation of a Christian America was reinforced because of the camp-meeting's connection to what historians have labeled the "holiness movement." Although interdenominational, that movement had an especially profound impact among Methodists, including those who founded Ocean Grove. Holiness advocates were conservative Protestants. They regarded the Bible as the revealed Word of God and rejected the "higher criticism" that subjected the book to historical analysis. Similarly, they opposed any accommodation between biblical thought and the theory of evolution. Their social concerns centered on the need to maintain moral order in an increasingly pluralistic urban-industrial nation. Holiness advocates believed it was possible to lead a perfect Christian life and specifically identified appropriate patterns of Christian behavior. They conceived of their movement as a means of bringing spiritual renewal to established churches that would then work to Christianize the entire nation.[5]

The holiness movement began long before the Civil War. During the first half of the nineteenth century, the search for Christian perfection was consistent with other significant intellectual and cultural trends. The United

States was a young nation striving toward economic and political maturity. Many Americans believed they were a chosen people. They were convinced that the country's democratic institutions and abundant natural resources offered all free and morally responsible individuals an opportunity to reach their full potential. The successful pursuit of individual goals would in turn secure the general welfare, and America would become a model for the rest of the world to follow.[6]

The holiness movement had a special appeal for the urban middle class, whose participation in revivalism had been inspired by the evangelistic work of Charles Grandison Finney. Finney recognized that these urbanites enjoyed the benefits expected in a land of opportunity but were troubled that economic and social change appeared to undermine traditional community and family values. Revivalism promised to eradicate the disquieting consequences of change and restore moral order by bringing together the diverse population of a city under the umbrella of old-time religion.[7] Holiness belief inspired many people to join the numerous voluntary organizations designed to rescue drunkards, free the slaves, uplift the poor, improve education, and address problems of health and sanitation in the nation's burgeoning cities. Like the individual striving for material success, the individual pursuing Christian perfection was expected ultimately to contribute to the general welfare. Holiness advocates appeared doubly qualified as productive citizens in a Christian America.

By midcentury the holiness movement had found its preeminent expression among Methodists, whose church had experienced a similar transformation. Once a denomination that drew its members from the lower end of the social scale, the Methodist Episcopal church became a decidedly middle-class institution in the last third of the nineteenth century. Revivals had increased membership vastly, and its elegant city churches showed Methodism's increasing prosperity and influence in urban areas. Rural migrants to the city were especially responsive to the efforts of holiness ad-

Fig. 2    Methodist camp meeting at Sing Sing, New York. *Harper's Weekly,* 29 August 1868.

vocates to combat the perceived worldliness and formality of urban Methodism. Most Methodist holiness ministers held pulpits in commercial and industrial towns after having served in country churches where simple revivalistic worship patterns were the norm. Along with their supporters, they longed to retain the evangelicalism of those churches "back home" within the new, elegant Methodist houses of worship. They fervently believed that a sanctified church would ultimately secure a converted world and thereby provide solutions for all the religious, social, and political problems that beset humankind. In short, holiness teaching was the key to creating a Christian civilization.[8] By 1870 holiness teachings were widely accepted within American revivalist Protestantism: in 1872 six of the eight new bishops elected by the Methodist Episcopal General Conference were favorable to the holiness cause.

The chief vehicle holiness advocates used to pursue their goals was an institution that had

fallen into disfavor among practitioners of an educated approach to the ministry—the camp meeting (fig. 2). In the camp meeting, a setting identified with the evangelicalism of rural Protestantism, holiness believers advanced on a journey toward Christian perfection that occurred in two stages. An individual first became a professed Christian and received forgiveness for past sins. The newly converted, however, was still plagued by a sinful nature which encouraged backsliding. Christian perfection was only achieved through the second blessing, also known as entire sanctification, perfect love, or Christian holiness. The second blessing was a direct, physically felt emotional experience, a manifestation of an actual visitation, or fiery baptism, of the Holy Ghost. Through it, the sanctified lost interest in worldly things which compromised their purity. In 1867 leading holiness ministers organized a National Camp-Meeting Association for the Promotion of Holiness to combat the "sad declension of spirituality in the

OCEAN GROVE SUPPLEMENT.

368   Where my Saviour Leads.

F. J. Crosby.                                    Arr. by Ira D. Sankey.

Fig. 3   *Church Hymns and Gospel Songs* (1898) contained thirteen favorite songs in an "Ocean Grove Supplement."

churches." At camp, holiness advocates had a platform from which to preach their message in a setting identified with the evangelicalism of rural Protestantism.[9]

Ocean Grove grew out of the National Holiness Camp-Meeting movement. The Ocean Grove Camp-Meeting Association (oga) was organized in 1869. It was specified that one-half of its twenty-six members would be Methodist ministers and the other half laymen. Among the founders of the oga were prominent individuals in the national holiness movement. Through a charter obtained from the state legislature, the organization was granted the powers of a municipal government to build and operate a permanent camp-meeting site on the New Jersey coast barely fifty miles from New York City. By the 1880s the summer population of this "Christian sea-

side resort" numbered between twenty and thirty thousand.[10]

The core clientele for Ocean Grove were business and professional men and their families. Their ability to afford a summer vacation was itself evidence of Methodist prosperity. What attracted these thousands who came to the Grove? For both oga officials and the majority of visitors, the religious element at the resort was always paramount. Among the strongest memories visitors took away with them, for example, was the congregational singing. In 1889 a shore correspondent reported that eight to ten thousand worshipers singing their praise of God could be heard a mile away, creating "such a volume of sound that the roar of the surf sounds like the bass notes of a distant organ."[11]

Congregational singing served the important function of uniting a large crowd in a group expression of shared belief (fig. 3). Recognizing its value, writers of holiness gospel songs created a body of work that both celebrated and contributed to the camp-meeting experience. One favorite theme was the experience of the second blessing as a metaphor for a believer's ultimate residence in the Promised Land, also called Canaan or Beulah. Camp meetings were held in the mountains or at the seaside, and holiness gospel songs placed the Promised Land in both locations. In 1875, for example, Edgar Page Stites wrote "Beulah Land" while en route to Ocean Grove. The song became a favorite at the resort. In the camp-meeting auditorium or at beach meetings, worshipers sang the refrain:

> O Beulah Land, sweet Beulah Land,
> As on thy highest mountain I stand,
> I look away across the sea,
> Where mansions are prepared for me,
> And view the shining glory shore,
> My heav'n, my home, for evermore![12]

The sentiments expressed in "Beulah Land" were repeated by those who remembered visiting Ocean Grove. Maria L. Chandler, for example, reminisced that both she and her husband were converted when young but never experienced the second blessing until they came to the Grove. "We found it indeed," she testified, "a land of Beulah in our experience."[13]

Mrs. Chandler's observation was not unique. As holiness camp-meeting sites like Ocean Grove evolved into comfortable vacation communities, increasing numbers of campers identified them as a foretaste of the Promised Land.[14] Holiness belief thus reinforced some already powerful attractions that resorts held for nineteenth-century Americans. The appeal of vacation communities has been linked with Leo Marx's concept of the "middle landscape"—the search for a middle ground between raw nature and untempered urbanism.[15] At a resort, the natural attractions of the mountains or seaside were combined with the comforts of a good hotel or summer cottage. "The hotel-keepers give us the conveniences of city life," a correspondent at one New Jersey resort wrote, "supplying the *urbe in rure*."[16]

At Ocean Grove there was a clear attempt to bring urban comfort to the countryside. Moreover, the attainment of Christian perfection was grafted onto a pastoral ideal that was pervasive in American culture. In the *Annual Report* of the OGA for 1890, for example, the Reverend Ellwood H. Stokes, the organization's first president, described the evolution of the resort. "Where there was utter desolation," he wrote, "there is now a City by the Sea." To this standard bit of pastoral imagery, Stokes added that the Grove was, in some degree, "our ideal of the harmonization of nature and grace, earth and heaven."[17] In short, this resort was not merely a middle ground between nature and the city; it was a mediating space between this world and the next (fig. 4). For many more than Mrs. Chandler, it was meant to be a land of Beulah in their experience.

This heavenly middle landscape comprised three-fourths of a square mile. It was laid out on a grid bordered on three sides by lakes and the ocean (fig. 5). Access from the west was blocked by a wooden fence with gates which

Fig. 4　The cover of the 1910 *Ocean Grove Annual Report* depicts the belief that Ocean Grove was a mediating place between the earthly and heavenly worlds.

were closed at midnight every evening and all day on Sunday. As at many respectable resorts, access to the community was restricted because the OGA hoped to exercise control over both the physical development and the moral atmosphere of the Grove.[18]

As would be expected at a "religious resort," the campground was the dominant district at Ocean Grove, and at its center was an auditorium. The first auditoriums built at the resort were covered frames which sheltered the preachers' stand and a congregation seated on benches (fig. 6). The auditorium still in use at the resort was completed in 1894. Built at a cost of close to seventy thousand dollars, with a capacity of nearly ten thousand, the building was described by a reporter as "the largest evangelical audience room in the world." Seven main iron trusses, each spanning 161

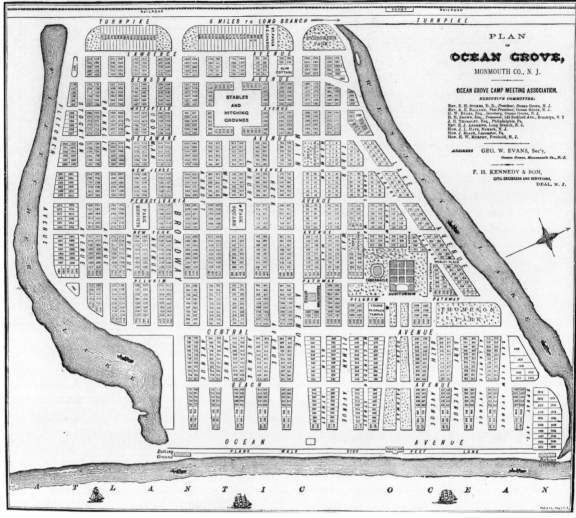

Fig. 5    Plan of Ocean Grove in the *Ocean Grove Annual Report* (1889).

feet, supported a roof of corrugated galvanized iron with sidewalls made of wood. The front facade of the building featured a main tower 119 feet tall flanked by two bell towers reaching a height of 62 feet. To insure the comfort of the audience and to retain the semblance of an open-air service, the vast majority of the building's 262 doors and windows could be opened to provide ventilation (figs. 7 and 8).[19]

The Grove's auditorium, at any stage of its evolution, was the focal point of the annual ten-day camp meeting each August which marked the high point of the summer season. Camp meeting as practiced at the Grove should not be confused with the gatherings

held before the Civil War. At the early camps, farm families gathered for a few days or weeks in a temporary enclosure to hear a series of preachers deliver fiery sermons. In an article on Ocean Grove, a newspaper reporter described their experience.

The campers of today have little conception of the wild, weird encampment of the olden times. The circle of tents (home-made and primitive [*sic*] in style), the barricade of trees and brush ten or twelve feet high, the elevated platforms placed at intervals about the encampment, where pine knots were piled high and lighted at night, formed a sight that once seen would be stamped upon the memory. Especially vivid would be the

Fig. 6    The Ocean Grove auditorium in 1880, which seated five thousand people and had standing room for a thousand more. *Ocean Grove Annual Report* (1889).

remembrance of the midnight sermon when the preacher thundered forth the terrors of the law and portrayed the final judgement.[20]

Responding to preaching "directed straight at the sinner's heart," participants at the early camps expressed the power of the Holy Ghost with shouts, groans, and tears. Some reclaimed sinners experienced "the jerks," a spasmodic quaking of the entire body. Many campers had never been in a group of more than several hundred people, but the great meetings attracted thousands. Both the anonymity of the crowd and the physical setting encouraged emotional release. At a midnight sermon, for example, firelight reflected off the trees and faces in the crowd as the preacher thundered forth the terrors of damnation. The voice of those seeking salvation washed over the entire campground and could be heard for several miles.[21]

Ministers who endorsed a cultured professionalism in preaching disapproved of these "wild, weird encampments." Along with

charges of religious excess, critics argued that the camps themselves offered opportunities for backsliding. The old-time camp meeting often attracted "a roving crowd bent on fun or mischief." In addition to those seeking salvation, hucksters, rowdies, gamblers, and prostitutes appeared on campgrounds. During services or at night, the narrow footpaths between tents were an especially attractive gathering place for those seeking and offering illicit pleasures.[22]

By contrast, camp meetings at Ocean Grove were of an "elevated character." Like urban evangelist Dwight L. Moody, who advocated an "old fashioned revival with modern improvements," holiness ministers placed a premium on orderly conduct on the part of worshipers.[23] Their audience wanted some of the religious fervor of the old days, which they found lacking in their city churches, but that enthusiasm was bounded by middle-class propriety. As practiced at the Grove, subdued revivalism became a form of ritual. While each

Figs. 7 and 8   Interior and exterior of the new Ocean Grove auditorium, built in 1894 with a capacity of nearly ten thousand. From the promotional photo booklet *Asbury Park and Ocean Grove* (1896).

believer was encouraged to express spontaneously felt religious emotion, the meetings followed well-established patterns in its expression. Both ministers and their congregations returned to the Grove year after year, each time executing virtually the same order of worship.[24]

A typical auditorium service at Ocean Grove included music, a scripture reading, and a main sermon. Demonstrative physical manifestations of the power of the Holy Ghost were discouraged. Even applause on the part of the audience was frowned upon, with the waving of white handkerchiefs encouraged in its place. The practice was followed at other respectable resorts and was known as both the "Chautauqua Salute" and the "Ocean Grove Wave." It was the highest accolade a speaker could receive.

Most speakers in the auditorium delivered inspirational sermons, focusing on fundamental themes that constituted a conservative defense against liberal theological thought. Only rarely was the doctrine of Christian holiness emphasized directly. Large public meetings were not conducive to leading individuals on their intense personal search for perfection. It was at "side meetings" attended by up to a few hundred where holiness was preached, exhortations offered, and personal testimony taken. Some meetings were identified with specific evangelists who conducted them for a decade or more. Others addressed the spiritual needs of a specific target audience. There were, for example, Mothers' Meetings, Women's Encouragement Meetings, and Businessmen's Meetings. In 1877 the Janes Memorial Tabernacle was constructed next to the auditorium to

house these gatherings. In the late 1880s Thornley Chapel and the Young People's Temple were constructed in Auditorium Square to serve the special spiritual needs of children (fig. 9).[25]

The ritualized pattern of worship and the ability of an evangelist to move an audience from joyous enthusiasm to subdued spirituality were perhaps nowhere more evident than at the closing of camp meeting. Each year the service followed a set pattern. There was an infant baptism in the morning followed immediately by the sacrament of the Lord's Supper. At the close of the service, several hundred ministers, the choir, and some members of the audience formed a procession. They circled the auditorium and its ancillary buildings twice, singing an appropriate hymn such as "We're Marching to Zion." After 1881 this cer-

emony became known as the "Jerusalem March" after a model of the biblical city that had been installed in front of the auditorium as an educational tool.

The songs, tears, and "rejoicings" during the march were among the emotional high points of camp meeting. When the ministers returned to the auditorium platform, they were greeted by "songs of triumphant joy" and the Ocean Grove Wave by those who were not in the procession. When all had reassembled in the building, however, "a holy hush" quickly descended on the crowd as the chief minister asked them to stand. Sometimes a song "as soft as angels sing" floated above the congregation as all attention was focused on the speaker's platform. "In the name of the Father, and the Son, and of the Holy Ghost," with the auditorium bell tolling after each name, the

Fig. 9    Thornley Chapel was named after the Rev. Joseph H. Thornley, superintendent of the Ocean Grove Sabbath School. *Ocean Grove Annual Report* (1889).

president of the OGA declared camp meeting closed.[26]

With the auditorium and its side buildings, the OGA had created facilities that served not only as a permanent camp-meeting site but also as a summer convention center for a variety of religious and reform organizations. Among the groups that regularly met at the Grove were the Women's Christian Temperance Union, the National Division of the Sons of Temperance, the New Jersey Sabbath Union, and the Women's Home and Foreign Missionary Societies. When the meetings, lectures, and programs sponsored by these and other organizations were added to those at camp meeting, the total could easily exceed one thousand for a summer season.

This oratorical feast comprised one of the resort's principal attractions, a summer of "intellectual treats" provided by "men of advanced thought" on a number of subjects (fig. 10). The resort hosted such luminaries as the

Reverend T. Dewitt Talmadge, Russell H. Conwell, and reformers Frances Willard, Anthony Comstock, and Jacob Riis. This summer program insured that visitors would be constantly exposed to calls for the creation of a Christian America. Perhaps no organization better exemplified how that would be achieved than the National Reform Association (NRA), which met annually at the Grove beginning in the 1880s. The OGA's *Annual Report* of 1887 listed the aims of the NRA:

> This organization takes up, and deals fairly and squarely, with the great moral and religious questions, which are now claiming so large a share of public attention, each one of which involves the whole idea of our national Christianity, viz.: Shall the liquor traffic continue among us? Shall our government respect the Lord's Day, and guard it from desecration? Shall we regard the law of Christ as the basis of our legislation touching the family and related interests? Shall we retain the bible, and unsectarian instruction in our public schools?[27]

The above agenda very nearly defined the entire program for those who wanted to Christianize American society. A Christian America had to reject the "rum evil." The "Puritan Sabbath" was an affirmation that religion still influenced the general culture. The family, along with the church, was the bulwark of conservative Christianity. Finally, the public schools, which communicated to students a decidedly Protestant brand of Christianity, were an important means of reaching the young.

Given this comprehensive reform program, the members of the NRA could hardly have found a more congenial spot than Ocean Grove for their summer meetings. Among respectable resorts, those operated by Methodist camp-meeting associations placed the tightest regulations on individual behavior. The Grove's notoriety, for example, rested in part on restrictions adopted by the OGA. In the well-known *Baedeker's Guide to the United States* (1893), the author marveled that thousands of vacationers willingly chose to spend their summer under "a religious autocracy, which is severe in both its positive and negative regulations."[28]

The sale of liquor was, of course, banned at the Grove. In addition to the prohibition of "demon rum," local merchants and hotelmen were forbidden to stock either tobacco or novels. "Light fiction" distracted visitors from pious devotions, and tobacco smoke had a long association with the saloon and the gambling den. Among the OGA's regulations, the Sabbath restrictions attracted the greatest comment. On Sunday, no business was conducted, no amusements allowed, and no newspapers delivered. The Grove's closed entrance gates prevented any vehicular traffic. The restriction on public conveyances even extended to the railroads serving the resort. The vigilance of OGA officials in defense of the Sabbath was revealed when they insisted that penny candy machines be emptied every Saturday night. These "slot machines" were a form of commerce which, like any business, had to cease on Sunday.[29]

This long list of restrictions was understandable in the context of the holiness movement. After conversion, the unsanctified believer had to recognize the need for the second blessing, and that recognition was evident through behavior. An appetite for alcohol and tobacco, an outburst of temper, or the surrender to worldly fashion was an indication of backsliding. The unsanctified believer was, in effect, expected to adopt the behavioral standards of a perfect Christian as evidence of the striving for Christian holiness. In short, holiness leaders equated inward purity with decorous behavior at every stage of spiritual development.

Because of this emphasis on external proofs of religious conviction, holiness advocates might be seen as quintessential Victorians. Developing strength after midcentury, the holiness movement maintained a symbiotic relationship with the period's official culture. The connection was hardly surprising. American Victorianism was middle class and Protestant; its adherents emphasized the virtues of sobriety and industry; and, finally, Victorians

Fig. 10    This "Oriental lecturer" spoke for three nights, illustrating what were called "hitherto obscure" passages of scripture to his audience. *Ocean Grove Annual Report* (1889).

were obsessively concerned with social practice. They devoured advice books which counseled them on everything from courtship and marriage to manners at table; they eagerly read tracts on subjects ranging from personal hygiene to the moral training of children.[30]

Holiness believers quite literally sanctified contemporary social usage. Good manners, according to advice book authors, were the "dress of character"; they were the "regalia of civilization" which marked a person as belonging to the "guild of ladies and gentlemen."[31] But holiness believers thought that behavior revealed much more: it marked a person as at least an apprentice in the guild of perfect Christians. It was as though, with each fiery baptism, the Holy Ghost delivered an etiquette book. In establishing the Grove's restrictions, OGA officials were merely demonstrating that they had read the chapters. As stated in the *Annual Report* for 1881, the association banned only those things pronounced by the "enlightened evangelical Christian Church" to be contrary to the Word of God. Its restrictions, therefore, were not oppressive, because they merely codified expected behavior in a Christian community.[32]

There were, of course, occasional violations of the regulations. In private homes and tents, novels were surreptitiously read, and an occasional bottle appeared from where it had been secreted in a suitcase. At the hotels, brass bands sometimes blared too loudly, or a cigar might be slipped to a guest when a clerk saw him drop a nickel into an unmarked box in the lobby. Despite such lawlessness, however, OGA officials were justifiably proud of "the perfect order among such multitudes as throng this place." They worried most about protecting the Grove from unwanted representatives of the "outside world." Local police spent most of their time patrolling the perimeter of the resort. Those excluded or put off the campground were cataloged in the annual reports. The list included intoxicated persons, tramps, organ grinders, Sunday bathers, brass bands, pack peddlers, Punch and Judy shows, and "noisy straw riding parties." The precise threat posed by those labeled "improper persons" was not specified.[33]

Professed high standards of personal conduct combined with reports of occasional backsliding made camp-meeting resorts prime targets for satire. In 1876, for example, *Puck* magazine revived the old charge that the physical layout of camp-meeting grounds actually fostered immorality. Many "good, nice girls," the magazine's editor conceded, came back from camp as good, nice girls, but many did not. Young people sleeping with only the wall of a canvas tent between them were more likely driven by the "childish folly in their heads" than the "calmer checking of their consciences." It was much easier to slip out from under a tent flap than down the creaking stairs past the "old folks" at home and indulge in "a moonlight ramble by the kissing waves."[34]

In fact, the built environment at Ocean Grove and similar campgrounds worked against the propensity for backsliding. The domestic life of cottagers and tenters was open to the perusal of neighbors and exposed to casual strollers on the grounds. On the Grove's small lots, measuring thirty by sixty feet, cottages and tents were erected close together and near the street (fig. 11). Windows and opened doors and tent flaps offered a clear view of sitting rooms or parlors. Thin cottage and tent walls did not muffle sound. Even if you could not see, you could often hear what your neighbors were doing. At night, shadows on tent walls indicated when family devotions were in progress. In 1874, recognizing that shadows revealed what went on in a tent, a newspaper artist pictured the silhouette of a young woman on a tent flap. The caption warned against lighting a lamp while in the process of disrobing.[35]

Ocean Grove was built for "neighboring," the informal socializing commonly practiced by people living in small towns. Both tenters and cottagers at the resort typically returned to the same summer residence season after season. Social relationships were forged through chance encounters repeated over a period of time by people living in the same neighborhood. As in any town, there were specific spaces where neighboring occurred. Among the best of such spaces was the front porch, a place for spontaneous interaction with passers-by. At the Grove, it was often just a few feet from the sidewalk to the porch of a cottage or tent. Moreover, a cottager or tenter could likely reach out an arm over the side of a porch and almost touch a neighbor's railing (fig. 12). The Ocean Grove porch was a platform suitable for intensive neighboring, both forward with passers-by on the street and side-to-side with those sitting on nearby verandahs.[36]

What passed across porch railings was, of course, conversation, or, more precisely, gossip. Gossip was crucial to neighboring, as a form of entertainment and a source of information. Grove gossip often focused on real or imagined cases of backsliding. In 1885, for example, it was widely whispered that billiard ta-

Fig. 11 The close living arrangements in Ocean Grove tents made residents aware of their neighbors' activities. *Asbury Park and Ocean Grove* (1896).

bles had been introduced into some private homes. OGA officials actually encouraged Grovers to develop the powers of observation needed to detect such alarming symptoms of frivolity and to report their findings to local officials. The officials also assumed that rum sellers, denied the right to operate openly, would almost certainly attempt to invade the resort by stealth. "Let every man's eye be like the eagle's," the *Annual Report* for 1880 advised, to detect any evidence of "the heaven-cursed rum traffic" in the Grove.[37]

Regarding one issue, the annual reports went beyond merely asking that Grovers be observant. This was the problem of persons, especially women, wearing "improper bathing clothes" on the beach (fig. 13). In general, bathing costumes worn at the resort were modest enough, although one reporter observed that they did "put trousers on the fe-

male form and make public demonstration of the fact that woman is a biped."[38] Against those who wished to demonstrate even more, the *Annual Report* of 1887 recommended that social pressure be brought to bear. "Let every person whose cheeks are not beyond the blush of modesty, frown all such persons out of respectable fellowship, and instead of seeming to favor the despicable practice by the slightest look or word, in the name of common decency, demand universal and immediate reform."[39]

This request acknowledged that the most effective agents of social control at the resort were Grovers themselves. The summer population was largely made up of individuals who were moral reformers, evangelical Protestants, or both. They were accustomed to looking for evidence of backsliding both in themselves and others. Moreover, the setting in which these

Fig. 12 A family using the front porch of its tent at Ocean Grove. *Asbury Park and Ocean Grove* (1896).

people found themselves, a community of tightly packed cottages and tents, facilitated looking out for their neighbors. At home, young folks had to sneak past the old folks. At Ocean Grove, they had to sneak past their parents, OGA officials, and thousands of eagle-eyed Christians living at close quarters. If the Grove was any example, the busybody was a bulwark of a Christian America.

Many of the restrictions at Ocean Grove related to leisure activities. Among operators of respectable resorts, Methodist camp-meeting associations maintained the longest list of proscribed amusements. Their policy was based on the paragraph on amusements in the Methodist *Book of Discipline,* written in 1872 by the Reverend Aaron E. Ballard, then vice president of the OGA. The paragraph classified activities that involved "imprudent and un-christian conduct," including drinking, gam-

bling, dancing, card playing, and going to the theater or circus.[40]

Ocean Grove was billed as a Christian seaside resort as well as a permanent camp-meeting site. In addition to prohibiting amusements, OGA officials had to identify what leisure pursuits were acceptable for vacationers. Was it possible to enjoy oneself in a Christian America? Given the restrictions at a place such as Ocean Grove, the question was a very real one. In the early 1880s, an answer was offered in an OGA-sponsored resort advertisement. Under the heading of "Pleasure," it was noted that boating, seabathing, and "kindred means of happiness" had been so connected with "modes of evil" as to make their indulgence by Christians suspect. At Ocean Grove, however, these activities were "put in their right relationships, and sanctified by the word of God and prayer."[41]

For middle-class Americans, pleasures taken in such a moral atmosphere were true "recreations." Beginning about midcentury, they evidenced a concern with the need for play in an urban-industrial nation. Recreation, as they understood the term, provided a respite from unhealthful aspects of city life, particularly from pressures in the workplace.[42] In 1883, Herbert Spencer, the father of Social Darwinism, preached this new "gospel of recreation" to an American audience. "The stern discipline of social life," he observed, "has gradually increased the aptitude for persistent industry." Americans, especially Anglo-Americans, displayed an "intemperance in work" which was undermining their health.[43]

Protestant clergy recognized that "intemperance in work," when it reflected an obsession with worldly things, could be as detrimental to an individual as intemperance in drink. To the stolid values of the Protestant work ethic—industry, sobriety, and thrift—they added another, the "duty to play." In an address on the history of Ocean Grove in 1875, the Reverend E. H. Stokes, president of the OGA, sounded a typical note of alarm. "The haggard brow, the tottering steps, the irritated nerves, the sudden paralysis, the multiplying victims of the insane asylum" were, according to Stokes, all traced to a single cause, "*Overwork!*"[44]

In contrast to recreations, however, there were "dissipations." As the word implies, dissipations were both morally and physically debilitating. The reader of almost any temperance tract, for example, discovered that a drunkard inevitably ended as both a physical and moral wreck. Ocean Grove was founded in part to provide a resort free from "temptations to dissipation." In his historical address, Stokes pointed out that its founders understood the connection between religion and recreation. "We knew that all recreation, or so called pleasure, divorced from religion, would degenerate into absolute sin, and instead of being rest, would become exhausting labor. . . . Religion and recreation should go hand in

Fig. 13    These bathing costumes indicate that although little girls could swim without wearing shoes, hats, or sleeves, women were required to dress more conservatively. *Delineator*, July 1884.

hand. Separate them, and religion grows morose, and recreation will soon become sinful. Blended both are beautiful."[45]

Within the Grove's landscape, Ocean Pathway symbolized the blending of religion and recreation (fig. 14). This thoroughfare stretched five hundred yards from Auditorium Square to the oceanfront. It was, in fact, two narrow streets with a park space sandwiched between them. The path was two hundred feet across at the auditorium end and widened to three hundred feet as it approached the beach. From the beach, a visitor looked toward the heart of a religious community. The view was especially striking after the construction of the Great Auditorium in 1894. Ocean Pathway converged on the building, which served as a gigantic visual magnet pulling visitors to the area of the town dedicated to the search for Christian perfection. Conversely, standing in front of the auditorium, a visitor had an unobstructed view of the sea as the Pathway wid-

Fig. 14    Ocean Pathway at Ocean Grove in *Asbury Park and Ocean Grove* (1896).

ened approaching the resort's principal public play space—the beach and boardwalk.

On any day but the Sabbath, a visitor would likely have seen the beach crowded with bathers. In an essay written in 1874, just two years after he had written the paragraph on amusements in the *Book of Discipline,* the Reverend Aaron E. Ballard left no question that seabathing was an example of invigorating recreation as practiced at the Grove.

> The long, rolling surf-waves . . . gently shock the frame and stir the sluggish blood to fresher motion. That motion rolls, and bounds, and leaps through the veins—anywhere, everywhere—routing all the host of peccant humors which have ambushed themselves in all possible hidden places. . . . The torpid liver finds itself compelled to join the general activity, and to work like a disused steam engine newly set in motion. The nerves respond to the body's school boy holiday, and scatter tingling sensations of pleasure all over the frame. . . . The surf lubricates the joints like oil; grave men fling out their limbs like colts in pasture; dignified women, from the very inspiration of necessity, sport like girls at recess; [and] aged people tumble among the waves till one would think they were only in their teens.[46]

Grovers took seriously the warning of physicians against dissipating the body's "vital force," its limited reserves of energy. As Ballard's description of seabathing illustrates, the Grove was to be a place where the human battery would be recharged. Physical rejuvenation achieved through true recreation was directly related to an individual's spiritual state. The ideal Christian, the Reverend George K. Morris asserted at camp meeting in 1886, was "a vigorous man whose nerves are in good condition." A Christian nation, after all, could never be secured by "namby pamby" believers.[47] Grovers were heirs to a tradition in place before the Civil War. They shared the vision, as

Harvey Green has described it, of "a truly Christian society as a sort of hygienic millennium, in which all citizens would have as perfect bodies as possible."[48]

Ocean Grove, where souls were touched by a fiery baptism and bodies reinvigorated by the surf waves, produced the kind of muscular Christians needed to serve God well. At the opening of the new auditorium in 1894, OGA president Stokes proclaimed Grovers to be "living epistles," providing a glimpse of the perfect Christian life for others to follow. They were also in the vanguard of an "aggressive evangelism." After a summer of religion and recreation, people would return home filled with the "old Crusader's spirit." For its founders, the Grove was both a refuge and a shining example of life in a Christian America. It was also a fortress where Christian soldiers rested, recreated, trained, and were inspired before invading "the territories of sin."[49]

Among the early visitors to Ocean Grove, James Adam Bradley was an excellent "living epistle" on the perfect Christian life. This wealthy brush manufacturer from New York was a moral reformer committed to temperance and protecting the "American Sabbath." He was also a health reformer interested in improving the sanitary condition of American cities and towns. Bradley understood the value of recreation. In 1870, he sought a respite by the sea at the Grove because his nervous system had been affected by "too close application to business."[50]

Within a year of visiting the camp meeting, Bradley purchased five hundred acres directly adjacent to Ocean Grove. Here he built Asbury Park, a resort named for Methodism's pioneer bishop in America, and created a community that would be an example of urban planning. He determined land use patterns by laying out wide streets and providing for generously sized house lots. He established a board of health, built the first comprehensive sewage system on the Jersey coast, and was among the first to introduce the electric trolley as a form of intraurban transit. Finally, he imposed restrictions on behavior similar to those

found at the Grove, establishing "The Park" as a temperance town with a set of Sabbath restrictions. In short, Bradley took on the ambitious task of demonstrating how both sin and sewage could be effectively discharged from a community. By the early 1890s his efforts were attracting between thirty and fifty thousand summer visitors.

Because of his role in shaping the resort, Bradley became known simply as "the Founder" at Asbury Park. As at Ocean Grove, the Founder laid out his city on a grid framed by lakes and the ocean on three sides (fig. 15). The city was organized around two main thoroughfares—Grand Avenue and Ocean Avenue. Grand Avenue, running parallel to the ocean through the center of the Park, was the resort's show street, the finest institutional and residential thoroughfare in the city. Several churches, one of the first large hotels, and the Asbury Park and Ocean Grove Library were built along its length. In 1877 Bradley moved Educational Hall from the Philadelphia Centennial Exhibition to a park along the avenue. It was the resort's first public auditorium. Like the Grove, Asbury Park would become a summer convention center for middle-class reformers.

Grand Avenue symbolized Asbury Park's claim to being a respectable community dedicated to Christian principles and committed to moral and intellectual uplift. The resort's other major path represented the city's primary function as a leisure community. Running parallel to the beach and boardwalk, Ocean Avenue defined a large, elongated public play space spanning the entire length of the resort. Unlike Atlantic City's famous boardwalk, "catch-penny booths" and technological amusements were banned along the oceanfront at Asbury Park. Bradley thus created the seaside equivalent of an urban park, an open space that would help "ventilate" the city's atmosphere. This space extended for several blocks into the resort along boulevards that widened to two hundred feet as they approached Ocean Avenue.

Writing as a correspondent for the *New York*

Fig. 15  Asbury Park, viewed across one of the lakes that framed the city. *Asbury Park and Ocean Grove* (1896).

*Tribune* in 1892, Stephen Crane described the crowd on the boardwalk bordering the avenue. "It is the world of the middle classes," he concluded. "Add but princes and gamblers and it would be what the world calls the world."[51] Asbury Park did have a core clientele similar to that of the Grove, but there were important differences as well. Bradley hoped to attract a cross section of the American middle class to his resort. These people shared in the broad consensus that identified a Christian civilization as desirable, but differed slightly as to what specific behaviors were acceptable within it. In order to attract a relatively cosmopolitan crowd, Asbury Park promoters had to avoid too close an association with Ocean Grove, because the entire set of restrictions at the camp-meeting resort was not endorsed by every Protestant.

Bradley himself brought to the attention of the public distinctions between the twin cities. In a local newspaper in 1876, for example, the Founder declared that Asbury Parkers supported those "mild restraints" on individual behavior typical in any "well-ordered and happy" community. The resort was not, however, a "religious institution" operated directly by a specific denomination or association.[52] The contrast between the "individual character" of Asbury Park and that of its camp-meeting neighbor was a frequent theme in promotional literature. In *Asbury Park and Ocean Grove with Their Points of Interest* (1892), for example, the author wrote,

> For the convenience of comparison, let us say here that Asbury Park is essentially a secular community, and that although the standard of morality is high and great care is taken to exclude objectionable residents and demoralizing institutions, there is no intimate association of "church

and state" in its government, and no claim is made that the surroundings and general "atmosphere" of the place are more religious than those of any other carefully and ably-governed Christian community.[53]

The paragraph on amusements in the Methodist *Book of Discipline* was too narrow a yardstick to measure proper recreation at "essentially secular" Asbury Park. In general, Asbury Parkers and Grovers raised the same questions regarding the appropriateness of a leisure activity: Did it provide the physical and mental rejuvenation typical of true recreation? Did it bolster or at least not compromise individual morality? Often the answers to these questions were the same at both resorts. Sport, for example, was easily justified as true recreation. Physical exercise built both strong bodies and character. In 1892 the striving for muscular Christianity was discussed by an opening-day speaker at Asbury Park's new athletic grounds. His discourse on "How to Grow Strong Morally" could have been part of an auditorium service at the Grove.[54]

In contrast to athletics, there were leisure activities accepted in Asbury Park that would have been reported to the authorities if detected in Ocean Grove. Holiness advocates, for example, did not play cards or dance, but these were common hotel entertainments in the Park. The *Book of Discipline* also banned going to the theater, but audiences regularly patronized Asbury Park's two opera houses. Finally, after-dinner strollers walked along the resort's boardwalk, fairly choking the wide promenade with fashionably dressed humanity (fig. 16). By contrast, Grovers interpreted fashion-consciousness as a surrender to worldliness, adding plain dress to the list of outward signs of Christian perfection. A correspondent for the *London Times* marveled at how they resisted "the temptation to extravagant dressing." In fact, it was not merely resisted, but "knocked down and trampled under feet."[55]

Ironically, leisure activities banned at the Grove but accepted at Asbury Park were justified according to a formula endorsed by the OGA. The association legitimated seabathing and "kindred means of happiness" by separating them from "modes of evil." Asbury Park promoters merely extended the list of appropriate pleasures taken in a moral atmosphere. Hotel ballrooms, for example, could be scenes of dissipation. Founder Bradley had himself once seen the "lascivious waltz" indulged in by intoxicated men in a manner "that should have caused the spectators to depart in shame." With the baleful influence of alcohol removed, however, dancing could be transformed into healthy socializing and exercise.[56] Presumably, this was the case in temperance-minded Asbury Park.

As in the ballroom, corrupting influences could be eliminated from the theater. After a performance of Gilbert and Sullivan's *Mikado* in 1886, for example, the manager of an Asbury Park opera house announced his intention "to provide the best and purest amusements that could be obtained." The eclectic mix included musical comedy, minstrel shows, and melodrama. The latter was an especially appropriate entertainment for Asbury Parkers. Melodrama employed a simplistic formula in which virtue and vice were easily identified. Characters such as Little Eva and Simon Legree in *Uncle Tom's Cabin* clearly personified goodness and evil. Melodrama thus reflected and reinforced the basic middle-class assumption that poverty, drunkenness, and disorder were the result of individual character flaws, not larger social and economic forces.[57] The conclusion followed that a Christian civilization was created by reforming many individuals and maintained by combating subsequent temptations toward backsliding.

Temptation was especially difficult to combat on the boardwalk, where strollers were cloaked by the anonymity of a crowd of diverse strangers primarily bent on enjoying themselves. Stephen Crane pondered the question of why people returned to Asbury Park's oceanfront evening after evening, why guests fled the huge wooden hotels, and why the boardinghouses seemed "to turn upside down and shake out every boarder." Cottagers made

Fig. 16    Asbury Park Boardwalk, as seen from Bradley's Pavilion. *Asbury Park and Ocean Grove* (1896).

ready for an evening stroll, as did local merchants and clerks who rolled down their sleeves and put on their jackets. According to Crane, the principal attraction was neither the view of the sea nor the music from the beach band: "The people come to see the people. . . . For there is joy to the heart in a crowd. One is in life and of life then. Nothing escapes; the world is going on and one is there to perceive it."[58]

Among these pleasure seekers, the one who received the most attention from newspaper correspondents and moralists was the "summer girl." With her bright talk, coquettish manners, and pretty dresses, she was "a creature of sweetness and all the light that is on sea or land." She was out for a good time with acquaintances of only a few weeks, whom she might never meet again after the summer.[59] The Reverend Charles H. Kidder was par-

ticularly concerned with the activities and vulnerability of Asbury Park summer girls. In 1886 he wrote a series of articles about the boardwalk in which he warned that "Mr. Pickup" was very fond of seaside resorts. As identified by Kidder and others, this "social pest" was attentive, well mannered, and well spoken, but his ultimate goal was debauchery.[60] These moralists warned that outward manners and fine appearance were not infallible signs of respectability. A polite, well-dressed young gentleman might in reality be "Mr. Pickup."

Mr. Pickup's deceit was made easier because he operated among strangers where first impressions were the sole basis for judging character and status. He was, in short, among the newly recognized confidence men who undermined a "cult of sincerity" which had once been one of the highest ideals of middle-class culture. After 1860 increasing numbers of middle-class urbanites had reached the conclusion that a mastery of the social graces was not necessarily a sincere expression of inner moral qualities. Like a perpetual stroll on the boardwalk, their lives were spent in a "world of strangers" where appearances could be deceiving and caution was advised.[61]

Beginning in 1890 the crowding of the boardwalk and Ocean Avenue by another group of pleasure seekers was institutionalized. On a July afternoon, the beach band stepped out to the strains of "Baby Mine," an appropriate tune to kick off Asbury Park's first annual Baby Parade. Bradley led a procession of two hundred infants wheeled along in carriages decorated with flowers, flags, and bunting.[62] This aggregation of "infantile loveliness and happy parents" was a perfect attraction for a respectable resort. In a *Handbook of American Pageantry* (1914), Ralph Davol argued that the essence of such pageants was "designed for the Puritan more than the Bacchanalian or Bohemian." Even if individual manner and appearance no longer revealed inner virtue, the collective activity associated with a pageant remained "a visible manifestation of the community soul." Outdoor pageants were especially beneficial because they were held in the "antiseptic sunlight and air" which killed "moral germs" as well as "disease germs."[63]

The Baby Parade reaffirmed the appeal of Asbury Park as a site for the enjoyment of true recreation. The parade program for 1906, for example, described the resort as a place of refined pleasures where "those seeking rest may find soothing quiet for tired nerves and weary bodies."[64] In particular, the parade reinforced the Park's reputation as a family resort, one of the chief attractions for all respectable middle-class vacation spots. This "great warm wave of infancy" served as a metaphor for the successful "cultivation" of children. Infants appeared as assorted blossoms and fruits. In 1912, for example, "Papa's Peach" appeared in the line of march. "Representing the pit in one half of a divided peach," a three-month-old infant lay

"beneath a tree bearing fruit, on a little grass plot."[65]

By 1912 the Baby Parade featured seven hundred infants and young children and attracted 150,000 spectators. It had been incorporated into a week-long schedule of events which included a "Children's Carnival" and the coronation of Titania, the queen of the fairies. By 1906 Carnival Week activities had been extended to Ocean Grove as the Great Auditorium became the site for "A Night in Fairyland." Under the light of Japanese lanterns, a chorus of one thousand children dressed as fairies performed. They were joined by a "chorus of Maidens" in Indian costume, the "Mandolin Club of young ladies," and the Boys' Rough Riders Company.[66]

While the Baby Parade continued well into the twentieth century, there was no denying that Asbury Park was experiencing subtle yet profound changes in its "community soul." Those changes generated conflict between the twin cities that belied the cooperative spirit evident during the "Night in Fairyland." After the turn of the century Bradley's control over Asbury Park was successfully challenged by a coalition of local hotel owners and businessmen. Their efforts at creating an "up-to-date resort" included the introduction of leisure practices that directly challenged the founding principles of the OGA. In response, the association's president increasingly identified the Park as within the "territories of sin."

The changes at Asbury Park, however, were far from sweeping. As the Children's Carnival indicated, the commitment to wholesome amusement remained strong at the resort. In addition, the tradition of city planning established by the Founder was carried on. Prior to the First World War the resort felt the influence of the City Beautiful movement. By 1905, for example, several large boardwalk pavilions had been erected in the Beaux Arts style. For City Beautiful advocates, Beaux Arts neoclassicism embodied the qualities of public order, cultural unity, and civic virtue.[67] In 1936 Mayor Clarence E. F. Hetrick linked Bradley with City Beautiful advocates while commenting on the history of comprehensive planning at Asbury Park. They both contributed to building "a city dedicated to health and happiness among wholesome surroundings."[68]

In 1912 the Asbury Park city council backed up the commitment to a City Beautiful by proposing a bond issue to pay for everything from "sewers to rhododendrons." That action was far less significant, however, than another event that occurred that spring. For the first time, regular Sunday train service was provided to the Asbury Park–Ocean Grove station. In order to protect the sanctity of the Sabbath, such service had been previously banned through an agreement between the OGA and the railroads serving the twin cities. After the turn of the century officials and businessmen at Asbury Park began serious appeals to state regulatory agencies in support of Sunday trains. In what must have seemed like a cruel irony to many Grovers, the breaking of the Sabbath restriction was heralded using revivalist terminology. It was part of the "Great Awakening" of Asbury Park.[69]

Sunday train service was not the only innovation sought at the Park. A coalition of local businessmen favored Sunday amusements and liquor licenses for the large hotels. They also supported a proposal to build a continuous Ocean Boulevard along the New Jersey coast in order to attract tourists in motorcars. This agenda was the culmination of a "liberal revolt" against Bradley and his "old guard" who were "imbued with conservatism." Its most prominent leader was Frank L. TenBroeck, the owner of one of the resort's major hotels. As a member of the city council, he clashed with Bradley on several occasions. In 1901 the Founder defeated TenBroeck in a race for mayor. Two years later, however, the hotel man won the position after a bitter campaign against a member of the "old guard."[70]

While leadership at Asbury Park was changing, the backgrounds and commitment of members of the OGA remained fixed. As the governing body at Ocean Grove, the OGA had a history marked by continuity. When the Grove

celebrated its twenty-fifth anniversary in 1894, for example, every member of the association had served for two decades or more. Because vacancies were filled by vote of OGA members, the selection of individuals sympathetic to the original aims of the organization was virtually assured. There was no real mechanism for a "liberal revolt" at Ocean Grove.

No one better represented the continuity of leadership at the Grove than the Reverend Aaron E. Ballard, who wrote the famous paragraph on amusements for the *Book of Discipline*. Ballard served as vice president of the OGA from the 1870s until 1907. In that year, at age eighty-seven, he became only the third president in the history of the association. It was Ballard who became the chief spokesman for Ocean Grove in its growing dispute with Asbury Park. By 1911 his position was that the Grove was "the vineyard of God," assailed on every side by "the powers of darkness."[71]

The OGA led the fight to preserve the ban on Sunday trains. The association also refused to participate in the Ocean Boulevard scheme, calling it a "race track" that would violate Sabbath restrictions. Like the trains, the noise from carriages and motorcars would disrupt the "other-worldly stillness" of an Ocean Grove Sunday. Finally, the OGA petitioned the state legislature to uphold a law banning the sale of intoxicants within one mile of a camp-meeting site. This would effectively stop the granting of liquor licenses to major hotels in Asbury Park.[72]

For more than a decade prior to 1912 Asbury Park newspapers reported on the growing tensions between the twin cities. "The partnership of Asbury Park and Ocean Grove is pulling apart," an *Asbury Park Press* correspondent observed, "one toward intolerance and the other toward liberty." Other newspapers carried comments on the bigotry, fanaticism, and "spirit of monopoly" represented by the "puritanical restrictions" imposed by the OGA.[73] In 1905 an editorial writer for the *Asbury Park Press* acknowledged that there were people "whose only entertainment is a quilting bee and who look upon anything that conduces to cheerfulness as a crime." If that were the only right way to live, however, resort towns could never prosper and furnish economic benefits to residents. The writer concluded by urging city councilors at Asbury Park "to do right and recognize the difference between healthful and elevating entertainment and the asceticism of the Middle Ages."[74]

As the above reference to "healthful and elevating entertainment" indicates, Asbury Park did not abandon its status as a respectable resort after the turn of the century. Its promoters were attempting, however, to adjust to cultural trends that were apparent even among church people. Their demand for Sunday amusements and train service, for example, reflected the continued relaxation of strict Sabbath observance. In 1900 the Methodist bishops acknowledged the trend in the report of their General Conference. "Obviously there is within the Church, as well as in the world without, a serious and rapidly increasing laxity of Sabbath observance. Unnecessary travel, unnecessary work, the Sunday newspaper, social visiting, excursions, and amusements encroach more and more on time which God has consecrated to sacred uses."[75]

Asbury Park had always been a place to get away from the pressures of work and the heat in the crowded city. Bradley had hoped to use the resort to demonstrate how the problems of urban life could be solved. After 1900, however, Asbury Park promoters increasingly emphasized merely the need to escape and valued respectable amusements as good business policy. They were no longer concerned with formulating moral and intellectual justifications for play in a Christian America. They were, however, interested in cashing in on the widespread acceptance of the "gospel of recreation." In so doing, they willingly compromised some of the original principles upon which the resort was founded.

The story at Ocean Grove was much different. The camp-meeting resort had been established during a period in which American evangelicalism was so influential as to be virtually a religious establishment. While extremely conservative, holiness advocates shared in the Protestant consensus that religion and civilization were intimately connected. In addition, their movement bore the unmistakable mark of the middle-class culture in which it originated. The cult of sincerity and the holiness movement had grown to prominence in tandem by the 1850s. Holiness advocates never abandoned the assumption that outward manners and appearance were sincere expressions of inner virtue. In fact, they sanctified the notion by linking behavior and dress with the striving for Christian perfection.[76]

In the 1870s holiness advocates were among the nation's respectable evangelicals. Fifty years later, they and other conservative Christians were a defensive minority. The reason for this change in circumstance was partly religious. By the turn of the century the influence of articulate liberal spokesmen was clearly increasing within American Protestantism. Rising to prominence after 1900, the social gospel movement was led by liberal-minded Protestant evangelicals who sought to rally Christians to deal with social problems resulting from industrialization and urbanization. Their approach called into question some of the basic religious assumptions that had inspired nineteenth-century efforts at reform.[77]

In particular, advocates of the social gospel challenged the individualism of nineteenth-century evangelicalism. They did not subscribe to the notion that individual character flaws were the sole cause of distress and disorder. The search for personal salvation alone did not appear sufficient to address major concerns in an era of big cities and big business. Conservatives, for example, viewed drunkenness as an individual vice and focused their efforts on reforming the drunkard. By contrast, social gospel advocates tended to regard drinking as a social problem, partially the result of the horrendous living and working conditions experienced by many Americans in the nation's industrial centers. Supporters of the social gospel argued that without ameliorating these conditions the problem of alcohol consumption could never be effectively addressed.

By the early twentieth century American Protestants appeared divided into two camps that historians have labeled "private" and "public" Protestantism. Supporters of "private Protestantism" seized the name "evangelical" and continued to emphasize personal salvation and individual moral conduct as the means to secure a Christian nation. These were the kind of people who made their summer homes at Ocean Grove. "Public Protestantism" was represented by the social gospel movement.[78] Whether operating a settlement house in an urban slum or championing the right of labor to organize, social gospel advocates measured their beliefs by their success in serving humanity. In addition to rejecting the individualism inherent in nineteenth-century evangelicalism, they often seemed to put a concern for civilization first, with their religious message serving as a means to an end. They still pursued the goal of creating a Christian America, but their priorities had been subtly reversed. As Robert Handy observed, "Men were being exhorted to be religious for the sake of civilization."[79]

The evangelicals' reaction to the social gospel is crucial to understanding important changes in their social views after the turn of the century. Even though religious conservatives represented "private Protestantism," they had no objection in principle to social activism. As the summer program at Ocean Grove illustrated, the holiness movement led many people to an interest in a variety of reforms. For holiness advocates and other conservative evangelicals, however, preaching the gospel was always the central aim. Support for social programs was seen as an outgrowth of the regenerating work of Christ operating through individuals. As Dwight L. Moody put it, the true Christian was imbued with "power for service" to his community. By contrast, proponents of the social gospel appeared to stress the need for service without adequately emphasizing the "power" behind it. Furthermore, in the minds of evangelicals, social gospel advocates were increasingly identified with liberal theology and the Progressive movement in politics through which they pursued many of their goals.[80]

In reacting to the social gospel, religious conservatives tended to become political conservatives as well. They increasingly concentrated their "power for service" on issues such as prohibition and protecting the Sabbath, leaving the larger field of social action to the liberals. For more than a century revivalist Protestants had followed fairly closely shifts in political thought, lending their Christian perspective to prevailing trends. At the turn of the century, however, this parallel development was interrupted. Conservative evangelicals fixated on a set of social and political views that had been characteristic of middle-class Americans before 1900. The concentration of the OGA on the issues of temperance and Sabbath observance in the dispute with Asbury Park illustrated this trend.[81]

As significant as their reaction to religious and political developments was the transformation evangelicals experienced in relation to the general culture. By the turn of the century, the genteel standards that marked Victorianism were confronted by a developing and vibrant mass culture.[82] Especially disturbing for such organizations as the OGA, some of the most striking examples of cultural change were found in the area of popular amusements. The movies, for example, moved from penny arcades and billiard halls in working-class neighborhoods to attract a middle-class audience. The new amusement parks such as those at Coney Island dazzled visitors with a variety of attractions, including technological amusements, dance halls, vaudeville theaters, and circus acts. Finally, the automobile contributed to the decline in strict Sabbath observance. A "Sunday drive" was itself a pleasure, and increased mobility made places of amusement all the more accessible on any day of the week. This was a fact well understood by Asbury Parkers who supported the Ocean Boulevard scheme.[83]

In the context of a changing culture, traditional religious beliefs and the behaviors associated with them were often perceived as quaint and outdated. Conservative evangelicals were becoming ideologically and socially "uprooted" in their own country. Like immigrants to a strange new land, they had to adjust to a different cultural setting. For people who had hoped to set the cultural agenda for the nation, it was an especially distressing situation.[84]

The difficulty evangelicals experienced in adjusting to that situation was apparent at Ocean Grove. Because of their religious convictions, Grovers were destined to be cultural conservatives from the day their resort was founded. By the 1860s increasing numbers of middle-class Americans had reached the conclusion that it was not always possible to determine inner virtue from outward appearance. Proper social forms remained important, but only because they defined social intercourse in polite society. In effect, everyone was expected at least to act as though they belonged in a Christian America.[85]

For holiness advocates, such a rejection of the cult of sincerity was difficult. An emphasis on social practice divorced from inner virtue smacked of a kind of vapid cultural formalism. It was like mounting the pulpit in a fine brownstone church and preaching a polished sermon that ignored the importance of the second blessing. It resembled a commitment to social and moral reform that failed to acknowledge fully the source of an individual's "power for service." Holiness advocates were opposed to the growing worldliness and formality of urban Methodism. They could hardly be expected to admire cultured manners devoid of sincerity just because they facilitated social relations in this world. As with the social gospel, the priorities seemed to be shifting subtly to an emphasis on the requirements of civilization at the expense of stressing the importance of genuine belief.

Having committed themselves to the cult of sincerity, holiness believers faced yet another difficulty. Once specific activities were identified as involving "imprudent and unchristian conduct," they could not very well become prudent and Christian at a later date. If drinking, dancing, and going to the circus were inherently sinful in 1869, they remained sinful in 1912. No matter how the general culture changed, holiness advocates remained rooted to fixed principles and the condemnation of specific immoral behavior. This was the source of the intransigence that Grovers displayed in their dealings with Asbury Park.

One nineteenth-century guidebook writer had compared Ocean Grove to a medieval fortified town ruled by an autocrat.[86] The analogy became increasingly appropriate after 1900. The intransigence of Grovers regarding change at Asbury Park was an example of the sharp militancy adopted by many evangelicals at the turn of the century. Bolstered by deeply held religious convictions, they refused to be willing participants in the process of cultural change. More than that, they employed the military imagery common to American evangelicalism to mount a holy war against change, as though defending the heavily fortified walls of Zion against attack.[87] Grovers saw the devil at the gate in the form of Asbury Park hotel owners who wanted to dispense wine or Sunday excursionists arriving aboard a train. Surrounded by these "powers of darkness," it was not surprising that a fortress mentality gripped the leadership of the OGA.

A firm commitment to "first principles" at Ocean Grove did not mean that every new form of entertainment was summarily dismissed by the OGA. After 1900 the old test that identified true recreations was still applied. An activity could be sanctioned if it was not "inimical to the cause of religion" after all "objectionable features" were removed. The OGA sponsored, for example, an annual series of concerts in the auditorium featuring works such as Handel's *Messiah* and such major operatic stars as Madame Nordica. Tali Esen Morgan, music director for the OGA, planned performances of both secular and sacred music. He pointed out that John Wesley himself had adapted street songs to religious purposes. "I believe that God deserves the best music we can give Him," Morgan insisted. In addition, a developed taste for "pure music" of every sort would especially benefit children by helping them resist "amusements of a corrupting kind" as they grew older.[88]

The concert series in the Great Auditorium served as an example of how culture could be blended with religion and thus contribute to enriching life in a Christian America. Alan Trachtenberg has identified this "sacralization" of American culture specifically with Chautauqua.[89] In fact, it was an objective shared by the developers of every type of respectable resort, with some important differences in emphasis. The mother Chautauqua in New York was established on what was once a camp-meeting site, but its founders had consciously eliminated revivalism from their enterprise. In 1895 a writer in *Forum* magazine credited them with creating an institution that was "educational without ceasing to be religious."[90] For Christians who regarded camp meeting as an important evangelical arm of the church, the Chautauqua program was disconcerting. Its focus was on popular education in art, science, and current events, although these were presented in a format patterned after camp meeting. But once again, the primary emphasis appeared to have shifted from religion to civilization.[91] Ocean Grove, on the other hand, attempted to keep its priorities in proper order. The OGA crafted a religious community which also provided educational and recreational attractions. As stated in the *Annual Report* for 1889, Ocean Grove "was not first a town, and then religion—but *first* religion and *then* a town."[92] As at other camp-meeting resorts, the OGA sought to keep summer residents focused on the primary purpose of the community. A constant round of religious services and meetings was one way of insuring that a "picnic" atmosphere would not predominate. This agenda did not exclude the Chautauqua program. In fact, under the auspices of the Ocean Grove Sunday School Assembly the OGA operated a Chautauqua institute. As with recreational activities, however, educational opportunities were always put in "their right relationships" to religion.[93]

Chautauqua has been credited with reinventing the camp meeting in a modern form. Stripped of the emotionalism and "backwoods frenzy" of the early camps, Chautauqua rationalized the binding together of culture and religion.[94] From the perspective of a nineteenth-century holiness believer, however, the claim might be disputed. It was at resorts such as Ocean Grove that camp meeting was truly reinvented by being raised to an "elevated character." Here was where evangelicals emphasized the primary role of religion in an effort to craft a Christian civilization. Revival services were not eliminated as at Chautauqua; the camp meeting was instead brought under control. Largely through the efforts of holiness advocates, the camp meeting was not a declining phenomenon after the Civil War, but the primary force behind a nationwide network of resorts and campgrounds for which Ocean Grove was a centerpiece.[95] As much as the Chautauquans, holiness believers were committed to "sacralizing" the culture. What they were not interested in was the "higher criticism" of the Bible, Darwinism, and a rationalized Christianity devoid of the fiery baptism of the Holy Spirit.

Because of their extreme conservatism, Grovers were unable to appreciate fully one of their greatest achievements. Along with the developers of other respectable resorts, they played a major role in bringing the Protestant middle class into the leisure revolution. These people already possessed both leisure time and disposable income. At places such as Ocean Grove and Asbury Park, they were provided with a rationale that justified the "duty to play" and a selection of suitable activities for their enjoyment.

What Grovers failed to acknowledge fully was the impact of these middle-class pleasure seekers on the growth and development of commercialized amusements. Entrepreneurs increasingly realized that middle-class participation was necessary in order to create a truly mass leisure industry. Building on the work of nineteenth-century proponents of true recreation, they explored the profit potential in respectable entertainment. After 1900, for example, promoters B. F. Keith and E. F. Albee perfected a network of continuous, inexpensive, and wholesome variety shows. This "high-class vaudeville" was respectable enough for Asbury Park opera houses. In the film industry, the domination of several large studios corresponded with the introduction of the "photoplay" that carried a moral lesson. This pattern of improving the moral tone of commercial entertainments was also evident in professional sport and at resorts and amusement parks. Entrepreneurs were intent on creating a broad-based and lucrative "American audience."[96]

After 1900 Asbury Park promoters insisted on the right to attract that audience, even if they arrived on Sunday trains. They did not intend to undercut the Park's reputation as a respectable resort. They just wanted it to be "up-to-date." More research needs to be done on respectable resorts in general, but a preliminary reading of the evidence suggests that the Park was representative of developments nationwide. According to the standard scenario, a resort was founded by individuals who espoused a commitment to maintaining a Christian civilization. Through dedication and hard work, a relatively prosperous vacation community was created. Sometime after the turn of the century, reform fervor was lost, but a comfortable family-oriented resort remained.

In relatively few cases did a resort survive with its "Methodistical restrictions" intact as at Ocean Grove. The ongoing success of the Grove was due to the continued support of a loyal core group of vacationers and like-minded conservative Christians. Prior to the First World War the commitment of these people to Christianize American culture hardly flagged, and their social and political views were barely altered. Whether seeking personal salvation and moral reform or merely seeking profits, however, promoters of a variety of respectable resorts all endorsed the slogan, "It Pays to Be Decent."

## Notes

1. *Shore Press,* 3 September 1903.
2. On respectable resorts, see Frederick E. Partington, *The Story of Mohonk* (Fulton, NY: The Morrill Press, 1911); Theodore Morrison, *Chautauqua: A Center for Education, Religion, and the Arts in America* (Chicago: University of Chicago Press, 1974); Charles A. Parker, "The Camp Meeting on the Frontier and the Methodist Religious Resort in the East—Before 1900," *Methodist History* 18 (1980): 179–92; Brenda Parnes, "Ocean Grove: A Planned Leisure Environment," in Paul A. Stellhorn, ed., *Planned and Utopian Experiments: Four New Jersey Towns* (Trenton: New Jersey Historical Commission, 1980); Glenn A. Uminowicz, "Sport in a Middle-Class Utopia: Asbury Park, New Jersey, 1871–1895," *Journal of Sport History* 11 (Spring 1984): 51–73; and Ellen Weiss, *City in the Woods: The Life and Design of an American Camp Meeting on Martha's Vineyard* (New York: Oxford University Press, 1987). See also the discussion of sanitariums founded by health reformers in Harvey Green, *Fit for America: Health, Fitness, Sport, and American Society* (New York: Pantheon Books, 1986), 132–36. The discussion of respectable resorts is based in part on Glenn A. Uminowicz, "It Pays to Be Decent: Marketing Respectability in the American Resort Industry, 1870–1915" (paper presented at "Leisure-Time Business: Sports, Resorts, and Commercialized Amusements, 1870–1920" symposium at the Eleutherian Mills Historical Library, Wilmington, DE, May 1984).
3. Dale A. Somers, "The Leisure Revolution: Recreation in the American City, 1820–1920," *Journal of Popular Culture* 5 (1971): 125–47.
4. Robert T. Handy, *A Christian America: Protestant Hopes and Historical Realities* (New York: Oxford University Press, 1984). See also Martin E. Marty, *The Righteous Empire: The Protestant Experience in America* (New York: Harper & Row, 1970).
5. On the holiness movement, see Timothy L. Smith, *Revivalism and Social Reform in Mid-Nineteenth-Century America* (Nashville: Abingdon Press, 1957), especially 103–34; Winthrop S. Hudson, *Religion and American Life* (New York: Charles Scribner's Sons, 1965), 342–45; Charles Edwin Jones, *Perfectionist Persuasion: The Holiness Movement and American Methodism* (Metuchen, NJ: The Scarecrow Press, 1974); Melvin Easterday Dieter, *The Holiness Revival of the Nineteenth Century* (Metuchen,

NJ: The Scarecrow Press, 1980); and George M. Marsden, *Fundamentalism and American Culture: The Shaping of Twentieth-Century Evangelicalism, 1870–1925* (New York: Oxford University Press, 1982), especially 72–101.

6. On the cultural beliefs of Americans and their relationship to revivalism, see William G. McLoughlin, *Revivals, Awakenings, and Reform: An Essay on Religion and Social Change in America, 1607–1977* (Chicago: University of Chicago Press, 1978), especially xiv; and Edward Pessen, *Jacksonian America: Society, Personality, and Politics* (Homewood, IL: The Dorsey Press, 1978), especially 4–32. The belief system of holiness advocates has been described as a kind of "evangelical transcendentalism." See Gerald O. McCulloh and Timothy L. Smith, "The Theology and Practices of Methodism, 1876–1919," in Emory Stevens Bucke, ed., *The History of American Methodism*, vol. 2 (Nashville: Abingdon Press, 1964), 609–18.

7. Pessen, *Jacksonian America*, 68–71; and Paul E. Johnson, *A Shopkeeper's Millennium: Society and Revivals in Rochester, New York, 1815–1837* (New York: Hill and Wang, 1978).

8. Jones, *Perfectionist Persuasion*, 17; and Dieter, *Holiness Revival*, 206.

9. Jones, *Perfectionist Persuasion*, 1–34; Dieter, *Holiness Revival*, 96–155; McCulloh and Smith, "Theology and Practices of Methodism," 608–18; and Dieter, *Holiness Revival*, 25–32, 57–63.

10. On the history of Ocean Grove, see Morris S. Daniels, *The Story of Ocean Grove* (New York: The Methodist Book Concern, 1919); Richard F. Gibbons, *History of Ocean Grove* (Ocean Grove: Ocean Grove Times, 1939); Richard E. Brewer, *Perspectives on Ocean Grove* (Ocean Grove: Historical Society of Ocean Grove, 1976); and Charles A. Parker, *A Study of the Preaching at the Ocean Grove, 1870–1900* (Ph.D. diss., Louisiana State University, 1959).

11. *New York Tribune*, 5 August 1889.

12. On the significance and symbolism of music in camp meeting, see Jones, *Perfectionist Persuasion*, 35–46. The full lyrics for "Beulah Land" are published in George D. Elderkin, *The Finest of the Wheat: Hymns Old and New* (Chicago: R. R. McCabe, 1890), 199.

13. *Twentieth Anniversary of the Ocean Grove Camp-Meeting Association* (Ocean Grove: Ocean Grove Record, 1889), 19.

14. Jones, *Perfectionist Persuasion*, 34.

15. Leo Marx, *The Machine in the Garden: Technology and the Pastoral Ideal in America* (New York: Oxford University Press, 1964). See also Howard P. Segal, "Leo Marx's 'Middle Landscape': A Critique, a Revision, and an Appreciation," *Reviews in American History* 5 (March 1977): 137–50. For a discussion of resorts, see Charles E. Funnell, *By the Beautiful Sea: The Rise and High Times of That Great American Resort, Atlantic City* (New York: Knopf, 1975), 124–25.

16. The remark was made regarding Long Branch, New Jersey, in the *New York Times*, 28 July 1868.

17. *The Annual Report of the President of the Ocean Grove Camp-Meeting Association for 1890*, 43–44. Published annual reports of the OGA are in the collections of the Monmouth County Historical Association, Freehold, NJ, and the Ocean Grove Historical Society.

18. Interpretation of the built environment of Ocean Grove and Asbury Park is in part based on an analysis of maps produced by the Sanborn Map Company and contained in the *New Jersey Coast Series* (Sanborn Map and Publishing Co., 1890 and 1905). Also useful is Chester Wolverton, *Atlas of Monmouth County, New Jersey* (New York: by the author, 1889). I have been influenced in my analysis by Kevin Lynch, *The Image of the City* (Cambridge: MIT Press, 1960); and Grady Clay, *Close-Up: How to Read the American City* (Chicago: University of Chicago Press, 1980).

19. Daniels, *Story of Ocean Grove*, 53–63; Gibbons, *History of Ocean Grove*, 17–20; and *Annual Report* (1894), 40–43.

20. *New York Tribune*, 23 August 1890.

21. John R. Stilgoe, *Common Landscapes of America, 1580 to 1845* (New Haven: Yale University Press, 1982), 231–38.

22. Reference to the "roving crowd" is found in the *New York Tribune*, 21 August 1889.

23. On Moody, see William G. McLoughlin, *Modern Revivalism: Charles Grandison Finney to Billy Graham* (New York: The Ronald Press, 1959), 166–281; and James F. Findlay, Jr., *Dwight L. Moody: American Evangelist* (Chicago: University of Chicago Press, 1969). Moody was among the most influential figures in nineteenth-century American Protestantism. In addition to the commitment to a subdued form of revivalism, holiness advocates shared other significant views with Moody. While the urban evangelist did not preach the second blessing, he did stress the role of the Holy Ghost in the process of conversion. In addition, both Moody and holiness advocates viewed revivalism as a rejuvenator of "dead churches" that were ineffective in serving the spiritual needs of their members and reaching the "unevangelized masses." Despite the professed commitment to reaching beyond the middle class, however, both Moody's revivals and holiness camp meetings remained identified with the "better sort of people."

24. Jones, *Perfectionist Persuasion*, 16–46. On increasing formalism in patterns of worship and on

revivalism as ritual, see McCulloh and Smith, "Theology and Practice," 627–36; and John L. Hammond, *The Politics of Benevolence: Revival Religion and American Voting Behavior* (Norwood, NJ: Ablex Publishing Co., 1979), 27.

25. Parker, *Preaching at Ocean Grove,* 160–267; and Gibbons, *History of Ocean Grove,* 21–25.

26. *Annual Report* (1887), 58–59, (1888), 62–63, (1890), 64, (1892), 73–74; *New York Tribune,* 29 August 1890; *Daily Spray,* 30 August 1893; *New York Times,* 31 August 1894.

27. *Annual Report* (1887), 48.

28. *Baedeker's Guide to the United States with an Excursion into Mexico* (New York: Charles Scribner's Sons, 1893), 222.

29. *New York Times,* 19 August 1888 and 3 August 1895; *Annual Report* (1879), 30–31, (1883), 44.

30. On American Victorianism, see Daniel Walker Howe, "American Victorianism as a Culture," *American Quarterly* 27 (December 1975): 507–32; and Harvey Green, *The Light of the Home: An Intimate View of the Lives of Women in the Victorian Era* (New York: Pantheon Books, 1983).

31. John A. Ruth, *Decorum: A Practical Treatise on Etiquette and Dress of the Best American Society* (New York: J. A. Ruth and Co., 1879), 12; and Maud C. Cooke, *Social Life; or, The Manners and Customs of Polite Society* (Buffalo, NY: The Mathews-Northrup Co., 1896), 17.

32. *Annual Report* (1881), 31–32.

33. *Annual Report* (1878), 23–24, (1880), 27, (1890), 30.

34. *Puck,* 10 September 1876.

35. *New York Daily Graphic,* 27 August 1874.

36. On neighboring, see John A. Jakle, *The American Small Town: Twentieth-Century Place Images* (Hamden, CT: Archon Books, 1982), 60–64. On the visibility of domestic life at a camp-meeting resort and on cottages arranged to heighten a sense of community, see Weiss, *City in the Woods,* 69–75.

37. *Annual Report* (1880), 28–29.

38. Quoted in *Annual Report* (1890), 66.

39. *Annual Report* (1887), 28.

40. T. Otto Hall and James P. Pilkington, "Methodist Publishing in Historical Perspective," in Bucke, *The History of American Methodism,* vol. 3, 162–63.

41. *Seaside Directory of the Jersey Coast* (about 1881), unpaginated.

42. Daniel T. Rodgers, *The Work Ethic in Industrial America, 1850–1920* (Chicago: University of Chicago Press, 1974), 108–54.

43. Herbert Spencer, "The Gospel of Recreation," *Popular Science Monthly,* January 1883, 354–59.

44. E. H. Stokes, "Historical Address," in *Annual Report* (1875), 31–32.

45. Ibid., 32.

46. A. E. Ballard, "Bathing," in *Annual Report* (1875), 59.

47. *Daily Spray,* 27 August 1886.

48. Green, *Fit for America,* 28.

49. *Annual Report* (1894), 76–78.

50. James A. Bradley, *Three Ways of Telling the History of Asbury Park* (Asbury Park: M., W., and C. Pennypacker, 1897), n.p. For more detailed information on James A. Bradley and the growth of Asbury Park, see Uminowicz, "Sport in a Middle-Class Utopia," 53–65.

51. Stephen Crane, "On the Boardwalk: Aug. 14, 1892," in Fredson Bowers, ed., *The Works of Stephen Crane: Tales, Sketches, and Reports,* vol. 8 (Charlottesville, VA: University Press of Virginia, 1973), 515.

52. *Asbury Park Journal,* 3 June 1876.

53. George F. Bacon, *Asbury Park and Ocean Grove with Their Points of Interest* (Newark, NJ: Mercantile Publishing Co., 1892), 27.

54. Uminowicz, "Sport in a Middle-Class Utopia," 65–70.

55. *London Times,* reprinted in the *Ocean Grove and Neptune Times,* 17 August 1885.

56. *Asbury Park Journal,* 22 July 1886.

57. On melodrama, see Robert C. Toll, *On with the Show: The First Century of American Show Business* (New York: Oxford University Press, 1976), 141–70; and David Grimsted, *Melodrama Unveiled: American Theater and Culture, 1800–1850* (Chicago: University of Chicago Press, 1968).

58. Crane, "On the Boardwalk," 515–16.

59. *Daily Spray,* 13 August 1889, 9 July 1892, and 29 June 1893.

60. *Asbury Park Journal,* 13 September 1879, 13 July 1886, and 20 July 1894.

61. On the cult of sincerity, see Karen Halttunen, *Confidence Men and Painted Women, 1830–1870* (New Haven: Yale University Press, 1982).

62. *Shore Press,* 25 July 1890.

63. Ralph Davol, *A Handbook of American Pageantry* (Tauton, MA: Davol Publishing Co., 1914).

64. *Children's Carnival and Baby Parade Souvenir Program* (1906), 18. Brochure in the collections of the Monmouth College Library, West Long Branch, NJ.

65. *Asbury Park Evening Press,* 22 August 1912.

66. *Children's Carnival Program* (1906), 26.

67. John F. Kasson, *Amusing the Million: Coney Island at the Turn of the Century* (New York: Hill and Wang, 1978), 17–23.

68. *Asbury Park Evening Press,* 11 June 1936.

69. Ibid., 1 April 1912.

70. For a discussion of politics in Asbury Park in the period, see *Asbury Park Sunday Press,* 17 June 1934.

71. *Annual Report* (1911), 9.

72. *Annual Report* (1901), 12–13, (1905), 75–77, (1908), 50–53, (1911), 69–70, (1912), 90–92.

73. *Asbury Park Press*, 1 June 1900; *Shore Press*, 9 April 1903, 24 April 1904, 26 July 1908; *Asbury Park Journal*, 15 June 1900.

74. *Asbury Park Press* quoted in the *Long Branch Record*, 24 March 1905.

75. *Journal of the General Conference of the Methodist Episcopal Church, 1900* quoted in Handy, *Christian America*, 145.

76. Jones, *Perfectionist Persuasion*, 1–6, 85–86.

77. On the social gospel and the conservative reaction to it, see Hudson, *Religion in America*, 310–15; Marty, *Righteous Empire*, 199–209; and Handy, *Christian America*, 156–70.

78. Marty, *Righteous Empire*, 177–87.

79. Handy, *Christian America*, 164.

80. Marsden, *Fundamentalism and American Culture*, 85–93. Marsden makes the important point stressed here that the distinction between "private" and "public" Protestantism should not obscure the contribution of nineteenth-century evangelicals to the tradition of reform. Private Christianity did not involve looking only at the next world and personal salvation. Dieter asserts, for example, that holiness believers directed the concept of individual freedom from sin outward toward the creation of a society freed from evil as well in *Holiness Revival*, 23–24. Their perfectionist idealism actually paved the way for later reformers, including advocates of the social gospel. Handy also notes that the social gospel was in many ways in continuity with "the old dream" of maintaining a Christian civilization in *Christian America*, 162. Nevertheless, the "social ethic" espoused by advocates of the social gospel did mark a sharp break with an earlier individualistic reform tradition that had in part been inspired by nineteenth-century revivalism. For a comparison between approaches to reform in the nineteenth and early twentieth centuries, see Paul Boyer, *Urban Masses and Moral Order in America*, especially 121–283.

81. Marsden, *Fundamentalism and American Culture*, 92–93; and Handy, *Christian America*, 143–54.

82. George M. Marsden, "From Fundamentalism to Evangelicalism: A Historical Analysis," in David F.

Wells and John D. Woodbridge, eds., *The Evangelicals: What They Believe, Who They Are, and Where They Are Changing* (Nashville: Abingdon Press, 1975), 129–34.

83. Kasson, *Amusing the Million*, 6–7; and Handy, *Christian America*, 146–47.

84. Marsden, "From Fundamentalism to Evangelicalism," 131–33.

85. Halttunen, *Confidence Men*, 187–89.

86. Gustav Kobbe, *The New Jersey Coast and Pines* (Short Hills, NJ: by the author, 1889), 52.

87. Marsden, "From Fundamentalism to Evangelicalism," 129–34.

88. *Annual Report* (1900), 65–69, (1906), 23–24.

89. Alan Trachtenberg, " 'We Study the Word and Works of God': Chautauqua and the Sacralization of Culture in America," in Sannia Weingartner, ed., *The Henry Ford Museum and Greenfield Village Herald* 13, 2 (1984): 3–11.

90. Albert Cook, "Chautauqua: Its Aims and Influence," *Forum*, 19 August 1895, 689.

91. Dieter, *Holiness Movement*, 110.

92. *Annual Report* (1889), 43.

93. *Annual Report* (1887), 47, (1894), 86–87.

94. Trachtenberg, " 'We Study,' " 5.

95. Dieter, *Holiness Revival*, 110, 126.

96. See, for example, Funnell, *By the Beautiful Sea*, 76–78; Steven A. Reiss, *Touching Base: Professional Baseball and American Culture in the Progressive Period* (Westport, CT: Greenwood Press, 1980); Robert Toll, *The Entertainment Machine: American Show Business in the Twentieth Century* (New York: Oxford University Press, 1982), 10–11; and Lary May, *Screening Out the Past: The Birth of Mass Culture and the Motion Picture Industry* (New York: Oxford University Press, 1980), 43–95. See also Peter Bailey, *Leisure and Class in Victorian England: Rational Recreation and the Contest for Control, 1830–1885* (Toronto: University of Toronto Press, 1978), 147–68. Bailey argues that the application of the discipline of the respectability to both audience and performers was part of the general rationalization of British music hall operation. The aim was to attract a "general audience" which included members of the middle class.

# "The Germans Take Care of Our Celebrations"

Middle-Class Americans Appropriate German Ethnic Culture in

Buffalo in the 1850s

DAVID A. GERBER

## The Problem in Context

By 1857 Buffalo's Fourth of July parade had come to reflect the city's recent march toward ethnic diversity. Foreigners were now a large majority of the city's people. German-speakers alone were nearly half the population.[1] Marching as members of ethnic fraternal, military, and craft associations, foreigners made up a constantly growing component of the procession, which was the high point of the municipality's official celebration. Their prominent role lent an exotic flavor to the festivities, and they were, for many Americans, variously a troublesome, paradoxical, or simply an objectionable presence at the national birthday party. There were native-born Americans for whom the situation symbolized Americans' loss of authority over their own culture and history and over the civic order their ancestors had created. In 1857 the Buffalo *Express,* the most outspokenly antiforeign (or "nativist") of the local daily newspapers, gave testimony to this troublesome development with an anecdote it published shortly after the commemoration of the Fourth. Editor Almon Clapp related overhearing one American "gentleman" say to another as the parade, with its promi-

nent representation of German marching bands and *Vereine* [associations], passed them, "The Germans take care of our celebrations and the Irish take care of our elections."[2] The operative word, of course, is "our," suggesting an anachronistic, proprietary feeling about an increasingly pluralistic public life.

This comment, which foreign editors such as Michael Hagan of the Irish-Catholic Buffalo *Sentinel* interpreted as simply another example of the unrelenting abuse to which their people were subject in Clapp's paper,[3] did indeed contain at least one especially potent source of antiforeign nativism, which in its political form, the American party, had been claiming the majority of the American vote since 1853.[4] There was no more disturbing development in the emergence of Americans' perception of being an increasingly powerless minority within their own national home than the power that Irish-Catholic Democratic politicians had skillfully been able to attain for themselves in local politics. Though only some 18 percent of the population, the Irish had been prepared for political competition in America through their struggle with Anglo-Saxon political institutions in colonized Ireland, and they were aided by their knowledge of English. Now, in America, with the opportunity afforded by political equality, they actually seemed capable of remaking the civic order in their own, foreign image.[5] In league with a few prominent American political families, they were successful in the later years of the decade in gaining control of the local party apparatus, getting local patronage jobs vastly out of proportion to their numbers, and even attaining national recognition, as well as enhanced political legitimacy, in consequence of some local federal appointments.[6] The majority of Americans strained bitterly under the burden of this incipient foreign regime. It was all the more unacceptable to them because of the rude, peasant ways of the large, impoverished majority of the Irish, whose reputation for shiftlessness, squalid living conditions, crime, violence, and alcoholism was unmatched, in American minds, by that of any other of the city's groups. And it seemed all the more dangerous because of Irish obedience to and public defense of the Catholic church. The old-world history and politics of the church were thought by most Americans to prove Catholicism inimical to the security of republican institutions.[7]

But this is not, by any means, the whole story. Americans themselves were to a significant extent the authors of their own dilemma. The illusive word "our" in speaking of contemporary public life offered Americans no protection against the pluralistic potentialities in the institutions and civic ideology they had been fashioning since the Revolution. The Fourth of July had come to reflect the city's new social pluralism, not because of immigrant impositions on native prerogatives, but rather because, in its formulation of citizenship and of the aspirations of republican institutions, the nation's American-crafted civic ideology was universalistic, cosmopolitan, and eclectic.[8] It did not allow Americans, in spite of their claims to the mantle of the Founding Fathers, to monopolize control over the nation's symbols. Moreover, while it was frequently alleged that the Irish were culturally

unprepared for republican citizenship, herded by ward heelers to the polls, and voting exactly as priests and venal ethnic leaders commanded, few Americans claimed the Irish had become citizens and voters by anything other than the quite liberal legal processes generously and idealistically conceived by American-controlled congresses and state legislatures.[9] Nor could it be said that what power the Irish had achieved was sustained only by corruption and violence. Rather it was the skill of the Irish at playing the political game already in place when they arrived and at creatively fashioning new roles for themselves within existing political institutions that caused irritation. The Irish were besting Americans at their own game and in the process staking their own claims to be Americans, if not by birth then by participation in the politics of the republic. Nativism was an effort, ill-tempered and wholly unsuccessful in its legislative aims, to change the rules of political participation in the middle of the game.

A similar American dilemma is evident when we consider more closely the role of Buffalo's Germans in all of the city's major "celebrations." The Fourth of July was not the only context in which Germans seemed to be organizing Americans' leisure time, though it was the most dramatic because of its potent symbolism. Indeed, at the very time nativist politics and temperance activism were asserting an increasingly powerful hold on American loyalties, Buffalo's Americans, seemingly contradictorily, were coming to embrace many elements of German ethnic culture, to which they were exposed as a consequence of the settlement of thousands of German refugees and immigrants around and among them. German folk songs and symphonic and chamber music had come not simply to dominate the local music scene. They actually *created* that scene, for previously there had been little musical performance beyond the occasional traveling tenor or soprano with accompanist and the semiprivate parlor recitals by local "professors." Americans thrilled to the gymnastic feats of the two associations of Buffalo *Turner* [gymnasts and the name of a formal organization], and partly under this influence they became more active in achieving physical fitness. Indeed, Germans had begun to offer Americans instruction in the development of their bodies. Americans, too, were coming to participate enthusiastically in the various German-organized *Feste*. These were day- to week-long celebrations, with multiform activities in several locations, that magically transformed the entire city into an adult playground, variously dedicated to song, to German cultural heroes such as Schiller, to the coming of summer, and, on one notable occasion, solely to sampling *Lagerbier*. Frequently held out-of-doors and always accompanied by good food and enough beer, said one local reporter, "to float a good-sized canal boat,"[10] these German festivals sometimes assaulted bourgeois attitudes about privacy and propriety. Yet in the process of surrendering themselves to German *Gemütlichkeit*, Americans would learn to question just such well-established cultural notions.

We must note that nativism and opposition to the consumption of alcohol were simultaneously exerting a powerful hold on Americans. It is clearly not enough, by way of explanation, to locate the presence of that accomplished trickster, irony, who conveniently allows us to mention contradictions without explaining them. Nor is it sufficient, though it is more promising, to look to the Americans' composite emotional response to the Germans, especially in comparison with their views of the Irish, to find an explanation. It is true that the American image of the Germans was considerably more positive. German craft and property-holding were recognized as civic virtues. The law-abiding behavior of individual Germans and the order reigning in German households and neighborhoods were widely praised. The German reputation for rational amusements stood the group in sharp contrast to the American vision of the drunken, brawling Irish.[11] It is true, too, that Americans recognized that about half the church-going Germans were Protestants and hence potentially more acceptable as citizens and voters, and that even the Catholic remainder had a different, less obedient style of sectarian loyalty, which focused not on the hierarchy but on the neighborhood parish.[12] Furthermore, though the majority of the city's Democrats were Germans, the Germans were too divided among themselves—between the various Protestant denominations, Protestants and Catholics, northerners and southerners, Alsatians and immigrants from the historic German states, and newcomers and older residents—and too inexperienced at democratic politics to become as menacing to American political interests as the Irish. German votes sealed Democratic rule, as they continually complained, but Germans themselves profited rather little from the power they exerted in local elections.[13] Finally, again unlike the Irish, who often seemed quite indifferent to what Americans thought of them, German ethnic leadership was skilled at impression management. We shall see this when we look at the ways in which these communal leaders courted and structured American participation at their various ethnic *Feste*.

Yet the Germans were still foreigners, and American nativists made no distinction between them and the Irish in seeking legislation to proscribe immigrant political power by changing the process through which one became a citizen (fig. 1). True, many Germans were Protestants, but the churches that claimed most of them (such as the Lutheran and Evangelical Reformed) had no American membership at all in Buffalo and few ties with American congregations. Then, too, within the generalized, positive, American image of the Germans, there were actually some troublesome elements. The stolid, cottage-owning German craftsman or building laborer was thought, for all his other virtues, to have a disturbing propensity both for radicalism when angry at his employer or at the government and for atheism and anticlericalism, which weakened his psychological resistance to extreme ideologies of the Left.[14] Furthermore, Germans were said by American contempo-

Fig. 1 In this political cartoon, Uncle Sam warns that immigrants will not be true Americans until they give up ties to their homelands. Germans' interest in beer is symbolized by St. Gambrinus—the mythical king of Flanders, inventor of beer, and Germany's patron saint of drinking. "Reform Is Necessary in the Foreign Line," by Thomas Nast, cover engraving of *Harper's Weekly*, 14 April 1877.

man things and to seek foreign alternatives to the world they themselves were then creating during the formative era of American modernization. If Americans of the middle classes allowed themselves to learn by the German example how to enjoy themselves—and this, more than the polemics of American cultural ideologists, was the mechanism by which the local, popular culture of recreation grew— what was it that readied them to be instructed? It is my perspective that the attraction of Americans to German ethnic culture, like the Americans' even more contradictory, simultaneous cycle of repulsion and attraction to the culture of Roman Catholicism, reflected a deep crisis in the psychology and culture of American bourgeois civilization.[16] At the heart of that crisis was the nagging, semiconscious perception of those Americans in the broad band of social strata we may call "the middle classes" that somehow the nation's tremendous economic and social development, of which they were justly so proud, was giving rise to a barren public culture that flattened and, in Max Weber's poignant phrase, "disenchanted" the world and made people alien to a significant range of their own needs. In seeking escape and release from the alienating, workaday functionalism of their nascent, urban business civilization, middle-class Americans reached out for vitalizing foreign and exotic sources of both ordinary recreation and aesthetic transcendence.

## The Rise of an American Urban Business Civilization and Its Consequences for Recreation

Buffalo's chief economic functions were dictated both by its location at the terminus of the Erie Canal and at the entrance to the continuously navigable portion of the Great Lakes and by its lack of convenient sources of cheap power. In contrast to Rochester, Utica, and Syracuse, which were then industrializing, Buffalo was a commercial city. It found its principal source of wealth in transshipping people and agricultural and finished goods be-

raries to be "lymphatic" (i.e., apathetic) on any question in which the public good was under debate. Only when their taxes were to be raised for the sake of some civic improvement did they seem to mobilize themselves, and then almost always to fight proposals many Americans regarded as progressive and in everyone's interest.[15] Clearly, then, the Germans did not win American respect for their ethnic culture simply by asserting claims to be extraordinary people with a superior style of life.

Something, therefore, had to be present, or perhaps better said, *lacking,* among Americans that led them to lessen their resistance to Ger-

tween the eastern seaboard and the Midwest.[17] There were some limited industrial spin-offs from the mammoth grain trade, and there were extensive shipyards and dry docks. But large-scale industrialization would have to await the development of hydroelectrification at nearby Niagara Falls at the end of the century.

The local growth generated by the Erie Canal, which opened in 1825, took place in essentially two phases. For the first decade, most of the shipping done out of Buffalo was made up of the movement of people and goods from the East to the recently settled states of the Old Northwest.[18] The trade of this decade gave rise to the construction of great warehouses and passenger depots and to the establishment of transfer and other businesses that provided services for cargo and passengers transferring from canal to lake craft. The rapid growth of this commerce put tremendous pressure on land values on the docks and in the nearby central business district. Wild speculation in land resulted. Highly complex and often quite fraudulent credit arrangements were necessitated by the ceaseless trading in lots as well as by a shortage of currency because of the inadequacy of local banking. Similar credit arrangements also characterized the booming commercial construction industry. The bubble burst in 1837 with the failure of the city's largest construction firm and the jailing of its owner on charges of forgery of notes of credit. The next year brought a national depression which deepened the local collapse.[19]

When recovery came in 1843, its sources lay principally in the inception of the ever-expanding trade of western agricultural goods, especially grain, shipped east via Buffalo, which by 1850 had become the world's busiest grain port (fig. 2). The grain trade placed heavy burdens on marine and warehouse facilities and necessitated massive private investment in such technological innovations as the grain elevator to solve the port's ever-increasing storage problems. The rise, too, of a ship repair and construction industry resulted from the need for carriers to transport the abundant quantities of grain shipped on the lakes to Buffalo.[20]

From late March to late November, from thaw to freeze, the great dock warehouses, shipyards, transfer businesses, grain elevators, and all the services attached to them usually maintained a six-day or six-and-a-half-day week of twelve to fifteen hours, depending on the amount of daylight and the volume of shipping. Shipping steadily increased throughout the season, but it reached its peak with the six-week fall harvests, during which ships might be unloaded all night under the light of the moon or lanterns in order to relieve pressure on the port. Superimposed on these seasonal and daily rhythms was the commercial schedule created by the competitive pressures of the shipping business. Business trips by commission merchants or their agents were required in the spring to firm up relations with suppliers and customers, and dozens of routine commercial chores accompanied the arrival and departure of each cargo.[21]

Leisure is ultimately a temporal concept. It is a state of being in time that is defined not by what we have to do to provide for our material needs but by our opportunities to recreate, to play, or to rest.[22] The nature of social time, and hence of middle-class recreation, in the Buffalo of the canal era was dictated by these rhythms and schedules. By late May when the docks routinely were busy fifteen hours a day, their influence in shaping the time of individuals spread out, in widening concentric circles, beyond the waterfront. Hard-pressed wives of businessmen and office workers found themselves having to serve two suppers each weeknight, one to children and the other to men arriving home from work after 9:00 p.m. Thus, many women or their servants were shopping for food once again after 6:00 p.m., and as long as they had to go out anyway, they used the opportunity to run errands at other shops. The situation grew so oppressive that the usually deferential American retail clerks began to complain publicly that they were losing their opportunity for renewal of mind and body. They issued an open letter to the "ladies of

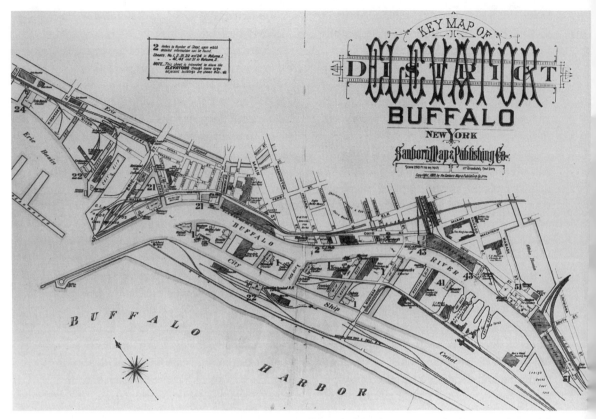

Fig. 2    This 1889 map shows the Elevator District in Buffalo, which by the mid-1800s had become the world's busiest grain port. Courtesy Buffalo and Erie County Historical Society (hereafter BECHS).

Buffalo," asking them to do their shopping earlier, and, after thinly veiled threats of a strike, succeeded in exacting promises from retail merchants that they would not have to work after 8:00 p.m. during the months between April and November.[23]

Everyone in Buffalo's commercial sector had the same complaints about long days and late hours during the eight-month shipping season, but most, employer and office worker alike, received little relief. By the time in late November that the shipping season had ended, the very cold, snowy weather had set in, and the days were greatly shortened. Though offices opened later and closed earlier as the pace of shipping slackened, opportunities for outdoor activity were at a minimum. People retreated to their homes, perhaps to long for warm weather and sunshine in the midst of a gloomy Buffalo winter. For many

middle-class men, however, there was the realization that the return of spring would find them once more immersed in their labors in the office. Only the triumph of the railroads over the canals, which allowed traders to space shipments throughout the entire year, would alleviate somewhat these coercive commercial rhythms. But that triumph would not occur until after the Civil War.

As powerful as work was in shaping the use of time among the middle classes, it was actually only one among several mutually reinforcing elements that constrained the acquisition and development of leisure among them. After all, Americans had also worked hard when they lived on the farms and villages from which they had migrated to Buffalo. But they had simultaneously enjoyed a rich array of rural amusements. Some of these, such as corn-shuckings and barn-raisings, had been integrated into their farm work; others, such as berry-picking, hunting, and fishing, provided both recreation and variety for the table; others still, such as swimming and hiking, existed solely for enjoyment. But these amusements had been lost upon resettlement in the city. This was so not simply because men allowed themselves to work as hard as they did and forced their households into becoming oriented around their work, but also because of the nature of city life itself. Urban office work did not admit to penetration by recreation, and urban space, which was developed in Buffalo along strictly functional lines, did not prove as malleable for play as the countryside. It may be said that these Americans worked as hard as they did because they had lost the amusements they had once enjoyed, and, as Foster Rhea Dulles noted long ago, had yet to find new ones shaped to their new requirements.[24]

Swimming and fishing, for example, were not taken up locally by middle-class Americans. Though Buffalo was bordered by Lake Erie and the Niagara River and bisected by the Buffalo River, the most accessible areas of the waterfront had been given over to commerce and to the development of residential neighborhoods for Irish dock workers, who, lacking horses or carfare, had to live near their work. Thus, an American tradition of the city's earliest decades, nude male bathing in an isolated area of the Niagara shore partly obscured by tall sand dunes, disappeared when the dunes were leveled and warehouses and grain elevators replaced them. Thereafter, it was the Irish poor who swam and fished in these increasingly polluted and congested waters.[25] Respectable middle-class Americans, on the other hand, now traveled out of the city, when they had the time, to take up one of these formerly easily accessible pastimes.

Much of American bourgeois leadership did exert counterpressures in the form of proposals for the development of a public park system against this narrow, functionalist development of public space, which was a conse-quence largely of their own business activities. Their efforts were prompted not only by the desire for a sylvan counterworld, with opportunities for walking and for quiet, therapeutic repose in the midst of the noisy, congested city, but also by an awareness that for all the wealth the city generated, it remained a rough-hewn place without beauty. Affluent Buffalonians who traveled to Europe had seen for themselves the carefully tended public parks and gardens of the continent's great cities. They knew their own hometown to be sadly deficient in comparison. Travelers to Buffalo also constantly berated the local urban landscape. As early as the 1830s such visitors as Frances Trollope and Harriet Martineau noted that Buffalo appeared aged and shabby, not, of course, because of the passage of time, but because of ill use and inattention to aesthetic improvements. The streets of the central business district and of the docks, the scene viewed daily by merchants and white-collar workers, were frequently littered and filthy. Too, the commercial buildings of both areas were often squat and functional and had an impermanent look (fig. 3). Public space was undeveloped, used and abused, and left to the ravages of neglect.[26] As the city entered the 1850s, a few small parks and private planted squares were all that provided the opportunity for repose and visual relief in the areas where most people lived and worked. But even these were laughably short of the mark, as the press bitterly complained. The Court House Park, the only one in the city's center, had a broken fountain and was so small—really no more than a lawn—that it could accommodate only a few benches. As it was, cattle sometimes grazed there, while servants beat rugs and laid out bedsheets to dry.[27] The potentially beautiful area called "The Churches," formed near the city's center by the conjunction of several streets joining at odd angles, contained several of the most prestigious Protestant churches and impressive private mansions on extensive lots with fine gardens and plantings. These streets, too, however, were littered, and they

Fig. 3    Lithograph entitled "View of Buffalo, N.Y. from the Old Light House," by E. Whitefield, 1847. Courtesy BECHS.

had evolved over the years into an unofficial farmers' market where wagoners hawked flowers, shrubs, and produce.[28] Buffalo was hardly an inspiring landscape for those seeking beauty.

As the city's bourgeoisie matured as a social group and sought increasingly to strike a socially responsible balance between civic stewardship and individual gain, it addressed the problem of what it now perceived to be an inadequate development of public space. It encountered powerful, mutually interreacting, material and political constraints. After lengthy, acrimonious debate, proposals for a large, centrally located public park that were favored by the daily press and, if the behavior of their elected officials is any indication, by most middle-class Americans, were defeated.

This struggle, which preoccupied much of the 1850s, was the most intense civic confrontation of the period, and it demonstrates the difficulties faced by those wishing to develop municipal recreation in Buffalo at the time. A wealthy American landowner had given the municipality an extensive tract of land, hoping, but not requiring, that it would be converted into a park. But the plan to use assessments on neighborhood taxpayers to de-

velop the property for that use met with opposition from two sources. A small group of American leadership was rigidly ideologically committed to a laissez-faire political economy when it came to any expenses it deemed less essential than improvement of the commercial infrastructure, and it sought to block the park proposal in the courts. These men found allies in the neighborhood's large population of German cottage owners, who demanded that the land projected for park development be used instead for a public market, where meats and groceries could be purchased at discount prices because of low overhead. Notably hostile when it came to facing tax assessments for any civic improvements beyond such essentials as paving, sidewalks, and sewers, Germans deemed parks a waste of money. Moreover, they had private ethnic pleasure and beer gardens, owned by their own countrymen, and saw no need to pay for public facilities they would not be using. In the end, through both their coordinated and separate activities, the two groups killed the park project.[29] No other proposals of this type would be forwarded by either private citizens or the common council during the balance of the decade, not only because of this lesson to American reformers in municipal democracy, but also because of the threats to the city's prosperity and interregional competitive position prompted by the 1857–1858 depression and the increasing challenge of the railroads to the Erie Canal. Both of these economic crises called for, according to the pre-Keynesian political economy of the time, municipal retrenchment and the diversion of private capital from commerce to manufacturing.[30] Parks now seemed a luxury even for their many exponents. In the last analysis, then, the compulsions of moneymaking and demands of economic stewardship in a capitalist system overtook sincere bourgeois strivings for high-quality urban life.

If the strictures of a capitalist political economy blocked the development of municipal recreational facilities, constraints from within the Americans' own culture limited the rise of private alternatives. In sharp contrast to the immigrant Germans and Irish, Americans manifested little ethnic identification. They were nationalistic and patriotic, to be sure, but they had a weak sense of common peoplehood. In consequence, they lacked the emotional bonds to develop the filiopietistic holidays that would have been the equivalent of the immigrants' saints' days. Beyond the Fourth of July, which, as we have seen, was quickly commandeered for representations of social pluralism, there was only George Washington's birthday, and the press protested that nothing was done to commemorate that day beyond a display of flags in a few shop windows.[31] Weak American ethnicity also inhibited the development of American ethnic voluntary associations equivalent to the Irish, English, and Scottish societies named for the patron saints of their homelands. These societies existed chiefly for the purpose of organizing a banquet or event to commemorate the annual birthday of St. Patrick, St. George, or St. Andrew, but occasionally, too, raised money for impoverished immigrant countrymen.[32]

It is true that, largely in reaction to the growing ethnocultural diversity around them, Americans in the 1850s began to develop some sense of ethnic consciousness in the form of interest in local history and in particular in the creation of a mutually binding pioneer legend. But it was testimony to how much those manifesting such ethnic aspirations had to struggle to see them realized that these efforts were also impeded by the practical requirements of commerce. In mid-December 1854, weeks after a brief but intense panic on the New York stock exchange, the first annual Pilgrims' Day banquet had to be canceled by those who organized it, the newly established New England Society, because of "the unusual absorption of the community in business."[33] The New England Society itself ceased to exist amidst the economic crises of the late 1850s. Too, it was not until 1862 that the long-standing desire to put local history on a solid institutional footing was realized with the founding of the Buffalo Historical Society.[34]

Even if not ethnic in their purposes, there were, of course, many ethnically exclusive American voluntary associations. But these were oriented only coincidentally and occasionally around recreation and festivities. Volunteer fire companies and temperance, fraternal, and church associations from time to time did sponsor celebrations of various types that helped to structure American leisure time, but they mostly pursued larger social and cultural aims such as reform, religion, and insurance for members. Only the American literary and lecture associations were exclusively concerned with recreation, which was in their case centered on the morally serious goal of self-improvement, rather than play for its own sake.[35]

Self-improvement, a well-known preoccupation of the American middle classes in the nineteenth century, was but a part of a larger moral culture that defined and constrained the possibilities for recreation. The roots of this moral culture are varied. Though it was given expression in the language of evangelical Protestantism, it was a product of Victorian gender ideology and of reactive attitudes produced by fears of the social disorder accompanying rapid urbanization and economic development. Its consequences for recreation were complex. It might be tempting to take as representative of this moral culture the views of one of its leading local ideologists, Methodist minister John Robie, editor of the weekly *Christian Advocate,* because he was so logically consistent in his stance toward recreation. At one time or another Robie denounced almost all forms of recreation—dancing, the theater, card playing, evening soirees, the consumption of liquor and stimulants, and almost all Sabbath activities except prayer and quiet conversation and reading at home.[36] But few Americans went as far as Robie in their views, and their behavior sometimes contradicted those views they did express. Americans wrote strong, bitter letters denouncing ethnic churches and associations that paraded with insistent band music on Sundays. But they defended on economic grounds the operation of Erie Canal locks on the Lord's day, a practice opposed by most of the evangelical clergy for many years.[37] Americans denounced violations of the liquor licensing and—for a brief time in the 1850s—prohibition laws by immigrant grocers and saloonkeepers. But they themselves drank quietly in their own homes, where they privately entertained themselves and their friends, beyond the oversight of the law.[38] Under any circumstance, many sensible and religiously sincere people could see no harm in card playing or in attending such occasional traveling theater as made its way to Buffalo. It was by no means apparent to the laity, therefore, that all of Robie's injunctions were the mark of a good Christian. No less is suggested by the frequency with which Robie felt himself forced to reiterate them.

Rather than attempt to list a number of self-proscribed behaviors, we would do better to understand the two values within American moral culture that most constrained recreation. The first, a condemnation of excessive stimulation, was prompted largely by concern for developing codes of social discipline appropriate both to the congested, interdependent world of the city and to urban office work. The fear of stimulation did not auto-matically translate into a code of behavior; it could be contracted and expanded to accommodate a considerable range of possibilities. Yet, because excessive mental stimulation was feared as much as the physical stimulation of, say, hard drinking or strenuous dancing in an overheated ballroom, this fear generally acted to limit options considerably. According to the most thoughtful Buffalo critic of American amusements, Presbyterian minister Grosvenor Heacock, what was needed was a "Christian" (by which he meant *Protestant*) philosophy of recreation. Its operative principle must be rationality, and it must ask whether an activity is "helpful to body, mind, and morals." It must reject, therefore, both dissipation and excessive mental and physical activity.[39] As we shall see, relatively few recreational pursuits were left to enjoy, at least in theory, after the application of Heacock's principle.

The second value, largely derived from Victorian gender ideology, was a delicacy about exposing women and children to public scenes of scandal and embarrassment. This greatly inhibited men from exploring new possibilities for public recreation with their families. Husbands and wives did attend lectures and the theater together. These were predictably safe contexts to the extent that those, such as sailors, canal boatmen, and immigrant laborers, widely deemed socially unrespectable, could not afford the price of admission and, under any circumstances, had their own amusements, among them the dockside gambling houses and taverns which often had live entertainment.[40] When such usually reliable contexts were likely to be morally compromised, gentlemen might be warned in advance against taking their wives. The sensationalistic lectures, usually by apostate Catholics, about the "secret lives" of the Catholic clergy, provide an example. Advertisements, such as one in 1848 for a lecture on "Popish Nunneries in Connection with the Intrigues of the Jesuits," alerted the especially scrupulous to the prospect of subject matter too shocking for respectable women. Women were also occasionally barred from public lectures. When

Edward Leahey, a former priest, spoke in 1851 on "The Treatment of Women in Convents by Male Priests," attendance by women was prohibited because of "the awful disclosures" that were expected.[41] In light of this delicacy and, in addition, of their fears of the effects of alcohol, it is no wonder that Americans had no equivalent of the German beer garden in which men drank alongside their wives, the children seated at the table with them, while talking, playing cards, and listening to music. One of the earliest and most pleasant American realizations about German recreation was that it was pursued mostly in family groups *and* in public.

Patterns of American middle-class recreation developed within the matrix formed by each of these constraints. In spite of, or, as we now know, *because of* the rigors of the climate, winter was the time of the most intense recreation. There was a full schedule of lectures and some theater and music, both of which competed with revivals at the evangelical churches. (Local preachers discovered soon after the canal opened that serious religious matters could not be addressed during the season of navigation.)[42] There were no organized or formal winter sports, though after every significant snowfall, sleighs could be seen making their way through the city, as much for fun as for transportation. But the principal location for most winter recreation was the home, and the usual participants were family members, local kinfolk, and friends who lived near enough to drop over for a visit. Much leisure time was spent informally in the family circle before the hearth. Here people read, conversed, or played board games and had the opportunity to enjoy the company of their children. Nothing more warmed the hearts of these Buffalonians than the security and comfort of this winter scene, which was so profoundly significant to the fulfillment of the emotional needs of the domesticated middle-class family. As the functions of family for so many new, urban, middle-class residents contracted to exclude cooperative, family-based work, affectional ties became the only bond that held families together.[43]

This cozy picture hardly exhausted the homebound pattern of recreation. The height of the winter social round was "the gay season." For the bourgeoisie, this was a series of "parties, balls, soirees, musical and other private entertainments, theatricals, and *tableaux vivants,*" which were held largely at home and mostly in December and January. Less affluent classes of Americans had their own version, with smaller guest lists, simpler refreshments, and perhaps less expensive new clothing for host and hostess. Fun and show though it was, "the gay season" also provided renewal for the communal social networks that sustained the middle classes but were allowed to lapse somewhat during the rest of the year because of the press of business. Furthermore, the intense partying presented opportunities for courting and making those matches that formed the basis of new families and households. No less is suggested by the number of visits during the winter from small-town nieces, granddaughters, and other young female friends and kin. These seasonal visits simultaneously served to strengthen the tight networks of female friendship that were a conspicuous part of nineteenth-century women's culture.[44]

Beyond the winter social round, few systematic diversions existed for the Buffalo middle class other than travel, near or far. In early spring and briefly at midsummer, especially during local cholera epidemics, those who could afford to, traveled to the cities of the seaboard and to the mountains and spas of upstate New York, sometimes combining business and pleasure trips. The "Grand Tour" of Europe was within the reach of a few wealthy people, such as Millard Fillmore. But grain merchants such as Merwin S. Hawley, who could not find the time for that, contented themselves with the neo-European environs of Quebec City.[45] For those who could not wander even that distance, there were nearby pleasure resorts and picnic grounds at both Niagara Falls and the suburban village of West Seneca, along the more bucolic upper reaches of the Buffalo River. People struggled to find picnic spots in the city itself, but they were not able to do much better in the mid-1850s than the cemetery grounds. When a few cricket and baseball clubs, which were largely composed of respectable young office workers and retail clerks who could get away for an evening or an afternoon a week, were organized in the late 1850s, their members, too, found a dearth of usable space in the settled portions of the city. They had to travel to play their matches to mowed farm fields in the countryside.[46]

Functional and not without its pleasures, this pattern of American middle-class recreation ultimately was as arid as it was limited. Its slavery to the seasonal rhythms of commerce meant that eight months passed with little in the way of formal or sustained diversion, while the remaining four months were filled with intense activity. The Reverend Grosvenor Heacock, for one, protested that such a schedule hardly fulfilled the need for balance between work and play.[47] Nor did this range of diversions provide anything for most American men and women in the way of organized physical activity, beyond the fervid dancing of "gay season" parties. Dancing, too, however, troubled Heacock, who believed that fresh air and routine, tension-releasing athletic exercises were healthier pursuits. He was not alone in decrying the dearth of systematic exercise. The local press joined a host of commentators throughout the North to criticize "the feeble American physique" and the high incidence of nervous illnesses bred by office work, and it spoke of the need for exercise among the overworked men who labored in the business district. Moreover, criticism of the dearth of parks was based not only on the absence of a quiet place to sit but also on the absence of a place to walk for exercise that was safely off the congested streets.[48] Had there been such a place, however, middle-class families would have had to suspend their fears of recreating in public and be willing to leave themselves open to the spontaneous experience that is a singular mark of urban social interaction. Finally, middle-class recreation offered no opportunities for aesthetic transcendence. Beyond traveling musicians and

theater companies, there was little art in Buffalo. Residents who traveled to Europe knew how little connected their city was to the Great Tradition of Western culture. Indeed, the Catholic church, for all its assumed evils, was actually the most evident connection. That was perhaps the greatest single reason why local bourgeois Americans gave money to the building of Bishop John Timon's magnificent cathedral, where they could attend lectures, even on religious themes, and performances of church music, and why they sent their children to expensive local private schools run by venerable European teaching orders.[49] Their travels probably succeeded only in convincing many Americans that life, real and profound, existed elsewhere. Travel thus came to represent not merely recreation, but also a therapeutic opportunity to escape the "blahs," that anemic feeling bred of a life structured by the workaday functionalism of the port. The *Commercial Advertiser* said as much in printing a bit of doggerel then apparently making the rounds: "Mrs. Bill is very ill, / And nothing can improve her / Until she sees the Tuileries, / And waddles through the Louvre." "Let her go," said the editor; her pursuit of "enlarged ideas and more correct tastes" was entirely laudable.[50] Yet such a pursuit did not necessarily assist Mrs. Bill to continue to live in Buffalo, as she knew it. She and others would have to begin to change their lives in the place where they lived.

## Americans Learn to Play, German Style

The large influx of Germans into Buffalo in the late 1840s and early 1850s transformed the local German community, and in the process deeply influenced American recreation. Prior to the late 1840s the local German population was largely composed of craftsmen and laborers of humble origin. They were socially conservative and not often educated beyond basic literacy, and they structured their American lives rather parochially around maintaining orderly neighborhoods and establishing church congregations. After the mid-1840s many such people continued to come to Buffalo, but a decided change also took place in the composition and social character of the German population. Political consciousness, expressed in a variety of ideologies, and pan-German cultural nationalism had grown in the Old World throughout the 1840s, and they provided the intellectual bases for the failed revolutionary movements of 1848. Both the voluntary immigrants and the political refugees who began to come to Buffalo in the mid-1840s manifested a deep ideological commitment to the public representation of German folk culture, the forms and attitudes of which, based in Christianity as they were, had been marshaled by revolutionaries of all views to express such universalistic values as equality and the dignity of common people that underlay their movements. Furthermore, a combination of political repression and economic crisis led to the forced exile or voluntary departure of significant numbers of educated middle-class students, professionals, writers, and artists who were just as passionately committed to German high culture, especially theater and classical music. They claimed that a unique, universalistic message of beauty, freedom, liberty, and the oneness of humanity was to be found in romantically inspired nineteenth-century German art.[51]

While the Germans who settled in the city prior to 1848, therefore, embraced without deep reflection a sustaining but parochial ethnic culture of daily life, calling their culture "German" largely in comparison to American ways, many of the new immigrants and refugees took an activist, missionary, and essentially ideological stance toward organizing German culture. The editor of the local German *Weltbürger*—an older settler—found these newcomers arrogant and condescending. Present in the country no more than a few years at most, they nonetheless had the audacity to think it necessary to awaken the long-resident German settler population from the cultural lethargy these self-proclaimed "oracles" arbitrarily said characterized its existence. In all their different class and ideological varieties,

the newcomers did have in common a direct and aggressive rhetorical style and an earnest, fervent, self-righteous, when not simply intolerant, public spiritedness. Both style and spirit could be offensive to the earlier German settlers who were making their own accommodations to American life, based, to their minds, on a longer, and hence superior, acquaintance with the new land.[52]

These asperities aside, however, there may be no doubt that the newcomers quickly transformed local ethnic cultural life. The number of *Vereine* dedicated to the arts and to recreation grew rapidly, and there was a proliferation of all sorts of public *Feste* and performances. In the process many of the old settlers themselves were vitalized, as indeed were many Americans, for the proud missionary attitude toward German folk and high cultures led the newcomers not only to seek to involve all of their own people, but Americans, too. Moreover, Germans were politically canny enough to understand the significance of making a good impression on Americans, who possessed so much of the city's money and power. Committed though they were to German culture as each group understood it, old settlers and newcomers alike recognized the value of accommodating themselves and their community to those aspects of the American cultural environment that could benefit them, such as learning English and other skills necessary to gain employment in American offices and American patronage at their shops. Their campaign for German culture among Americans, therefore, was an effort to broaden, rather than to commandeer, the mainstream, and in the process to help themselves by raising the status of Germans among Americans.

By the mid-1850s it was apparent that Americans were deeply impressed with German culture. Americans had begun, for example, to compare their own feeble efforts to organize leisure time events with the efforts of these activist Germans. The nativist *Commercial Advertiser* routinely admitted that American businessmen and professionals were too engrossed in commerce to organize the astonishing array of *Feste,* excursions, picnics, musical performances, and gymnastic exhibitions which lately had become a feature of not only German, but the entire local population's daily life. Americans were increasingly attending these events, and to their surprise they were learning to enjoy themselves in ways new to their experience.[53]

No more important source existed for Americans in acquainting themselves with German forms of recreation than the series of German popular festivals of the 1850s: the 1854 and 1858 *Turnerfeste,* the 1860 *Lagerbier Fest,* and, above all, the multiform, annual St. John's Day *Feste.* All of these events enjoyed substantial American attendance.

Established in Buffalo in 1851 by the German Young Men's Association—a literary, debating, and library society dedicated to propagating German culture—St. John's Day was an ancient European folk festival marking the coming of summer.[54] It had not been celebrated communally by the first wave of German settlers, but now it became a true people's festival and a synthetical showcase for all of German popular and high culture. There were thousands of active participants from the German fraternal *Vereine,* bands, choral and drama groups, and *Turner* associations, all of whom had a place on the program, and many more thousands of casual participants and spectators drawn from the city-at-large. As the years passed, the program expanded and became more varied, and eventually it consumed the entire day.[55] There was no hiding the sense of anticipation in the American press as the day approached. Particularly eager was the nativist editor of the *Commercial Advertiser.* On the eve of the 1854 celebration, he remarked, "These reunions of our German fellow citizens are always pleasant entertainments, and a happy time can be passed by visitors as well as by those more directly involved. . . . A German festival is always full of life, spirit and fun; and men, women and children enter into amusements with a zest fully refreshing to behold."[56]

The sources of the rave reviews Americans gave the annual summer *Feste* were varied. The exotic, multiform program was attractive and offered a wide range of activities from choral singing and ballroom dancing to foot races and games, such as *Sackhüpfen* [sack race] and *Wurstschnappen,* ["steal-the-sausage"] that everyone could play. The *Turners'* precise and graceful gymnastic feats of strength were frequently commented upon by Americans (fig. 4). They were fascinated by the athletic activities of these "gentlemen in brown Hollands," though they probably would have been horrified, had they the skills in German to follow their speeches and publications, to learn how radical *Turner* politics were. *Turner* gymnastics, said the *Commercial Advertiser* in 1858, are "so foreign to our native sports that their observance is a novelty not lightly to be missed." The German program committee did attempt, however, to incorporate familiar American themes and activities to attract the native-born. It soon added, for example, horse racing and fireworks, as well as various representations, such as in *tableaux vivants,* of American patriotic symbols. Moreover, the organizers of the *Feste* deliberately sought to make Americans feel welcome. They invited the mayor and the entire common council to the festivities and gave them a guided, explanatory tour through the exclusively German parts of the program.[57]

But the attraction went deeper than the program. As an American complained in 1856, the city was so lacking in public parks that Forest Lawn Cemetery was thronged with picnickers, and its managers had begun to sell tickets to control access to the consecrated grounds. But, he added, through attendance at St. John's Day festivities, Americans were learning about Westphal's Garden, a private park and beer garden in a woods in the northern section of the city. The principal location of the annual *Feste,* Westphal's was not, as some Americans had expected, "a sort of territory devoted to the foreign population and teutonically tabooed." Americans attending the *Feste* were told they were welcome to come back if they wished.[58] Westphal's was also a compelling site because American men were able to bring their families there, just as respectable Germans routinely did. "Unlike Americans," said the *Commercial Advertiser* of Westphal's on the day of the annual *Fest,* "but just like sensible people, [German men] take their wives and children with them on these occasions, and make it a day of pleasure for all." What allowed American men to come to Westphal's in full certainty that their wives and children would witness nothing untoward was "the perfect order" prevailing at the *Feste,* which were always free of scandal and aggressive drunkenness. The German organizers were privately concerned that the longed-for increase in attendance by *Americans* might nonetheless result in rowdiness by drunks. Germans held the lower classes of Americans in contempt for being unable to hold their liquor and conduct themselves decently in public. Indeed at the 1859 festivities, the only drunks observed, the *Commercial Advertiser* noted, were Americans. That no serious disorder on the part of that or any other source ever did occur at Westphal's on the day of the *Fest* may well have been the result of the deliberateness with which the local *Vereine* patrolled the grounds in search of miscreants. But on other days, too, Westphal's was just as orderly, and it seems clear that the convivial, scandal-free mood reliably found there was the product of the standards of orderly public behavior common among Germans.[59]

Americans sought to understand why these standards routinely prevailed. How is it, said the *Commercial Advertiser,* reflecting on the extent to which "these festivals display the German character in a favorable light," that the Germans were able so easily to do what Americans could not: "enjoy themselves in a simple, hearty manner?"[60] The explanation for Americans seemed to lie in the relationship Germans had to alcohol. Beer allowed Germans to drink without suffering the frightening physical and psychological effects produced by distilled spirits. In the context of American preoccupation with self-control and fear of stimulation, this insight offered Americans the basis for a hopeful, middle position

Fig. 4   This 1905 photograph of members of Buffalo's German *Turnverein* marks not only German assimilation into American culture, but the Americans' assumption of aspects of German ethnic culture as well. Courtesy BECHS.

between moderate, relaxing indulgence and destructive drunkenness (figs. 5 and 6). Unlike American alcoholic staples, "maddening, corroding . . . brandy, liver-eating gin, and stomach-destroying rum," the paper said at the time of the broadly popular *Lagerbier Fest,* German beer is "more a kindly sedative than a stimulus." Middle-class men frequently mentally overstimulated from incessant labors at their desks could easily "bear a little muddling without injury."[61] On the basis of just such beliefs, which apparently many American men tested annually at Westphal's on St. John's Day, and of an examination of neighborhood arrest data, the editors of both the *Republic* and the *Commercial Advertiser* actually came to favor selective enforcement of the antialcohol laws. In the Irish First Ward, said the *Commercial Advertiser*'s editor, drink and disorder were "synonymous," as was evident every St. Patrick's Day. Stern police measures were thus needed. But in German wards "where a riot of any kind is a rare occurrence," the laws might safely "be cancelled to national custom and habits which have become a birthright."[62] Even the *Christian Advocate,* which customarily used phrases such as "vile monster" to refer to

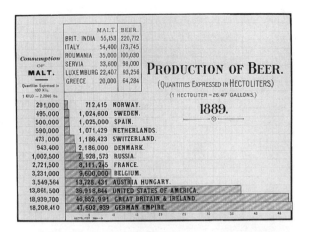

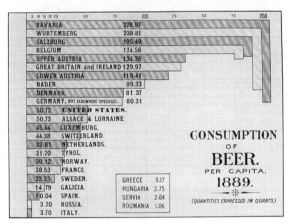

Figs. 5 and 6   *Twenty-five Years of Brewing, with an Illustrated History of American Beer* (1891) used graphs to display the excess of beer production over consumption in the United States in 1889.

alcohol, had recently begun to write of *lager-bier* in an anthropological and historical, rather than a moral, way.[63] This was just the impact on American opinion for which the German organizers of the *Lagerbier Fest* had hoped in deciding to make ample stocks of free samples available to American visitors.

Presented with these models of rational recreation and self-control amidst pleasure, Americans began tentatively to copy them in their own lives and communal activities (fig. 7). By 1855 many respectable German and American families alike were spending the balance of the Fourth of July, after the procession and speeches, at Westphal's listening to music and drinking beer.[64] Too, influenced in all likelihood by the *Turners'* public example of mas-

culine athleticism, Americans also developed a taste for German exercise. Some Americans were now attending several downtown gymnasiums Germans were operating for office workers. As the *Courier* said of one gymnasium, "The exercises are strength-giving, invigorating, and Doctor-cheating, especially for accountants, bookkeepers, and the whole sedentary tribe."[65]

Another American desire, for art, was also enhanced by the opportunities Germans created for musical and theatrical performance. Most German immigrants of this era considered the United States "a land without music." Immigrant musicians and intellectuals alike noted critically that performances were few, music seemed completely isolated from daily life, and indigenous musical traditions were thin.[66] The newer German settlers set out very deliberately to organize their own musical life, and in the process they rectified some of the deficiencies they found in the city's music scene. By the mid-1850s, as a result, musical performance of some sort was almost always in the offing in Buffalo. Concerts were arranged by local German agents, who booked German performers into halls in ethnic neighborhoods and downtown. There were touring German chorales and orchestras, such as the renowned Germanians, whose romantic personal histories of revolutionary activity and exile were almost as compelling as their exquisite renderings of the classical repertory. There were also the local German professionals, such as the private orchestra created by the conductor and teacher Gustav Poppenberg, and amateur groups, particularly the many singing societies, of which the *Liedertafel* [glee club; here also the formal name of a local association] was the most prestigious. Together with Karl Adam, the director of the *Liedertafel*, Poppenberg organized a number of memorable productions of sacred music, usually in the accepted tradition of Mozart and Beethoven. He avoided the newer and controversial music associated with Liszt and others. The two men courted American patronage. They advertised in the American press and for especially important performances rented elegant St. James Hall. Adam also gave explanations of the music in English to American audiences before concerts. Americans responded with marked enthusiasm, for the music Adam and Poppenberg chose expressed a unique and culturally potent mixture for them, as Alan Levy has said, of freedom within boundaries and feeling proscribed by reason. It was proper, disciplined, and solid, but it expressed the deepest yearnings of the soul. That many of these performances were held on Sunday and that beer was sold in the lobby did little to curb American attendance, though evangelical opinion was certainly not pleased.[67] Nor would Sabbath performances and the availability of alcoholic refreshment discourage American attendance during the decade at the first locally staged, high-quality dramatic events—the acclaimed full productions or readings in English of Schiller and Shakespeare put on for profit by local German companies and for charity by the German Young Men's Association.[68]

These musical and theatrical developments culminated in the city's two great antebellum festivals of the arts, the 1859 *Schillerfest* and the 1860 *Sängerbundfest.* Here, too, the organizers courted American attendance. They advertised in the American papers and arranged the schedule of the most impressive events, including concerts and the readings of Schiller done in English, to accommodate office workers and entrepreneurs. They included on the program some of the less artistic, popular activities—massive processions, sampling of ethnic foods, and *tableaux vivants*—that Americans found particularly appealing in the annual St. John's Day program.[69] But without such features, these *Feste* would still have been impressive. The festival of song, which brought German singing societies from throughout North America to Buffalo to compete in public performances, was capped by a "monster concert," unlike anything Buffalo or most other American cities had ever seen. The concert had to be held at the railroad station to accommodate a sixty-five-piece orchestra, a

Fig. 7   As beer became more popular, the brewing industry increasingly identified its product with American themes. This stoneware stein, made in Germany for the American market around 1900, features three scenes from Rochester, New York.

choir of six hundred, and ten thousand spectators. It was said that the concert was attended by "the elite of Buffalo," who were afterwards invited by the organizers to attend a banquet of German delicacies at St. James Hall. But if the ten thousand figure is correct, it could hardly have been only the elite within the American population that was in attendance.[70]

Activities such as these *Feste* did more than simply succeed in bringing Germans and Americans together in an amiable setting, and hence speed the process by which the former, though recently arrived foreigners, became acceptable to the latter. To be sure, had the *Feste*

Fig. 8    A political cartoon from *Puck*, 3 October 1883, celebrating "A Family Fest—the 200th Birthday of the Healthiest Lad among Uncle Sam's Adoptive Children."

accomplished only that, their historical importance would be assured. They also greatly broadened American cultural horizons and gave an important seal of legitimacy to immigrant contributions that proved vital to American recreational life. At the time, to be sure, this broadening of horizons was taking place within distinctly German cultural molds. It is a fitting comment on the completely derivative nature of these new American horizons that when in 1858 Americans created their first society for the encouragement of the performance of classical music, they named it "The Mendelssohn Association."[71] But under the prestigious American imprimatur, the boundaries of the public culture of recreation were being widened in ways that would have been unimaginable without the ethnic festivals and entertainments Germans established in Buffalo. With a curiously divided consciousness, middle-class Americans were seeking to repress the Germans within the civic community, while allying with them in a process of

accommodation and democratization that would create the foundations for a genuine urban, melting-pot culture. But then, antebellum middle-class Americans would certainly not be the last native-born defenders of the vision of a socially homogeneous America who grudgingly allowed foreigners to enrich their lives (fig. 8).

## Notes

1. Laurence A. Glasco, *Ethnicity and Social Structure: Irish, Germans and Native-Born of Buffalo, New York, 1850–1860* (New York: Arno Press, 1980), 20. Foreign-born men and women were 73.3 percent of the population of household heads in 1855. German-speakers were 38.6 percent, while the French-born, who were almost all German-speaking Alsatians, were another 5.3 percent of the household heads. The story of antebellum social pluralism in Buffalo is told in my own *The Making of an American Pluralism: Buffalo, New York, 1825–1860* (Urbana: University of Illinois Press, 1989).

2. Buffalo *Express*, quoted in Buffalo *Sentinel*, 11 July 1857. For previous celebrations of the Fourth, see Buffalo *Patriot*, 3 and 10 July 1821; Buffalo *Daily*

*Buffalonian,* 12 July 1839; Buffalo *Courier,* 3 and 13 July 1847, 30 June 1849, 29 June 1850, 15 May 1851, 5 July 1852, 23 June 1853, 23 May 1854.

3. Buffalo *Sentinel,* 11 July 1857.

4. Buffalo *Commercial Advertiser,* 8 November 1854, 2 September 1855, 10 June 1857; Buffalo *Demokrat und Weltbürger,* 6, 7, and 14 June 1855; Buffalo *Republic,* 5 November 1856; Andrew Yox, "Decline of the German-American Community in Buffalo, 1855–1925" (Ph.D. diss., University of Chicago, 1983), 47.

5. Glasco, *Ethnicity and Social Structure,* 20; Edward M. Levine, *The Irish and Irish Politicians: A Study of Social and Cultural Alienation* (Notre Dame: University of Notre Dame Press, 1966), 5, 32–38, 39–51, 91–92, 127, 129, 155–202; William V. Shannon, *The American Irish: A Political and Social Portrait* (New York: Macmillan, 1963), 60–67; James A. Reynolds, *The Catholic Emancipation Crisis in Ireland, 1823–1829* (New Haven: Yale University Press, 1954); T. D. Williams, *Secret Societies in Ireland* (Dublin: Gill and Macmillan, 1973).

6. Buffalo *Express,* 4 September and 10 November 1855, 3 January, 6, 17, and 28 July, 2 and 3 August, and 13 October 1858, 13 October 1859; Buffalo *Commercial Advertiser,* 30 October 1855, 25 April 1857, 1 November 1859; Buffalo *Demokrat und Weltbürger,* 16 and 21 May 1857.

7. The negative stereotypes of the local Irish were so generally held by Americans that it is possible to draw elements of them from *all* of the city's major American dailies. Independent of partisan affiliation, and even of nativist or anti-nativist opinions, Buffalo's *Courier, Commercial Advertiser, Express,* and *Republic* all agreed on the strengths and especially the weaknesses of the Irish, and their views were no different from the well-known national American consensus.

8. Arthur Mann, *The One and the Many: Reflections on the American Identity* (Chicago: University of Chicago Press, 1979), 80–81, 89–90; John Higham, "The Immigrant in American History," in Higham, ed., *Send These to Me: Immigrants in Urban America* (Baltimore: Johns Hopkins University Press, 1984), 20.

9. James H. Kettner, *The Development of American Citizenship, 1608–1870* (Chapel Hill, NC: Institute of Early American History and Culture, 1978), 225–37, 245–47. For the common charges against the Irish for their political activities, see, for example, Buffalo *Republic,* 25 November 1853, 14 August and 14 November 1854; Buffalo *Courier,* 27 March 1852; Buffalo *Commercial Advertiser,* 1 November 1859.

10. Buffalo *Commercial Advertiser,* 16 April 1856.

11. Ibid., 9 December 1853, 24 June 1854, 9 April 1857, 29 August 1859, 6 January 1860, 22 July 1876; Buffalo *Republic,* 5 October 1857; Buffalo *Christian Advocate,* 6 February 1859.

12. David A. Gerber, "Modernity in the Service of Tradition: Catholic Lay Trustees at Buffalo's St. Louis Church and the Transformation of European Communal Traditions, 1829–1855," *Journal of Society History* 15 (Summer 1982): 655–89; Buffalo *Christian Advocate,* 6 and 20 July 1853, 19 October 1854, 15 July 1858, 17 November 1859; Buffalo *Commercial Advertiser,* 23 June 1853, 27 June 1854, 10 March and 23 April 1860.

13. Glasco, *Ethnicity and Social Structure,* 20; Buffalo *Weltbürger,* 26 January and 9 and 16 June 1839, 13 February 1841, 7 May 1842, 3 March 1843, 9 April and 22 September 1845; Buffalo *Demokrat und Weltbürger,* 4 November 1858, 28 May and 15 August 1859; Buffalo *Commercial Advertiser,* 1 November 1859.

14. Buffalo *Weltbürger,* 20 January 1838; Buffalo *Demokrat und Weltbürger,* 19 May 1859; Buffalo *Commercial Advertiser,* 21 March 1846, 27 November 1855, 14 November 1857; Buffalo *Christian Advocate,* 7 August 1851, 27 April 1854, 22 March 1855, 14 July 1859; Buffalo *Republic,* 18 and 20 May 1854.

15. Buffalo *Courier,* 23 August 1843, 2 October 1850; Buffalo *Commercial Advertiser,* 20 April 1854, 12 February 1855, 22 May 1856 (quotation), 3 March and 14 November 1857, 22 August 1859.

16. I have attempted to explain the ambivalence toward Catholicism in very similar terms in "Ambivalent Anti-Catholicism: Buffalo's American Protestant Elite Faces the Challenge of the Catholic Church, 1850–1860," *Civil War History* 30 (June 1984): 120–43. Also see Jackson Lears, *No Place of Grace: Anti-Modernism and the Transformation of American Culture* (New York: Pantheon Books, 1981), 147, 151–52, 159–62, 184–216, 241–42, 251.

17. Richard Larry Ehrlich, "The Development of Manufacturing in Selected Counties in the Erie Canal Corridor, 1815–1860" (Ph.D. diss., State University of New York College at Buffalo, 1972); Marvin Rapp, "Buffalo and the Great Lakes Trade, 1825–1900," pt. 1, *Inland Seas* 17 (Spring 1969): 18–24; Buffalo *Courier,* 3 November 1847; Paul E. Johnson, *A Shopkeepers' Millennium: Society and Revivals in Rochester, New York, 1815–1837* (New York: Hill and Wang, 1978), chap. 1; Mary P. Ryan, *Cradle of the Middle Class: The Family in Oneida County, New York, 1790–1865* (New York: Cambridge University Press, 1981), 10.

18. Ronald E. Shaw, *Erie Water West: A History of the Erie Canal, 1792–1854* (Lexington: University of Kentucky Press, 1966), 14–83; Marvin Rapp, "The Port of Buffalo, 1825–1880" (Ph.D. diss., Duke University, 1947), 9–13.

19. Roger Whitman, *Queen's Epic: Benjamin Rath-*

bun and His Times (Buffalo and Erie County Historical Society [hereafter BECHS], typescript, 1942);
Guy Salisbury, "The Speculative Craze of 1836," Buffalo Historical Society Publications 4 (1896): 317–37;
Verna G. Walker, "Banking in Buffalo before the
Civil War" (M.A. thesis, University of Buffalo, 1933),
30–51.

20. John G. Clark, The Grain Trade in the Old
Northwest (Urbana: University of Illinois Press,
1966), 117; Arthur Markowitz, "Joseph Dart and the
Emergence of Buffalo as a Grain Port, 1820–1860,"
Inland Seas 25 (Fall 1969): 183–92.

21. Merwin S. Hawley to Elijah Hawley, 25 January
and 1 April 1851, 18 March 1852, Hawley Papers,
BECHS; Merwin S. Hawley, Autobiography (BECHS,
manuscript, 1872), 16–18, 24, 28–29; Samuel Welch,
Home History: Recollections of Buffalo . . . ; or, Fifty
Years Since (Buffalo: Peter Paul and Bro., 1891), 170;
Rapp, "The Port of Buffalo," 149; Buffalo Commer-
cial Advertiser, 15 January 1855.

22. The source of my understanding of the concept
of leisure, as well as of both recreation (the purposeful seeking of physical or mental renewal and refreshment) and play (activity that is informal, spontaneous, and has an element of make-believe) is
Max Kaplan, Leisure in America: A Social Inquiry
(New York: Wiley, 1960), 19–25.

23. Buffalo Courier, 16 and 24 June 1851; Buffalo
Commercial Advertiser, 2 July 1851.

24. Foster Rhea Dulles, America Learns to Play: A
History of Recreation, 2d ed. (New York: Irvington
Publishers, 1965), 22–43, 67–83, 136–37; Peter
Levine, "The Promise of Sport in Antebellum
America," Journal of American Culture 2 (Winter
1980): 625.

25. Welch, Home History, 26–27; Henry H. Baxter
and Erik Heyl, eds., Maps, Buffalo Harbor, 1804–
1964 (Buffalo: BECHS, 1965), 10–19, 30–31.

26. Frances Trollope, Domestic Manners of the
Americans, vol. 2 (London: Printed for Whittaker,
Treacher and Co., 1832), 270–73; Harriet Martineau,
Retrospect of Western Travel, vol. 1 (London: Saun-
ders and Otley, 1838), 90–91; Buffalo Commercial
Advertiser, 27 March 1854, 8 and 11 April 1856,
31 October 1860; Quackenboss and Kennedy, Direc-
tors, Map of the City of Buffalo, New York, Surveyed
under the Direction of Quackenboss and Kennedy
(New York, 1854); Edward Hildebrandt, Street in
Buffalo, New York, 1844 (painting), reproduced in
Hugh Honour, The New Golden Land: European Im-
ages of America from the Discoveries to the Present
Time (New York: Pantheon Books, 1975), 202.

27. Buffalo Commercial Advertiser, 16 July 1851; Buffalo Courier, 17 June and 31 July 1852; Buffalo Express, 13 May 1853; Buffalo Republic, 9 September
1854, 19 July 1856.

28. Buffalo Commercial Advertiser, 31 October 1860.

29. Ibid., 19 and 27 August and 3, 8, and 9 September 1851, 16, 17, 21, and 22 November and 12 December 1854, 21 February 1855, 18 August and 9 and
29 September 1856; Buffalo Demokrat und Weltbürger, 20 September 1853, 16 February, 18 and
24 March, and 23 October 1854, 27 December 1855,
2 January, 25 March, 8 July, 15 and 18 August, 9, 10,
and 26 September, and 16 December 1856, 15 and
23 September 1858; Buffalo Republic, 21 November
1854, 27 May, 14, 15, and 18 August, and 6 September
1856, 3 October 1857.

30. Sandford B. Hunt, "Buffalo: A Glance at Its
Progress Down to the Present Time," in The Man-
ufacturing Interests of the City of Buffalo (Buffalo:
C. F. S. Thomas, 1866), 13–17; Buffalo Commercial
Advertiser, 4 and 15 February 1860; Buffalo Express,
19 January 1858.

31. Buffalo Commercial Advertiser, 22 February 1856.

32. The activities and larger social functions of these
societies over the course of the many years of their
local existence are discussed in Gerber, The Making
of an American Pluralism, chap. 5.

33. Buffalo Commercial Advertiser, 22 December
1853, 19 December 1854. The Buffalo Republic believed that commercial preoccupations routinely
impaired adequate planning of July Fourth celebrations (see 9 June 1853). So did the Buffalo Courier,
21 June 1851.

34. Seventy-Fifth Anniversary of the Founding of the
Buffalo Historical Society (Buffalo: Buffalo Historical Society, 1937).

35. Welch, Home History, 84, 340–47; Commercial
Advertiser Directory of Buffalo, 1855 (Buffalo, 1855),
17, 19, 20–22, 23–25; Buffalo Courier, 27 January,
6 May, and 17 July 1844, 10 January and 29 April
1847, 18 July 1849, 1 March, 1 July, and 3 December
1850, 2 July and 27 August 1852, 2 February 1853;
Buffalo Christian Advocate, 28 February 1850, 23 December 1852, 6 March 1856, 5 March 1857, 11 March
1858, 27 January 1859.

36. Almost any issue of the Buffalo Christian Advocate, from its inception on 1 January 1850, contains
some sort of moral admonishment, but ibid.,
14 March 1850, is representative. Here the Reverend
John Robie simultaneously denounced Sabbath des-
ecration, bowling alleys, saloons, billiard parlors,
and the theater ("that vestibule of ruin").

37. Shaw, Erie Water West, 225–26; Buffalo Courier,
16 March 1849, 28 June 1852; Buffalo Christian Advocate, 27 November 1851, 3 March and 27 October
1853, 27 April and 11 May 1854, 15 November 1855;
Buffalo Commercial Advertiser, 11 December 1857,
23 March 1859.

38. Buffalo Christian Advocate, 14 March and 19 December 1850, 21 February 1856; Buffalo Commercial
Advertiser, 7 October 1859.

39. Grosvenor Heacock, Sermon Preached at Central

*Presbyterian Church, March 20, 1859: Subject—The Christian Law of Amusements* (Buffalo: Phinnege and Co., 1859). On the problem of stimulation as contemporaries understood it, see Harvey Green, *Fit for America: Health, Fitness, Sport, and American Society* (New York: Pantheon Books, 1986), 44, 67–68, 137–38; Hillel Schwartz, *Never Satisfied: A Cultural History of Diets, Fantasies, and Fat* (New York: Free Press, 1986), 70; Stephen Nissenbaum, *Sex, Diet and Debility in Jacksonian America* (Westport, CT: Greenwood Press, 1980), 120.

40. Rapp, "The Port of Buffalo," 219–44; Charles Termini, "The Sailortown of Buffalo" (Seminar paper, State University of New York College at Buffalo, 1983, in the possession of David Gerber).

41. Buffalo *Courier,* 7 October 1848, 28 September 1851.

42. Busby Torrey to Charles Grandison Finney, 28 February 1831, quoted in Whitney Cross, *The Burned-Over District: The Social and Intellectual History of Enthusiastic Religion in Western New York, 1800–1850* (Ithaca: Cornell University Press, 1950), 155. Many years later, the Buffalo *Christian Advocate,* 1 April 1858, protested that local Americans had come to believe that "religion is something for the winter months."

43. Buffalo *Courier,* 28 November 1848; Dr. Bryant Burwell, *Diary* (1838–1845), BECHS.

44. Buffalo *Commercial Advertiser,* 7 October 1859; Merwin S. Hawley to Elijah Hawley, 25 January 1851, 24 February 1852, Hawley Papers, BECHS; Heacock, *Sermon Preached at Central Presbyterian Church, March 20, 1859,* BECHS; Carol Smith-Rosenberg, "The Female World of Love and Ritual: Relations between Women in Nineteenth-Century America," *Signs* 1 (Autumn 1975): 1–29.

45. Welch, *Home History,* 170; Hawley, *Autobiography,* 16–18 and passim; Buffalo *Commercial Advertiser,* 2 February and 4 June 1857; John T. Horton, et al., *History of Northwestern New York,* vol. 1 (New York: Lewis Historical Publishing Co., 1947), 164.

46. Buffalo *Courier,* 13 July 1847; Buffalo *Commercial Advertiser,* 16 July 1856; Buffalo *Republic and Times,* 11 June and 17 and 25 September 1858, 26 May 1859.

47. Heacock, *Sermon Preached at Central Presbyterian Church, March 20, 1859.*

48. Ibid.; Buffalo *Courier,* 8 April 1853; Buffalo *Commercial Advertiser,* 4 August 1856, 8 March and 24 June 1858; Green, *Fit for America,* 28, 85; Levine, "Promise of Sport in Antebellum America," 629.

49. Thomas Donohue, *History of the Catholic Church in Western New York* (Buffalo: Catholic Historical Publishing Co., 1904), 200–201, 202–4, 319–24; Robert J. Rayback, *Millard Fillmore: Biography of a President* (Buffalo: Published for the Buffalo Historical Society, 1959), 407, 409; Buffalo *Courier,* 4 January and 28 April 1851, 24 November 1857,

30 January 1858; Buffalo *Commercial Advertiser,* 28 November 1853, 17 May and 23 and 25 August 1856, 23 February and 3 August 1857, 30 January, 26 March, and 13 April 1858, 29 June 1859.

50. Buffalo *Commercial Advertiser,* 4 June 1857.

51. *Geschichte der Deutschen in Buffalo und Erie County, New York* (Buffalo: Reinecke and Zesch, 1897), passim; H. Perry Smith, *History of the City of Buffalo and Erie County,* vol. 2 (Syracuse: D. Mason and Co., 1884), 150–79; Ismar Ellison, "The Germans of Buffalo," Buffalo Historical Society *Publications* 2 (1880): 117–44; Yox, "Decline of the German-American Community in Buffalo," 1–97; Donohue, *History of the Catholic Church in Western New York,* 114–27, 212–32, 242–43, 245, 248, 256–57; David A. Gerber, "Language Maintenance, Ethnic Group Formation, and Public Schools: Changing Patterns of German Concern: Buffalo, 1837–18/4," *Journal of American Ethnic History* 4 (Fall 1984): 31–45; Carl Wittke, *Refugees of Revolution: The German 48ers in America* (Philadelphia: University of Pennsylvania Press, 1952); Bruce Carlan Levine, " 'In The Spirit of 48': German-Americans and the Fight over Slavery's Expansion" (Ph.D. diss., University of Rochester, 1980).

52. Buffalo *Weltbürger,* 9 January 1847, 19 April 1848, 27 May, 28 June, and 16 October 1849, 26 and 30 January, 2 February, 10 and 27 August, and 20 November 1850, 8 March, 27 August, and 15 October 1851, 27 April 1853.

53. Buffalo *Commercial Advertiser,* 31 January, 8 June, and 14 October 1854, 14 November 1856, 22 January, 13 and 31 March, and 6 April 1857, 7 January, 10 March, and 24 November 1858, 14, 15, and 21 June, 22 July, 29 August, and 8 November 1859, 8 and 10 May, 28 June, 21–26 July, and 29 October 1860. The Buffalo *Christian Advocate* began to make similar remarks late in the decade; see 17 November 1859 and 26 July 1860. Also see Roberta J. Park, "Healthy, Moral, and Strong: Educational Views of Exercise and Athletics in Nineteenth-Century America," in Kathryn Grover, ed., *Fitness in American Culture: Images of Health, Sport, and the Body* (Amherst, MA, and Rochester, NY: University of Massachusetts Press and the Strong Museum, 1989), 138, 141.

54. Buffalo *Weltbürger,* 18 June 1851; Peter Burke, *Popular Culture in Early Modern Europe* (London: New York University Press, 1978), 180–81, 194–95; Smith, *History of Buffalo and Erie County,* vol. 2, 157–58.

55. Buffalo *Weltbürger,* 18 and 28 June 1851; Buffalo *Demokrat und Weltbürger,* 24 June 1853, 3 June 1854, 30 June 1855, 24 June 1856, 24 June 1857, 18 June 1859, 23 June 1860.

56. Buffalo *Courier,* 20 June 1851, 25 June 1853; Buffalo *Commercial Advertiser,* 24 June 1854, 23 June

1855, 24 June 1857, 24 June 1858, 15 June 1859.

57. Buffalo *Weltbürger,* 18 June 1851; Buffalo *Demokrat und Weltbürger,* 24 June 1853, 30 June 1855, 18 June 1859, 23 June 1860; Buffalo *Commercial Advertiser,* 26 June 1857 (quotation), 24 June 1858 (quotation), 14 June 1859, 26 June 1860.

58. Buffalo *Commercial Advertiser,* 16 July 1856. Also, Buffalo *Republic,* 19 July 1856, which gives Germans credit for developing alternatives in the absence of municipal parks.

59. Buffalo *Weltbürger,* 28 June 1851; Buffalo *Demokrat und Weltbürger,* 15 April and 3 June 1854, 30 June 1855, 15 March 1858, 19 December 1859; Buffalo *Commercial Advertiser,* 24 June 1857 (quotation), 21 June 1859.

60. Buffalo *Commercial Advertiser,* 21 June 1859.

61. Ibid., 14 August 1856.

62. Buffalo *Republic,* 17 July 1855, 4 August 1858; Buffalo *Commercial Advertiser,* 6 January 1860.

63. Buffalo *Christian Advocate,* 27 August 1854.

64. Buffalo *Demokrat und Weltbürger,* 5 July 1855.

65. Buffalo *Courier,* 8 April 1853; Buffalo *Demokrat und Weltbürger,* 26 March 1858.

66. LaVern J. Rippley, *Of German Ways* (Minneapolis: Dillon Press, 1970), 283; Charles Hamm, *Music in the New World* (New York: Norton, 1983), 209–10. These immigrant criticisms marked the inception of a venerable polemic in American musicol-

ogy; see Gilbert Chase, *America's Music: From the Pilgrims to the Present* (New York: McGraw-Hill, 1955), 325, and the somewhat more balanced H. Wiley Hitchcock, *Music in the United States,* 2d ed. (Englewood Cliffs, NJ: Prentice Hall, 1974), 54–55, 65.

67. *Geschichte der Deutschen,* 118–20; Alan Howard Levy, *Musical Nationalism: American Composers' Search for Identity* (Westport, CT: Greenwood Press, 1983), 3–6; Hitchcock, *Music in the United States,* 86; Buffalo *Courier,* 25 February and 16 March 1850, 6 June 1851, 29 June 1852, 14 March, 7 April, and 23 June 1853; Buffalo *Commercial Advertiser,* 31 January, 9 February, 8 June, and 14 October 1854, 14 November 1856, 22 January, 13 and 31 March, and 6 April 1857, 7 January, 10 March, and 24 November 1858, 8 May 1860; Buffalo *Demokrat und Weltbürger,* 2 January and 14 and 15 September 1857.

68. Buffalo *Commercial Advertiser,* 5 January 1847; Buffalo *Courier,* 25 February 1850.

69. Buffalo *Commercial Advertiser,* 11, 23, 24, and 26 July and 8 and 17 November 1859; Buffalo *Christian Advocate,* 26 July 1860; Buffalo *Demokrat und Weltbürger,* 2, 7, and 11 November 1859, 18, 23, 24, 25, and 26 July 1860.

70. Buffalo *Commercial Advertiser,* 21 and 25 July 1860.

71. Ibid., 22 June 1858.

# Roller-skating toward Industrialism

DWIGHT W. HOOVER

In their classic study, *Middletown* (1929), Robert S. and Helen Merrell Lynd described Muncie, Indiana, in 1885, just before the discovery of gas had caused the town to boom.

> The thin edge of industry was beginning to appear, though few people thought of the place then as anything but an agricultural county-seat: a bagging plant employed from a hundred to a hundred and fifty people, making bags from the flax grown in the surrounding countryside; a clay tile yard employed some fifteen; a roller-skate "company" in an old barn up an alley, perhaps eight; a feather-duster "factory," five or six; a small foundry, half a dozen; and a planing mill and two flour mills, a few more. It was still for Middletown the age of wood, and a new industry meant a hardwood skewer shop, a barrel-heading shop, or a small wooden pump works.[1]

This is only one of two references to roller-skating in the book, the second being an item taken from a newspaper in 1890 that mentions roller-skating only tangentially:

> Among the business class small dances in fashionable homes on New Year's Eve and other holidays were not uncommon; this group, moreover, patronized Professor Daisy's fortnightly dancing lessons at the skating rink, culminating in a "ball and German with fifty society couples and seventy-five spectators, the latter watching with interest the fancy dancing, heel and toe polka, then the German."[2]

By this time, it would appear skating was no longer popular in Muncie, and that Munsonians had put the rinks to other uses.

Yet roller-skating was more important in Muncie in 1885, both as recreation and as an exemplar of growing industrialization, than the Lynds' depiction suggests. Why the Lynds noted only one skate manufacturer in the town in 1885 is difficult to understand, since there were three at the beginning of the year and five by the end. Roller-skate manufacture was different in kind from the manufacture of other products in the town at the time, and it signaled the transition from a pioneer agricultural village to a burgeoning industrial city. The experience of those involved in the industry served to prepare them for the gas boom industrialization that soon followed. Further, the manufacture of skates raised the horizons of their producers from a local and regional market to a national and international one. Finally, those who frequented the roller rinks were part of a group seeking commercial entertainment, entertainment that, according to Gunther Barth, separated city people from those of town, village, and farm. The actions of both manufacturer and skater moved the community in the direction of an industrial city.

The transition can best be seen in the personal history of a prominent Muncie family, the Neelys. The differences between the founding father, Thomas Neely, and his son, Thad, illustrate the changing character of the community and the varying attitudes of two generations, reflecting changes in the modes of capital generation and investment. The former made his fortune in traditional land speculation; the latter made his in new industrial products.

Thomas S. Neely was born on a farm in Adams County, Pennsylvania, on September 13, 1811. After a three-year apprenticeship to a blacksmith, he worked as a smith in several small villages in western Ohio, returning to Pennsylvania to marry. The Neelys moved to Muncie in 1839, when the town was but twelve years old.[3] Although it was the county seat of Delaware County, the community still had only a handful of residents.

After a short-lived venture in the grocery business, Neely returned to blacksmithing as a partner with Madison Whiteside, a blacksmith in a nearby shop.[4] "Hard times and little money in circulation" dissolved the union four years later, though both men continued in the trade separately.[5] However, Neely was more successful and, a few years later, bought Whiteside's house and lot.[6]

This transaction was only one of a series of land deals for Neely. In the 1840s, he became a builder, constructing the first county seminary jointly with his brother Moses in 1846.[7] At the same time, Neely had become a leader in community affairs. He became a deacon in the Presbyterian church in 1845; elected to the Board of County Commissioners in 1842, he served six years.[8] Neely's most notable contribution came in 1847 when he held a series of meetings to promote the need for a rail connection to Muncie. The resultant publicity aroused the support of the community and helped convince out-of-town investors to make Muncie a stop on the Indianapolis and Bellefontaine Railroad.[9]

By 1850 Neely owned real estate assessed at $1,650 and personal property at $250.[10] His net worth placed him in the upper stratum of the community, as few individuals owned more than one thousand dollars of real estate, and he continued to profit from the need for new facilities as the town grew.

In 1851, for the first time, Neely appears in the R. G. Dun Credit Reports when he asked for credit for the building that was to house the hardware store of Neely and Davis. It failed to prosper and soon closed.[11] He also collected funds to build a district (one-room) school and then served as director. In 1858 he was the successful bidder for the contract to erect a new jail (the second in the county) and sheriff's residence. That same year he changed major vocations, closing his smithy and opening a photographic studio, the first in the town, in his own brick building.[12]

Neely's career was a paradigm of business in pioneer Muncie (fig. 1). Beginning as a craftsman serving primarily rural customers, Neely invested his profits from that trade and from construction of needed public facilities in real estate. As the town grew, so did his fortune. In middle age he changed business, taking advantage of a new need and invention.

Although motivated by the same desire to become rich, Neely's son Thad had a different career. The Muncie to which he returned after serving in the Civil War had changed considerably from the town his father had first seen in 1839. By 1860, for the first time, the census recorded individuals in the category of unskilled laborers, thus marking the beginnings of a more stratified society. Five years later, Muncie had become an incorporated city and had elected its first mayor and city council. The town's growth continued in the next two decades at an ever-accelerating pace, despite the serious national financial panic of the 1870s. By 1870 Muncie had a population of 2,992, almost double that of ten years earlier.

The size of the town almost doubled again in the next decade, reaching 5,219. During this time the number of unskilled workers continued to increase as the proportion of proprietors and skilled laborers declined, indicating business consolidation and signs of early industrialization.[13]

The town prospered because of revenue derived from its governmental function as county seat and from providing goods and services for the farmers in the immediate region. What manufacturing did exist largely consisted of mills which ground grain or sawed wood, blacksmith shops and carriage works which built wagons and carriages for farmers, and a packing house to process the hogs grown in the region. One business made furniture out of local lumber; another used feathers purchased from farmers to make feather dusters. The largest employer in the city in the 1870s was James Boyce, who operated a factory producing flax bagging and tool handles.[14] Boyce was an exception in the town since he sold his bags to southern farmers and had a market beyond the confines of the region. No other manufacturer in town had a national market, nor was any product produced in Muncie likely to have other than local appeal.

There were, however, indications that the town's growth was achieving enough critical mass to support a larger population and to attract others to it. Muncie built its first city hall in the 1870s, thus replacing the vacant stores that had previously housed city services. In 1872 the town began gas lighting from an artificial gas works, and, although the early street lights were inadequate, they gave the community a more citified look (fig. 2). In 1874 a free public library opened. In 1880 the Muncie High School moved to a new building from its previous home in various church rooms.[15] By 1880 seven new churches had organized and had constructed new buildings or purchased old ones. There was also a YMCA (which had an avowed goal of "improving society" as an "auxiliary of the Christian Church"), a chapter of the Women's Christian Temperance Union, and two other temperance organizations—the

Fig. 1   Thomas Neely, about 1870. Courtesy Dwight Hoover.

Broad Ax Temperance Lodge and the Murphy Movement. Women of Muncie conducted sixty-nine temperance crusades in 1874 alone. Law enforcement officers cracked down on social order offenses (drunkenness, frequenting prostitutes, etc.), an effort that led to the highest rates of such crimes charged in the community's history.[16]

The attempt to clean up the town was accompanied by the appearance of groups of residents determined to move Muncie "toward the higher civilization." As historian Andrew Yox has noted, "Outside the churches, the city in 1875 was a cultural desert with dirt roads and makeshift dwellings. In a state of disorganization, the civic elite began their offensive to bring art to town. The professional and business leaders were united in their belief that Muncie needed a better image."[17] In 1878 seven lawyers, five physicians, three educators, and two ministers met in the mayor's office and formed the Literary and Scientific Society to improve Muncie's image. Their organization was patterned after the Women's Literature

Fig. 2   Muncie, Indiana, in the late nineteenth century. Courtesy Dwight Hoover.

Club, created two years earlier. Music lovers joined together in the Musical Association of Muncie in 1879. There were a few oases appearing in the cultural desert.

However, these cultural opportunities were confined mainly to business and professional men of the community and their wives and daughters. They were the ones who also patronized the few public entertainments that Muncie afforded. Muncie was on the circuit of traveling troupes that visited towns in the Midwest, but it suffered from a lack of facilities for staging performances. Until 1863 plays could be seen only in the courthouse; in that year, however, Walling's Hall opened in a building across the street with a "grand dance." After the Universalist church was built, it also became the site of "dramatics" in 1867. In 1872 Jacob Wysor opened his first opera house. The plays presented varied in their intended audience. In 1882 Denier's Humpty Dumpty company opened the remodeled op-

era house with light farce, but county historian G. W. H. Kemper noted that Minnie Maddern played in *Caprice* to a small audience in 1882 and that the main attraction in 1885 was *The Mikado*.[18] Few of these cultural attractions appealed to the majority of Muncie's population, composed as it was of unmarried young people in whose ranks were increasing numbers of unskilled and only slightly educated workers. In 1880 the median age of the population was twenty-two years, women outnumbered men by 50.7 percent to 49.3 percent, and single persons outnumbered married by 56 percent to 38 percent.[19]

In this postwar economic and social climate, Thad Neely's first business efforts failed, just as had his father's original attempt. In 1872 he opened a lumberyard with a partner named Brown. Both men were single and, according to a Dun credit reporter, "lived pretty fast." Thad still resided at home with his family and had little net worth, but the reporter recommended credit extension because of the elder Neely's wealth, now estimated at fifty thousand dollars. In 1873 Brown left the business and Thad, aided by his father, struggled on another year alone. Early in 1875 he opened a boot and shoe store, a common enterprise, took a partner three months later, and then sold his interest three years after that.[20] At the same time, Thad, like his father, had become involved in civic affairs. In January 1873 he helped organize Muncie's first fire department; James Boyce, leading businessman and owner of the bagging factory, appointed Thad Neely chief. As chief, Neely demonstrated a talent for invention. He devised a method for automatic halter removal to speed up the harnessing of horses to the steam pumper, he installed an improved fire-alarm telegraph, and he invented a device to seal leaks in burst fire hoses quickly and easily.[21]

Neely then turned his inventive talents toward improving the roller skate. He did not invent the skate nor introduce it into American society, and roller-skating was not new when Neely became involved with it. Although sources disagree as to exactly when the sport was introduced into this country, they do agree that James L. Plimpton, an Englishman, first popularized it in New York City in 1863.[22] Its popularity spread quickly and, according to Foster Rhea Dulles, a pioneering historian of recreation, its devotees became wildly enthusiastic. One even claimed that "what the sewing machine is to our industrial wants and the telegraph to our commercial pursuits, this new system of exercise has become to society's physical and social wants."[23]

Plimpton envisaged the sport as an upperclass diversion, and it quickly caught on among rich New Yorkers who skated avidly in the summer in Newport. But it soon became popular among other classes. Rinks threw open their doors to all comers. In New Orleans, Major E. D. Lawrence converted a hall he owned into a rink and first invited only the best families in the city. He was soon overwhelmed by other patrons and abandoned his original plans for exclusivity.[24] The boom in

Fig. 3    In the mid-1880s, roller-skating became so popular on Sundays that church attendance dropped. This cartoonist offered "a hint to pastors with slim congregations on how to fill their churches." Courtesy The Bettmann Archive.

roller-skating came, however, in the 1880s (fig. 3). The reason, according to historian Douglas A. Noverr, was improved technology.

> Roller-skating became a rage in the 1880s, and almost every town and city came to have its own rink. Once again, technology had made a sport popular since it was the introduction of metal wheels with pin bearings which made for smooth skating. The activity was popular with girls and women, and at its peak in 1885, over $20 million worth of roller-skating equipment was sold.[25]

Richard D. Mandell and other theorists have also offered a technological explanation for the rise of roller-skating's popularity. They attribute much of the explosion of interest in physical activity, play, and sports after the Civil War to innovations in equipment, combined with advances in mass communications, the popular press, and the telegraph to encourage popular participation. Mandell extends his argument to claim that bicycling later displaced roller-skating because bicycles were more complex technically and, hence, more attractive to the user.[26]

Other theorists probe deeper to find reasons for the growth of sports in the social structure of the country at that time. As Benjamin G. Rader has argued, an emergent national consciousness envisaged sports as a means to unify the country: "Sports can be a national language and a civil religion that binds the diverse nation together and satisfies a common need for liturgical enactments of beauty, excellence, and grace."[27] Rader has also contended that sports gave status and a sense of commonality to ethnic subcommunities, as was manifest in the proliferation of baseball teams, men's clubs, and yacht clubs in the late nineteenth century.[28]

Perhaps the oldest explanation for the rise of the attraction of physical sports is that of Frederic Logan Paxson, who first articulated his thesis in the seminal article "The Rise of Sports" in the *Mississippi Valley Historical Review* in 1917. Paxson claimed that sports served as a safety-valve to bleed off social stresses after the frontier, which had previously served this function, had closed. His adaptation of the Turnerian thesis has proved quite popular; many sports historians begin with Paxson's paradigm, claiming that these social stresses were products of a developing urban-industrial society.[29] John Higham has even maintained that American culture experienced a reorientation in the 1890s as Americans sought a way "to break out of the frustration, the routine, and the sheer dullness of an urban-industrial culture."[30] For Higham, this reorientation evidenced itself in the bicycling craze of that period, particularly among women who, for the first time, energetically participated in sports.

Donald J. Mrozek also attributes part of the interest in sports to a changing definition of women's role in American society as it moved toward "an energetic dynamic style in all aspects of life." This shift revealed itself in almost every aspect of the culture from industrial capitalism to philosophy. Women began to exercise as vigorously as men (fig. 4). And sports offered a new opportunity for social unity: individuals of differing ethnic or national origins and of varying socio-economic groups mingled together, thus setting off a process of vertical integration. Mrozek has argued that "once sport achieved a certain frequency and distribution, it tended to generate new conditions and advance its own acceptance. It thus became part of the background presence of the culture, a piece in the whole of community life, and one whose very strength inhered in its complexity and seeming self-contradictions."[31]

Although these explanations for the growth of sports may be valid for the United States as a whole, they appear to fit less comfortably in the case of Muncie. Technological advance may help explain the rise in the manufacture of skates, but it fails to explain why citizens flocked to rinks. Further, although Muncie was in the process of becoming an industrial town, it had not yet reached that level. Its new residents came from farms and villages surrounding the area; they came in part because of the excitement of the town and had not yet experienced the stultifying routine of factory labor. Moreover, they shared a common bond of social origin and class with older residents. Munsonians were overwhelmingly not ethnic, not first-generation Americans. They did not need sports to unify them.

Norbert Elias's explanation for the rise of sports explains Muncie's situation more effectively. Postulating the presence of an instinctual craving for excitement in all humans, Elias claims that modern society, as it grew more rational and civilized, damped that instinct by emphasizing emotional control. The tension between societal demands for such control and the individual need for emotional excitement explains the growth of socially approved "moderate" excitement found in "mimetic" leisure-time activities. These activities relieve the rational and stale routinized aspects of life that are not just confined to the factory floor but permeate many other areas of existence.[32]

The evidence is clear that in preindustrial Muncie of the 1870s, the old frontier town, with its lack of religious or legal controls on citizens' behavior, was changing. In all aspects,

Fig. 4 Part of roller-skating's immense popularity came from its appeal to women and children. Courtesy The Bettmann Archive.

the town was less free than before. No longer could drunks lie in the street or saloons operate with impunity. The repression of these activities had to be balanced by other kinds of excitement, and one kind of excitement happened to be roller-skating (figs. 5 and 6).

Neely's success with roller skates was meteoric. He had met another inventor, W. F. Cornelius (also a fire chief), at a nearby town in 1878. The two entrepreneurs became partners, patenting the Muncie Roller Skate on March 25, 1879, and beginning manufacture of it in Portland. Both claimed credit for the new product, which featured a superior method of clamping to the skater's shoes.[33] Later in 1879

the firm moved to Muncie to a room in the opera house and completed between 150 and 175 pairs of skates. On September 25, 1880, Neely bought out his partner's interest and moved the plant to the Neely house. Cornelius remained at the old location with a new associate.[34]

At the time of the split, Neely's assets were only twenty-five hundred to three thousand dollars, including an investment of between twelve and fifteen hundred dollars in the skate business. He was still single and living at his parents' home, but with expanded capital and confidence, Neely moved ahead rapidly with the Muncie Roller Skate. By the end of 1881 he

UNION HARDWARE CO.
STEEL TOP LEVER RINK ROLLER SKATE.
Nos. 78 & 79.
Patented August 28, 1883.

Sizes.—8¼, 9, 9½, 10, 10½, 11, 11½ inches.

TRADE PRICE LIST.                              69

UNION HARDWARE COMPANY.
NEW PATENT RINK SKATE.
No. 75.
Patented May 16, 1876; Aug. 1, 1876; Sept. 5, 1876; Oct. 10, 1876.

Sizes.—8¼, 8, 8½, 9, 9½, 10, 10½, 11, 11½ inches.

Figs. 5 and 6   These illustrations show two of the five styles of roller skates offered in an 1886 trade catalog. One bowed to advancing technology by advertising adjustable size, fit, and "stiffness of the spring" while the other featured simple leather straps and a wooden platform. William M. Cornwall, *Trade Price List of Fishing Tackle* (1886).

had sold five thousand pairs. By 1882 his net worth had climbed from three to five thousand dollars; by 1883 he had finally married. By 1884 he was worth five to ten thousand dollars. By 1885 his net worth was twenty thousand dollars, an amount that would place him in the top 10 percent of all property holders in the city.[35] He had become rich in four short years.

So spectacular was his rise that a promotional book, *Resources and Industries of Indiana: Wayne, Henry, Delaware and Randolph Counties* (1884) credited him with almost single-handedly creating the boom in roller-skating in the United States:

Scarcely two decades have passed since the roller skate was first introduced to the notice of the American public, and it was not until many years later that it became popular with the masses. In fact, it was not until Mr. Thad A. Neely, of the city of Muncie, perfected and patented what is now known in America and Europe as the "Muncie Roller Skate" that the pastime of roller skating was raised to the rank of one of the most graceful, healthful, and elegant accomplishments of modern times and had become immensely popular with all classes of the community.[36]

The directory continued with a description of the merits of the Muncie Roller Skate. Its most significant feature was that it had an adjustable bottom which allowed the skate to be fitted tightly to either foot. The directory went on to praise the quality of the product and its manufacturer.

In the year 1880 Mr. Neely established in the city of Muncie a manufactory for the production of these skates, and although there are at present four similar works in the United States, he has secured a trade extending to all sections of this country and Europe, which will exceed in fourfold proportion that of any of his contemporaries, his annual output at this time being from 40,000 to 50,000 pairs, which range in price from $1 to $20, the latter being exquisitely finished and gold mounted, suitable for a prize or presentation. Mr. Neely occupies a two story building, 20 x 60 feet in dimensions and furnishes employment to a force of about 25 men, in what is technically known as "assembling" or putting together the various parts which are manufactured at other points, many nations and foreign lands being tributary to even so delicate a contrivance as this beautiful skate. Mr. Neely is a native and lifelong resident of Muncie, and to his ability, enterprise and integrity may be attributed the world wide reputation which has been attained by our beautiful inland metropolis within the past four years.[37]

Even disregarding the hyperbole, roller skate manufacture was clearly a modern industry (fig. 7) and, contrary to the Lynds' contention, Muncie was not fixed in the age of wood. Neely's firm did not rely on local sources for materials or on local markets for

Fig. 7 Roller skates, manufactured by Barney and Berry, Springfield, Massachusetts, 1876–1883. The key at the back turns to lengthen or shorten the size of the skate.

sales. Both parts and finished skates were elements in national and international networks. Unlike his father, who crafted farm tools by hand of wood and iron from the region to sell to local consumers, Neely had a global perspective. Moreover, he utilized capital from outside the community, something his father had done only later in life and sparingly at that. By all these standards, Neely's business was a prototype of those to come.

Neely's success prompted competitors. By 1885 other entrepreneurs had stepped forward to challenge his lead. Each claimed to have invented a new skate, and each had located capital to exploit the improvement. On January 9, 1885, the three Heath brothers announced that they had patented a new skate, had obtained credit from a Cincinnati firm, and had rented a "room just east of Citizen's Bank, on Jackson St., and commenced manufacturing." Four days later Cornelius went public with news that he had invented an improved skate, his third, and had opened an office and workroom at a new location on Walnut Street. Less

than two months after the Heaths' announcement, a third individual entered the lists with his new improved skate version: Charles J. Becktel had begun to assemble skates in a building near a lumber mill.[38] The last to go public was J. F. Schafer, whose trip to Cincinnati in April 1885 inspired this article from the *Cincinnati Enquirer:*

> The roller skate business is still on the boom. We are informed by reliable authority that Mr. J. F. Schafer, an old traveler and citizen of this city, at present general manager of the Victor Roller Skate Company of Muncie, Ind., has just closed a contract with Post & Co. of Cincinnati, for the manufacture of 50,000 pairs of the New Victor Climax Nickle-Plated Club Skates. This is a self-lubricating, anti-friction skate, and it is thought will cap the climax.[39]

Roller skate factories also sprang up in nearby communities, a phenomenon that was to be repeated by glass plants a few years later after the discovery of natural gas.

The boom in roller-skating not only caused

the proliferation of manufacturers but also a proliferation of skating rinks. At first, these rinks were either converted stages or temporary facilities. On September 12, 1881, for example, Thad Neely's brother Lon opened a skating rink in the Boyce building, a block that contained a theater on whose stage presumably skaters could hone their skills. Other entrepreneurs constructed temporary facilities, such as the Skating Rink, a 50-by-150-foot tent with a hardwood floor located on a vacant lot at Jefferson and North Streets.[40] Not until 1885 was there a push for new, more permanent rinks for the increasingly popular sport. When entrepreneurs decided to build, they all decided at once; as was the case with the manufacture of roller skates, everyone wanted to get into the act. The first announcement about rink building appeared in the *Muncie Daily News* on February 23, 1885.

> Mr. John Little and Mr. Longstreth will as soon as the weather permits, commence the building of a rink on the corner of Main and Mulberry streets on the property lately purchased from K. G. Sample. The building will be 60 x 110 feet giving a skating surface of nearly seven thousand square feet. The floor will be of the latest octagonal pattern and all conveniences will be added to make it complete in every particular.[41]

No sooner had this announcement appeared than another businessman indicated his intention to build a rink. Jacob H. Wysor, a pioneer settler and man of considerable means, had come to Muncie as a child in 1834 and entered the milling business as an adult. Like Thomas Neely, he was a real estate speculator and a railroad promoter, and he had served as president of the Muncie and Granville Turnpike Company. Recognizing the need for an adequate meeting place and for entertainment, Wysor had built Muncie's first opera house in 1872.[42] The newspaper announcement of Wysor's plan for a rink indicated an impressive edifice: "The Rink when completed will for political or other meetings seat eight thousand people." It was to be 200 by 125 feet

and to be lighted by a Brush electric plant, making it one of the most attractive in the state, according to a local newspaper,[43] and one of the first to use electric lighting in the city.[44]

Thad Neely made his move the next day. In cooperation with A. L. Johnson, who later in the year was to become a competitor in assembling roller skates, Neely planned a rink with a stage at one end, a raised floor on each side, and a gallery for spectators. The *Muncie Daily News* noted with evident amazement that "within the last few days there has [*sic*] been numerous rumors of the erection of rinks until nearly every capitalist of Muncie was reported to have under consideration plans and specifications tending in the direction of a rink."[45] The day following this announcement, in fact, Will Patterson traveled to Indianapolis to visit rinks in that city in order to get ideas for one he wished to build in Muncie.[46] Three weeks later, Patterson revealed plans for a building similar in size to Neely's. He hedged his bet, however, by saying that he would so construct his building "that in the event it should cease paying as a rink it can be made two or three stories high and converted into business rooms with offices above."[47]

Together, the proposed capacity of the three rinks was fourteen thousand persons, certainly adequate for a town whose population was only 5,219 in 1880. In order to fill them, individuals from the hinterlands had to be enticed to come to Muncie. This the promoters did with aggressive advertising, as the example of Neely's Royal Rink shows. The Royal Rink first opened its doors on April 8, 1885, after an advertising campaign aimed at all ages and sexes. Local merchants tried to capitalize on the new excitement; Leon and Metzger touted its plaid skating caps for boys at a cost of only twenty-five cents, while Wachtell & Son pushed its skate bags for ladies. The grand opening was a great success, with more than one thousand persons attending. The rink was a Neely-controlled one: Thad owned half, and his brother Lon was the manager. This arrangement was short-lived, however; Thad sold his interest in the building to his partner, A. L. Johnson, and leased the land to him for one year with a five-year option. Later the same day, Johnson sold Neely's interest to S. M. Highlands and W. P. Jenkins, Johnson's partner in the manufacture of skates.[48] Lon Neely remained as manager.

Neely was fortunate to leave the business so quickly: the fad faded and almost disappeared by 1886. In New Orleans "by 1888, when several young men met in the Crescent City Roller Skating Rink to organize the Southern Athletic Club, the rink was inhabited by nothing but cobwebs and a few enterprising bats."[49] Neely later had to close his skate factory, but he continued to prosper in other lines of business. In 1885, he entered into a partnership to build carts with George Kirby and Jasper A. Sprankle, both well-known and financially secure capitalists worth collectively more than seventy-five thousand dollars.[50] The Muncie Cart Company soon went bankrupt, but Neely then became involved in real estate. He was a founder and charter member of the Muncie Business and Manufacturing Association, created on May 22, 1885, to erect "buildings for the purpose of manufacturing and promotion of manufacturing in Muncie and in the vicinity."[51] After the discovery of natural gas in 1886, he helped charter the Board of Trade, a forerunner of the Chamber of Commerce, which strove to bring in new industries; and, on November 17, 1887, he chartered the Cooperative Fuel and Gas Light Company of Muncie, a corporation designed to find a market for natural gas. When he died of a stroke in 1904, he was eulogized as one of the most influential figures in Muncie's industrial growth.[52]

Neely's career after leaving the skate business documents Muncie's transition from a country town dependent upon the surrounding community for its economic livelihood to a manufacturing center with larger regional and national markets. Having successfully entered the national market, Neely helped to attract other entrepreneurs with the same vision and ambition. He aided in the recruitment of the five Ball brothers whose glass plant sold kerosene containers and jars for home canning throughout the country. The Balls were joined by other industries such as Republic Steel, which made nuts, bolts, and turnbuckles, and Warner Gear, which made gears for automobiles. These companies, all of which were integrated into a national economy, took advantage of the available labor, the physical resources (particularly natural gas), and the boom psychology of the town fostered by the roller-skating mania. As a result, the town would never revert to its earlier role; for better or worse, it was now an industrial community.

Roller-skating also had a considerable impact on those who indulged in it. A sport primarily aimed at young adults, not children, and offering entertainment without liquor or shady ladies, roller-skating capitalized on the demographics of the town. Its combination of physical participation with spectator sport was attractive to both sexes and to all classes. Its competition—the opera house, the public dance, or the party at home—seemed less exciting and varied than the skating rink. Even before the installation of permanent facilities, the entertainment element was obvious. On May 11, 1882, for example, the Skating Rink, a tent with a hardwood floor, advertised as its main attraction a grand exhibition of the Nellie Leslie Company of spirit mediums, consisting of Miss Leslie, Harry Herman, a seven-year-old medium, and Dr. White, a mesmerist.[53] Skating here took a back seat. When the entertainment was local, it could be hazardous, adding the spice of danger. The Skating Rink featured on certain nights "Scalp the Indian" as a main attraction. At this event, a select group of skaters would race through an obstacle course composed of four barrels at each side of the rink. If skaters failed to duck as they sailed through, they would be "scalped."[54]

By 1885, even before the opening of the

Royal Rink, attendance had become so common in the Skating Rink tent that the local newspaper routinely reported it as social news. The April 14, 1885, *Muncie Daily News* featured several such news items on its front page.

> Barrel Race at the Rink to-morrow night.
>
> Several new skaters were on the floor Saturday night.
>
> There was a good crowd at the rink on Saturday night.
>
> Quite a party of school girls skated on Saturday afternoon at the hall.
>
> The crowd at the rink Saturday night was the largest and most enthusiastic of the season.
>
> Quincie Walling went to the rink to have a time and he got it, if he did try to reach the ceiling with his heels.
>
> Ed Rickenberg could not enjoy the fun at the rink on account of a severe cold.[55]

Perhaps the best example of the kind of programs rinks usually offered is that provided at the opening night of the Royal Rink on April 13, 1885. One thousand people paid fifteen cents each to enter at 8:00 p.m., stand (the three hundred chairs for spectators failed to arrive in time), and watch the grand march of forty couples who crossed and recrossed the hall on skates. Charles Beeson and Frank Ives then did trick and fancy skating, and the Robinson Brothers turned somersaults and handsprings on skates. Then it was time for all to join in a general skate before the closing at 10:00 p.m. The newspaper reported the events in full detail the next day and created a new feature, "rinkles," which told of happenings at the rinks. In the first edition of the new feature, the paper reported such items as "Lee Lacy made a bold effort last evening and succeeded in going around the rink several times without a fall."[56]

The rink needed a continual influx of talent, just as vaudeville did, to keep interest high. The Royal Rink's ad for the second night after its opening assured readers that its program changed every night and that its next attraction would be Miss Alma Willard, who did rope tricks and the toespin on her skates. Not all the talent was on skates. The same night that spectators at the Royal watched Willard spin, the Wysor Opera House presented Barlow and Wilson's Mammoth Minstrel Show, and the Skating Rink had the Champion Roller Skaters in a burlesque show. The Royal countered the following night with its own musical show, the Snow Drift Quartette, a local group that had earned its name from being snowbound in Michigan the winter before. (Included in the quartette was Lon Neely, the manager of the Royal).[57] In addition to the extra entertainment, the rinks had special nights for skaters alone. One example was the Royal's Masquerade Carnival, where 150 persons came in masks and carnival attire.[58]

The rinks also spawned a new sport based on polo but played on skates—roller polo. The rinks developed their own teams which then sometimes became identified with the town. The first roller polo game in Muncie was played on April 22, 1885, between the Royals and Stars, and the sport invaded the Muncie High School.[59] In 1894 it was one of only four interclass sports played there (the others were tennis, football, and baseball).[60] Because the high school lacked a gym, the sport was often played elsewhere in town and persisted until well into the early twentieth century (fig. 8). Roller polo became institutionalized into a spectator sport as local merchants or rink owners sponsored teams which utilized whatever public facilities were available; high school students imitated these teams in their interclass competition.

Bicycling acts began appearing in Muncie rinks in 1885. On May 1 of that year, George Jones, Indiana's champion bicyclist, gave an exhibition of fancy riding. He was followed later by female performers on bicycles, including a twelve-girl drill corps executing military formations and the Sylvester Sisters, who did fancy and trick skating, handkerchief tricks, and clog dances.[61]

When Patterson's Rink opened on May 18, 1885, the competition intensified. Patterson brought in the Lockwood Band, Muncie's

Fig. 8   The Wachtells Royals roller polo team. *Muncie Morning News*, 8 March 1900.

finest musical group, which enjoyed the sponsorship of the Musical Association of Muncie.[62] Moreover, Patterson's Rink remained open until midnight, switching to dancing after 10:30 p.m. Even this was not enough to attract sufficient crowds; sustaining attendance required the scheduling of ever more spectacular or zany acts. On succeeding nights, Patterson offered football, Peck's Bad Boy and his Pa, and three Mormon giants, all on skates.[63] The management even featured two bicyclists in a spectacular show, as the advertisement for the event indicates.

> Don't miss seeing the contest between Wells and Jones Tuesday evening. See Wells ride the large wheel alone over logs, 15 foot see-saw, up and down stairs. Wells will go through the manual of arms on a bicycle 12 feet from the floor. To see

Jones do the plate spin on the bicycle is wonderful. Jones will turn the bicycle a complete summer-sault, ride the large wheel backwards and give his complete exhibition.[64]

Patterson's Rink also brought in a contortionist who juggled and walked a tightrope while blindfolded and on skates. It sponsored the city skating championship, trapeze artists, and, as always, Lockwood's Band. By June 1885 the Royal Rink succeeded in scheduling the band, which then alternated between the two rinks. The competition between rinks appeared to diminish the business of each, and it was apparent that enthusiasm for skating was dying. Only twenty-five couples paraded for Patterson's Mother Hubbard Party on June 17, a much smaller number than had previously skated.[65]

The rinks closed in early fall in 1885 but re-opened in November. By this time, the owners used other inducements to attract customers. The Royal offered a five-hundred-dollar reward to anyone who could match the twirling of a heavy gun by Harry W. Overman, who performed on skates and claimed to be champion Zouave of America. Patterson's Rink offered prizes for the best costumes at its fancy dress carnival. Ladies could win a silver watch or a hand-painted fan; gentlemen competed for a silk umbrella or a satin muffler. Increasingly, the schedule at the Royal included polo matches between the Royal's own polo club and those from other communities, while group skating became less frequent.[66]

Perhaps the ultimate advertising gimmick came on Thanksgiving Eve, when Patterson's Rink offered free turkeys in a skating contest. The event was not for the timid. The *Muncie Daily News* reported that "the turkeys will be suspended from the ceiling above the heads of the skaters who will be blindfolded and started on the hunt. Any one catching the turkey gets it. The turkeys will be suspended in different parts of the rink. There will be a separate Turkey Hunt for the ladies."[67]

The Royal Rink countered with its own extravaganza. New manager Charles J. Brown, who had replaced Lon Neely, planned a Grand Hat Carnival on Thanksgiving Day to open the Royal for the winter season. The all-day affair began with a two-hour skate in the morning for women and children; in the afternoon, the rink scheduled two acts—Marie Carlyle playing the violin while performing difficult feats on skates and Princess Ke-Ku-Ko doing mikado dances on skates in full Japanese costume. The Grand Hat Carnival was a three-and-a-half-hour skate at night with prizes of a hat for the best hat, a pair of skates for the second best, and a season ticket to the rink for the third best.[68]

The spectacle was repeated at Christmas time and extended for a week. On Monday and Tuesday, December 21 and 22, the Royal featured Indiana State League Championship Polo games between the Muncie Royals and the Indianapolis team. On Wednesday and Thursday, the rink spotlighted the Stirk Family of skaters and five English bicyclists. On Christmas Eve, there was a Masquerade Carnival with prizes for the winners. The prizes were not as good as at the Thanksgiving skate, which reflects the decline of the sport's popularity.[69]

The great roller-skating craze vanished almost as quickly as it had come, leaving so few traces that the Lynds missed it entirely. It was a failure so rapid that it led the Lynds to misjudge the character of the town by discounting its industrial development. Rather than being a sleepy county seat town in 1880, Muncie was a community well on its way to becoming an industrial center. Alexander E. Bracken has said, "If Muncie had not yet developed an 'industrial culture' by 1880, it did possess an economic system based on manufacturing interests. . . . Muncie was not yet a complete industrial city by 1880, but it was well on its way even before the tremendous expansion brought on by the gas boom five years later."[70] Roller-skating pushed the town even farther down the road.

Why did the roller-skating boom collapse? There appear to be several reasons. The gas boom occurred the next year; the excitement of economic expansion plus excursions to the gas fields provided entertainment for many. Other forms of amusements grew; the town had a semiprofessional baseball team, and everyone was bicycling. Moreover, in part, the sport had fallen victim to its own development. Introduction of more and more vaudeville-type acts into the rinks had induced a reaction from the churches, which began to attack the sport. As a result, roller-skating became more and more relegated to children, to be played on sidewalks and in the home but not in a public rink. The skating fad, which had fed on itself, collapsed.

The roller skate did not disappear completely from Muncie. Roller polo continued for some time. Appropriately enough, three days after Thad Neely died, the Indianapolis team defeated Muncie in roller polo ten to five.[71] Even before Neely's death, the old Royal Rink served primarily as a meeting hall. Its biggest crowd of two thousand came to hear the noted black leader Frederick Douglass; at other times, it hosted temperance meetings of the Murphy Society.[72] By 1900 Munsonians could no longer sing the great minstrel Dochstadter's famous skating song, "That Ain't No Lie."

Went to the roller rink for to skate,
Thought to tumble would be my fate:
Stopped on the way to get a bracer of gin,
Took two or three before I went in.
Asked the skate man for the skates to try.
He looked at my feet and says he with a sigh,
"There ain' a skate big enough in the lot,"
Says I, "What's the matter with the skate I've
    got?"
[Refrain:]
I'm a natural born skater,
I'm a natural born skater,
A regular high roller,
That ain't no lie.[73]

## Notes

1. Robert S. Lynd and Helen Merrell Lynd, *Middletown* (1929; reprint, New York: Harcourt, Brace & World, 1956), 12–13.

2. Lynd and Lynd, *Middletown,* 282.

3. Dick Greene, "Our Neighborhood," *Muncie Star,* 15 June 1976.

4. Thomas B. Helm, *History of Delaware County, Indiana, with Illustrations and Biographical Sketches* (Chicago: Kingman Brothers, 1881), 226; G. W. H. Kemper, ed., *A Twentieth Century History of Delaware County, Indiana* (Chicago: The Lewis Publishing Co., 1908), 37; Frank D. Haimbaugh, ed., *History of Delaware County,* vol. 1 (Indianapolis: Historical Publishing Co., 1924), 210; and Muncie *Morning Star,* 10 August 1901.

5. Kemper, *Twentieth Century History,* 37.

6. Ibid.

7. Delaware County Deed Book, vol. 6, 324, vol. 7, 511, and vol. 8, 18, 26, and 632; Haimbaugh, *History of Delaware County,* 141, 187, 313.

8. Haimbaugh, *History of Delaware County,* 345, 347.

9. Helm, *History of Delaware County,* 227; and Muncie *Morning Star,* 17 August 1901. Helm claimed that Neely pushed for the railroad in order to have a more convenient method of transporting iron for his smithy from Cincinnati.

10. Delaware County Tax Duplicates, 1850, 347. The 1850 census listed fifty-seven percent of the native-born citizens as property holders. Of that number, sixty-four percent owned property valued at less than one thousand dollars and seventeen percent owned property worth between one thousand and twenty-five hundred dollars. United States Census Office, Seventh Census, 1850, *Indiana,* Population Schedules of the Seventh Census of the United States, 1850 (Washington, DC: National Archives, National Archives and Records Service, General Services Administration, 1963–1964), tabulated in Alexander E. Bracken, "Middletown as a Pioneer Community" (Ph.D. diss., Ball State University, July 1978), 173.

11. R. G. Dun Credit Reports, Baker Library, Harvard Business School, vol. 22, 206.

12. Helm, *History of Delaware County,* 227; Haimbaugh, *History of Delaware County,* 174; and Muncie *Morning Star,* 17 August 1901.

13. Bracken, "Middletown as a Pioneer Community," 25–35.

14. Wiley W. Spurgeon, Jr., *Muncie and Delaware County* (Woodland Hills, CA: Windsor Publications, 1984), 32–35; Andrew Yox, "Art and the American Community: Middletown 1875–1950" (Center for Middletown Studies, Muncie, IN, February 1988), 11.

15. Spurgeon, *Muncie and Delaware County,* 29.

16. Theodore Caplow, Howard Bahr, and Bruce Chadwick, *All Faithful People* (Minneapolis: University of Minnesota Press, 1983), 47–48; Kemper, *Twentieth Century History,* 123; and John D. Hewitt and Dwight W. Hoover, "Local Modernization and Crimes: The Effects of Modernization on Crime in Middletown, 1845–1910," *Law and Human Behavior* (Winter 1982): 321.

17. Yox, "Art and the American Community," 12–15, 17, 21, 84.

18. Ibid., 120, 122, 166, 168–69.

19. Bracken, "Middletown as a Pioneer Community," 34–35.

20. R. G. Dun Credit Reports, vol. 22, 156, 219.

21. Helm, *History of Delaware County,* 198–99.

22. Melvin L. Adelman, *A Sporting Time: New York City and the Rise of Modern Athletics, 1820–70* (Urbana: University of Illinois Press, 1986), 262; Foster Rhea Dulles, *America Learns to Play: A History of Popular Recreation, 1607–1940* (New York: D. Appleton-Century Company, 1940), 193. Adelman says the roller skate was introduced in 1838 while Dulles says the date was 1863.

23. Dulles, *America Learns to Play,* 182.

24. Ibid., 193–94; Dale A. Somers, *The Rise of Sports in New Orleans, 1850–1900* (Baton Rouge: Louisiana State University Press, 1972), 213–14.

25. Douglas A. Noverr and Lawrence E. Ziewacz, *The Games They Played: Sports in American History, 1865–1980* (Chicago: Nelson-Hall, 1983), 33.

26. Richard D. Mandell, *Sport: A Cultural History* (New York: Columbia University Press, 1984), 186. See also Stephen Hardy, *How Boston Played: Sport, Recreation, and Community, 1865–1915* (Boston: Northeastern University Press, 1982), 14–15.

27. Benjamin G. Rader, "Modern Sports: In Search of Interpretations," *Journal of Social History* 13 (Winter 1979): 310; see also Mandell, *Sport: A Cultural History*, 188.

28. Benjamin G. Rader, "The Quest for Subcommunities and the Rise of American Sport," *American Quarterly* 29 (Fall 1977): 361–63.

29. See, for example, the bow to Paxson in Hardy, *How They Played*; Donald J. Mrozek, *Sport and American Mentality, 1880–1910* (Knoxville: University of Tennessee Press, 1983); Rader, "Modern Sports"; and Dale Somers, "The Leisure Revolution: Recreation in the American City, 1820–1920," *Journal of Popular Culture* 5 (Summer 1971): 138, 146.

30. John Higham, "The Reorientation of American Culture in the 1890s," in John Weiss, ed., *The Origins of Modern Consciousness* (Detroit: Wayne State University Press, 1965), 27.

31. Mrozek, *Sport and American Mentality*, xvi–xvii, 119, 231.

32. Norbert Elias and Eric Dunning, *Quest for Excitement: Sport and Leisure in the Civilizing Process* (Oxford and New York: Basil Blackwell, 1986), 63, 65–69, 73, 93, 115, 120.

33. R. G. Dun Credit Reports, 208; Haimbaugh, *History of Delaware County*, 724; Helm, *History of Delaware County*, 202; and *Resources and Industries of Indiana: Wayne, Henry, Delaware, and Randolph Counties* (Cincinnati: Historical and Statistical Publishing Co., 1884), 126. The latter states, "Some years ago Mr. W. F. Cornelius invented a roller skate, which at the time appeared to meet the requirements of the time. The skate is now manufactured and controlled by another firm."

34. Helm, *History of Delaware County*, 202; and Charles Emerson, *Muncie Directory, 1881–82* (Indianapolis: Carlon, Hollenbeck, Printers and Binders, 1881), 149.

35. R. G. Dun Credit Reports, 321; *Muncie Daily Herald*, 4 December 1904; and Helm, *History of Delaware County*, 202.

36. *Resources and Industries of Indiana*, 134.

37. Ibid.

38. *Muncie Daily News*, 9 and 13 January and 2 March 1885.

39. Ibid., 4 April 1885.

40. Ibid., 10 September 1881, 11 May 1882.

41. Ibid., 23 February 1885.

42. Ibid., 24 February 1885; and Haimbaugh, *History of Delaware County*, 329–30.

43. *Muncie Daily News*, 24 February 1885.

44. David Nye, "Electrifying Muncie" (Center for Middletown Studies, Ball State University, Muncie, IN), 3–4. The other user was James Boyce in his Boyce Block, which contained a skating rink. See *Muncie Daily News*, 8, 10, and 13 April 1885.

45. *Muncie Daily News*, 25 February 1885.

46. Ibid., 26 February 1885.

47. Ibid., 20 March 1885.

48. Ibid., 8, 10, 13, and 14 April 1885.

49. Somers, *The Rise of Sports in New Orleans*, 214.

50. R. G. Dun Credit Reports, 100.

51. Kemper, *Twentieth Century History*, 169.

52. Ibid., 170, 188; and *Muncie Daily Herald*, 4 December 1904.

53. *Muncie Daily News*, 11 May 1882.

54. Ibid., 5 January 1885.

55. Ibid., 14 April 1885.

56. Ibid.

57. Ibid., 19 April 1885.

58. Ibid., 25 April 1885.

59. Kin Hubbard, ed., *A Book of Indiana* (n.p.: Indiana Biographical Association, 1929), 460.

60. *Zetetic* (Muncie: Muncie High School, 1894).

61. *Muncie Daily News*, 1, 8, and 11 May 1885.

62. Yox, "Art and the American Community," 21; Helm, *History of Delaware County*, 106; and *Muncie Daily News*, 22 March 1879.

63. *Muncie Daily News*, 21, 23, and 29 May 1885.

64. Ibid., 2 June 1885.

65. Ibid., 9, 16, 17, and 20 June 1885.

66. Ibid., 29 September, 27 October, and 7 and 8 November 1885.

67. Ibid., 24 November 1885.

68. Ibid.; Kemper, *Twentieth Century History*, 169.

69. *Muncie Daily News*, 18 December 1885.

70. Bracken, "Middletown as a Pioneer Community," 39–40.

71. *Muncie Daily News*, 27 January and 2 February 1887; and *Muncie Daily Herald*, 7 December 1904.

72. Kemper, *Twentieth Century History*, 171.

73. Dailey Paskman and Sigmund Spaeth, *"Gentlemen, Be Seated!": A Parade of the Old-Time Minstrels*, rev. ed. (New York: C. N. Potter, 1976), 226.

# American Angling

The Rise of Urbanism and the Romance of the Rod and Reel

COLLEEN J. SHEEHY

In a 1960 episode of the television series "The Twilight Zone" entitled "A Stop at Willoughby," the scene opens on a corporate board room where one man—the president of the company—is hammering a pencil on the table. The other man—the account executive—holds his stomach, his ulcer acting up, while the boss yells, "This is a push business. Push. Push. Push." Just then, Rod Serling, the omniscient narrator gesturing with cigarette in hand, steps in from stage left with that familiar introduction: "This is Garth Williams, aged 38, ad agency executive, who, in just a moment, will move into the Twilight Zone in a desperate search for survival." The next we see of Garth Williams, he is taking the train home, presumably in some eastern city. When he falls asleep on the train, exhausted from his ordeal at work, he wakes up to find the train stopping at the small town of Willoughby in 1888, where the first things he sees are two barefoot boys with fishing poles over their shoulders walking through the town square. He says to himself, "I've never seen such serenity. It must have been the way people lived a hundred years ago." Williams becomes so attracted to the slow life in Willoughby that he gets off at this imaginary town, leaving his briefcase—symbol of urban business—on the train. He goes to join the boys fishing. With Serling's usual sardonic twist, the episode ends with the train's porter calling out that a man had just jumped off the train while yelling something about "Willoughby," which turns out to be the name of a funeral home. Serling's concluding moral ties Garth Williams's delusion of a nineteenth-century town where barefoot boys can fish all day to the threat of the modern world "that moves too fast," and leaves us to wonder if the Twilight Zone is the imaginary town or the modern world.[1]

Despite the episode's strange ending, this television story reflects a good deal about the values that came to be associated with fishing in the nineteenth century, values that persist to the present day. As immigration began to swell the borders of eastern cities at midcentury and as the lives of upper- and middle-class men became more routinized in corporate work, nineteenth-century Garth Williamses increasingly took up the rod and reel. Recreational fishing provided an escape from urban life and a retreat to an innocent and simple activity. Over the course of the nineteenth century, fishing was transformed from being predominantly a way of gathering food and supplementing food supplies to a sport, a change that meant an emphasis on certain fishing methods, the development of a code of sportsmanship, and eventually the passage of laws regulating fishing practices. As angling became more popular, it became the locus of highly charged values, a respite from urban life and business pressure. A new fascination with boyhood as a carefree time of play and idleness developed at the same time, and images of boys fishing served as emblems of longing for a time prior to adulthood. The barefoot boy later became a common way of remembering nineteenth-century America, just as Rod Serling depicted him in the "Twilight Zone" episode.

The story of how fishing came to be practiced the way it is today and of how Americans began to associate new values with it began in the mid-nineteenth century in the complex intersection of growing cities, a receding frontier, expanding railroads that made remote areas accessible for settlers and travelers, a changing attitude toward nature, and, as the century progressed, a growing concern with conservation. The story began in the eastern United States, where cities and their attendant urban problems first grew, but the story also involves the West as a place that fueled the development of new attitudes toward nature and also as a place that nurtured alternate fishing practices and values to those promoted by the new sports fishing. The transformation of fishing from a subsistence activity to a leisure-time sport practiced by broad segments of the population occurred over the course of the nineteenth century yet gained new urgency in post–Civil War days with the rise of industrialism, rapid urban growth, and increasing recognition of wildlife depletion. As a result, a sport that previously had been practiced primarily by the upper classes became codified for the general populace through the passage of state laws regulating fishing methods.[2]

Fishing with rod, line, and hook (or angling), as compared to other fishing methods using nets or spears, was not unknown in America prior to the nineteenth century, as Charles Goodspeed acknowledged in his 1939 book *Angling in America,* one of the few histories of this sport. Angling had been part of the genteel tradition in Great Britain, chronicled as early as the seventeenth century in Sir Izaak Walton's famous *The Compleat Angler.* That gentlemanly tradition came to colonial America but was not widely practiced before the nineteenth century.[3] Goodspeed, in scouring old newspapers, biographies, and other eighteenth-century print materials, uncovered numerous references to colonial fishing practices, including some accounts of angling. John Rowe, a Boston merchant, wrote in his diaries of the 1760s and 1770s about his fishing expeditions in eastern Massachusetts, where he caught pike, perch, and one "fine red trout of fourteen inches." And Lyman Beecher, father to Harriet Beecher Stowe, Catharine Beecher, and Henry Ward Beecher, wrote of his boyhood fishing experiences in the late eighteenth century when he used a stick, brown thread, and a crooked pin. Pictorial evidence, such as the M. F. Cormé painting of Peter Oliver of Salem, Massachusetts, from the late eighteenth century, shows the angler, book in hand, posed beside a bamboo cane pole with fishing line tied to its tip and two hooks attached to the line. And tackle advertisements appearing in eighteenth-century newspapers also confirm a market for rods and tackle, usually products imported from England.[4] Fishing prior to the nineteenth century, however, usually meant catching fish for subsistence or for commercial sale to markets by any effective method, including netting, spearing, shooting, setting a line with multiple hooks, hooking the fish's body, catching fish with one's bare hands, and sometimes, in the case of large fish such as sturgeon, even riding a fish to shore in shallow waters. The key act was catching fish, not how one caught them.

Angling with hook and line increased markedly by the 1830s and 1840s as clubs of gentlemanly anglers began to multiply. The earliest example of these fraternal clubs was Philadelphia's Schuylkill Fishing Company, established in 1732 in a forested region far enough beyond the city's streets to provide a rural retreat for fishing and conviviality among Philadelphia's business and political leaders. From the first of May through October, they met fortnightly for fishing and an afternoon meal, when they were joined by "the ladies." A typical meal in those days might have consisted of a four-foot-long sturgeon or seventy dozen assorted white perch, striped bass, catfish, and shad washed down with a toast of the famous Fishhouse Punch, concocted of Jamaican rum, peach brandy, and cognac. Thus began America's longest-standing sporting club, one that still exists today and of which a written record has been preserved. As Philadelphia grew in the early nineteenth century, and as urban development brought the construction of waterworks and industrial pollution, the Schuylkill Fishing Company retreated farther downstream. In 1822 members moved their meeting grounds to Rambo Rock, where they erected a club building called "the Castle," and in 1887 the Fishing Company moved off the Schuylkill entirely to the Delaware River. As American cities grew generally—in 1820, only 7 percent of Americans lived in urban centers, in 1870, 25 percent, and in 1920, 50 percent[5]—anglers elsewhere sought fertile fishing grounds further removed from urban areas. Aided by the growth of railroads, especially after the Civil War, anglers traveled to Long Island, the Adirondacks, Maine, and to points west such as Michigan, Wisconsin, and Minnesota, where trout and bass still could be found in profusion.[6]

The gentlemen of the Schuylkill Fishing Company were not angling purists; they valued mostly the social occasion. Though they fished primarily with rod and line, using a handheld net to catch fish or setting a long line with many hooks and bait across the river were not completely frowned upon.[7] Nonetheless, the company served as a model for later fishing associations that emphasized fishing with hook, line, and rod to a greater degree.

The Schuylkill Fishing Company is the most famous fishing association, but by the 1830s fishing clubs had also sprung up in Cincinnati, Boston, New York, and Philadelphia. Comprised of upper- and middle-class men, often those in positions of power in government, business, or the church, these clubs aimed "to blend amusement with recreation," according to the toast proffered by the president of the Cincinnati Angling Club at its first anniversary dinner in 1831.[8] Clearly, by this time, fishing was beginning to be regarded by these groups as a leisure activity, a time away from work when one could enjoy the beauty and bounty of nature and get together with fellow anglers for good talk, a pipe, brandy, and a fine repast. Sporting clubs ranged from those with controlled membership, usually the domain of the elite, to loosely organized groups of sportsmen such as the Happy Days Club in Minnesota, formed in the 1890s.[9] When fishing spots close to urban areas became depleted, some wealthier clubs purchased their own preserves, as did the Blooming Grove Park Association, which established a summer resort area in 1871 only a four-and-a-half-hour train ride from New York City. Its members gained privilege to their summer grounds by buying at least one share at $450, an amount slightly less than the entire annual salary of the average urban worker of the day.[10] With their emphasis on angling with rod and line, these associations opposed taking fish with nets and spears because those methods were considered unsportsmanlike and threatened to deplete fish populations. By the end of the century, many sporting clubs organized increasingly to promote conservation, although the social and sporting aspects remained important.[11]

Besides joining for outings, members of sporting clubs shared their knowledge of the newest and most effective tackle. Fishing equipment became increasingly available in greater variety during the nineteenth century as more American manufacturers began producing their own rods, reels, lines, hooks, flies, and lures for a market that had been dominated by British imports (figs. 1 and 2). As

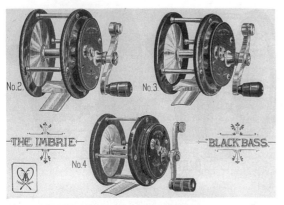

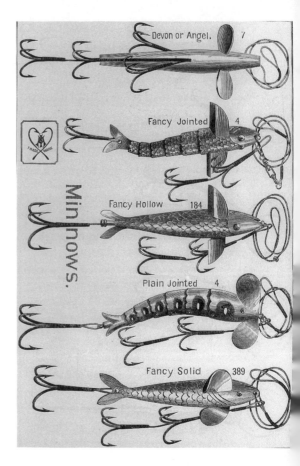

Figs. 1 and 2   Imbrie "Black" Bass reels and minnow-type lures. Abbey and Imbrie trade catalog *Fine Fishing Tackle* (1884).

sports historian Stephen Hardy has noted about athletic goods for competitive sports, throughout the nineteenth century several sources provided sporting goods—homecrafting, local artisans, European imports, and large manufacturers—and the same was true for fishing tackle. Homecrafters fashioned poles from tree branches and string as well as spliced together finer rods of dogwood or hickory, following instructions from angling books and sporting magazines. Tackle retailers such as Edward Pole of Philadelphia (a business later owned by George R. Lawton) offered imported bamboo rods, horsehair, silk, and linen lines, and an impressive array of artificial flies and live bait in the late eighteenth and early nineteenth centuries. A contest held in 1849 between two American tackle manufacturers—Ben Welch and John Conroy of New York City—to determine which one could make the best fishing rod marked a tone of general confidence in the quality of American tackle manufacturers by that time.

Reels had become an increasingly essential piece of fishing equipment by the 1830s. Multiplying reels, developed in England in the late eighteenth century, allowed the angler to achieve a greater reach because the reel could hold more line than could be attached to the end of a pole, the earlier method of using a rod and line. English reels were imported for sale in the United States, but native manufacturers

such as George Snyder of Kentucky also contributed to the development of more versatile and reliable reels by applying crafts technology from watchmaking to the reel. Finely crafted rods with nickel and silver ferrules or joints would have been within the budgets of only wealthy anglers during antebellum days, but by 1895 anyone with thirty-five cents could buy a fine bass rod through the Montgomery Ward catalog, or a three-piece bamboo pole for fifteen cents, high-grade trout flies for ten cents each, and a multiplying reel for ninety cents. Unlike competitive sports that were marked by increasing standardization of equipment and related standardization of sporting practice, fishing tackle became more diversified as fishing became a sport (fig. 3), a characteristic that continues to the present day.[12]

As the rise of fishing clubs and the availability of tackle attest, angling as a sport was booming along the East Coast by the 1840s as disenchantment with the industrializing cities increased and as nature began to be viewed in more benevolent terms. One place we find evidence of a sudden increase in angling is in the painting and popular imagery of the day. Painters of the Hudson River School such as Thomas Cole, Thomas Doughty, and Asher B. Durand reflected and helped to generate a new vision of nature's benevolence in such works as Doughty's *In Nature's Wonderland* of 1835, where the American wilderness appears grand and inspiring. Along with the nature poetry of William Cullen Bryant and the writings of Emerson and Thoreau, who regarded the natural world as the means to spiritual truth and renewal, an earlier fearful view of nature was changing.

The fisherman in nature expressed this new relationship. In 1852, for example, John Frederick Kensett painted *Trout Fisherman,* which shows a man and boy dwarfed in a golden, cathedral-like space, their fishing rods nearly invisible in the forest's shadows. That same year the popular lithographers Currier and Ives produced several prints featuring angling scenes, including one drawn by Frances F. Palmer called *The Trout Stream,* where one gentleman plays a trout with his supple, fifteen-foot rod, while another watches from the forested banks (fig. 4).[13] If fishing imagery centered on trout fishing in the eastern states, out West in the frontier lands of Missouri artist George Caleb Bingham was depicting a rougher kind of fishing in his 1851 work *Fishing on the Mississippi.* These fishermen used trimmed tree branches and sturdy cord rather than hickory rods and flies, and Bingham's Mississippi men may have been fishing for channel cats rather than trout. Nonetheless, as Kensett and Currier and Ives prints did, he presented fishing as a restful and innocent activity that immerses the angler in nature and brings time to a near standstill. Along with Bingham's other work that glorified midwestern frontier life, his *Fishing on the Mississippi* presents the crude fishing of the working class as every bit as noble as fly-fishing by Eastern gentlemen.[14]

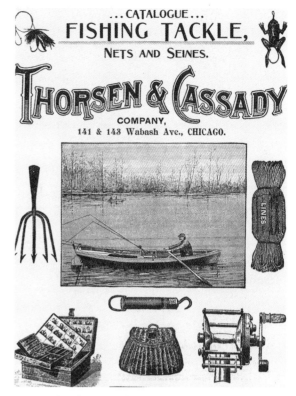

Fig. 3    The Thorsen and Cassady trade catalog *Fishing Tackle, Nets and Seines* (Fall and Winter 1894) illustrates the diverse array of fishing paraphernalia available as the popularity of fishing increased.

At the same time that artists were increasingly fascinated with American landscape and men in the landscape, the popular press was burgeoning through the introduction of the steam-powered press, producing an array of mass periodicals and newspapers. Several of these early publications covered the nascent world of American sports, such as the *American Turf Register and Sporting Magazine* (first issued in 1829) and the *Spirit of the Times.* Begun by sporting enthusiast William Porter in 1831, the *Spirit of the Times* devoted its attention to the world of leisure, covering horse racing, fashion, theater, and angling, among other pursuits. American publications became more specialized in post-Civil War decades, when several started up that were completely devoted to field sports. Among these were *Forest and Stream,* started in 1873 and edited by

Fig. 4 "The Trout Stream," Currier and Ives lithograph drawn by Frances F. Palmer, 1852, in Harry T. Peters, *Currier & Ives: Printmakers to the American People* (1942).

the prominent sportsman Charles Hallock; *Western Field and Stream,* started in 1896 and shortly thereafter renamed *Field and Stream;* and the first American publication devoted entirely to fishing, the *American Angler,* begun in 1881. Filled with piscatory adventures, these magazines fed a growing audience that wanted to learn about and share fishing techniques, equipment, and tales of fishing throughout the United States. Letters and articles from readers provided much of their content.

Like their visual counterparts that glorified fishing and nature, the piscatory press railed loudly against the city and extolled recreational fishing as an antidote to urban life. In an article from 1877, Thomas Alexander voiced what had by that time become a common attitude about fishing among urban men. He said, "It is an amusement especially adapted to the

present day, and to the American manner of living and working 'at high pressure,' taking heed only of present result and not counting the true cost of the excessive physical and mental strain required to secure them." He recounted the current maladies afflicting "civilized" Americans and recommended fishing as an activity that "withdraws the weary and worn from the crowded, unhealthy cities, leading him among nature's pleasantest places, along the flowery bank of the sparkling brook or upon the broad bosom of the fresh glad lake."[15] Another correspondent identified only as "J. W." in an 1881 edition of the *American Angler* wrote that fishing was a "healthy diversion" from the pressures of the business world, providing "an agreeable incident in life to return to some secluded locality, where, forgetful of the formalities, cares, and anxieties of city life, one may wear his old clothes and go fishing."[16] In 1896 Isaac McLellan, a poet often published in *Field and Stream,* wrote in "The Angler's Pleasure":

The angler's joy we celebrate—the sports
That lure him from tumultuous scenes of life
    That win him from the city's noisy street
From mart, from wharf, from avaricious strife.[17]

And in 1903 civic and religious leader Henry Van Dyke, also a popular angling author, prefaced his book of "essays in profitable idleness" entitled *Little Rivers* with the poem, "An Angler's Wish in Town":

When tulips bloom in Union Square,
And timid breaths of vernal air
    Are wandering down the dusty town
Like children lost in Vanity Fair;

When every long, unlovely row
Of westward houses stands aglow
    And leads the eyes toward sunset skies,
Beyond the hills where green trees grow;

Then weary is the street parade,
And weary books, and weary trade:
    I'm only wishing to go a-fishing;
For this the month of May was made.[18]

Along with the mass periodicals, a body of fishing literature grew from the 1840s onward, written mostly by upper-class men, that compiled knowledge about American fish species and promoted a code of sportsmanship. John J. Brown published *The American Angler's Guide* in 1845, the first volume on American fish and fishing, though apparently much of it was derived from British authors. In 1847, the first American edition of Izaak Walton's *The Compleat Angler* appeared, edited by minister, scholar, and sportsman George Washington Bethune, with additions on American fishing. The British aristocrat-turned-American, Henry William Herbert, published the popular *Frank Forester's Fish and Fishing of the United States and British Provinces of North America* in 1859, writing under the nom de plume of "Frank Forester" to lend the work a more convincing American tone.[19] In 1864 Thaddeus Norris, who became known as "the American

Walton," published *The American Angler's Book.* Robert Barnwell Roosevelt, uncle to Theodore, published *Superior Fishing* in 1865; sportswriter Charles Hallock published *The Fishing Tourist* in 1873. The appetite for this fishing literature, which ranged from scientific treatises on American fish species to travel essays and instructional manuals on fly-fishing, continued unabated into the early twentieth century. Charles Goodspeed noted that nearly one hundred books on American fishing were published between 1870 and 1901.[20]

The angling press and literature played a key role in promoting a new code of sportsmanship that encompassed methods for fishing, standards for the most prized fish, and guidelines for conduct in the field, principles that previously had been tacitly agreed upon by gentlemen anglers, though even among that group, adhered to rather loosely. These codes can be viewed to some extent as measures taken by the socially elite to distance themselves from the coarse fishing methods of the lower classes, though, to be fair, the elite's promotion of angling was also motivated by genuine concerns about the depletion of fish stocks if netting and spearing continued unabated.[21] With the promotion of certain means of catching fish—rod-and-reel fishing and, particularly, fly-fishing—a debate raged about exactly which fish should be sought. Discussion increased on the subject of which fish deserved the status of "game" fish and which fish were "rough" or "coarse." As the rhetoric reveals, these debates about fish were often veiled discussions about the social status and class of the fishermen. Not by taste alone, insisted Henry William Herbert in the guise of Frank Forester, should game fish be known, but by their "character." Game fish were those that would take natural or artificial bait "and which when hooked have sufficient rigor, courage and velocity to offer such resistance, and give such difficulty to the captor, as to render pursuit exciting." Herbert warned those who thought that bait fishing through holes in the ice or hauling in the seine or using a set line was "fishing" to avoid his book.[22] Charles

Hallock in *The Fishing Tourist* explicitly connected fish status to social status. "Define me a gentleman," he stated, "and I will define you a game fish; which the same is known by the company he keeps, and recognized by his dress and address, features, habits, intelligence, haunts, food, and manner of eating. . . . other coarse fish might 'pass in a crowd' as the shabby genteel frequently do."[23] According to his status hierarchy, salmon was considered the noblest freshwater fish, followed by trout and bass, while catfish, sturgeon, and pike were among the lowly.

Angling authors spent a good deal of time delineating "the true angler"—who was indeed a gentleman—as distinguished from "the prowlers, poachers, and pot-hunters."[24] Norris described him as a virtuous and modest man, comfortable in nature and knowledgeable about fish, a man who did not insist on a huge catch but enjoyed practicing the art of angling as much as landing fish.[25] And R. B. Roosevelt in *Superior Fishing* added several qualities to the list of necessary attributes:

> A genuine sportsman must possess a combination of virtues which will fill him so full that no room can be left for sin to squeeze in. He must be an early riser—to be which is the beginning of all virtue—ambitious, temperate, prudent, patient of toil, fatigue, and disappointment; courageous, watchful, intent upon his business; always ready, confident, cool; kind to his dog, civil to the girls, and courteous to his brother sportsmen.[26]

Not only did "the true fisherman" use rod and reel and possess a constellation of moral virtues; the true fisherman was a fly fisherman (fig. 5). R. B. Roosevelt stated, "Therefore to his many other qualities, the true sportsman must add a thorough knowledge of fly-fishing, and only the use of artificial fish or fly . . . should be termed SUPERIOR FISHING."[27] Nearly thirty years later, argument between bait and fly fishermen still raging, Charles Hallock added his opinion by claiming, "Fly-fishing is all ethereal, vitalizing, elevating. There is nothing groveling in fly-fishing—

nothing gross or demoralizing. But bait fishing? Well—it is cruel to impale a minnow or a frog. It is vulgar and revolting to thread a worm. Worms! bah! let them go to the bottom."[28] Hallock's contempt for worms revealed a curious squeamishness, considering that angling has generally been considered one of the "blood sports."

Practiced in the nineteenth century, as now, primarily by well-to-do men,[29] fly-fishing held great status appeal given its connections to British aristocratic sporting traditions. It also appealed to the amateur scientist, common in upper-class circles, because it required a thorough knowledge of the seasonal diets of different fish, of the stages of insect life, and of the varied natural settings the angler fished. Frank Forester insisted that one needed "to study much and long . . . how to adapt and blend the various materials used in the construction of a fly, how to construct the fly on certain defined rules; and lastly, how to select your flies, thus carefully and correctly constructed, in accordance with the state of the sky, the color of the water, and the peculiar habits of the fish in different rivers."[30]

Nineteenth-century angling literature devoted numerous chapters and articles to the art of fly tying. The loving attention given to details of materials and techniques reveal the craftlike aspects of this activity. Frank Forester recommended a litany of materials that the fly-fisher needed, among them "Berlin wools, the same of pig's wool, or mohair, various colors and tints, of furs, you require Musk-Rat, Field-Mouse, Black Squirrel, Mink, Martin, young Fox, ditto coon, Green Monkey, Porcupine-belly, Red Squirrel, the ear of the English Hare, and ditto Polecat."[31] The guides provided step-by-step instructions for creating flies with names like Kinmont Willie, the Blue Dun, the Great Dark Drone, and the Jenny Spinner.[32] At a time when men were increasingly removed from working with their hands and when their working world was becoming more highly technical and industrialized, fly tying recalled the simplicity of craft traditions. The technology was easy to master, even if the skills of casting and the knowledge of appropriate flies took considerable experience. After all, one only needed a pin vice, gut line, wrapping silk, some fabric or fur, and the incredible patience and good eyes needed to tie the infinitesimal fly. A little creativity was even encouraged, as the "fancy flies" popular in Victorian times did not mimic insects but were whimsical concoctions of bits of fur, feathers, and tinsel.[33]

Angling literature and mass periodicals helped to promote angling methods and spread the gospel of sportsmanship in the latter half of the nineteenth century, for they circulated throughout the country and carried articles and letters from all sections. Part of their function was to share information about good fishing spots as anglers wrote to tell of their travels. Many anglers went west along the Great Lakes or north along the Mississippi to try their lines in the bountiful waters of Minnesota, land of ten thousand lakes, birthplace of the Mississippi, and border to Lake Superior. As early as the 1850s, tourists from the East and South traveled to St. Paul and Minneapolis to stay at the resort hotels and to fish.[34] And many learned about Minnesota fishing in the late 1860s when ex-Civil War officer Oliver Gibbs wrote a series of letters to General Spinner, then United States treasurer, that were printed in the *Spirit of the Times* and later collected into a volume called *Lake Pepin Fish-Chowder*.[35] Gibbs praised the landscape of Lake Pepin, a wide expanse of the Mississippi south of St. Paul, and gloried in the river fishing, where he sometimes had to borrow the neighbor's wheelbarrow to carry his catch home. Railing against the "pot fishers" who netted fish by the wagonloads, Gibbs promoted fishing with rod and reel. Truth be known, however, Gibbs used live bait and was not a strict fly fisherman, though he did help to start the Lake Pepin Sportsmen Club in 1876 that held casting contests and helped to enforce the state game laws.

During the late nineteenth century, the bounty of America's frontier was still a reality, though an endangered one, in Minnesota.

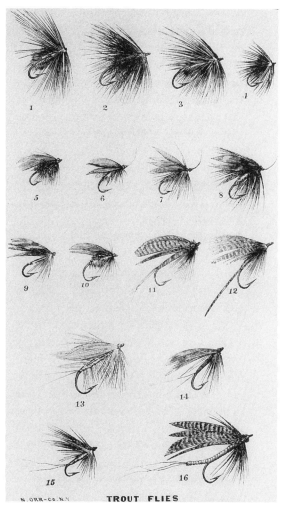

Fig. 5 "Frank Forester" (Henry William Herbert) illustrated an assortment of trout flies in his 1856 book *The Complete Manual for Young Sportsmen.*

Railroads carried fishing tourists throughout the state, where, without any limits yet imposed, they could take whatever they could catch through just about any means. Even though in its first session ever in 1858 the state legislature had passed a law banning the netting of trout, no numerical limits on fish catches were imposed until 1893.[36] Fishing methods in this sparsely settled area only slightly removed from wilderness remained rough-and-ready; it was a place where giant sturgeon were ridden to shore, where shooting fish was still legal, and where prodigious catches made even tall tales true.

We find this intoxication with Minnesota's

bounty in print form in newspapers, which carried almost unbelievable stories about fishing catches, and in visual sources into the early twentieth century. Nineteenth-century Minnesota newspapers often noted the catches of residents and visitors and often had to deny that their accounts were "a fish story" in the face of such incredible numbers. One story carried by the *Minneapolis Tribune* in 1882 took the form of a sworn statement by a witness, Westley Austin, that two fishermen from St. Louis had caught on one July day 213 fish—86 pickerel, 123 bass, and 2 crappies—coming to a total of 146 pounds of fish.[37] Visual equivalents of the tall-tale fishing stories abounded as fisherfolk photographed huge catches or concocted postcards to emphasize just how good the fishing was in Minnesota.[38]

Despite the plenty of Minnesota's fish, state leaders were sensitive to warnings that unregulated fishing could deplete a seemingly inexhaustible supply, just as the once-plentiful beaver had been nearly trapped to extinction in the state. R. B. Roosevelt, like his nephew after him, was an early conservationist. He headed the New York State Fish Commission from 1868 to 1888 and greatly influenced the courses taken by state governments to the west. Minnesota established a Fish Commission in 1874, which initially oversaw the distribution of fish stock, bringing new species, like carp, to Minnesota for propagation. Increasingly the commission took an active role in promoting restrictions on fishing practices, outlawing nets except for licensed commercial fishermen, outlawing the sale of game fish, and constructing fishways to assure the passage of fish up and down streams. This was the wave of the future: in the fifteen years from 1875 to 1890, the number of states with fish commissions more than doubled.[39] At the commissions' urging, state legislatures passed laws that set limits on certain fish, established fishing seasons, regulated fishing methods, designated certain species game fish or rough fish, and required sporting licenses.

Even with some regulation, Minnesota's north country provided an arena where men could be challenged by nature, where they could gather with their own for fishing, hunting, drinking, tale telling, and joking. And that was exactly what many men did as the male fishing vacation became a tradition—like the one written about by Percy Field, a Kansas City newspaperman who traveled to Minnesota's Leech Lake with his buddies in 1916 and wrote about it in a book called *The Syndicate*.[40] Yet other fishing experiences existed side by side with this dominant one—widely practiced traditions of families who fished together, of women who fished, of women who waded into the water with long dresses, of little girls and little boys who fished, and of women who taught little boys to fish.[41] But these practices were not recognized or addressed to any degree in the sporting literature (figs. 6 and 7).

If one side of the romantic ideas about fishing was the opportunities the sport offered for a vigorous, manly experience in the wilderness or at least outside the city, another facet was captured by the image of the barefoot boy with a branch for a pole and a bent pin for a hook. This image multiplied during the nineteenth century, and continued into the twentieth century, as Serling's "Twilight Zone" indicates. Boyhood itself was reconceptualized during the nineteenth century, changing from the idea that children were miniature adults and part of the adult world to the notion that childhood was a special time of life deserving appropriate separation from the adult world.[42] Influenced by Jean Jacques Rousseau's ideas about childhood innocence and the Romantic movement's fascination with childhood, boyhood became associated with the natural world, a world separated from the city and civilization and free from the responsibilities of adulthood. In literary and visual sources, the barefoot boy with a fishing pole became an emblem of a longing for boyhood, and fishing became a time to relive a boy's experiences.

An early example of this growing fascination with boyhood was provided by the portrait painter Thomas Sully in *The Torn Hat* of 1820, where a disheveled and winsome young lad gazes at the viewer, a fishing pole surely

Fig. 6   Although not widely discussed in sporting literature, it was not uncommon for Victorian women to participate in fishing expeditions. "The Fishing Party," by Winslow Homer, 1869.

just out of frame. In Doughty's 1835 painting *In Nature's Wonderland,* it is through the eyes and experiences of the child in the foreground, the picture suggests, that we can most fully appreciate the natural world. The Virginia painter John Gadsby Chapman created an early image of a boy fishing in *The Lazy Fisherman* of 1845. Here the boy languishes on the river's edge, as though time does not exist and no responsibilities wait. By 1872 the motif was circulated by Currier and Ives in a print called *The Barefoot Boy,* again by Frances F. Palmer, the artist who depicted the earlier fishing scenes.[43] Barren of shoes that suggest the constraints of civilization, this stylized boy looks somewhat like the Romantic English poet Byron, though he has the manly calves of Daniel Boone.

In literary sources, the motif of the boy with his branch and bent pin are common in the childhood reminiscences of angling writers. In one article called "A Fisherman's Reverie," lawyer Grace Lincoln Hall wrote of going "off on a fishing expedition and indulging in day dreams." Fishing, he stated, "has always been a favorite pastime of mine ever since my days of barefoot boyhood when a bent pin served as a successful hook," and he told of how "a fishing pole and a bent pin" caused him to run away from school. He finished by lamenting that he could not take his daydream back to "the hurry and struggle" of business life.[44]

Artist Winslow Homer most closely conveyed Hall's desire to recapture childhood in numerous images of boyhood. His works show straw-hatted boys protected forever from the world of the city and the adult cares that await them, as though Homer wished they would never grow up. Homer's disenchantment with urban life is well known, as he

Fig. 7    Three generations of fishers display their catches in this turn-of-the-century trade card for Lake View House in Woodville, New York. The family hotel advertised "unsurpassed opportunity for . . . fishing in season."

spent much of his adulthood fishing and hunting in rural New York State, Maine, and Florida. His boys often linger in the afternoon sun, savoring their aimlessness, as in *The Nooning*, after an engraving of 1873. Similarly, in his many depictions of boys fishing, full of figures with faces obscured by hats or turned away from us, fishing is presented as a magical realm, separate from the world of the viewer outside the painting, as in Homer's well-known engraving for an 1874 *Harper's Weekly*, *Waiting for a Bite* (fig. 8). Unlike the works of artist John George Brown who depicted street urchins, newsboys, and bullies analogous to the boys with luck and pluck in Horatio Alger's stories, Homer's boys could not survive in the urban world; they belong forever in the fields or by the sea or out fishing.

If Homer's boys portray a certain languor and immobility, one of his contemporaries created barefoot boys who never seem to stop moving—Mark Twain's Tom Sawyer and Huckleberry Finn.[45] Twain drew on the al-ready established tradition of barefoot boys, though his characters both capture the innocence of those figures and achieve a mischievousness that the visual images lack. In Twain's novels fishing does not figure centrally, though it does take place in both of his major stories, as is shown by one of E. W. Kemble's illustrations from the original 1884 edition of *The Adventures of Huckleberry Finn*, where Huck and Tom fish together as they plot Jim's escape at Aunt Sally's (fig. 9). Yet fishing seems to exist just in the background of the stories, as though Huck and Tom would be fishing on the Mississippi with branch poles and bent pins if they hadn't been caught up in these adventures. The straw-hatted Huck, with a grin that somehow combines equal amounts of innocence and hell-raising, became a prototype for this imagery into the twentieth century. And Twain's ornery critique of "sivilized" America also added a more explicit critique of modern life to this imagery.

In the early twentieth century Norman

Fig. 8    "Waiting for a Bite," by Winslow Homer, *Harper's Weekly,* 22 August 1874.

Rockwell created the most perfect visual match for Twain's characters, fully capturing their puckish charm. He drew many boys for the covers of *Boy's Life,* the publication of Boy Scouts of America, illustrated the 1913 *Boy Scout Hike Book* and the Boy Scout camp books, and drew for *Country Gentleman, St. Nicholas Magazine,* and, of course, the *Saturday Evening Post.* Rusty Doolittle, a character often appearing on *Country Gentleman,* seems like Huck incarnate and was certainly based on Kemble's illustrations, which Rockwell knew well. Rusty and his brother Chuck provided a continuing narrative, often with their city-slicker cousin, Reginald, serving as the foil. In one 1919 sequence, Reggie's snooty fly-fishing gear is no match for Rusty and Chuck's crude poles and can of worms. Rusty appeared again that year on the cover of *St. Nicholas* magazine, with his straw hat and fishing rod. When Rockwell illustrated *The Adventures of Tom Sawyer* in 1936 and *The Adventures of Huckle-*

*berry Finn* in 1940, Kemble's images came full circle. In these illustrations Rockwell made the characters' connections to fishing more explicit, as seen in his title page for *Tom Sawyer* and the table of contents page for *Huckleberry Finn.* Rockwell repeated the image of a boy fishing throughout his career. In 1975, three years before Rockwell's death, his drawing of a barefoot boy fishing provided the model for a porcelain figurine in the "Joys of Childhood" series.[46]

The varied echoes of John Gadsby Chapman's, Winslow Homer's, and Mark Twain's images of boys and fishing have persisted in the twentieth century, becoming a way of saying "long ago," in childhood, or before life got so complicated, or started moving so fast, or when the country was young. The imagery might refer to pre–Civil War days, or to the late nineteenth century, or to the early twentieth century, or just to some mythical time. Examples are numerous, but one that seems

# Chapter

"We was feeling
fast, and r
over the riv
and had a g
at the raft
and got h
found thei
worry they
they was si
go right o:
was done a
us what th
let on a w
but didn'i
knowed as

Fig. 9   Huck Finn and Tom Sawyer fishing, by
E. W. Kemble, in Mark Twain's *Adventures of Huckleberry Finn* (1884).

particularly fitting comes from a slim volume
by President Herbert Hoover called *Fishing for
Fun—And to Wash Your Soul.* Hoover stated in
his dedication that people who fish "escape—
or cast off—the trammels of life into a land of
enchantment. Perhaps this [his book] will extend the moments in that land of joys and illu-
sions." And in his chapter "The Affinity of
Boys and Fish," he began by asserting, "Every
true fisherman must have an affection for his
neighbors, and especially the barefoot boy
whence we all started our fishing careers. I was
a boy in the days before our civilization became so perfect, before it was paved with ce-
ment and made of bricks. Boys were not so
largely separated from Mother Earth and all
her works."[47]

Hoover's comments on fishing as a "land of
enchantment" match Rod Serling's enticing vision of the town of Willoughby in 1888. For
Garth Williamses of the nineteenth century
and of today, fishing provides both actual and
imaginary places that run counter to the rush
and bustle of modern life. If sports fishing
practices and codes during the nineteenth century served to distinguish elite and working-
class groups, in the twentieth century the
sports fishing ethos began to emphasize the
democratic nature of the activity. Later references to the barefoot boy with a fishing pole
would highlight the leveling of class groups
that supposedly happened when men cast off
their workaday cares to go fishing, where they
returned to the state of nature and of childlike
innocence. Today the cultural roots of sports
fishing continue to inform its rhetoric and imagery, as did a recent billboard displayed in the
inner city of Minneapolis, featuring a lone
fisherman silhouetted against the sunset, that
invited viewers to "Play Hooky. Escape to
Wisconsin," conjuring visions of Huck Finn
lighting out for the territory.

## Notes

1. This "Twilight Zone" episode was originally
broadcast on 5 May 1960 and was included in "Mas-
terpieces from the Museum of Broadcasting" shown
at the Walker Art Center, Minneapolis, MN, July
1985.

2. For useful analyses on the development of sport
and its relationship to urban life, see Stephen
Hardy, *How Boston Played: Sport, Recreation, and
Community 1865–1915* (Boston: Northeastern University Press, 1982); and Melvin L. Adelman, *A
Sporting Time: New York City and the Rise of Modern
Athletics, 1820–1870* (Urbana: University of Illinois
Press, 1986). Both studies examine relationships between industrialization, urbanization, and the rise
of sports, mostly organized athletics. Sports fishing
shares with organized athletics some reasons for its
development and the implementation of regulations governing its practice. However, it differs
from organized sports in that it remained, and is
practiced even today, as part of a private, regional,
folk cultural activity rather than as a corporate
spectator sport, even while participating in the big
businesses of tourism and tackle manufacturing.

3. The term "angling" comes from the word "angle," an obsolete word for fishhook, which goes
back to Old English roots. Its antecedents "ank" and
"ang" mean bent, crooked, or hooked. Angling,
then, originally meant using a fishhook and line.
See *The American Heritage Dictionary of the English
Language,* school ed., s.v. "angling"; Charles Good-

speed, *Angling in America: Its Early History and Literature* (Boston: Houghton Mifflin, 1939), 14. Little scholarly attention has been devoted to the history of fishing even though primary sources—for example, fishing literature and sporting magazines—are extensive. Goodspeed's book is a valuable compilation but not analytical or interpretive—he is primarily a fishing enthusiast.

4. Goodspeed, *Angling in America,* 84, 91; Paul Schullery, "The Colonial Angler," in *American Fly Fishing: A History* (Manchester, VT: Nick Lyons Books and the American Museum of Fly Fishing, 1987), 13–17.

5. Sam Bass Warner, *The Urban Wilderness: A History of the American City* (New York: Harper & Row, 1972), 70.

6. See the chapter "The Fly-Fishing Exploration" in Schullery, *American Fly Fishing.* For a discussion of the values that mid-nineteenth-century urban travelers took with them on their fishing and hunting travels in the Adirondacks, see Philip G. Terrie, "Urban Man Confronts the Wilderness: The Nineteenth-Century Sportsman in the Adirondacks," *Journal of Sport History,* Winter 1978, 7–20. For travels along the Great Lakes, see Robert Barnwell Roosevelt, *Superior Fishing; or, The Striped Bass, Trout, and Black Bass of the Northern States,* introduction by Ernest Schwiebert (St. Paul: Minnesota Historical Society Press, 1985).

7. Susan A. Popkin and Roger B. Allen, *Gone Fishing: A History of Fishing in River, Bay and Sea* (Philadelphia: Philadelphia Maritime Museum, 1987), 8–11; Goodspeed, *Angling in America,* 29–53.

8. Goodspeed, *Angling in America,* 109.

9. "Happy Days Club of St. Paul," *Western Field and Stream,* June 1896, 60–61. For the impact of class on the formation of sports clubs, see Adelman, *A Sporting Time,* 7–8; Schullery, *American Fly Fishing,* 126. For information on the increase of sports clubs in the 1870s, see Donna R. Braden, *Leisure and Entertainment in America* (Dearborn, MI: Henry Ford Museum, Greenfield Village, 1988), 251. The role of sporting clubs in the reformation of urban life in the nineteenth century is discussed in Benjamin G. Rader, "The Quest for Subcommunities and the Rise of American Sport," *American Quarterly* 29 (Fall 1977): 355–69.

10. Charles Hallock, *The Fishing Tourist: Angler's Guide and Reference Book* (New York: Harper and Brothers, 1873), 224–99; annual wages cited in *Historical Statistics of the United States from Colonial Times to 1970* (Washington, DC: U.S. Department of Commerce, 1975), 165.

11. "Minnesota Game and Fish Protective Association," *Western Field and Stream,* September 1896, 118.

12. Schullery, *American Fly Fishing,* 23, 32–42; Stephen Hardy, " 'Adopted by All the Leading Clubs': Sporting Goods and the Shaping of Leisure, 1800–1900," in Richard Busch, ed., *For Fun and Profit: The Transformation of Leisure into Consumption* (Philadelphia: Temple University Press, 1990). Hardy argues that the standardization of equipment made by major manufacturers in the late nineteenth century limited the range of sports and standardized their practice. See *Montgomery Ward and Co. Catalogue, 1895* (reprint, New York: Dover Publications, 1969), 489–92.

13. For a discussion of Kensett's *The Trout Fisherman,* see Barbara Novak and Elizabeth Garrity Ellis, eds., *The Thyssen-Bornemisza Collection of Nineteenth-Century American Painting* (New York: Vendome Press, 1986), 82; see *Currier and Ives: A Catalogue Raisonné* (Detroit: Gale Research, 1984), 643, for a reproduction of Palmer's print. For a discussion of changing attitudes toward nature during the nineteenth century, see Roderick Nash, *Wilderness and the American Mind* (New Haven: Yale University Press, 1967), especially the chapters "The Romantic Wilderness" and "The American Wilderness"; for a discussion of how changing attitudes were expressed in American art, see Barbara Novak, *Nature and Culture: American Landscape and Painting, 1825–1875* (New York: Oxford University Press, 1980).

14. See Albert Christ-Janer, *George Caleb Bingham: Frontier Painter of Missouri* (New York: Harry N. Abrams, 1975).

15. Thomas Alexander, "Fish and Fishing," *The Lakeside Library* 4, 90 (Chicago: Donnelley, Lloyd and Co., 1877), 543. Located in the Minnesota Historical Society Library Collections, s.v. "Fishing."

16. "Fishing Tackle and Its Use," *American Angler,* 15 October 1881, 5.

17. *Western Field and Stream,* June 1896, 67.

18. Henry Van Dyke, *Little Rivers: A Book of Essays in Profitable Idleness* (New York: Charles Scribner's Sons, 1903), 3–5.

19. John Dizikes, *Sportsmen and Gamesmen* (Boston: Houghton Mifflin, 1981), 77.

20. Goodspeed, *Angling in America,* 269; for a useful review of this angling literature, see Paul Schullery, "Hope for the Hook and Bullet Press," *New York Times Book Review,* 22 September 1985, 1, 34–35.

21. Working-class resistance to fishing regulations arose in part from fears that laws would limit their access to game, still an important supplement to other food supplies, while preserving access for the wealthy, as happened with regulations in England. See Adelman, *A Sporting Time,* 248. Native Americans found fishing regulations completely at odds with their fishing practices and relationship with

nature. The imposition of sporting regulations on Native Americans met much resistance, as documented, for instance, by the fines levied against them and recorded in late nineteenth-century reports of the Minnesota Board of Game and Fish. With negotiation of treaty rights, many Native American tribes could continue to practice their methods of netting and spearing fish on reservations and in other designated areas.

22. Henry William Herbert, *Frank Forester's Fish and Fishing of the United States and British Provinces of North America* (New York: W. A. Townsend and Company, 1859), xxii–xxiii, 17.

23. Hallock, *Fishing Tourist,* 25.

24. Ibid., 53.

25. Thaddeus Norris, *The American Angler's Book* (1864; reprint, Philadelphia: Porter and Coates, 1884), 33–36.

26. Roosevelt, *Superior Fishing,* 19.

27. Ibid., 21.

28. Hallock, *Fishing Tourist,* 22.

29. Schullery, *American Fly Fishing,* 236. Schullery refers to a 1983 readers' survey for *Fly Fisherman's* magazine, which found that the average income of those surveyed was $62,590 and the average value of their homes was $135,903.

30. Herbert, *Frank Forester's Fish and Fishing,* 441.

31. Ibid., 442.

32. Roosevelt, *Superior Fishing,* 215–27.

33. Schullery, *American Fly Fishing,* 77–82.

34. See the Works Progress Administration Subject Files under "Natural Resources—Fish" and "Hotel and Tourist Trade—Resort" at the Minnesota Historical Society's Division of Archives and Manuscripts, St. Paul, MN.

35. Oliver Gibbs, *Lake Pepin Fish-Chowder in Letters to General Spinner* (New York: H. D. McIntyre and Company, 1869).

36. June Holmquist, "Fishing in the Land of 10,000 Lakes," *Minnesota History,* Summer 1953, 252.

37. "Minnetonka News. A Fish Story," *Minneapolis Tribune,* August 2, 1882, located in the Works Progress Administration Subject Files under "Fish," Minnesota Historical Society Division of Archives and Manuscripts, St. Paul, MN. The numbers are correct as quoted from the source.

38. For a discussion of tall-tale postcards and their significance for the Upper Midwest, see Karal Ann Marling, *The Colossus of Roads: Myth and Symbol along the American Highway* (Minneapolis: University of Minnesota Press, 1985), 64–81.

39. Minnesota Board of Game and Fish Commission, *Annual Report* (Minneapolis: Harrison and Smith State Printers, 1891), 22–24.

40. Percy Field, *The Syndicate* (Kansas City, MO: Smith Grieves Company, 1916).

41. Photographs from the late nineteenth century onwards provide good sources of documentation for fishing traditions among others than the male sportsman. Author's sources for the practices of women, children, family, and community groups have been drawn primarily from the photography collection in the Audiovisual Library, Minnesota Historical Society, St. Paul, MN.

42. For an excellent discussion of changing conceptions of childhood during the nineteenth century, see Mary Lynn Stevens Heininger, "Children, Childhood, and Change in America, 1820–1920," in Heininger et al., *A Century of Childhood, 1820–1920* (Rochester, NY: Margaret Woodbury Strong Museum, 1984), 1–32. T. J. Jackson Lears discusses the fascination with childhood as part of a widespread cultural shift at the turn of the century, especially among upper- and middle-class men, in the chapter "The Morning of Belief: Medieval Mentalities in a Modern World," in Lears, *No Place of Grace: Antimodernism and the Transformation of American Culture 1880–1920* (New York: Pantheon Books, 1981), especially 144–49.

43. *Currier and Ives: A Catalogue Raissoné,* 41, 52.

44. Grace Lincoln Hall, "A Fisherman's Reverie," *Western Field and Stream,* June 1896, 58.

45. Twain's work on Tom Sawyer and Huckleberry Finn was contemporaneous to the increased appearance of barefoot boy imagery found in Currier and Ives prints and in Homer's work. *The Adventures of Tom Sawyer* was published in 1875. Twain had written half of *The Adventures of Huckleberry Finn* by 1876 when he put that manuscript aside. He then wrote *The Tramp Abroad, The Prince and the Pauper,* and *Life on the Mississippi* before finishing *Huckleberry Finn* and publishing it in 1884.

46. See Laurie Norton Moffatt, *Norman Rockwell: A Definite Catalogue,* 2 vols. (Stockbridge, MA: The Norman Rockwell Museum at Stockbridge, 1986); and Thomas S. Buechner, *Norman Rockwell: Artist and Illustrator* (New York: Harry N. Abrams, 1970).

47. Herbert Hoover, *Fishing for Fun—And to Wash Your Soul,* ed. William Nichols (New York: Random House, 1963), 35–36.

# "Another Branch of Manly Sport"

## American Rifle Games, 1840–1900

RUSSELL S. GILMORE

Henry William Herbert, America's first sporting writer and very nearly its first sportsman, expected that before the nineteenth century ended rifles would be obsolete in the United States. The "utility and honor" of weapons disappeared with the animals they killed, so that even in 1848 rifles were rare on the East Coast and shotguns certainly would become so when the small game gave out.[1] Herbert proved no prophet. By 1900, the rifle's honor, if not its utility, had greatly advanced—had in fact turned into a cultish adulation.

Nearly all military weapons before the middle of the nineteenth century were loaded from the front, or muzzle. They also did without the helicoidal grooves, or rifling, which could spin a bullet and create real accuracy, because such grooves slowed loading. Herbert assumed that the basic military weapon would always be a smoothbore—no great wonder because American experiments with the undersized Minié bullet, which would speed the loading of rifles, had not begun when he wrote. Yet seven years later, in 1855, rifles became standard issue in the American army, bringing a revolution as important, if not as dramatic, as military breechloaders would

during the Civil War. The Minié bullet (whose hollow base expanded, under the force of powder gas, to grip rifling grooves) quintupled effective range, but its potential remained unrealized. The usual view seems to have been that shooting skill, while desirable in a recruit, was only a few men's birthright. After a little desultory firing to learn the mechanics of their new weapon, most regular army companies fired no more.[2] Civilians knew even less and in 1860, at the outbreak of the first great war of the rifle, turned anxiously to the few hobbyists who could offer instruction or formed themselves into groups and together attempted to master the machine that was to be central to their lives.[3]

Early battles established that the average northerner did not sit his horse very firmly and in most other ways seemed less fit for military life than his Confederate opponent. As part of a general feeling of inadequacy, Union troops—or at least Union newspapers—assumed that the enemy also shot better. In fact, the general level of marksmanship on both sides was so low as to make comparison pointless.[4] Specific complaints mentioned snipers, whose "unerring rifles" picked off Union officers. But only selected soldiers with specialized equipment served as snipers. The North had them, too, whole regiments of them, and probably those who did the most spectacular mankilling on either side served the Union as Berdan's Sharpshooters. Detached to special duty whenever opposing lines became firm, they shot from platforms in trees or carefully constructed "nests," sometimes killing from a half-mile off. The weapon for such work was heavy—occasionally too heavy to hold[5]—and fitted with a telescopic sight. The Federal Ordnance Bureau apparently purchased only a half-dozen during the whole war, but recruits to a sharpshooters' unit often brought their own, and ballistic experimenters donated privately owned "slug guns," giving up an esoteric hobby to contribute their bit to the carnage.[6]

Most Americans who knew rifles before 1861 learned either in hunting or casual targetry. Informal match shooting with rifles of the pre-Minié kind, generally considered too slow in battle, had long been commonplace, especially on the frontier. Competitors usually fired three shots apiece at twenty rods (about 110 yards), each measuring the distance of his bullet holes from the target's center with a piece of string. The shortest string won cash, whiskey, or beef. On the Atlantic Coast, an occasional "American" club[7] shot similar matches with more precise rifles for less consequential prizes. Such clubs had no military features, held no parades, and were generally inconspicuous. But they contributed many of the Civil War sharpshooters who, when they carefully squeezed triggers, expected to see men die.

The other organized bodies of American marksmen were showy and less serious but vastly more important in numbers. During the burst of enthusiasm for gorgeously uniformed volunteer militia units in the 1830s, New York firemen formed the first "target companies," the elite of which differed from the militia elite chiefly in devotion to shooting practice. At a time when state troops often served out seven-year enlistments without firing their weapons, clubs such as the Pocahontas Guards assembled "the best shooters in the city" for frequent target excursions into the suburbs and, even allowing for their casual discipline (members occasionally looted shops along the line of march), were probably more effective military units.[8] By 1850, one estimate put the members of New York City target companies at ten thousand, "thousands" of whom had volunteered for the Mexican War. Not all were firemen, because the employees of individual factories, foundries, and shipyards had begun to get up target excursions after the same pattern, and some companies formed as ward organizations.[9] At least from the 1840s, armed bands parading the streets left respectable New Yorkers uneasy, and after the Draft Riot of 1863 the Quality spoke increasingly of disarming the lower orders, or at least of subjecting those who toyed with rifles to soldierly discipline. Colonel William Conant Church of the *Army and Navy Journal* heartily wished "target companies might decline and militia companies be built up on their ruins."[10]

No one seems to have been uneasy about the other block of shooting organizations in New York City, the *Schützenbünde* (fig. 1), and Mayor John T. Hoffman clearly had targeteers in mind when he congratulated his Germanic brethren on establishing that "love of the rifle is not incompatible with respect for the law."[11] During the period when it was sniping at target societies, the *Army and Navy Journal* endorsed *Schützen* as serious marksmen and a complement to the militia, quoting with approval a banner motto which read, "A sharp eye and a steady hand guard our right and Fatherland."[12] (Presumably Colonel Church concluded that as the sentiment was in English, the Fatherland referred to was the United States.) Describing the 1864 meeting of the New York *Schützen* Corps, a newspaper assured its readers that efficient police and the shooters themselves patrolled the grounds so that no one need leave his family at home for fear of disturbances. Another time, *Harper's Weekly* observed that although there was "a flowing beer keg under nearly every tree . . . no man was seen to be intoxicated."[13]

The only widespread quarrel with *Schützen*

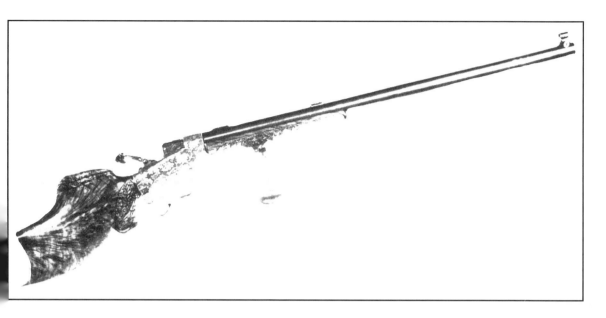

Fig. 1   This custom *Schützen* rifle was of the sort used for gallery marksmanship indoors and for outdoor shooting at ranges of 200 yards or less, chiefly by German-American hobbyists. Elaborate stocks and accessories caused many long-range shooters to regard *Schützen* weapons as impractical or as toys. Courtesy Frank De Haas, *Single Shot Rifles and Actions* (1969).

riflery seems to have been over its *Gemütlichkeit,* which was offensive to some and probably seemed inappropriate to most non-Germans. The typical *Schützenfest* started with a parade of uniformed marksmen, each brilliant with ribbons and decorations (fig. 2). After an elaborate meal, the club president began competition by firing several shots at a traditional wooden eagle target, the first for the president, then the governor, and finally for the *Schützen* corps and himself. Each member then took a turn and claimed prizes associated with whatever bits of the eagle he dislodged. The man lucky enough to break the final fragment was *König,* immediately smothered in flowers and kisses by as many as fifty blond maidens. Gamblers liked the novelty targets, such as a full-scale iron stag pursued by an iron dog, pulled suddenly along rails from one bank of bushes to another. To hit the deer was to win five dollars; to hit the dog was to forfeit that much, as well as a twenty-five-cent match fee. The women's contest used no rifles but a lance swinging on wires and paid off in parasols, combs, and the like. Serious shooting at a minutely divided twenty-five-ring mark some-

times inspired magnificent prize lists. One "honor target" at Shell Mount Park in San Francisco offered winners twenty-five thousand dollars in goods of all sorts.[14]

But social and fraternal features of the *Schützenfeste* seemed more important to most present, because often thousands listened to the Tyrolean singers or patronized the merry-go-rounds and lottery booths while only hundreds shot. The marksmen brought their much-extended families. Grandfathers drank beer and told stories; daughters danced (with whomever took their fancy—no one had to be introduced) while their mothers sat nearby darning socks. *Schützenbünde* often had women's auxiliaries, benefit societies, secret grips, and other trappings of the lodge, though as they expanded in the years after the Civil War, they seem to have become more cosmopolitan. By the turn of the century, German maidens occasionally found themselves obliged to crown and engarland an Irishman or other non-Teuton.

Unlike target companies, which never spread beyond New York and New Jersey,[15] *Schützen* clubs flourished before 1860 in every

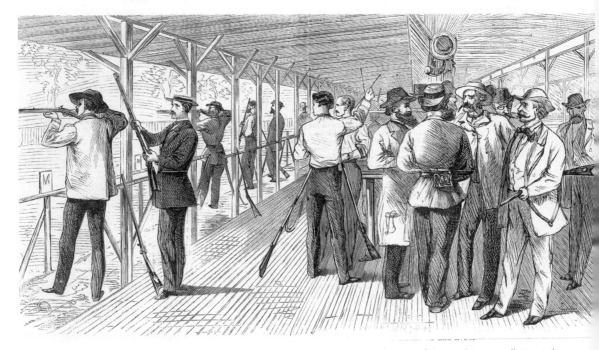

Fig. 2 "The Schützenfest—shooting-gallery at Jones's Wood.—Sharp-shooters firing at the targets," *Harper's Weekly*, 18 July 1868. *Schützen* riflery attained considerable popularity even among non-Germans by the turn of the century, but association with "the Hun" killed it during World War I.

East Coast city with a noticeable German population, and in Buffalo, Cincinnati, Chicago, Milwaukee, St. Louis, and San Francisco as well. During the eighties and nineties, midwestern federations seem to have been the most vital, and they continued to add new clubs into the present century, as did those in California. The New York *Bünde* met early competition from other ethnic social and fraternal organizations of the sort that finally displaced *Schützen* clubs altogether, but, despite complaints over apathy, the Independent Corps (one of five New York City leagues) chartered a whole steamer for members and their families attending a European contest in 1890, and the 1895 fest at Glendale Park, Long Island, proved the largest to that date. Though *Schützen* riflery declined in the twentieth century, it continued to be important until 1917, when amused tolerance of German shooting ended abruptly. Even when it had been counted harmless, Americans had never been drawn to Germany's variant on target

practice, which remained ethnically narrow and in the popular mind a sort of saturnalia.[16]

Yet if more Irishmen had been willing to compete for garlands and kisses in German parks, respectable New Yorkers would have been more comfortable. Instead, during the years following the Civil War, Irish in increasing numbers assembled as frolicsome and sometimes drunken bands for target parades into the suburbs. Such affairs took on a sinister look after the 1871 Orange Riot, in which Catholic Irish, organized under the cover of a grand picnic and "target excursion," tangled with a Protestant Irish parade. Revolver shots out of the crowd brought indiscriminate return fire from National Guard regiments assigned to protect the Protestants. When the shooting ended, fifty people lay dead or dying. The Orange Riot sped modern arms into the hands of the guard and helped create the National Rifle Association to teach their use.[17]

Two months after the riot, Colonel Church formally organized the NRA in his newspaper offices, but George Wood Wingate, a New York City lawyer and guard officer, actually created it. He had been a partisan of military rifle training ever since witnessing the marksmanship of Civil War volunteers. Wingate taught a British-inspired system which had attracted almost no attention in the United States before the Orange Riot. Now other guard officers pressed him for information and help. Wingate seized the chance and soon found himself supervising construction of the NRA's splendid Creedmoor range on Long Island, intended chiefly to train the New York Guard.

While studying range construction in England and Canada, Wingate had inquired into long-range targetry and on his return helped organize the Amateur Rifle Club, sixty-two New Yorkers interested in more precise shooting than the sort intended for the militia. Alonzo Alford, a representative of the Remington Arms Company, sat as chairman of their first meeting, which elected Wingate president. The Amateur Rifle Club did nothing until Creedmoor opened officially in June 1873 and thereafter confined itself to conducting a match for a gold medal at five hundred yards, considered a great distance by American riflemen (both target companies and *Schützen* corps usually stopped at two hundred) but only half that of the most important British shooting.

In this untried state, the Amateurs accepted a challenge from the Irish victors of Great Britain's Wimbledon match who, having won by a previously unparalleled score, looked to be champions of the world.[18] New York's *Forest and Stream* called it an example of "supremest American cheek."[19] The British game of small-bore shooting had evolved from military riflery into a fiendishly complex and demanding enterprise.[20] Though huge charges drove heavy projectiles with the maximum energy available from black powder, beyond half a mile the bullets deviated wildly due to crosswinds. Changing light affected sighting. Its devotees counted small-bore riflery a science, but

as practiced in Great Britain it was nearer an art, requiring delicate sensibilities and extensive practice. Arthur Blennerhassett Leech, captain of the Irish team, called it "the poetry of shooting."

Not only had no member fired at Wimbledon distances, but the Amateur Rifle Club possessed not a single weapon suitable for practice. The five-hundred-yard rifles at Creedmoor had inappropriate stocks which raised egg-sized welts on the shoulder and sights without even the crudest lateral adjustment. But George Wingate, not one to underestimate the importance of equipment, almost certainly had a promise from his friend Alford before taking up the Irish challenge. Both the Remington and Sharps arms companies came forward immediately with pledges of weapons right for the contest and together put up the five-hundred-dollar stake that the Amateur Club had agreed to post.[21] The great international rifle contest was to try not only America against Britain but the best American machine-made breechloaders against the best handmade muzzleloaders of Europe. Weapons that loaded from the rear were much more convenient, especially for military use, but seemed to be inherently less accurate than weapons whose projectiles were pushed down from the muzzle. United States devotees of the older arm prophesied disaster, pointing out that even at Creedmoor muzzleloaders had won every match that admitted them. New York's *Turf, Field and Farm* feared that the Irish would "have a competition scarcely sufficient to make it interesting."[22]

The arms argument added to an already considerable excitement. One month after the challenge, a Michigan letter writer observed that the international rifle match had become the principal subject under discussion in sporting clubs throughout the country, and *Forest and Stream,* which felt sure that riflery was to be a great national preoccupation, began a seven-part series titled, "How to Shoot at Long Range."[23] George Wingate announced that the Amateur Club had

THE INTERNATIONAL RIFLE MATCH AT CREEDMOOR, LONG ISLAND—LAST DAY'S PRACTICE OF THE AMERICAN AND IRISH TEAMS.

Fig. 3    Both prone and supine positions are illustrated in this sketch of practice before the first great International Rifle Match in 1874. *Harper's Weekly*, 10 October 1874.

accepted the challenge not for ourselves alone but in behalf of the riflemen of America. We have therefore sent out a number of circulars, intended to reach all classes of individuals interested in rifle practice. . . . From New Orleans, Philadelphia, Massachusetts and the far West we have received response and during the summer we may expect to see a great assembly . . . at Creedmoor.[24]

In that hope, Wingate was entirely disappointed, though national interest—at this stage largely confined to sportsmen—continued to grow, and many agonized over the low initial scores turned in with the new breechloaders.

As team captain, Wingate had tested the rifles and knew they were capable of astonishing accuracy, but he knew also that American marksmen could not equal the experienced Irish man for man. If he organized his people thoroughly and synchronized their sights, however, team members could assist each other, the best judges of wind and light going first to determine settings for the others (fig. 3). By the end of the summer, Wingate had rationalized rifle shooting nearly as thoroughly as Remington and Sharps rationalized rifle production. At the time of the challenge, the Chicago *Inter-Ocean*, which believed, as did

nearly everyone, that the Amateurs would be trounced by the Irish, printed an editorial that in retrospect seems ironic on every count.

> While these riflemen who have carried away the shield at Wimbledon have been practicing under scientific teachers, and popping away at a bullseye in a carefully constructed gallery, our boys have been shooting buffaloes upon the plains or taking a wild turkey on the wing. . . . It will be a contest between trained efficiency and native skill, between the dainty hand of the city and the rough grasp of the woodsman. Should the result prove contrary to our confidence in the shooting qualities of our trusty marksmen, it will be because they are unaccustomed to be trammeled by any rules, or tied down to any particular form or custom.[25]

Canadians had essayed team organization (though their system was not nearly so rigorously worked out), and Wingate almost certainly got the idea from them. They offered him another bit of help in a letter from someone identified by the editor of *Forest and Stream* as "a distinguished Canadian rifleman." Be certain, said "Royal," to "keep your oldest and coolest shot for last."

It was a fine day and a fair crowd at Creedmoor on September 26, 1874, and the excur-

Fig. 4   Thousands of spectators attended the international competitions in the mid-1870s. *Historical Register of the Centennial Exposition* (1876).

sion trains brought thousands of new spectators as telegraphs reported the United States ahead at eight hundred yards, still a little ahead at nine hundred (fig. 4). Clearly the Amateurs had a chance, though the Irish normally did better at the greatest range. When an American prepared to fire the final shot at one thousand yards, the match hung on it (fig. 5). Colonel John Bodine, unlike the other members of the team a lifelong hunter and marksman, took his position with an unperturbed air. A friend offered him some ginger beer. As Bodine reached for it, the "unpoetic" (but melodramatic) bottle exploded, driving splinters of glass into his right palm. Doctor J. B. Hamilton of the Irish team rushed to him, pronounced the wound serious, and suggested delaying the final shot. Bodine declined and took up his position with a bloodstained handkerchief around his hand. Nearly ten thousand people fanned out down the range,

providing a corridor through which he made a bull's-eye.[26]

The unexpected and cliffhanging win caused a sensation. Irish team members did not go directly home but stayed to participate in a gala and then traveled west with Charles Hallock, editor of *Forest and Stream,* for prairie chicken shooting and the usual unconscionable buffalo hunt, giving the rest of the United States a chance to gape and throng. If their own exploits were not enough, the Lord Mayor of Dublin and two people with titles accompanied them. As for the Americans, a writer who wanted to obtain for the rest of sport riflery's newly acquired prestige described a remarkable shift:

The few men who met at Creedmoor . . . were of slight importance three years ago. Their doings were carelessly chronicled and respectable people who think that all sport savors of evil, only knew them to avoid them. Suddenly they are the asso-

T. S. DAKIN.   HENRY FULTON.   L. L. HEPBURN.   H. A. GILDERSLEEVE.

G. W. YALE.   THE BADGE.   THE CUP.   JOHN BODINE.

Fig. 5    Members of the 1874 American team with the silver cup and badges brought by the Irish team for the victors. Colonel John Bodine, whose bull's-eye won the match for the Americans, is at the lower right. *Harper's Weekly*, 10 October 1874.

ciates of archbishops and college dignitaries and rivals of princes of the blood and ministers of state. Ah, how good it is to be a rifleman.[27]

The sensation owed something to the nation's postwar interest in and increased approval of games, but it owed more to nationalism. Representatives of the United States had achieved no such triumph over foreign opponents since 1851, when the *America* won its cup at Cowes, and this was victory not in a piddling boat race but a miniature formalized war. Prematch philippics in the sporting press demanding intense training and a win "no matter what it costs" revealed that in the minds of the writers this game involved profound psychological risks. Judge N. P. Stanton

at a prematch banquet made an explicit—though of course playful—statement of the emotional investment in mock battle when he said "the representatives of two great nations are now to meet at Creedmoor with deadly weapons."[28] If, as Konrad Lorenz suggests, all sport has origins in "highly ritualized but still serious" fighting,[29] riflery must surely be closer to those origins—and therefore closer to the bone—than other contests between peoples. Perhaps it was appropriate that blood trickled down Colonel Bodine's arm as he fired the winning shot.

Though the victory had been wonderful, American sporting magazines seemed a little uncertain just whom we had beaten. The Irishmen were Great Britain's champions of

Fig. 6    The Irish team from the first international competition. Team captain, Arthur B. Leech, is seated, second from the left. *Harper's Weekly,* 10 October 1874.

course, but did they represent a middle class for whom riflery offered patriotic exercise and escape from city cares, or gentlemen of leisure such as had no counterpart in the United States? One editorial in *American Sportsman* somehow held to both views in succeeding paragraphs, but most outdoor journals favored the second characterization. Arthur Leech and his fellows did have aristocratic trappings. Photographs of the two squads show Irishmen cradling custom-built weapons and languidly sprawled in Norfolks and deerstalker caps, while Wingate and his men look the efficient team they were, posed matter-of-factly in business suits (figs. 6 and 7). The Irish actually comprised two country gentlemen, three merchants, two gunmakers, and a jeweler, not an especially distinguished crew

though more prosperous than better shots who had been unable to afford the trip. The typical American team member was a New Yorker, a business or professional man with officer rank from the Civil War and a current interest in the National Guard. Only in his martial experience and concerns did he differ noticeably from the Irish. The press, however, preferred to see a contest between commercial civilization and aristocracy, pointing to the fact that of the Americans, General Thomas S. Dakin alone lacked employment—and that was because he had retired from an executive career. Comparison of Remington's foreman Hepburn, the nearest thing to a working man on either team, with John Rigby, who owned the Irish gun company, allowed the claim that it was democracy's victory as well.[30]

Fig. 7    The 1874 American team, reproduced in John Durant and Otto Bettmann, *Pictorial History of American Sports* (1952).

But political philosophy got less play in the press than business civilization, perhaps because nobody doubted that a man could be a republican and a fighter—Americans had proved that to themselves a hundred years earlier. Moreover, Herbert Spencer had half convinced business that its virtues were incompatible with those of the soldier. Hence the celebration that "our clerks, merchants and men of business have shown that they are not disqualified from equality and fraternity with the gentlemen of Europe in another branch of manly sport. . . . Our capacity to be first in commerce does not militate against our being men of war, when we have something to fight for."[31] At worst, riflery promised to "keep alive in a mercenary age some spark of the old martial spirit."[32] Gentlemen, even those themselves engaged in business, frequently contrasted the discipline and self-sacrifice of military service with the greed and self-indulgence of life in the Gilded Age. And those more comfortable with the laissez-faire capitalism of the day

could see shooting as the logical complement to business militant: "Though we have no privileged classes . . . whose life is the pursuit of pleasure, we can cultivate athletic and field sports, and can mingle the use of arms and the growth of physical fiber with the unpoetic but world-controlling duties of the desk and factory."[33]

American riflery successes represent an early—perhaps the first—triumph of a re-United States, but a triumph with flaws. Sporting papers of the West and Midwest complained that easterners hogged the glory, offering the example of a Chicago man who qualified for but did not shoot in the international match marking the nation's centennial. Wingate explained that the candidate had demanded one thousand dollars to participate. *Chicago Field,* the major sporting magazine published outside New York, became champion of the inland clubs, energetically disputing *Forest and Stream*'s contention that western riflemen were imaginary. What *Forest and*

*Stream* claimed and *Chicago Field* denied was that gentlemen shooters were an East Coast phenomenon. No one doubted the existence of the hunters of the West, but their place in the nation's mythology did seem to be under attack.

Eastern newspapers printed smug accounts of city men's preeminence in riflery, the most "intellectual" of outdoor sports. The New York press even berated frontiersmen for failing to respond to Wingate's call, though few could be expected to travel two thousand miles at their own expense, especially as the best shots supported themselves precariously by hunting. If westerners would not come east, Major Henry Fulton, Creedmoor's champion, could go west, where he sought out and defeated a number of local deadeyes, much to their discomfort. Whether because of that or a more general resentment of the East's presumptuousness, W. F. Carver, a professional hunter and later a famous trick shot, hated "those Creedmoor boys." Carver told his biographer that when he and a friend came upon one hunting buffalo, they seized his rifle and threw away the breechblock.[34] Other plainsmen vented their disgust with "fancy Creedmoor target popping" in half-literate letters to the sporting press.

The reticence of marksmen in the former Confederate states created an even bigger problem than western resentment. Perhaps the members of the NRA Centennial Match election committee actually would have been willing to pay for Dudley Selph of New Orleans, the South's best long-range shot, but they never had that chance. Their letter of invitation offered him an opportunity "to revive the feelings of fraternity between North and South which we are anxious to foster,"[35] but he replied that the New Orleans team rejected his participation. He would be present to watch but not to shoot.[36] Carping from the West and aloofness in the South did not, however, keep the great small-bore matches of the 1870s from bringing national glory, especially when United States teams established a pattern of success, winning both at home and in Great Britain, in all weather, four times in a row (fig. 8).

There was a good deal of nativist self-congratulation. Nathaniel Southgate Shaler, the Harvard geologist who fancied American autochthons superior even at the vegetable level, observed in an essay that the inhabitants of this country excelled in the three "leading diversions of the open air, yachting, horsemanship and 'sharpshooting.' "[37] An *Army and Navy Journal* editorial later explained the win in similar terms, theorizing that the vast distances of America train eyesight to accuracy. George Wingate himself laid the rifle progress of New York Guardsmen, who in two years achieved scores the British had just attained after two decades, mostly to our "intelligence."[38] When the Amateur Club organized a return match in 1875, announcements emphasized that only native-born riflemen could try out for the team—American superiority henceforward would be even more clear-cut. During the Centennial Match a reporter saw decided contrasts between teams according to their members' place of birth. "The rapidity of the Irish fire, the slow sure aim of the Scotchmen, the steadiness of the American champions, afforded an interesting comparison of national character."[39] For many, international rifle successes proved America's special virtue.

Some preferred to emphasize the community of interest created by riflery. At first they tended to Britishers. As early as 1875, the London *Sporting Gazette* observed that while the arts of peace had not created a "bond of union" within the English-speaking world, shooting now bid fair to achieve it.[40] Because only Anglo-Saxons seemed to excel at long-range target practice, more generous or more Anglophilic Americans expanded their self-congratulation to include the rest of the race. At the very least, small-bore riflery constituted another "sweetmeat on the table of Anglo-American reconciliation."[41] Sir Henry Halford, captain of the British teams of 1877 and 1882, recalled that on his first visit Americans received him cordially, but on his second they showed real warmth (fig. 9). He felt certain

Fig. 8 "Presentation of prizes to the American team at Gilmore's Garden, September 15th—cheering the foreign teams." *Historical Register of the Centennial Exposition* (1876).

that fondness for Britain was growing among "the thinking part" of the country (by implication, the unthinking part was Irish).[42] And as the London *Times* observed, international friendships can be cemented as private friendships are, in shared amusement—perhaps in "a slight affair like a rifle match."[43] On the eve of American involvement in the First World War, a U.S. officer recalled in *Scientific American* that Germans had never participated in "the noble sport of long range rifle shooting"[44] but stuck to their frivolous *Schützen* targetry. He attempted to explain the fact that British soldiers shot better than Germans; he suggested by his tone that a shared amusement may indeed have fostered fraternalism between the United States and Britain.

Besides revived nationalism and closer ties with the Empire, long-range riflery contrib-

uted a good deal as martial symbol and inspiration, though it had about as much direct military application as the international yacht racing to which so many compared it. Small-bore zealots required a weapon that cost half a workingman's yearly earnings (fig. 10) and had to be cleaned after every shot.[45] They normally fired from contorted back positions, using delicate sights—as precise as micrometers—mounted at the buttplate (fig. 11). Perfection in the game demanded almost full-time practice, as Henry Fulton, the star of the Americans, discovered to his distress.[46] Even at the height of the frenzy only a few hundred men shot seriously, and the NRA never had many to choose from when putting together a team. Faddishness probably drew most marksmen—though long-range riflery also offered peculiar psychological satisfactions.[47] Among the more clear-headed participants were National Guard officers who valued small-bore contests largely because the publicity devoted to what Leech had called the poetry of shooting greatly benefited the prose of guard recruitment.[48]

The high social class of long-range marksmen helped make their doings more newsworthy and invested the whole game with glamour. A month after the 1874 win, Chicago had the beginnings of four long-range clubs, one boasting a general, a judge, and a doctor of divinity. New York's Irish Rifle Club enrolled one of the nation's leading dramatists and a famous musician, as well as several journalists, invaluable boosters. The other New York clubs also attracted luminaries, though National Guard officers predominated.[49] Upper-class men in other cities from Maine to Florida to California had clubs a year after the first international match, and even United States citizens in Peru formed a long-range squad. Most observers seemed to regard the sport as not only rather nobby but notably clean and vaguely patriotic—the mayor of New York suggested that perhaps one of the city's long-range marksmen might some day pick off the general of an invading army.[50] The spillover of national interest certainly benefited the National Guard, as Wingate had hoped, but it extended much further into American life (fig. 12).

Before the Civil War, shooting had been regarded as the province of aristocratic triflers or underclass "woods loafers," but by 1875 riflery had become so worthy that it was endorsed by preachers and practiced by women. In their basements, churches set up ranges patronized by both sexes. Sporting magazines reported and welcomed such developments. "It has become quite the fashion," reported *Forest and Stream,* "for ladies to practice rifle shooting. At many fairs regular matches are shot between teams of young ladies selected according to nationality or otherwise."[51] Before 1880 several cities had all-women clubs. Target practice was a much more liberating hobby than croquet, women's first post–Civil War enthusi-

Vol. XVIII.—No. 929.]  NEW YORK, SATURDAY, OCTOBER 17, 1874.  [WITH A SUPPLEMENT. PRICE TEN CENTS.

Fig. 9   In a Thomas Nast cartoon entitled "Hibernia's Shot," Columbia demonstrates to Ireland that, though losing the first great international match, she has pierced the heart of America. *Harper's Weekly,* 17 October 1874.

asm, invading a masculine prerogative and encouraging the sort of practical clothing that bicycles later required. And female participation did not render shooting a less "manly" activity in the view of American sporting journals. True, targetry cultivated masculine spirit and assertiveness, but American women needed such qualities for self-defense, said the *Chicago Field.* The only change women brought to the game was a higher moral tone.[52] Target matches open to both sexes became a usual way to raise money for fresh air funds, hospitals, and the like.

The new wholesomeness transformed a minor American institution. Shooting galleries, the hangouts of drunks and ruffians, had existed in American cities since at least the 1830s. Except for a brief period before the Civil War when gentlemen needed to learn killing, none had attracted many respectable custom-

LONG RANGE "CREEDMOOR."

The Remington Breech-Loading Rifle used by Dakin, Fulton, Bodine, Hepburn, Coleman, Farwell, Canfield, Hyde, Rathbone, Crouch, Sanford, Weber, and many others.

**PRICE.**

A—Pistol Grip Stock, Vernier and Wind Gauge Sights..................................................$100 00
B—Plain Stock, Flat Butt Plate, Vernier and Wind Gauge Sights......................... 75 00
C—Military Stock, Vernier and Wind Gauge Sights.................................................. 55 00
D—Same as A, except Rubber Butt and Tip, and Checked fore-end, including Spirit Level and 2 extra Discs............... 125 00
E—Same as A, except selected curly polished stock, and extra finish throughout.................................. 150 00
Spirit Level, extra, when not mentioned above.......................................... 5 00
Wind Gauge Sight Discs, extra, each............................................. 1 50

HIGHLAND, N. Y., March 28, 1876.
D. G. WILD, Esq.—DEAR SIR:—Replying to yours of the 20th inst., without entering into details on the subject of rifles, I beg to say, that having had thirty years experience in their use, and now owning a number from the most prominent manufacturers, both foreign and domestic, I unhesitatingly pronounce the Remington Breech-Loader superior to all others yet produced. Their accuracy and power at long range, up to twelve hundred yards, is astonishing, even to those most familiar with their use. Very truly yours,
COL. JOHN BODINE.

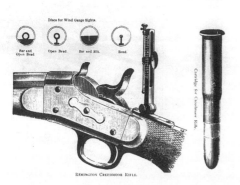

Fig. 10    The Remington and Sharps Companies made the first breech-loading long-range rifles. As this price list indicates, such weapons were expensive. Just the sighting equipment for a Creedmoor rifle cost as much as most guns of the period. The endorsement letter is from Colonel John Bodine, the hero of the famous 1874 match. Courtesy Frank De Haas, *Single Shot Rifles and Actions* (1969).

Fig. 11    Long-range practice by the Amateur Rifle Club. In the 1874 match, the American and Irish competitors used the prone and more usual back positions while firing at distances of up to 1,000 yards without telescopic sights. Reproduced in Durant and Bettmann, *Pictorial History of American Sports* (1952).

ers.[53] Now, though the scruffy sort persisted, several ranges in New York City appealed to serious marksmen, "the preRaphaelite school of Creedmoorites," and to less fanatic gentlemen shooters. Zettler's Gallery, opened in 1874, drew mostly purists, who used long-range rifles modified for indoor use. Conlin's, an older establishment which had been burned out with each of P. T. Barnum's unlucky museums, relocated and upgraded that same year. Its owner introduced the "safety-range," an index of the higher social class of his new customers because it required a lackey beside each marksman to load and watch for carelessness. Most of the customers of these new ranges counted as gentlemen only by comparison with earlier gallery habitués—journalists and insurance underwriters seem to have constituted a high percentage of the suddenly "huge and urgent" downtown patronage. Really prosperous shooters established private galleries, of which the New York Rifle Club may have been typical. "On entering," noted *Forest and Stream*, "the visitor is in a parlor or reception room with its piano and soft yielding carpet, its heavy window curtains, elaborate chandelier, bronzes and works of art displayed on the walls."[54] The actual shooting room was almost as sumptuous, done up in "obtrusively naturalistic Eastlake style."[55] Galleries, both plebeian and plush, constituted a purely American extension of the shooting mania. British critics dismissed them with sarcasm and counted short-range guns "vanities."[56]

Fig. 12 "Rifle practice at Creedmoor," in *Harper's Weekly,* 24 September 1881. By the 1880s, long-range shooting had begun to become an adjunct to military practice rather than a civilian spectator sport.

Yet college galleries and short outdoor ranges seem to have helped transform both the military training promoted by the 1862 Morrill Act and student attitudes toward soldier skills. During the spring and summer before the first international match, William Conant Church exchanged worried letters with an army captain assigned to Bowdoin College, who encountered a "hornets' nest" when he attempted to teach drill.[57] The undergraduate response to military instruction usually leaned more toward indifference, yet after the first international match students at Harvard, Yale, Columbia, and a number of other universities, colleges, and schools formed rifle clubs and applied to local militia officers for training. As if to underscore the parallel between the playing fields of England and those of the United States, the club at Columbia challenged other college teams to an annual contest modeled on that between Cambridge and Oxford.[58] A few school matches held at Creedmoor with full-power military rifles attracted attention, but most undergraduates had to make do with reduced loads at short ranges. *Forest and Stream,* from the first the most passionate proponent of college riflery, thought that considerably better than nothing.

Editor Charles Hallock's discussions of the intercollegiate rifle contests sponsored by his journal usually began with a homily about the cool nerves, diligence, and other manly qualities shooting conferred and praised it as a sport among other sports. But Hallock occasionally acknowledged that he hoped riflery would be the basis of a serious college program of military training. All of his prizes promoted "military shooting with military rifles."[59] In 1888 nearly fifty schools and colleges drew government ammunition and taught marksmanship. Harvard's president Charles W. Eliot proclaimed target practice the finest sport available to young men; no other had proved such a builder of coordination and self-control. Secretary of War William C. Endicott suggested raising the ammunition allowance for schools, as it might require nothing more to make shooting as popular with inland colleges as boat racing was on the seaboard.[60]

Outside the schools and the military, however, interest in target marksmanship dropped during the 1880s with the end of international small-bore contests and the growth of other sports.[61] Polo, another game promoted by James Gordon Bennett, Jr., during the 1870s, had more charm and long-term appeal for the typical member of the class that had first taken up long-range riflery. Old soldiers continued to meet for casual competition that today would be styled "plinking." In a community near Indianapolis,

> it was nothing unusual for half the merchants of the little town to shut up shop in the middle of the afternoon and, together with the lawyers, doctors and, yes, the preachers, to repair to some vacant lot and shoot impromptu matches with anything from old "pepperboxes" to the latest rifles. At that time and in that place practically all the "men" were veterans of the Civil War and this shooting business was part of their gospel.[62]

Targetry appeared in a degenerate form in the Wild West shows, which popularized trick shooting and brought fame to Annie Oakley and other adepts. William Cody contrived a set of targets connected to piano keys which allowed him to play "Yankee Doodle" with bullets, an unrivaled combination of "music, marksmanship and patriotism." Though much of the shooting at such shows was helped along with wires or was otherwise fraudulent, Americans took to it and to gimmicks such as the skating rifle match, which became surprisingly popular in the winter of 1884.[63] As interest in conventional shooting fell and real estate values rose, rifle clubs began to sell the tracts of metropolitan land that they had acquired for ranges. Galleries often became beer gardens. It was a starving time for the National Rifle Association, which died obscurely in 1892.

But it did not stay dead. The Spanish-American War brought a rush of trade to surviving city galleries, and early Boer successes against the British in South Africa persuaded many that civilian rifle experts armed with the new smokeless powder repeaters could out-soldier regulars. (A tremendous technical leap in arms occurred just before the turn of the century. Black powder, which allowed limited velocities and created great clouds of sulfurous smoke, was replaced by a new propellant that produced little smoke and burned progres-sively, accelerating the bullet to much higher velocities. Effective range doubled.) The present National Rifle Association, born at the turn of the century, came into an America where sporting magazines called for chairs of marksmanship at major universities and "chic summer girls" would soon crowd the shooters at the government's new National Matches. The rifle was headed toward its World War I apotheosis in the hands of Sergeant York.

Rifled arms had more than merely escaped the extinction predicted by Henry William Herbert in 1848. And yet he had been right about the disappearance of game. By the turn of the century, the sort of animals hunted with high-power rifles had nearly ceased to exist everywhere but the far West.[64] Although it had killed away its "utility," why had the rifle's "honor" so vastly increased? Target practice offered a sport justifiable in Calvinist terms, a sport chiefly improving and patriotic and only incidentally (if at all) fun. Control and repetition are essential in target shooting as in few other games. In fact, riflery with its discipline and exactitude hardly seemed recreation, even to many of the men drawn to it. Americans, unlike Germans, did not appear able to enjoy the range, reflected the sporting press, but strove on it as relentlessly as in their offices. Its partisans urged marksmanship for character building more often than for sport, and "the arm of precision" truly demanded Protestant virtues, including temperance, because alcohol and even tobacco interfered with success.[65] As for patriotism, small-bore shooters constituted at least a cadre of top-quality minutemen and perhaps a whole new weapon. Some enthusiasts expected infantry to advance under the cover of long-range rifle fire rather than artillery.[66] The rigor and patriotism of shooting did much to render sporting contests respectable during the 1870s; once respectable, such contests could take other forms with more spectator interest.

Targetry, retreating into its justification, became ever more military as the century progressed. The 1880s saw international matches between amateur soldiers replace civilian small-bore contests. During the early 1890s, marksmanship became "virtually a religion" in the United States Army.[67] And the shooting craze that arrived with the new century was almost wholly military in inspiration, even though some of its devotees saw the end of regular armies in it. All that represented the norm. In most times, few people care about target shooting outside a military context. The hugely aberrant international matches of the 1870s revealed more than a still-Calvinistic people's dalliance with mass sport. They signaled a still-sundered nation's return to self-assertion and presaged the Anglo-American alliance of our own century.

## Notes

1. Frank Forester [Henry William Herbert], *Frank Forester's Field Sports of the United States and British Provinces of North America* (New York: Stringer and Townsend, 1848), 29. Herbert, an upper-class Englishman resident in New York, wrote gunning books and essays between 1848 and 1858. Rifles had been used by specialized military units for centuries, but their bullets had to be forced down grooves rather than dropped down a smooth interior. The extra time and trouble could be justified only in units of sharpshooters.

2. Henry Heth, *The Memoirs of Henry Heth,* ed. James L. Morrison, Jr. (Westport, CT: Greenwood Press, 1974), 142; *The National Rifle Association: 1873 Annual Reports and Regulations for Rifle Practice* (New York: E. A. Kingsland and Company, 1873), 6.

3. *Forest and Stream,* 2 October 1879, 691; *Shooting and Fishing,* 16 May 1901, 95.

4. See, for example, Colonel Henry A. Gildersleeve's remarks in *Spirit of the Times,* 18 May 1876, 136. Any edge which southerners may have possessed disappeared in the lower quality of their equipment.

5. The most massive had to be fired from a bench or other rest.

6. Claud E. Fuller, *The Rifled Musket* (New York: Bonanza Books, 1968), 258; Charles Winthrop Sawyer, *Our Rifles,* vol. 3 of *Firearms in American History* (Boston: The Cornhill Company, 1920), 87.

7. So called to distinguish them from the *Schützenbünde,* discussed later.

8. Augustine E. Costello, *A History of the New York Fire Department, Volunteer and Paid* (New York: Augustine E. Costello, 1887), 753. Earlier, some militia made once-a-year excursions, but the custom lapsed among them in the 1840s when semimilitary societies took it up with fervor. Colonel Emmons Clark, *History of the Seventh Regiment of New York: 1806–1889,* vol. 1 (New York: Published by the Seventh Regiment, 1890), 339.

9. Emmeline Charlotte Elizabeth Stuart-Wortley, *Travels in the United States During 1849 and 1850* (London: R. Bentley, 1851), 298–99.

10. *Army and Navy Journal,* 13 April 1867, 50. Colonel Church, a successful journalist in New York City and Washington, D.C., had established his paper in 1863, chiefly to serve the Union army's officers. By 1867, he spoke authoritatively for the military and would continue to do so through an extraordinary editorship that ended only with his death in 1917.

11. *Army and Navy Journal,* 16 May 1869, 621. Though a Tammany man, Hoffman as city judge "had done good service in punishing participants in the Draft Riot." *The Diary of George Templeton Strong: The Civil War, 1860–1865,* ed. Allan Nevins and Milton Halsey Thomas (New York: Macmillan, 1952), ix.

12. *Army and Navy Journal,* 620. *Schützen* guarded their respective parts of Germany for centuries before they brought their sport to America in the 1840s. The form had not changed appreciably since days when practice was with crossbows.

13. *New York Times,* 28 July 1864; "A German-American Fete," *Harper's Weekly,* 13 July 1895, 664.

14. *Shooting and Fishing,* 4 July 1901, 233.

15. *New York Times,* 24 April 1857. Private military societies attained considerable popularity in the South and Midwest but did not style themselves target companies. Many practiced fancy marching inspired by the Zouave drill of Colonel Elmer W. Ellsworth's Chicago troop. Theodore G. Gronert, "The First National Pastime in the Middle West," *Indiana Magazine of History* 29, 3 (September 1933): 180.

16. Newspaper accounts of *Schützenfeste* tended to be ironic, as reporters had difficulty believing that serious shooting could go on amidst such a carnival. The most native of Americans, a band of Indians, protested in war paint the fireworks set off by New York's Independent *Schützen* Corps during a fest at Lake Hopatcong, New Jersey. *Shooting and Fishing,* 7 July 1892, 215. Other Americans of old stock sometimes objected almost as strongly. *Forest and Stream,* 18 October 1888, 586.

17. "National Guard" was a term first borrowed from the French to apply to New York's volunteer militia. A militia convention in Richmond, Virginia, in 1877 created the National Guard Association. After that, the term "National Guard" was generally used for volunteer state troops. Russell F. Weighly, *History of the United States Army* (New York: Macmillan, 1967), 282. Units were used mostly

for maintaining public order (to include, frequently, strike breaking). It was not until the Dick Act of 1903 that the National Guard was effectively incorporated into the national defense.

18. Arthur Blennerhassett Leech, captain of the Irish team, had heard of neither the American NRA nor the Amateur Rifle Club, but he did know James Gordon Bennett, Jr., innovative editor of the *New York Herald,* whose bankrolling of Stanley's expedition had impressed him. Leech placed an ad in the *New York Herald* which the NRA's board of directors voted to ignore as "a mere newspaper letter" despite Wingate's pleas. Arthur B. Leech, *Irish Riflemen in America* (London: Edward Stanford, 1875), 101.

19. *Forest and Stream,* 2 August 1883, 4.

20. Modern "small-bore" shooting uses .22 rimfire cartridges at short ranges and ought not to be confused with its nineteenth-century namesake. Military weapons of the 1860s usually had bores of .50 caliber or larger. Only by comparison were .44 and .45 caliber rifles small.

21. G. W. Yale, superintendent of Sharps Rifle Company, and L. L. Hepburn, foreman of Remington's Mechanical Department, each had a place on the final team.

22. *Turf, Field and Farm,* 26 June 1874, 440.

23. *Forest and Stream,* 24 January 1874, 267.

24. Ibid., 11 April 1874, 21.

25. Chicago *Inter-Ocean,* 28 November 1873, 2.

26. "The International Rifle Match," *Harper's Weekly,* 10 October 1874, 838.

27. *Rod and Gun,* 21 August 1875, 312. When, having won the return match, team members called on Victor Hugo in Paris, the *New York Times* (8 August 1875) counted that front-page news.

28. *Forest and Stream,* 6 April 1886, 212.

29. Konrad Lorenz, *On Aggression* (New York: Harcourt, Brace & World, 1966), 280.

30. *Rod and Gun,* 19 June 1875, 188.

31. *American Sportsman,* 10 October 1875, 24.

32. *Turf, Field and Farm,* 30 July 1875, 91.

33. *American Sportsman,* 10 October 1874, 24.

34. Not that they rejected pointless killing of buffalo, because they then chased the small herd and destroyed it in flight to educate the Creedmoor boy in western ways. Carver and Texas Jack Omohundro were guiding an Englishman at the time and apparently left the animals to rot. Raymond W. Thorp, *Spirit Gun of the West: The Story of Doc W. F. Carver* (Glendale, CA: Arthur H. Clark, 1957), 58.

35. Letter of 23 July 1877 signed by George W. Wingate, D. D. Wylie, and Joseph G. Story, printed in the *New Orleans Daily Picayune,* 30 July 1877, quoted by Dale A. Somers, *The Rise of Sports in New Orleans: 1850–1900* (Baton Rouge: Louisiana State University Press, 1972), 204.

36. *Turf, Field and Farm,* 10 August 1877, 221.

37. Nathaniel S. Shaler, "The Summing Up of the Story," in *The United States of America,* vol. 2, ed. Nathaniel S. Shaler (New York: D. Appleton, 1894), 622.

38. *Army and Navy Journal,* 18 August 1906, 1415.

39. *Spirit of the Times,* 16 September 1876, 154.

40. Quoted in *Turf, Field and Farm,* 30 July 1875, 91.

41. W. H. Nelson used this phrase to describe Sir George Otto Trevelyan's *The American Revolution,* 4 vols. (1899–1907).

42. *Forest and Stream,* 14 December 1882, 394.

43. Quoted in *Forest and Stream,* 23 September 1875, 104.

44. Edward Crossman, "German Military Rifle Practice," *Scientific American* 116, no. 5 (3 February 1917): 126.

45. One hundred dollars would buy the basic rifle. One could spend twice that much. And there were expensive accessories in addition. One dollar a day was a fair wage at the time.

46. *Army and Navy Journal,* 23 September 1876, 105.

47. Long-range riflery "imparts to him who perfects himself in the accomplishment a sense of power and self-dependence which cannot be otherwise attained. The accomplished long-range rifleman knows that the weapon he bears is a magic wand by whose power he holds at his mercy the life of any enemy, be it man or beast, that ventures in the radius of half a mile from the spot whereon he stands, and the consciousness of such power is no ordinary sensation." *Rod and Gun,* 4 September 1875, 340.

48. Wingate gave that as the reason for his own involvement. *National Guardsman,* 1 March 1878, 141.

49. *Forest and Stream,* 7 January 1875, 344.

50. *Rod and Gun,* 28 August 1875, 325.

51. *Forest and Stream,* 21 December 1876, 314.

52. *Chicago Field* 50, 19 July 1880, 300.

53. Early galleries often sold alcoholic drinks at attached refreshment stands. *Rod and Gun,* 3 April 1875, 4.

54. *Forest and Stream,* 8 April 1880, 190.

55. Ibid.

56. Ibid., 19 March 1874, 90.

57. The Morrill Act stipulated that instruction in military tactics was to be included at land-grant colleges. In fact, such instruction could be provided by army officers to any college with 150 male students.

58. *Turf, Field and Farm,* 8 January 1875, 21.

59. *Forest and Stream,* 9 December 1875, 286.

60. Lieutenant A. C. Sharp, USA, "Military Training in Colleges," *Journal of the Military Service Institute of the United States* 8, 32 (December 1887): 411; *The Rifle,* 1 February 1888, 157; *Report of the Secretary of War,* 50th Cong., 2d sess., 1888, Ex. Doc. 1, 17.

In a letter to a fellow University of Wisconsin re-gent that same year, an opponent of military training assumed marksmanship had become its essence. "That discipline which savors least of culture or mentality and most of brute passion and war, is being pushed most persistently and vigorously. To study classics is choice or whim—to train with a gun and know how to shoot is a requirement." George H. Paul to John C. McMynn, 7 January 1888, McMynn Papers, State Historical Society of Wisconsin, quoted by John Frank Cook, "A History of Liberal Education at the University of Wisconsin: 1862–1918" (Ph.D. diss., University of Wisconsin, 1970), 122.

61. *Turf, Field and Farm,* 30 May 1884, 418. The NRA knew well the publicity value of international small-bore contests, but foreign teams could not be tempted once they saw they had no chance to win. In 1882 and 1883 National Guardsmen and British Volunteers held practical matches, but those drew hundreds where small-bore contests had drawn thousands. *Forest and Stream* said the 1882 competition was "a military affair. . . . There were no scenes of excitement or enthusiasm" (21 September 1882, 152).

62. Herbert W. McBride, *A Rifleman Went to War* (Plantersville, SC: Small Arms Technical Publishing Company, 1935), 2.

63. *Forest and Stream* believed the fad dangerous, because shots fired while flashing over a frozen pond often went wild (14 February 1884, 40).

64. Deer began their comeback not long after 1900, thanks partly to closed seasons and partly to government and private game preserves. By the 1920s many eastern and midwestern states had more than their forests could support. James B. Trefethen, *Crusade for Wildlife* (Harrisburg, PA: Stackpole Books, 1961), 338ff.

65. "Rifle practice carries with it self-denial, sobriety, and iron nerve." *Rod and Gun,* 31 July 1875, 264.

66. *Army and Navy Journal,* 3 February 1883, 599.

67. Captain H. C. Hale, USA, "The New Firing Regulations for Small Arms," *Journal of the United States Infantry Association* 1, 1 (July 1904): 14.

# A Room with a Viewer

The Parlor Stereoscope, Comic Stereographs, and the Psychic Role of
Play in Victorian America

SHIRLEY WAJDA

Charles Dickens called it "an extremely pretty
toy that is of no use except as an elegant and
valuable illustration of a train of scientific rea-
soning." Queen Victoria was indeed amused
when she peered through one at the Great Exhibition at the Crystal Palace in 1851. What "it"
was, was the stereoscope. Along with a basket
of stereographs, this rather awkward-looking
viewing device constituted an important element of the showcase of symbolic objects
found on the typical Victorian parlor center
table throughout the last half of the nineteenth
century. The German visitor Dr. Herman
Vogel testified to the stereoscope's popularity
when he observed, on his third visit to America in 1883, that "the stereoscopic picture is
much more esteemed in America than in Europe; I think there is not a parlor in America
where there is not a stereoscope."[1]

The sheer number of stereoscopes and stereographs manufactured in the United States
in the nineteenth century underscores the pastime's popularity. By 1901 the successful publishing firm of Underwood and Underwood,
for instance, was producing twenty-five thousand stereographs daily and selling three
hundred thousand stereoscopes annually. Al-

though exact numbers are not known, collec-
tors have placed the total number of negatives
produced in the years between 1854 (the year
in which the stereoscope was introduced in
America) and 1920 at somewhere between
three and four million. If only one hundred
copies were reproduced from each negative, at
least three hundred million stereographs were
issued in these years. Undeniably, the variety
of views rendered with the illusion of three-
dimensional reality provided a fascinating and
enduring pastime for many an American Victorian family.[2]

Yet the perceptions and uses of this pastime and, by extension, of leisure in general,
changed over time. At its introduction at midcentury, the stereoscope and stereographs were
hailed as a didactic tool for home amusement,
serving both to educate and to entertain the
family. Successful stereographers captured a
range of images that fit popular notions of
correct and uplifting subject matter—American and foreign scenery, newsworthy events,
and famous personages. Prominently displayed on the parlor table, the stereoscope and
stereographs symbolized the proper Victorian
family's commitment to perfecting society by

perfecting moral character through the acquisition of knowledge about the world around it.

After 1890, however, this ideal began to give way to a different view of home and the family. Advice writers advocated a more easygoing and relaxed style of life to replace the emphasis on decorum and the social primacy of the home and family. Importantly, women and children were urged to become more independent, which in practice translated to engaging in activities outside the house. The domestic sphere had to be redefined to accommodate the changing needs of the individual members of the family. Leisure occurring wholly within the domestic sphere was also affected by—indeed, helped to effect—the change. The world of play provided one "place" to which late-century Americans displaced their ideals and where the tensions inherent in the shift to modernist twentieth-century culture could be articulated and negotiated.[3]

This cultural transformation is manifested in much of the material culture evidence of the era.[4] One indicator of this cultural shift is the discarding of the parlor and what it symbolized. Late-century housing and design reformers, rejecting the parlor as stuffy and useless, advocated a new type of space, a living room in which family members could retreat from the world and rejuvenate themselves. What Americans were actually discarding was the parlor as the very public symbol of "character," the proper social face with which to present oneself and one's family to the world. Contemporary stereographic images, both factual and "fictional," recorded this shift. One such set of multicolored lithoprint stereographs, entitled "Comic Series," was advertised by Sears, Roebuck and Company as "laughable hugging and kissing scenes, humorous scenes of domestic tribulations, amusing bathing scenes, photographs of children engaged in childish occupations." Though these studio-produced images portrayed a fictionalized reality, they simultaneously depicted a form of real action that had taken place in front of the camera lens. Taken together, the views in the Comic Series collapse the shifting nature of late Victorian play into accessible material evidence—the cardboard stereograph—and a reenactable viewing process.[5]

What follows is an analysis of the Comic Series in relation to the cultural shift—from a Victorian world view to a modernist one—underway in the years between 1890 and 1920. By considering image, text, and context in relation to one another, we can begin to understand how many late Victorian Americans coped with cultural change and how the domestic sphere and the concept of play served as an idealized arena for this change.

The home as we conceive it today is not the same entity that our mid-Victorian counterparts understood. "Home, properly regarded, is the grand institution of social life," asserted *Frank Leslie's New Family Magazine* in 1859. "It is the birth place of the affections, the centre of every genial influence; and in building up a home, regard should be had to all that can contribute to its happiness and comfort."[6] Moreover, the family was integral in the quest for a perfect society. "The family is the best school for the development of character," asserted one editor. "The child can be better trained at home than abroad, and the man and the woman find a discipline in the relationships of home which life outside can never supply. This is indeed the function of the family—to perfect individual character."[7] Without a doubt, the home—the domestic "sphere" held to be under woman's authority—was the most important institution in Victorian America.[8]

The stereoscope and the basket of stereographs on the parlor center table were popular symbols of the Victorian dedication to self-improvement through didactic pursuits. "It were strange indeed if many parlors were without them," noted the *American Journal of Photography* in 1858. "What is better adapted to enlarge the attention of a visitor whilst temporarily delayed, waiting for the appearance of the lady of the house? What better interlude during an evening party than to fill up a pause with a glance at a fine stereoscopic view?"[9] The nature of this and other suggestions in domestic journals leads to the conclusion that the basket of stereographs and the stereoscope on the parlor table acted as symbols of a cosmopolitan family.

The interest in knowing the world—being cosmopolitan, "at home" in the world—as a characteristic of a middle-class identity had its roots in the late eighteenth century. Travel journals described the world by offering engraved illustrations as well as written description. The *Universal Traveller,* published in 1836, appealed to its readers by speaking to their aspirations: "It is the privilege of but few, to visit distant countries and different nations . . . the majority are necessarily cut off from this species of amusement and information. . . . We will hold up a picture by which, in the comfort of your homes, you may see whatever is worthy of inspection, just as the literal traveller would see it."[10] The subject matter of the stereograph also fit this intention. In 1853 the Boston daguerreotype firm of Southworth and Hawes offered in its "Grand Parlor Stereoscope" whole-plate stereoscopic scenes of Boston and its surrounding area. Patrons enthusiastically embraced the invention, buying season tickets to the changing displays, which took place in the firm's daguerreotype parlor.[11] The three-dimensionality afforded by the magnifying stereoscope offered what was widely believed to be the truest representation of reality. Indeed, stereoscopic photography was considered the medium in which hidden truths revealed by the camera were made to "surface."[12]

Colonial Americans had learned about the world through many visual means. Eighteenth-century print sellers displayed their wares in shop windows. Early nineteenth-century artists employed novelty in their display of panoramas of the Mississippi River, of Versailles, and of Niagara Falls. Stereographs and stereoscopes specifically may be considered the nineteenth-century successor of perspective views. These views, nonsensical in the original, could only be made rational through a perspective glass. These eighteenth-century prints were popular among the genteel classes and were placed on tables in drawing rooms or, more often, libraries. The limitations of the devices—perspective glasses and stereoscopes accommodated one viewer at a time—rendered them useful for education and contemplation and fit well the emerging emphasis on visual literacy.[13] Visual literacy was a vital component of nineteenth-century pedagogy and was due in great part to the technological revolution in illustration and publishing. Even learning to write was related to the ability to visualize correctly and to draw accurately. In May 1839, the *Common School Assistant* carried an editorial commenting on the use of pictures: "There are some who would use engravings . . . to cultivate the taste, the imagination and the habits of attention and observation."[14] Learning through pictures was advocated most strongly for childhood education. The Centennial Exhibition, for example, was acknowledged as a capsulated version of world cultures and of history accessible through pictures (fig. 1). In articles entitled "The Exhibition as a School" and "The Home-Uses of the Exhibition," mothers in particular were advised to take advantage of this once-in-a-lifetime opportunity by using pictures of the event to instruct their children.

> There is a chance, too, for the school-boy and girl to gain a knowledge which no book can afford, of countries which they in all probability will never visit. . . . Here are Europe and the East within our gates. . . . But to comprehend these living pictures, a child will require an intelligent guide . . . , the mother [who] . . . will best know how to carry it into practice.[15]

Card stereographs, introduced in the 1850s, were printed with descriptive texts and often came in small sets (ranging in number from four to twelve) that created a narrative structure, thus appealing to the growing and popular habit of reading and the emphasis on visual literacy. The stereograph's educational function, signaled by the introduction of boxed sets sold as "libraries" at the end of the nine-teenth century, is undoubtedly the primary reason for the pastime's long-lived popularity.

It is little wonder, then, that we find the stereoscope and stereographs occupying a privileged position on the parlor center table. The parlor, as a public and family space, served to display the family's refinement as well as its cultural commitment to the perfection of character. The instrument that had so captivated Queen Victoria when it was displayed at the Great Exhibition in 1851 became a middle-class "must-have" almost overnight. Within three months of the queen's "sanction," nearly twenty-five thousand stereoscopes were sold in London and Paris. In America, a similar reception occurred. Of course, few Americans could afford the $1,160 price tag of Southworth and Hawes's piano-sized "Grand Parlor Stereo-scope." Many Americans opted instead for the Brewster stereoscope (fig. 2). Sir William Brewster in 1850 had perfected the lenticular stereoscope, a box containing two adjustable lenses placed at the top that allowed the viewer to look at a stereo-daguerreotype (or stereo-ambrotype) positioned on the floor of the box. One or both sides of the box could be opened to admit light. It was this type of stereoscope Oliver Wendell Holmes characterized when he warned, "Twenty-five glass slides, well inspected in a strong light are *good* for one headache, if a person is disposed to that trouble."[16] And it appears that many were so disposed. *Harper's New Monthly Magazine* humorously documented the "typical" family's reaction to the miracles of the Brewster stereoscope, a reaction that must have been shared by many American families (fig. 3). Any modern-day stereoscope user can testify to the eye strain experienced when using the instrument. Stereoscopic viewing consists of looking through two lenses separated by a septum to force the eyes to combine the images of two pictures taken from slightly varying points of view (usually two to two-and-a-half inches apart). This refocusing process—which is an acquired ability—produces the three-dimensional effect

Fig. 1  "Kansas State Exhibit, Kan. & Col. B'l'd'g.," Centennial Photographic Co., 1876. Except for figures 2 and 4, illustrations are in the collection of the author.

of depth and solidity, similar to pop-up pictures found in many children's books. Contemporary experts noted that the fatigue or pain experienced in the viewing process was the result of a lack of adjustment of the focal distance between the picture and the eye.

The cheaper and, historically, most popular stereoscope, the handheld one devised by Oliver Wendell Holmes and Joseph L. Bates in 1860—the one still found in attics and at flea markets—was the version that found the route to the parlor table (fig. 4).[17] Its simple construction made the instrument affordable to nearly everyone. It also featured an adjustable sliding card holder and a hood to block out extraneous light. The simultaneous developments in the 1850s of card stereographs and of the stereocamera, making production of stereographs faster and cheaper, virtually guaranteed the pastime's success.

The central attraction of the stereoscope, the illusion of three-dimensionality, appealed to the Victorian eye. As Kenneth L. Ames and Katherine C. Grier have noted, Victorians tended to create similar effects within their homes, adding mirrors so as to watch motion or designing vistas through various rooms,

Fig. 2    This Brewster-type stereoscope holds both lantern slides and stereographs. English, papier-mâché and mother-of-pearl, about 1850.

niches, and doorways.[18] Within the lenses of the stereoscope, the viewer could feel "part" of the scene quite literally at hand. The best stereographers capitalized on the effects of depth and solidity by composing views that emphasized them. Generally, these effects were created by the use of a long slanting line extending into the background of a picture, as in three-point perspective drawing. The use of floral wreaths as borders that stood out in relief around portraits was another device to create a sense of depth (fig. 5).

Historians who have primarily been interested in the wealth of images produced for the stereoscope have not addressed how people used the instrument. Primary accounts of stereoscope viewing are few and offer even fewer specifics about that use. But the limits of the stereoscope were implicitly acknowledged in the ways its use was advocated. References to use are presented in combination with uses of leisure time: time on one's hands was never to be wasted. As *Scribner's Monthly* advised the mistress of the house,

> While you are arranging a parlor, just have a thought for the visitors who must sometimes wait to see you, and carefully refrain from putting every object of interest out of reach. . . . The late magazines, a book of good engravings, a household volume of poetry, a stereoscope and

views, photographs of foreign scenes . . . are all good aids to the occupation of stray minutes.[19]

The offer of didactic amusements to single visitors was a gesture that signaled the family's commitment to cosmopolitanism through the pursuit of knowledge. Family time also fell into this category. In "Huldah the Help. A Thanksgiving Story" from the same magazine, the narrator reveals that the time after the holiday meal we now so devoutly spend watching football was utilized in more worthwhile pursuits.

> We had eaten dinner and had adjourned to the warm bright parlor. I have noticed on such occasions that conversation is apt to flag after dinner. Whether it is that digestion absorbs all of one's vitality, or for some other reason, at least so it generally falls out that people may talk so brilliantly at the table, but they will hardly keep it up for the first half-hour afterward. And so it happened that some of the party fell to looking at the books and some to turning the leaves of the photograph album, while others were using the stereoscope. For my own part, I was staring at an engraving in a dark corner of the parlor.[20]

As one editor warned, "People are incessantly talking of killing time, unmindful that it is time that kills them. . . . Even if killing time be the sole object, it is just as easy to kill time to advantage as to disadvantage."[21] The constellation of objects on the parlor center table—books of poetry, portfolios of art engravings or foreign scenery, photograph albums, and Bibles—reminded visitors and family members alike of the Victorian abhorrence of idleness.[22]

One popular etiquette manual was very direct on this point, advising its readers to "employ that leisure which others waste in idle and corrupting pursuits, in the acquisition of those branches of knowledge which serve to amuse as well as instruct; natural history, for example, or chemistry, or astronomy, or drawing, or any of the numerous kindred branches of study."[23] Stereographers acknowledged this demand by supplying the appropriate subject matter. The overwhelming favorite was Ameri-

Fig. 3   "Stereoscopic Slides," *Harper's New Monthly Magazine*, November 1860.

can and foreign scenery. Taking cues from the travel magazine, the scenic stereograph provided the allure of letting one "visit" anywhere without leaving the comfort of home. "To look in the quiet of one's parlor," enthused the *Photographic Times,*

upon the incomprehensible Pyramids, the wondrous tombs of Egypt, the ruined temples of India, the old abbeys of England and Scotland, the dismal dungeons and castles of Spain, the glories of the Rhine, the fascinations of the Alps, the bewildering beauties of the Himalayas, and of all that history has made interesting, is a pleasure which none who know of it will relinquish.[24]

Furthermore, such views could serve as souvenirs of travel for those who dared to venture

out of their parlors. "Nothing affords a more convenient and pleasing memorial of scenes visited in travels than a collection of stereoscopic views," remarked one author, linking the stereograph with the nascent pastime of touring.[25] "Almost every place of note in the country has its local stereographer and every tourist carries away some pictures to remind him of his visit," claimed *Anthony's Photographic Bulletin*.[26]

The pastime's growth in popularity was also due in great part to developments in the stereograph industry. Early stereographers, encumbered by heavy equipment and complicated techniques, could produce only limited quantities of views. As Howard S. Becker has noted, the first audiences of stereographs were

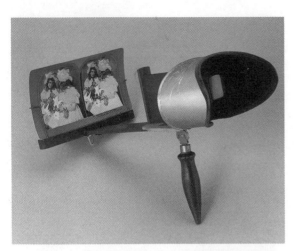

Fig. 4  This Holmes-Bates style of stereoscope was manufactured about 1900 by Underwood and Underwood, a company that also made stereoviews.

the instrument along with telescopes and microscopes. A stock of stereographs could only enhance business.) Stereographs were also sold at popular tourist attractions, such as Niagara Falls, the White Mountains, or the Delaware Water Gap. With the rise of large companies after the Civil War, however, stereographs were marketed by door-to-door canvassers (often college students on summer vacations) and through mail-order houses. In 1898 the halftone screen printing process, in which an image is composed of small printed dots, resulted in the development of multicolored "lithoprint" stereographs. Although these color-printed views were cheaper to produce, not all the major companies adopted this method. These lower-priced stereographs were not sold by salesmen; rather, they were offered through mail-order companies or were sold wholesale to drugstores, bookstores, department stores, and stationers, who would then retail the cards or offer them as premiums. After 1903, Sears, Roebuck and Montgomery Ward promoted boxed sets, usually issued in numbers of fifty or one hundred, of multicolored lithoprint stereographs of selected subject matter.[28]

The disintegration of Victorian didactic leisure is articulated by the separation of its serious and purposeful dimension from play through the categorization of subject matter in boxed stereograph sets. Boxed sets of images of foreign, historic, or cultural sites, for example, were numbered to follow the same sequence of sights an actual traveler might encounter. Accompanied by an extended caption on the reverse of each card, the images gave the stay-at-home, in essence, a guided tour. Advertisements for religious scenes and Bible stories were geared toward church organizations and Sunday schools. In 1898 the Keystone Stereoview Company began to market sets designed specifically for school instruction. Created by educators, oriented to grade levels, and accompanied by teacher's manuals, these sets illustrated such topics as costume, history, geography, commerce, and nature. The diversification of subjects heralded the separation of education from the home and, perhaps to a

small, localized ones, since most early images were those of local events, places, and people. By the Civil War, however, the demand for stereographs increased to the point that several photographic firms organized large-scale production facilities. Large, national companies soon replaced these local professional or amateur stereographers, with twelve separate national companies established in the years between 1880 and 1914. These large publishing companies bought negatives from local stereographers or hired their own staff to produce specific views in response to demand. Regular upgrading of assembly-line production methods throughout the last half of the nineteenth century increased output. For example, in 1862 the Kilburn Brothers of Littleton, New Hampshire, could manufacture an average of three thousand stereographs a day. With a half-century of improvements, the H. C. White Company of North Bennington, Vermont, could boast in 1907 that its mechanized plant could produce fifteen thousand stereographs a day.[27]

At the outset of the stereograph's long-lived popularity, photographers sold views out of their studios, or through art supply shops or at opticians. (Stereograph sales at an optician's? Remember that opticians, skilled in grinding the glass lenses of the stereoscope, often sold

lesser but still noticeable extent, the secularization of the home. The traditional duty of the mother to instruct her children on matters academic and religious now began to fall to other authorities. The home was slowly expelling these serious pursuits and was being redefined as a servantless, private, family-centered retreat.[29]

This reorientation of the domestic sphere is characterized in the "Comic Series," a boxed set of one hundred multicolored lithoprint stereographs (many copyrighted by T. W. Ingersoll of St. Paul, Minnesota, a major regional producer of stereographs). In 1905 Sears, Roebuck advertised the Comic Series in its catalogs. Such staged anecdotal or sentimental scenes, commonly referred to as "groups" at midcentury, had historically constituted only a small percentage of subjects depicted in stereo. These "groups" had satisfied the mid-Victorian criteria for didactic leisure. The photography historian-theorist M. A. Root promoted these "tableaux vivants," or living pictures, as both uplifting and amusing.

> The models . . . may serve . . . to entertain and instruct the public, by composing and exhibiting "tableaux vivants." In these spectacles may be presented the sublimest and loveliest scenery of all lands, and the grandest and most beautiful monuments of human genius, skill, and labor, in both the ancient and modern worlds. . . . The most thrilling and critical scenes . . . that are commemorated in history or imagined in romance, together with the heroes or geniuses, the sages or saints or martyrs, may be reproduced before the contemplations of the present generation. . . . What incalculable means and materials of instruction, of refinement, and of elevation, not less than recreation and amusement are here represented.[30] (Fig. 6)

In contrast, the scenes depicted in the Comic Series are not reenactments of historical or allegorical events, nor are they necessarily depictions of grand moral tales. Rather, these photographic images, through more realistic staging (the portable "detective" camera was invented in 1888; the rapid rise of amateur photography and the "snapshot aesthetic" no

Fig. 5 "The Cottage Door," no. 367 in Stereoscopic Treasures series, F. G. Weller, Littleton, NH, 1872.

doubt influenced both pose and subject), depict contemporary anecdotes or simply ordinary scenes of ordinary persons doing ordinary things. Gone is the midcentury "staginess" of purposeful poses and attitudes in which actors "play" to the camera. Yet the images of the Comic Series belie their studio origin in an attempt to capture reality. Sears, Roebuck's advertisement for the boxed set did not stress its educational value. It stressed only the realism and entertainment value of the series:

> *These one hundred pictures are all photographed from life.* There are no copies of paintings or drawings, but every picture is made with a camera direct from life. The coloring in these comic views is exceptionally good and our new process has enabled us to bring out the details and present the subjects in the most realistically lifelike manner. Great care has been exercised in selecting the subjects for this set so that only unusually good views are included. There is not a vulgar picture in the entire set, not a picture to which the most refined could possibly object, but at the same time every picture in the set is interesting, and they will be looked at over and over again, forming a never failing source of pleasure and relaxation.

Fig. 6   "NO. 925 Yosemite Fall, Yosemite Cal," Kilburn Brothers, Littleton, NH.

Fig. 7   "Chasing Butterflies in the Daisy Field" (53).

*Everybody likes a good laugh,* and every picture in this big set is good for one big hearty laugh.

Laughable hugging and kissing scenes, humorous scenes of domestic tribulations, amusing bathing scenes, photographs of children engaged in childish occupations—

*Funny, entertaining and laughable pictures.* They will amuse you and help to entertain your friends. Understand, this big set contains one hundred comic colored views, every picture a good one.[31]

How do these images chronicle the transition from Victorian to modernist culture at the turn of the twentieth century? The details of the images and of the extended captions tip the historian to the historical and cultural meaning produced by both. As Oliver Wendell Holmes, medical doctor, celebrated author, and enthusiastic advocate of the stereograph, posited, these "lesser details . . . often [give] us incidental truths which interest us more than the central object of the picture."[32]

The pastime itself reinforces the attention to detail. The hood of the stereoscope blocks out peripheral light and vision. The extended captions also serve in part to indicate details and to emphasize the viewing process itself. "Chasing Butterflies in the Daisy Field," for example, reinforces the phenomenon of three-dimensionality by directing the stereograph viewer back to the image: "The longer one looks at this picture the more beautiful it grows. The blades of grass and the flower stalks stand out in the most natural fashion" (fig. 7). And the text of "The Goat Carriage. Driving in the Park" emphatically bids the stereograph viewer to notice the image's artistic play of light and color: "And look at those trees! Notice the exquisite effects of the light on the leaves, from silvery white to deepest green, and the purple shadows below!" (fig. 8). The middle-class emphasis on visual literacy and an understanding of beauty is conveyed explicitly in " 'Look at the F[r]oggies' ": "It is a dull child indeed, that does not stop to cast a second glance at the pond mirroring the beeches with their delicate foliage and silvery trunks, at the stately swan with its gracefully posed neck, showing the line of beauty, or at an exquisite bit of scenery like the one shown in this picture" (fig. 9).

One detail quickly discovered is the duplication of props and locations in the Comic Series views. The interiors especially serve to fix these scenes as studio creations. Note, for

Fig. 8  "The Goat Carriage. Driving in the Park"
(15).

Fig. 9.  " 'Look at the F[r]oggies' " (73). T. W. Ingersoll, copyright 1899.

example, the table and lamp in " 'Just Like Grandma Does' " and in " 'I Just Knew It Would Be a Boy' " (figs. 10 and 11). The advertisement's assertion that these views were "made from life," therefore, refers to both the stage of the studio and the staged human comedy. These staged productions employ conventions for the theatrical frame noted by sociologist Erving Goffman. As in any form of theater, a frame of offstage, real activity is transformed into one of staged being. But the conventions between the real and the staged differ. In the theatrical frame, the spatial boundaries of the stage are cut off from the real world (in the stereograph, the audience is also divorced from the action by time). Staged productions open up rooms to the audience by "removing" the ceiling and one wall. The difference between a staged drama and its stereographic counterpart, however, is crucial. Because the stereograph viewer enters into an activity in progress, he must be informed— that is, given situational cues, through devices such as pose, props, and location—in order to decode the scene. Conversely, the viewer also brings to the activity his cultural "decoder ring"—the sum knowledge of his social and cultural environment—that he shares with the creator of the scene.[33]

A late nineteenth-century comic stereograph, entitled "Bridget and the dev'lish mouse," may serve as an example of this process (fig. 12). A disrupted dinner is depicted: two armed men on all fours hunt for the culprit rodent; one woman claims the higher ground of the dining table and suffers from a severe case of dishabille. Notice, too, the potatoes scattered about the floor. Of course, the scene is humorous for the antics of the actors. But there is something more to this picture that we in the late twentieth century cannot readily apprehend but that our nineteenth-century counterparts easily could. The stereographer obviously knew the popular anecdote about the mistress and her new Irish maid. The mistress had instructed the maid, recognized as Irish by the use of the stereotypical name "Bridget" or "Biddy," to bring the potatoes to the dinner table undressed—that is, without the jacket skins. In a laughable misunderstanding of her mistress's orders, the *undressed* maid serves the potatoes—still "*dressed*" in their jackets—only to be upset by a mouse scurrying through the dining room.

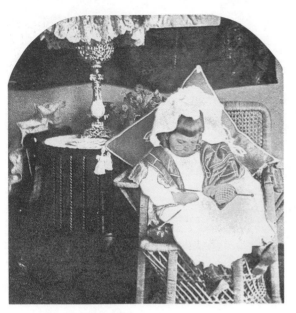

Fig. 10 "'Just Like Grandma Does'" (22).

Fig. 11 "'I Just Knew It Would Be a Boy'" (64).
T. W. Ingersoll, copyright 1898.

Obviously, the joke was widely known and underwent several permutations; in "Biddy and the Rat," for example, the potatoes are missing but the maid remains undressed (fig. 13). The situational cues—undressed maid, men armed with silverware, and baked potatoes—provide the stereograph viewer with evidence to reconstruct the story line—the totality of the assumptions and actions of the actors—encapsulated within one stereographic frame.

Thus, nothing in these stereograph scenes is insignificant—including the caption. In a theatrical performance, the script and the action provide the needed information. In the stereograph, the title or caption tenders information and orients the stereograph viewer toward a specific message based on the social conventions of the producer and consumer. The message, however, may be multivalent. "Bridget and the dev'lish mouse" amuses because of the antics of the actors, but the humor also relies on an unflattering ethnic stereotype that both articulated and reinforced Victorian ethnocentrism.[34]

In the Comic Series, the extended descriptive text found on the reverse of each stereograph serves both to introduce and to complete the action being depicted. The picture of

"Undressed Kids," for instance, tells little (fig. 14). The caption, however, contextualizes the image: "The miller's two grandchildren. His daughter their mother, came home with them for a visit, and on this hot day has decided to keep them as cool as possible. They are waiting for mama to superintend their bath in the millrace, of which they heard her talk so much on the way from town."

The extended prescriptive text on the reverse of each stereograph of the Comic Series reinforced prevailing Victorian behavior as the images simultaneously documented daily life. Yet that daily life was undergoing rapid change in fin de siècle America. Taken as a whole, the Comic Series presents the historian with a static and cohesive world view. Broken down into constituent parts of image, text, and audience, however, the tensions inherent in late Victorian culture become apparent.

There are no scenes of work or the work place in the Comic Series. Rather, the domestic sphere—the home and its seasonal extension, the family summer retreat from the city—provide the conceptual settings. It is useful to note here that the physical attributes of the ideal Victorian house served its inhabitants by dis-

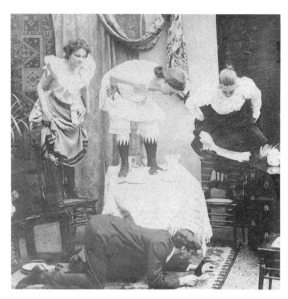

Fig. 12　"Bridget and the dev'lish mouse" (4527). C. H. Graves, copyright 1897.

Fig. 13　"Biddy and the Rat" (253). Webster & Albee, Publishers, Rochester, NY.

playing and reinforcing such virtues as sobriety, integrity, frugality, tidiness, comfort, and, of course, morality. As Simon Bronner and Kenneth L. Ames have noted, the arrangement of the house is a response to manners and customs and corresponds to perceived social needs. Front/back zones corresponding to a syntax of formal/informal, public/private spaces are evident in the physical layout of the typical Victorian house. The public rooms—parlor and dining room—used for entertaining and receiving guests and where the family gathered in the evening were located at the front of the house. The private rooms, such as the back parlor on the first floor but especially the second-story bedrooms, served family needs. Between these spaces was the hall, which mediated the spheres and preserved the intended functions and integrity of each. Finally, the production spaces located at the rear of the house—kitchen, back porch, back yard, and related work spaces—comprised an autonomous realm populated by servants. Within each of these spheres, certain rules applied to the types of persons, be they family, servants, or guests, interacting there. Against these domestic backgrounds and through play, ideal Victorian social roles were reinforced. Thus, in

the Comic Series, humorous or embarrassing situations occur when the decorum of a space is broken by a character normally not "seen" in that space, or when a character, through indecorous behavior, contradicts "correct" behaviors associated with a space.[35]

Because the Comic Series takes place in the domestic sphere, nearly all the images contain women and children. As may be expected, children's play is most often portrayed. Sometimes spontaneous and always sentimental, these stereographs convey a romanticized view of childhood. Children and pets are "playmates" and, as Mary Lynn Stevens Heininger has pointed out, references to children as "pet," "kitten," "lamb," "pup," and in similar terms became popular after 1850.[36] Children are portrayed as happy, innocent creatures whose play is natural and healthy (figs. 15 and 16).

Later childhood and adolescence (a new life-cycle stage "discovered" around 1910) are depicted as a period of learning to live in the adult world. Girls assume adult roles as caregivers and also, it seems, as ornaments. For both boys and girls, most formally posed scenes—that is, scenes in which the children acknowledge the camera's presence by assum-

Fig. 14 "Undressed Kids" (45). T. W. Ingersoll, copyright 1900.

Fig. 16 "Jealous Pets" (40). T. W. Ingersoll, copyright 1898.

Fig. 15 "Comrades. Maud and Max" (72).

ing a "public" demeanor—occur only in contexts in which they are deliberately play-acting adult roles. In "Brave Boys in Blue, Starting for Manila," for example, the young actors dressed in military uniforms indicate their awareness of the camera (the scene also conveys the nationalistic fervor brought by the Spanish-American War). Only young girls, by contrast, are put on display simply as themselves, preparing for their adult roles as ornaments to a scene (figs. 17 and 18).

On the other hand, males of all ages quite simply were allowed to be boys throughout their lives. To a certain extent, boys' mischief—and, for that matter, that of girls—was seen as normal and ultimately harmless in childhood. Getting caught skinny-dipping in a forbidden pond for the second time, the boy of " 'What Did I Tell You If I Caught You Again?' " will receive leniency from a sympathetic judge (fig. 19). Yet an adolescent boy could go too far—for instance, when he puts a toad in his mother's dresser drawer and thus must meet with the "Board of Education" (fig. 20). Adolescence was a trial-and-error learning period and, according to Heininger, in part formed the arena in which the battle for new social norms was fought.[37]

Boys' mischief, however, grew into men's mischief. In scenes of married life, drunken new husbands return home after a night out with the "boys" and are attended to by understanding, nurturing wives, who learned their roles early in life. Compare these scenes of mischief—the antics of the adolescent pair in

Fig. 17 "Brave Boys in Blue, Starting for Manila" (2). T. W. Ingersoll, copyright 1898.

Fig. 19 "'What Did I Tell You If I Caught You Again?'" (54). T. W. Ingersoll, copyright 1898.

Fig. 18 "'All Aboard'—A Big Wheelbarrow Load" (21). T. W. Ingersoll, copyright 1902.

Fig. 20 "The Special Meeting of the Board of Education" (75). T. W. Ingersoll, copyright 1902.

"Celebrating the Great and Glorious 4th of July" and "The Day After the 4th of July Celebration" and the action of the young married couple in "'Oh, My Dear, I'll Be Home Early'" and "2 A.M. And He Rolls in Quite Early" (figs. 21–24). Both designate prescribed roles: in the last scene, we learn that "she will put him to bed and pull off his boots, and in the morning she will appease his rebellious stomach with hot milk." Yet men's mischief had its limits: in "Mrs. Brown Returns; Unexpected," what is here a false analogy to mischievous— and therefore forgivable—behavior forms the basis of the text:

Fig. 21 "Celebrating the Great and Glorious 4th of July" (26[a]).

Fig. 23 "'Oh, My Dear, I'll Be Home Early'" (58[a]). T. W. Ingersoll, copyright 1898.

Fig. 22 "The Day After the 4th of July Celebration" (27[b]).

Fig. 24 "2 A.M. And He Rolls in Quite Early" (59[b]). T. W. Ingersoll, copyright 1898.

"Apples," said a learned judge, "were made for boys, and boys were made to eat apples. So if a boy cannot get a certain apple without stealing it, I will not punish him for taking it." But this is a different proposition, and the judge may not be learned, but she "knows the law," and is going to administer it with a strong and impartial hand. Her erring hubby will feel it on his cheek in a

second, and the girl will be out of the house in just five minutes. (Fig. 25)

The depiction of the private side of life—of retreat from public display and interaction—is an important feature of the series. The related concepts of "play" and "retreat" are themselves associated with the domestic sphere. For in-

Fig. 25 "Mrs. Brown Returns; Unexpected" (44). T. W. Ingersoll, copyright 1898.

Fig. 26 "Reducing the Surplus. 'Now, Pull Hard!'" (86). T. W. Ingersoll, copyright 1899.

stance, advice writers' recommendations of a female retreat from public display within the house and the responsibilities of entertaining and maintaining the household find actualization in the series. Nearly all the scenes of women are depicted to take place within the home, and a good number take place in the private spaces—the dressing rooms and bedrooms—in which women prepared for or repaired from public display. For example, "Reducing the Surplus. 'Now, Pull Hard!'" and "The Toilet Powder and Puff" detail the secrets of a "society belle," while the texts of "After the Ball Is Over" and "Dream After the Ball" tell of "victories" won through "thought and painstaking work . . . spen[t] in . . . preparations" (figs. 26–29).[38]

Men in the role of fathers—patriarchs—rarely appear in the series' images. They are in fact supplied by the text. Indeed, their role as provider for leisure consumption is made explicit while hidden from view. The text of "Hard at Play," for instance, characterizes play as an earned privilege, provided by the father:

These children have been very careful in selecting their parents. Their father is none of those shiftless men that spend all their earnings for drink

Fig. 27 "The Toilet Powder and Puff" (35[b]).

or betting on the ponies, and then marry some unfortunate, poor girl and live in two rooms in a back street where the children grow up among ash barrels and rubbish heaps. He did not pop the question until he had a fat salary and few thousands in government bonds and gilt edge mortgages, and the girl he chose had a fortune in her own right. Why shouldn't your children have the same privileges as these? (Fig. 30)

Fig. 28   "After the Ball Is Over" (38).

Fig. 30   "Hard at Play" (25).

Fig. 29   "Dream After the Ball" (97).

Single (read pre-patriarchal?) men do appear in courting scenes. Posing before people, or equipoise, an important tenet of Victorian culture, is the implicit subject of courting scenes. These scenes take place only in the summer in the series and depict secret trysts, in defiance of and humorous compliance with these social roles. Lovers are ever on guard against discovery. Thus, "Idle Hours With His

Summer Girl" (fig. 31) are interrupted (fig. 32, " 'Oh! Some One is Coming!' "); rendezvous occur in out-of-the-way places or are humorously betrayed. These actions defy contemporary etiquette manuals which warned young women against "compromising positions [that] are easily fallen into," cautioning them to be "constantly on . . . guard" and forbidding them from appearing in public places unescorted.[39] Women are warned against men who would prey on their virtue, and women are "possessed" by their beaux (note the point of view in the title "Idle Hours With *His* Summer Girl").

Did the Comic Series merely reinforce the paternalism that undergirded Victorian culture? At this point in the analysis, the answer appears to be "yes." The series' fascination with the domestic sphere is a paternalistic one, when paternalism is defined as a system in which an authority supplies needs and regulates conduct of those under its control. In practice, this authority asserted what was best and natural for those within its boundaries. Reciprocity was necessary and expected of those who received, and benefited from, paternal benevolence. As Sarah Josepha Hale, the editrix of *Godey's Lady's Book*, stated, "The

Fig. 31 "Idle Hours With His Summer Girl" (47[a]). T. W. Ingersoll, copyright 1899.

Fig. 32 " 'Oh! Some One is Coming!' " (48[b]). T. W. Ingersoll, copyright 1899.

province of the man, then, is to find the means—it is the duty of the woman to use these means in such a manner as will secure the best interests and purest enjoyments of the household with which she stands connected."[40] The home provided security from an increasingly turbulent and uncertain world, the ultimate retreat. "The Sultan's Favorite" recognized this "need" of women: "Say what you will about her being in a gilded cage, she doesn't feel that way. If you pity her, you may be sure that she reciprocates, if she ever hears about your way of living" (fig. 33).

This paternalism is also reinforced in the Comic Series through the "voice" of the texts. Although the images depict the breaking of rules or theretofore private or unmentionable events, the prescriptive text "traditionalizes" the contemporary image. The use of prescription—be it in the form of etiquette manuals, popular women's and domestic journals, or stereographs—was designed to alleviate the stress of social interaction and facilitate order. Prescriptive literature codified social behaviors, admonishing readers to adhere to and to maintain traditional values. Ironically, the formulaic nature of prescriptive literature impeded change at the same time as its tradi-

Fig. 33 "The Sultan's Favorite" (80). T. W. Ingersoll, copyright 1898.

tional function attempted to accommodate change. The Comic Series still retains the authoritarian—male—voice of didacticism in its instruction of social roles. The audience, comprehending these views by "hearing" the "traditional" voice of the text, elides the modern meaning rendered by the stereographic image alone. In other words, the subtle, often

Fig. 34 "Come to Grief" (66). T. W. Ingersoll, copyright 1898.

Fig. 35 " 'I Wonder If I Can Do It That Way?' " (88). T. W. Ingersoll, copyright 1899.

imperceptible, changes our late Victorian counterparts accepted as part of everyday life we today recognize as historical details of cultural change.[41]

A telling example is found in "Come to Grief," where Mrs. Brown has fallen off her bicycle (fig. 34). Bicycling, traditionally regarded as an activity reserved only for men, was not attempted by and considered acceptable for women until the turn of the century. Yet the text predicts that this fall will not be the last. The same pessimism is conveyed in " 'I Wonder If I Can Do It That Way?' " in which a novice female swimmer attempts the dive of the man whose feet we see. "His body formed a perfectly straight line as it shot into the water, and the lady wishes she might be able to go in as gracefully. She is going to try, and, of course, the first time she will strike the water as flat as a board and it will hurt" (fig. 35). These scenes of woman-as-athlete stand apart from other depictions of women in the series, although the commentary remains consistent. Humor is used to ridicule in these scenes only, apparently an effort to retain social control. Having yet to achieve mastery of "masculine" sports, these "New Women" are implicitly

chastised for their attempts, which visually chronicle the transition to new social roles.

Of course, one could argue that the Comic Series, as a family-oriented leisure commodity, needed to address multiple audiences. Images in advertisement for the series support this assessment. Illustrations of home life that accompanied descriptive ad copy recalled earlier prints of domestic life, like that of "The Morning Lesson," an 1876 frontispiece of *Godey's Lady's Book* (figs. 36 and 37), in which mothers perform traditional roles of instruction. Images apart from the texts appealed to younger children who could not read, while older children, with the approval of parents who purchased the series, learned social lessons from the texts. Yet something more fundamental occurs in these images, and it has to do with the "voice" of the texts which guided the way our Victorian counterparts viewed the images.

It is easy to forget that the Comic Series reached its popularity with the rise of mass amusements—Coney Island, vaudeville, nightclubs, and motion pictures—that eventually replaced the stereoscope and home-centered amusement in the twentieth century. Historians concerned with the transformation of

Fig. 36    Advertisement for stereoscopic views, "a most delightful entertainment," in Sears, Roebuck & Co. catalog (1908).

Fig. 37    "The Morning Lesson," frontispiece in *Godey's Lady's Book,* January 1876.

American culture at the turn of the century approach the problem by lumping together categories of ideas or objects to characterize synchronically a culture or era. More often than not, these historians are interested in the innovations—motion pictures provide a prime example—and how these innovations were accommodated to a culture. Sometimes we learn how these innovations displaced their traditional predecessors, which are themselves, however, most often simply ignored. Modern mass culture arose outside the home, and Victorians simply surrendered their long-cherished ideals and changed their lives to accommodate the new social mores. But we know from lived experience that cultural change is never rapid, and never complete. Innovative ideas, usually viewed as having a forward thrust, effect lateral changes as well, causing both contradiction and compromise.[42]

The inherent contradiction and compromise of the Comic Series lie not only between image and text, but between the lived realities of the creator/viewer and image-as-ideal as well. Remember that men-as-patriarchs do not appear in these images but are provided by the texts. Although we know little about the creation of the texts, we do know that at least two owners, Ben Kilburn of Kilburn Brothers, and B. L. Singley, the founder of the Keystone View Company, composed the texts and captions for their companies' stereographs. William C. Darrah notes that these captions reflected "personal patriotic, religious and moral values."[43] Given what we know about the nineteenth-century photography industry (for example, women were, as a rule, hired only as factory labor to manufacture stereographs) and about the nature of the work force in general, we may assume that the author(s) of the Comic Series texts and the photographer(s) were male.

If men created these images, why did they choose to portray the domestic sphere? More important, why did they choose humorous domestic scenes that broke the traditional social rules (rules that, from our late twentieth-century perspective, favored men), even as the prescriptive texts maintained them? The reason may have been the wish to attract multiple audiences, including one for which motion pictures and the affordability of cameras created competition for this pastime. Comic stereographs as a genre achieved their greatest popularity after 1898, coinciding with the rise and commercialization of motion pictures. The early "shorts" presented audiences with the same subjects as the stereoscope had. Many of the scenes of domestic life in which children and women are playing are presented in a style similar to the "snapshot aesthetic." In essence, these images present individual frames of action that necessitate a storyline to complete the action. Whereas short movies completed stories by portrayal, stereographs could not. Competition with nickelodeons may have been at least a partial spur for the modern and humorous subjects for the stereograph. In this case, the Comic Series is a compromise product, attracting audiences with modern pictures and traditional viewpoints.

The year 1898 also marked a reintroduction, of sorts, of the picture postcard and the beginnings of a card collection craze that lasted until 1915. Before 1898 the United States Post Office had retained control of postcard printing and rates. Private postcard printing was allowed, but the card was considered a letter and rated as such if inscribed. Congress in 1898 authorized the extension of the postcard rate to privately printed cards on which messages were confined to the view side of the card, and in 1906 that body also authorized messages on one-half of the address side of the card.

Postcards, benefiting also from the multicolor lithoprint process, were framed and hung as works of art in parlors, and, importantly, were collected and saved in albums. Many postcard series were numbered to abet the collecting craze. This "Postal Carditis," as one commentator dubbed it, no doubt also influenced the decision of major stereograph companies to retain their market and take advantage of the collecting craze by offering numbered sets, especially those of American and foreign scenery.[44]

Competition alone, however, does not provide a sufficient reason for the creation and popular reception of comic stereograph views.

The domestic sphere and all its components—retreat, women, children—represented the most cherished ideals of American Victorian culture. That the family and home were perceived as disintegrating was a matter of public record and grave concern. The choice of domestic subject matter parallels to some degree the work of social reform photographers in urban slums. The well-known work of Jacob Riis, in *How the Other Half Lives* (1890), provides an interesting benchmark for the way in which middle-class domestic life was portrayed in the Comic Series. Middle-class life was not invaded by the camera in the series as New York tenement life was in Riis's work, where both class and ethnic lines were crossed; the middle class was too near and accessible. The realism that Riis, or William Dean Howells, or Hamlin Garland sought was present in the images of the set. And social concerns—shared by both mothers and fathers—were still present: in "'Look at the F[r]oggies,'" for example, the viewer is reminded that "parks are more necessary for a healthy development of our children than schools, at least in a large city where the child is shut out from the beneficent influences of nature" (see fig. 9). These images served to reinforce the work ethic and consequent good fortune (and, incidentally, the increasingly suburban location) of the middle class. "How much one such day would mean to a poor boy all through his life!" reads the caption of "'Say, but This Is Fun!'" "You man of wealth, would you like to see such ecstasy in reality? Give the children of your poor neighbor a similar outing and earn their undying gratitude! It will do you as much good as them" (fig. 38). The paternalistic voice of the series' text is that of early twentieth-century Progressive reform. In fact, it may be better termed a "public" voice, one that was traditionally male and one that still adhered to the Victorian hortative style of oratory and authorship.

Yet the Comic Series used humor through images as a lens in which to promote a classic form of self-criticism. Perhaps such a close examination of middle-class life could only take place within the displaced realm of comic play. The viewer sees his or her counterparts with their "hair down," even catching them with their "pants down." What is presented in the set is a critical mirror of the late Victorian in the process of reevaluation. And that critical mirror contains a male reflection of self and the world. The paternalistic voice of the didactic texts leads the viewer into these domestic scenes, scenes that presented familiar and comfortable surroundings and activities. The camera is allowed to intrude—or rather is invited—into the private spaces of the house, the private lives of the typical American Victorian. The subjects of the camera do not "mind" the camera's presence. Women in boudoirs are not shocked or surprised by the camera's presence; children play in serene self-absorption, unfearful of a strange camera. Very much like the benevolent father figure—the ideal of Victorian manhood—who is at the same time at the center and periphery of the domestic sphere, the camera enters into rooms freely and familiarly.[45]

The disintegration of the sociospatial spheres within the Victorian house, suggested by the camera's and the viewer's access into private spaces—and manifested after 1890 in housing reform and in new house forms such as the bungalow—allows the viewer also to gain an understanding of the private side of character. And despite the prescriptive social norms implied by the text, the image is conveyed in a presentation of self in many cases theretofore unseen in the modern medium of photography. Short stories structured around the custom of women looking under the bed for intruders before retiring had first appeared in popular journals at midcentury.[46] This popular tale of a man found under a woman's bed, when recorded in the Comic Series, however, provided a visual and literary conceit in which to consider public and private behaviors: "When suddenly confronted by one of the perplexing problems of life, our true nature asserts itself, and we act regardless of the character in which we are accustomed to pose before people" (fig. 39).

Fig. 38    "Say, but This Is Fun!" (13).

This preoccupation with the self, Warren Susman has noted, provides evidence of a cultural shift, in this case from the Victorian modal type of "character" to the modern "personality." Ideas of a new self-consciousness developed in late nineteenth-century American society, a society well aware of the fundamental change underway. This process of objectification and analysis was manifested in the sudden spate of "how-to" personality literature after 1900. These manuals, adopting the traditional form of etiquette and household advice manuals, now stressed self-development over societal and moral imperatives and urged improvement that could best be achieved in leisure time.[47]

The Victorian idea of home and vacation as retreat, as explored in the Comic Series, may also be seen as a psychic retreat from the public self. The exploration of the sociospatial spheres within the house countered the widening distance between work and home, between the public self and the private, and between the family and the individual. Concern for this growing and widely perceived dilemma is echoed in "Reflection. Told by the Glass": "Everybody has three characters: There is your real one, the one you wish other people to

Fig. 39  "'A Man! At Last, a Man!'" (68[b]). T. W. Ingersoll, copyright 1899.

Fig. 40  "Reflection. Told by the Glass" (85). Copyrighted, 1898, by T. W. Ingersoll.

think you possess, and the one these other people ascribe to you. If the two first named are nearly identical, the third will not vary much from them, but most people are more or less hypocrites" (fig. 40).

The social role demanded of all in the new culture of personality, argued Susman, was that of a performer, who made the most of his or her physical appearance, wit, and charm. It was within leisure time—time off, play—and the domestic sphere that the evolution of the modern self could take place. (Indeed, every definition of "play" in the *Oxford English Dictionary* is referenced in this series.) Scenes of rejuvenation through play and glimpses of private realms, in which people revealed their "true" selves, offered Americans a new but familiar mirror in which to view themselves. The need for retreat was essentially one of self-preservation; this introspective act fueled the search for an all-purpose identity which made use of once-private behaviors and, more importantly, acknowledged these behaviors. To go, hesitantly, one step further: that act of introspection was a necessary one for American men in the attempt to adjust to new roles demanded by the concomitant changes in the

roles of women and of children, and in the nature of the marketplace.

The distinctive attributes of a Victorian world view conveyed in the Comic Series—the paternalistic voice, the emphasis on domestic subjects—suggest that many late-century Americans were not turning en masse to modern amusements. The Victorian ideals associated with the domestic sphere were displaced to a world of images and texts constructed for leisure instruction. The tensions apparent in the real world were safely articulated and negotiated in the paper world of the Comic Series. Yet that world, depicted through the "objective" medium of photography, was once action taking place in front of a camera lens. The very facts that actors and actresses were willing to re-create private moments and that an audience could view these point to a new, if somewhat hesitant, relaxation of social mores, permissible in one conceptual "place"—the play of the domestic sphere—but apprehended through traditional means—the lenses of the stereoscope. Stereographs of characters involved in self-*re*-creation provide historians with clues to the roots of modernist culture.

The Comic Series, then, in revealing the implicit nature of photography to be "truthful" despite the "traditionalization" of the images through text, chronicles the tensions of late Victorian culture. Play was hard work, indeed.

## Notes

1. Charles Dickens quoted in William C. Darrah, *The World of Stereographs* (Gettysburg: Times and News Publishing Co., 1977), 5; Vogel quoted in Edward W. Earle, ed., *Points of View: The Stereograph in America—A Cultural History* (Rochester, NY: Visual Studies Workshop, 1979), 60.

2. For figures see Darrah, *World of Stereographs*, 6 (I've used a more conservative estimate than Darrah, who has placed the number at six million). For estimates, see also Richard N. Masteller, "Western Views in Eastern Parlors: The Contribution of the Stereograph Photographer to the Conquest of the West," *Prospects* 6 (1981): 55–71.

3. On Victorian culture in general, see Daniel Walker Howe, "American Victorianism as a Culture," *American Quarterly* 27 (December 1975): 507–32. Studies of Victorian culture and the domestic sphere include Karen Halttunen, *Confidence Men and Painted Women: A Study of Middle-Class Culture in America, 1830–1870* (New Haven: Yale University Press, 1982); Katherine C. Grier, *Culture and Comfort: People, Parlors, and Upholstery, 1850–1930* (Rochester, NY: The Strong Museum, 1988); Marilyn Ferris Motz and Pat Browne, eds., *Making the American Home: Middle-Class Women and Domestic Material Culture, 1840–1940* (Bowling Green, OH: Bowling Green State University Popular Press, 1988). The origins of the ideology of domesticity are delineated in Kathryn Kish Sklar, *Catharine Beecher: A Study in American Domesticity* (New York: Norton, 1976). The transition in America from a Victorian to a modernist culture is analyzed in Alan Trachtenberg, *The Incorporation of America: Culture and Society in the Gilded Age* (New York: Hill and Wang, 1982); Robert Wiebe, *The Search for Order, 1880–1920* (New York: Hill and Wang, 1967); T. J. Jackson Lears, *No Place of Grace: Antimodernism and the Transformation of American Culture* (New York: Pantheon Books, 1981); and Warren I. Susman, *Culture as History: The Transformation of American Society in the Twentieth Century* (New York: Pantheon Books, 1984).

I use the term "modernist" to refer to early twentieth-century culture for the simple fact that every culture, every age, perceives itself as "modern."

4. For a synopsis of the material culture approach to American civilization, consult Thomas J. Schlereth, ed. and comp., *Material Culture Studies in America* (Nashville: American Association for State and Local History, 1982).

5. As Peter Plagens has written about current photography, "photography is inevitably an uneasy combination of objectivity (a mechanical and chemical imprint of the real world) and subjectivity (the loves and hates swirling in the photographer's soul)." The case is no different for photography of another era. ("Into the Fun House," *Newsweek,* 21 August 1989, 52.)

6. "Home," *Frank Leslie's New Family Magazine,* January 1859, 91. The concept of home has an interesting history and is related to the origins of the middle class: see Witold Rybczynski, *Home: A Short History of an Idea* (New York: Penguin Books, 1987).

7. Quoted in Clifford Edward Clark, Jr., *The American Family Home, 1800–1960* (Chapel Hill: University of North Carolina Press, 1986), 36. *Scribner's Monthly*'s (hereafter cited as *SM*) "Home and Society" column carried suggestions for family-centered winter and summer amusements: "Parlor Games," *SM,* April 1871, 678–79; "Two New Parlor Games," *SM,* February 1872, 495–96; "Acting Rhymes," *SM,* February 1875, 507–8; "The Children's Hour," *SM,* August 1875, 316–17; "A Family Journal," *SM,* March 1876, 745; "Woman's Winter Amusements," *SM,* November 1877, 125–27; "A Successful Experiment," *SM,* June 1878, 293–94; "Parlor Plays," *SM,* October 1879, 939–40.

8. The most cited article on "woman's sphere" is Barbara Welter, "The Cult of True Womanhood: 1820–1860," *American Quarterly* 18 (Summer 1966): 151–74. Linda K. Kerber's "Separate Spheres, Female Worlds, Woman's Place: The Rhetoric of Women's History," *Journal of American History* 75, 1 (June 1988): 9–39, discusses the use of the metaphor "separate spheres."

9. *American Journal of Photography,* 1 August 1859, 82. Also quoted in William Welling, *Photography in America: The Formative Years, 1839–1900* (New York: Thomas Y. Crowell Co., 1978), 12.

10. Quoted in Earle, *Points of View,* 9.

11. Robert A. Sobieczek and Odette M. Appel, *The Spirit of Fact: The Daguerreotypes of Southworth and Hawes, 1843–1862* (Boston: David R. Godine and International Museum of Photography, 1976), xvii–xix. See also Robert Taft, *Photography and the American Scene* (1938; reprint, New York: Dover Publications, 1964), 178.

12. The notion that the photograph form captured a piece of reality was debated in the early years of the invention. See Richard Rudisill, *Mirror Image: The Influence of the Daguerreotype on American Society* (Albuquerque: University of New Mexico Press,

1971). Oliver Wendell Holmes, "The Stereoscope and the Stereograph," *Atlantic Monthly,* June 1859, 738–48, offers a clue to the contemporary reaction to the instrument and the illusion of three-dimensionality.

13. Visual literacy includes instruction not only in and through seeing, but in drawing: see Diana Korzenik, *Drawn to Art: A Nineteenth-Century Dream* (Hanover, NH, and London: University Press of New England, 1985); and Peter C. Marzio, *The Art Crusade: An Analysis of American Drawing Manuals, 1820–1860* (Washington, DC: Smithsonian Institution Press, 1976). Thomas Eakins, like all students at Philadelphia's Central High School, was required to take drawing as part of the curriculum and used Rembrandt Peale's *Graphics,* first published in 1834 and reprinted several times: see Elizabeth Johns, "Drawing Instruction at Central High School and Its Impact on Thomas Eakins," *Winterthur Portfolio* 15, 2 (Summer 1980): 139–50.

14. "The Picture System of Education," *Common School Assistant* (New York, May 1839), 1, quoted in Earle, *Points of View,* 11.

15. "The Home-Uses of the Exhibition," *SM,* May 1876, 127; "The Exhibition as a School," *SM,* July 1876, 438.

16. Holmes, "The Stereoscope and the Stereograph," 747. For the development of the stereoscope, consult Sir David Brewster, *The Stereoscope: Its History, Theory and Construction* (London: John Camden Hotten, 1870); Darrah, *World of Stereographs,* 1–5; Harold F. Jenkins, *Two Points of View: A History of the Parlor Stereoscope* (Elmira, NY: World in Color Productions, 1957); and Roy W. Mabie, *The Stereoscope and Stereograph* (New York: privately printed, 1942).

A word about early photograph forms: the daguerreotype, perfected in 1839, was a positive print on a polished, silver-coated copperplate. In the 1850s, several other materials and processes were developed, all leading to the overall success of the medium. The cheap ambrotype and tintype, both positive prints on (respectively) glass, the reverse surface of which was painted black or purple, and japanned tin, were edged out when the negative printing process, which could produce multiple images on treated paper, was introduced later in the same decade.

17. Because Holmes never patented this stereoscope, the simply designed instrument was easily copied and manufactured by others, leading to greater availability to Americans.

18. Kenneth L. Ames, "Meaning in Artifacts: Hall Furnishings in Victorian America," *Journal of American Culture* 3, 4 (Winter 1980): 619–41; Grier, *Cul-ture and Comfort,* 154–62, 256–59 (in which Grier discusses the portière as a "stage curtain" of the parlor).

19. "Odd Minutes of Waiting," *SM,* February 1874, 500.

20. "Huldah the Help. A Thanksgiving Story," *SM,* December 1870, 189–96.

21. "Killing Time," *SM,* September 1874, 627.

22. This constellation of objects, read as an entity, gives meaning to the individual objects that comprise it. Grant McCracken discusses this "Diderot unity"–"highly consistent complements of consumer goods"–in *Culture and Consumption: New Approaches to the Symbolic Character of Consumer Goods and Activities* (Bloomington and Indianapolis: Indiana University Press, 1988). See especially chap. 8, "Diderot Unities and the Diderot Effect: Neglected Cultural Aspects of Consumption," 118–29.

23. *Decorum; a Practical Treatise on Etiquette and Dress of the Best American Society* (New York: Union Publishing House, 1879), 49.

24. "Some of the Modern Appliances of Photography," *Photographic Times* (1 March 1871): 33. See also Oliver Wendell Holmes, "Sun-Painting and Sun-Sculpture; With a Stereoscopic Trip Across the Atlantic," *Atlantic Monthly,* July 1861, 13–29.

25. Austin Abbott, "The Eye and the Camera," *Harper's New Monthly Magazine,* July 1869, 482.

26. *Anthony's Photographic Bulletin,* December 1872, 766, quoted in Earle, *Points of View,* 50.

27. See Howard S. Becker, *Art Worlds* (Berkeley: University of California Press, 1982), 315–18, 322–26, 328–29, 334–39, 349–50; and Becker, "Stereographs: Local, National and International Art Worlds," in Earle, *Points of View,* 89–96. For a history of the industry, see Reese V. Jenkins, *Images and Enterprise: The Technology and the American Photographic Industry, 1839–1925* (Baltimore: Johns Hopkins University Press, 1975).

28. See Darrah, *World of Stereographs,* 53–56.

29. For a brief discussion of the Keystone View Company's educational sets, see ibid., 49–50.

30. M. A. Root, *The Camera and the Pencil* (1864), 445–49, quoted in Darrah, *World of Stereographs,* 59.

31. Catalog, Sears, Roebuck and Company (1905), 367–69.

32. Holmes, quoted in Earle, *Points of View,* 14.

33. Erving Goffman, "The Theatrical Frame," chap. 5 in *Frame Analysis: An Essay on the Organization of Experience* (New York: Harper Colophon Books, 1974), 123–55.

34. For discussions of the problems in reconstructing cultural meanings in photographs, consult

Allan Sekula, "The Traffic in Photographs," *Art Journal* 41, 1 (Spring 1981): 15–25; and Alan Trachtenberg, "Albums of War: On Reading Civil War Photographs," *Representations* 9 (Winter 1985): 1–32. I have utilized here Roland Barthes' formulation. According to Barthes, the relation of the text to its image is twofold. First, he writes, "the text most often simply amplifies a set of connotations already given in the photograph"; second, it invents "an entirely new signified which is retroactively projected into the image, so much so as to appear denotated there." Quoted in Earle, *Points of View,* 14.

35. Simon J. Bronner, "Manner Books and Suburban Houses: The Structure of Tradition and Aesthetics," *Winterthur Portfolio* 18 (Spring 1983): 61–68; Kenneth L. Ames, "Meaning in Artifacts"; and Clark, "Dreams and Realities," chap. 2 in *American Family Home,* 37–71. For a full discussion of front and back regions, consult Erving Goffman, *The Presentation of Self in Everyday Life* (Garden City: Doubleday, 1959), chap. 3; also see Halttunen's application of Goffman's thesis in *Confidence Men and Painted Women,* 104–5.

36. Mary Lynn Stevens Heininger, "Children, Childhood, and Change in America, 1820–1920," in Heininger et al., *A Century of Childhood, 1820–1920* (Rochester, NY: Margaret Woodbury Strong Museum, 1984), 15.

37. Ibid., 26–28.

38. One cannot help noticing the prurient quality of these stereographic images of women in their boudoirs. In fact, when I gave this paper in an abbreviated form at the American Studies Association meeting (hereafter cited as ASA) in New York in 1987, members of the audience could not help commenting (in discussions after the session) on this fact over and over again. For those who argue that I am missing the point here, a word about process is in order. When I set out to research and write an essay on the stereoscope as pastime, I chose the Comic Series as an example because it depicted implicit and explicit definitions of "play" and fit well Johan Huizinga's analysis of play in *Homo Ludens: A Study of the Play-Element in Culture* (1949; reprint, Boston: Beacon Press, 1967). I assumed a popular reception for comic views based on the number of images and on the popularity of later stock vaudeville and early motion picture characterizations. Thus my analysis elides the issues of ideology and power that currently interest historians.

Edith Mayo (National Museum of American History) and James Curtis (University of Delaware), panel commentators at the ASA, suggested that these private scenes allowed for the actualization of "safe"

Victorian prurient interests. This, too, assumes a male gaze. Because I had been thinking about *how* the Comic Series used the concept of *play,* I ignored the ideational aspects at the point of creation in these images, a process the implications of which I can only hint at in this essay.

39. The overwhelming number of etiquette manuals published in the nineteenth century gave this advice. For a synopsis of these advice books, see Arthur M. Schlesinger, *Learning How to Behave: A Historical Study of American Etiquette Books* (1946; reprint, New York: Cooper Square Publishers, 1968).

40. Quoted in Clark, *American Family Home,* 32. See also a woman's role in the creation of domesticity in Sklar, *Catharine Beecher.*

41. I wish to thank Karin Calvert and Katherine C. Grier for pointing out the implications of the formulaic and repetitive nature of nineteenth-century prescriptive literature. The idea that texts may simultaneously conform and betray a cultural ideology (such as domesticity) was made clear to me in Joanne Dobson, "The Hidden Hand: Subversion of Cultural Ideology in Three Mid-Nineteenth-Century American Women's Novels," *American Quarterly* 38 (Summer 1986): 223–42. See, of course, Jane Tompkins, *Sensational Designs: The Cultural Work of American Fiction, 1790–1860* (New York: Oxford University Press, 1985); and Janice A. Radway, *Reading the Romance: Women, Patriarchy, and Popular Literature* (Chapel Hill and London: University of North Carolina Press, 1984).

42. For the rise of modern mass culture, see Lewis A. Erenberg, *Steppin' Out: New York Nightlife and the Transformation of American Culture, 1890–1930* (Chicago: University of Chicago Press, 1981); Lary May, *Screening Out the Past: The Birth of Mass Culture and the Motion Picture Industry* (Chicago: University of Chicago Press, 1980), especially chaps. 1 and 2; and John F. Kasson, *Amusing the Million: Coney Island at the Turn of the Century* (New York: Hill and Wang, 1978).

43. Darrah, *World of Stereographs,* 49.

44. Steve Dotterrer and Galen Cranz, "The Picture Postcard: Its Development and Role in American Urbanization," *Journal of American Culture* 5 (Spring 1982): 44–50.

45. As Peter G. Filene argues, "The men were more than carpenters of the pedestal and then audience to its occupants. They played their own roles in the drama of the sexes—as sons, husbands, fathers, or simply men. No one was off stage." See *Him/Her/Self,* 2d ed. (Baltimore: Johns Hopkins University Press, 1986), 69. The "woman question" mandated a reconsideration and reconfiguration of manhood as

well. Filene continues: "The concept of manliness was suffering strain in all its dimensions—in work and success, in family patriarchy, and in the area that Victorian Americans did not discuss aloud, sexuality" (69–70).

46. "Looking Under the Bed," *Harper's New Monthly Magazine,* November 1866, 789–92.
47. Susman, " 'Personality' and the Making of Twentieth-Century Culture," in *Culture as History,* 271–86, especially 273.

# Ladies of Leisure

Domestic Photography in the Nineteenth Century

MADELYN MOELLER

"Photography combines the exactness of scientific truth with the keen pleasure of artistic effort," Catharine Weed Barnes wrote in "Photography from a Woman's Standpoint" in the January 1890 issue of *American Amateur Photographer*. Barnes, soon to be an editor of this magazine, was an ardent promoter of photography as an ideal recreation for women. "I cannot speak too strongly as to a woman's taking up photography; it has far more in its favor than many of the so-called 'fads' devised to kill time."[1] She was right—photography afforded middle- and upper-class women excellent opportunities to expand their domestic sphere after 1880. Faced with an unprecedented amount of leisure time—time that was expected to be consumed in prescribed rituals that bespoke the acceptance of a certain framework of social values—the more adventurous women capitalized on this new recreation. Photography was not only challenging; it contained creativity lacking in other endeavors, such as needlework and other "hearth" crafts. It also enabled women to emerge from the physical confines of the home. Like other forms of recreation, such as biking, tennis, golf, and dancing, photography broke gender barriers, and the enthusiasm with which women embraced it exemplifies their changing role in America at this time.

Becoming a photographer was a deliberate choice, the way one chose to spend leisure time. Recreational photography fulfilled creative needs, and the photographs in turn reflected the world view of their maker.[2] Photography provided the means by which talented adventurous women consciously used the domestic ideology of the time to emerge from their private world and enter into the public arenas usually reserved for men. From this perspective, the artistic values and the aesthetic quality of the pictures they produced are of relatively less interest than how the role of women in photography became socially acceptable, how they learned the science of the process, and how the subjects of their images reflect the prevailing cultural ideology.

Under the semblance of domesticity, photography allowed these women to emerge from a private world into a quite different public space. Barnes was thirty-seven years old and an unmarried lady of means when she took up photography. She was atypical in the degree to which she became involved with the medium, but her personal background is exemplary of those women who pursued photography for its recreational and artistic benefits. Her friends initially considered her interest in the medium only "a craze." For Barnes, however, photography became something considerably more than a pastime as she was thrust into the limelight through her published images and columns on photography. "I have gained a broad appreciation of the world," she observed.[3] So, too, did other "ladies of refinement" who chose a camera and makeshift darkroom over needlework or other domestic crafts.

Photography and domesticity were compatible—one could dabble in photography while at home caring for children or others. The same qualities desirable in a fine photographer were those necessary to operate a well-managed household—"rigid attention to cleanliness, [with a] delicacy of manipulation and patience."[4] With no perceived duties beyond the domestic circle, women had more time to "easily attend to the duties of the dark room."[5] They made the best of primitive conditions. Women contributors to *American Amateur Photographer* told how bathrooms, empty closets, and kitchen corners could be adapted to darkroom work. Catharine Barnes was one of only a few with a regular studio. When first experimenting with a camera, women turned to their immediate world and recorded a literal view of their home life. The camera soon became a vehicle, however, to extend oneself beyond the domestic realm. Women quickly moved away from the traditional concentration on the home and began to record real life on the streets and in the fields as well as the family and recreational activities. They also pursued other themes with their photographs—the posed genre scene or artistic creation. Although they began with naive images of home interiors, women soon created skillful scenes and experimented with light and multiple images, and they expected their photographs to compete with those composed and taken by men. The ratio of women to men involved with this recreation is unknown, but the number of extant collections by women and the quantity of published articles and photographs by them in photographic journals is indicative of their extensive participation in this new recreation.[6] Whether their photographic self-expression concentrated on straight documentary shots or on pictorial images, photography was seen as a respectable domestic activity while at the same time it provided a release from domesticity.

Significant advances in the photographic process in the late 1870s enticed both men and women into experimenting with recording and preserving images of their everyday lives. The introduction of commercially prepared dry-plate glass negatives provided the means for the amateur to pursue what up to that time had been mostly a commercial endeavor (fig. 1). Unlike the individually prepared wet plate that required immediate developing in a portable darkroom, this manufactured glass plate carried a gelatin that was ready to be exposed and could be developed days or months later. It eliminated the immediate need for messy chemicals away from home or studio. Developing and printing still required a degree of proficiency, but the process was far more forgiving than the wet plate process was. Its appearance coincided with the phenomenal growth of a leisured class in America, those people who had the extra time and money to spend on entertainment.

George Eastman is appropriately associated with the mass marketing and tremendous growth of photography for the general public. After several failed attempts to market his new flexible film for the commercial market, in 1888 Eastman introduced a "key conceptual change" in who "was to practice photography"—he decided to "reach the general public and create a new class of patrons."[7] Eastman popularized photography—his "new class of patrons" was hobbyists, not serious amateurs, who produced records of their travels and families which required no skill and minimum financial investment. Eastman's new camera was reasonably priced, and the buyer simply pushed the button, returned the camera intact

Fig. 1 Alice Austen's maid washing photographic prints at the pump in the Austen yard, about 1886. Even with the recent advances in photographic technology, the Austens' lack of indoor plumbing challenged the amateur photographer. Courtesy Staten Island Historical Society.

to Eastman's company, and received by return mail the developed pictures and the camera reloaded with new film. The serious amateur may have experimented with flexible film but continued primarily to use glass negatives and large cameras on tripods.

Many women photographers were serious amateurs. They were not hobbyists, those people using Eastman's Kodak, nor were they professionals, the men and women with studios whose major income came from their photographic skills. The serious amateur shared a characteristic of the novice in that she chose photography as a leisurely hobby, but, like the professional, she desired the superior quality produced from using glass plates. These amateurs also sought the challenge of doing their own developing and printing and often pre-

pared their own papers. They were amateur only in the sense that they did not support themselves through their photographic efforts—each had sufficient means and leisure time to pursue photography as a recreational and artistic hobby.

Amateur photography evolved earlier in Victorian England than it did in America. The introduction of a perfected photographic process was made by Louis Jacques Mandé Daguerre before the French Academy of Sciences in January 1839 and almost simultaneously in England by W. H. Fox Talbot.[8] Both Daguerre and Talbot were anxious to protect the patent rights for their inventions and required practitioners to be licensed in most countries. Therefore, in England, the majority of those working from the earliest introduction of photography in 1839 through the 1850s were amateurs, not commercial photographers. But having retained the patent right for his process in England, Daguerre did not retain these rights in America. As a result, American entrepreneurs used the daguerreotype process to make a fast dollar recording the likenesses of thousands. People who were unable to afford painted portraits could afford a photograph. While the cost of equipment was not beyond reach, few Americans had the leisure time necessary for such a hobby and so photography remained almost solely a commercial enterprise. In England, on the other hand, there was an enlightened monied aristocratic class who could afford to purchase a license from either Daguerre's or Talbot's agents and to buy the equipment necessary to dabble in the new art/science. American commercial photographers of the 1850s are remembered mostly for their superior daguerreotype portraits, whereas British amateur photographers produced images of landscapes and monuments and casual photographs of their families and friends, usually by Talbot's paper negative-positive process.[9] Despite the success of photographic business ventures in America, the amateur photographer did not appear on the American scene to any noticeable extent until the 1880s.

Amateur photography was part of the mass commercialization of leisure after the Civil War. Information on where to buy equipment and how to take, develop, and print photographs appeared in magazines directed at both male and female audiences. Manufacturers of photographic materials quickly realized the enormous market potential in appealing to women at home with leisure time. The image of a woman with a camera was a central feature both in the advertising of the photographic products and for the promotion of leisure itself.[10] A popular image was a woman in ruffled constricting garments, with her hat set at a proper angle, standing behind a camera on a tripod, which not only associated women with operating a camera but also indicated that photography could be practiced

with ease. The Scovill Manufacturing Company also explicitly directed much of its advertising to women, noting in one of its annual photographic manuals that "here, as well as abroad, amateur photography is destined to be taken up by Ladies of refinement and quick artistic perception."[11] Other journals and magazines praised Scovill's contribution for making the hobby available to so many.[12]

Popular magazines, in particular *American Amateur Photographer,* were open to publishing the work of and articles by women. The percentage of female subscribers to these journals is not known, but much of the material was directed at them. Photographic magazines made a major contribution to expanding the available information and encouraging women to participate in this increasingly popular activity. Fifteen of the first thirty-six frontispieces in *American Amateur Photographer* were photographs by women, nine of them by Catharine Weed Barnes.[13] These ladies were competing with some of the best-known photographic luminaries of the time, Alfred Stieglitz and Rudolf Eickelmeyer, Jr., whose work also appeared. The photographic work by women prominently displayed in a leading journal became an inspiration for women working at home on arts and crafts knickknacks made to decorate the home. They, too, could create an aesthetically pleasing "picture" *and* develop and print it with a degree of expertise.

Although the manufacturers of cameras and equipment recognized the vast female market and directed much of their advertising toward them, and although women's publications also provided rudimentary instructions, most women actually learned the basics of photography from a male relative. The instructions in ladies books and journals are similar to the advice and patterns on producing other crafts in these journals—they lack depth and often are very vague. They read like recipes of the period, and the details are seldom exact or true. In the 1880s the help and encouragement of another photographer was usually needed in order for a beginner to understand the most fundamental requirements.[14] Women learning the fine points of photography from a male relative shared a similarity with female artists; as other forms of apprenticeship were denied them, they profited from their study with kin.[15]

By 1884 there were numerous flourishing and growing photographic societies, but initially only a few—those in Pittsburgh, Chicago, and New York—admitted women.[16] Most were considered male smoking clubs. Catharine Barnes, the leading woman contributor to *American Amateur Photographer* and within a year of its founding its assistant editor, maintained that these societies were "indispensable to real progress" and beginning in 1889 wrote on the right of women to enter these private clubs. Having been denied admission in her hometown of Albany, she eventually joined the New York society. One of her earlier articles in *American Amateur Photographer* concerned "Why Ladies Should Be Admitted to Membership in Photographic Societies." Women were refused admission not because of the quality of their work but because of their sex, Barnes argued. Because women obviously could not subject themselves to "cigars and earthy language," they were denied new knowledge of the scientific and artistic improvements available to men. Although some cities had clubs specifically for women, Barnes was against this arrangement. She also wanted photographs by women to be judged competitively with those taken by men.[17] "Let no ladies thrust aside [from joining societies] think it best to organize a society of their own. This may be considered independence, but it is far wiser to join a club that allows them to win their way by fair competition," she wrote in December 1889.[18]

Club-sponsored photographic competition divided categories into specific and challenging topics for the men but simply "Woman's Work" for the women. Barnes was particularly adamant in arguing against this division. "The day is coming," she wrote, "where the question will be asked of any photographic work—'Is it well done?'"[19] Other contributors to *American Amateur Photographer*, both male and female,

also urged female participation in photographic societies.[20] As local clubs allowed women into membership, the classifications for judging competitions became only topical, without division between sexes; by the end of the century, competition was no longer gender-specific.

Acceptance into men's clubs and equal recognition in competitions were major achievements for those women seeking activities beyond the domestic sphere, but these circumstances could not have come about if venturing about with a camera and spending time in a darkroom had not already come to be viewed as an acceptable activity for women. Middle- and upper-class women used their leisure time in the context of domesticity. The proliferation of printed material during this period provided the "gentler sex" with a vast array of ideas and specific instructions on socially acceptable ways to fill their days. Books and magazines on ladies' fancy work, aimed at enriching home adornment, were common by the 1870s. For example, the preface of *Ladies' Fancy Work, Hints and Helps to Home Taste and Recreations*, published in 1876, states that the purpose of the text is to improve home life while providing recreation. The attractive little pleasures made by women in the home would "make the Little Rhealm [sic] more enticing."[21] A general survey of women's magazines and how-to books reveals that many of these crafts were of little functional value and the instructions were often exceedingly difficult. The projects did not demand creativity on the part of the maker, and the assembly process must have been extremely frustrating, yet the maker was expected to produce an exact replica of the object. In 1873, in *American Women in Society*, Abba Goold Woolson called women who undertook such projects "ornamental young ladies" who waited gracefully upon mankind and used their time to "braid Christmas slippers, hem handkerchiefs, and stitch cigarcases." Woolson also noted that needlework, which had once been creative, had ceased to be so when manufacturers began to supply everything with the figures complete; the seamstress had only to fill in the uniform background.[22] Painting, another popular entertainment, provided creative recreation, but, like all other endeavors in the domestic sphere, it was expected to be an amateur pursuit. *The New Recreation, Amateur Photography* in 1884 suggested photography for ladies as a means to recall the memories of the day but also as a record for the "dabbler" to re-create the scene in oil or water color.[23] Only "dabbling" in paint was acceptable at a time when fine arts were largely closed to women.[24] Women were not only constrained by domestic responsibilities; they were limited in the types of leisure activities considered acceptable for them.

Beginning in the early 1880s, limited instructions on making photographs appeared in a wide variety of women's how-to books. Found among chapters on interior decoration, handiwork, recipes, general health, and training children were chapters on making photographs for both amusement and profit.[25] Photography, in many ways, became an extension of the pursuits they were already following— one could paint on a photograph one had made or use the photograph to recreate on canvas a scene one had observed at an earlier time. The appearance of instructions for photography in these publications indicate that the taking and developing of a picture had become a socially acceptable recreational activity for women. Like other forms of ladies' fancy work, photography could occupy time, and photographs made by women were an effective form of decoration for a home. Unlike the manufactured needlework that belittled a woman's creative instincts and other "home adornments" devised to waste time, photography afforded scientific challenge and artistic opportunities.

Referring to photography as domestic "work," just as home crafts were called "fancy work," added to its respectability. Catharine Barnes published a monthly column in *American Amateur Photographer* titled "Woman's Work." ("Field Work" was another regular column on outdoor photography.) Readers were often reminded that camera work was hard

work, but worthwhile. Another of Barnes's columns, titled "Woman to Women," suggested to "work when fresh" to produce the best pictures. Barnes also noted that photography was "hard work—moving things about" and advised that ladies "do not do any unnecessary labor."[26]

In September 1889 *American Amateur Photographer* featured the first of many photographs made by Catharine Barnes on the frontispiece. The picture was of an "elegant parlor interior" with the "arrangement, lighting, exposure and development done by an experienced hand." The editor continued: "Photographing interiors . . . should be a subject of special interest to ladies, as they may perpetuate the many different arrangements of furniture, painting, wall-paper, etc, which in the course of time are sure to occur, forming a valuable record to refer to."[27] Indirectly, the magazine justified women's photography on the grounds that women could record their "work"—they produced the domestic setting. In the same issue, Barnes wrote a three-page article on "The Study of Interiors," encouraging women to try their hand at photographing their own homes.[28]

The careful reader would have noted that Barnes did not take the image for the frontispiece in her home but in "her new portrait studio" with a "home-like arrangement of furniture."[29] The new studio, a separate spacious building on the lawn, was probably furnished in a manner not unlike her own parlor, but the studio permitted better lighting and eliminated the clutter of daily life. The image provided an example of a type or style of photograph others could duplicate, and it demonstrated Barnes's artistic ability with arrangement and her technical skills with lighting.

While the average woman engaged in photography as a leisurely pursuit and recorded family records and home life, Catharine Weed Barnes made her domestic interiors for public viewing. Unmarried and supported by her widowed father, a prominent Albany attorney, she had the time to create the ideal parlor and to promote photography for women in a national magazine. But this ideal parlor was an extension of woman's sphere, whether it was a studied recreation like hers or the real thing. Barnes appears to have felt interiors were the proper place for women to practice their skills. Interiors were suitable for ladies, she wrote, "unlike city scenes where the ubiquitous small boy predominates and seems to rise from the earth at the sight of a camera."[30] Domestic photography helped maintain the proper decorum in that it did not challenge women's accepted place—in the home and not out on the street. By concentrating on subjects that were considered suitable, domestic photography conformed with definitions of ideal womanhood. It is not surprising, then, to find a few pictures of interiors in most amateur collections. It was only natural that the Victorian home—the symbol of marriage and family revered by nineteenth-century moralists—be the focal point for many women's introduction to photography. These images of home usually appear in the family album as a record of objects treasured by the photographer, just as she treasured friendships and family.

We often think of amateur photography as the ubiquitous family album, devoid of meaning to anyone beyond the immediate participants. Prior to the 1880s, however, family images were stiff, formal studio portraits recorded by a stranger. The "new" family pictures were made in one's own surroundings and showed a changed relationship between the subject and the nineteenth-century "camerist." As the family is usually shown to advantage, these photographs are not completely objective. Often neglected are the normal and sometimes more negative features from everyday life—work, arguments, daily customs, and crying babies. Images made by an amateur photographer reflect the general character of the person, however, far more than the make-believe world of the portrait photographer.[31] When Harriot Curtis photographed three of her children playing in the Atlantic surf and Catharine Barnes created a series of photographic illustrations, they were unaware of how their actions and the actions of thousands

of others would change the social role of photography. The Curtis children were far more relaxed for their mother than they would have been for a professional photographer, and Barnes persuaded her friends to pose in costumes performing actions most improbable in an outsider's studio. Photographs became personal reflections of the photographer's point of view; they were no longer the impersonal products of a stranger's vision.

Between 1884 and 1888, Curtis assembled an album of photographs composed primarily of her family at their country house in Manchester, Massachusetts. The enormous house, known as "Sharksmouth" and situated on one hundred acres bordering the Atlantic, was home to the family nine months out of the year. The rest of their time was spent at the Curtis's Boston home on Beacon Hill. Harriot Curtis was the daughter of one of the wealthiest men in Massachusetts, but no amount of money would have secured a professional photographer that could have captured these children in the act of play as did their mother. Their dress and grooming fit the leisurely country home environment; they are not formal or artificial. The older children occasionally look a little disgruntled, but, for the most part, they seemed to accommodate their mother's bidding. Curtis caught her children at play in the surf, the family at dinner, and her family and friends performing extravagant theatricals.[32]

The mother of ten, Curtis posed her children year after year in numerous stairstep images that she titled "Ten in a Row" (fig. 2).[33] She posed them climbing trees, still in birth (or perhaps size) order, and seated on a bench outdoors holding photographs of themselves. She preserved memories of theatricals, lawn tennis, croquet, excursions to the beach, and children going off to school (fig. 3). The image of Elinor Curtis with the waves breaking over her head as her brothers look on from the shore could easily be interpreted as capturing the antics of children at play at a much later time, but it is significant because it was taken in about 1885 (fig. 4). This was a period of high

Fig. 2    Curtis children, "Ten in a Row," 1886. Photograph by Mrs. Greely S. (Harriot) Curtis (1841–1923). Curtis Collection, Society for the Preservation of New England Antiquities (neg. 12810-B).

Fig. 3    Harriot Curtis's daughter Elinor in tableau, 1887–1888. Photograph by Mrs. Greely S. (Harriot) Curtis (1841–1923). Curtis Collection, Society for the Preservation of New England Antiquities (neg. 12850-B).

Fig. 4 Bathing place at Manchester-by-the-Sea, Massachusetts, about 1885. Photograph by Mrs. Greely S. (Harriot) Curtis, (1841–1923). Curtis Collection, Society for the Preservation of New England Antiquities (neg. 12818-B).

youth mortality, and for many parents the only picture they had of their child or children was taken after burial preparations. Instead, Harriot Curtis captured her three scantily dressed children at normal play.

In interior views, the Curtis children are usually in motion. In one 1887 series of pictures, the family is seen at meal time. The maid is serving the meal, and the children are wiggling in their chairs (fig. 5). The motion is due to the lengthy exposure time necessary without a flash.[34] The explosion of powder required extensive knowledge of chemicals and was often dangerous. Most women photographing their interiors would have used natural lighting, mounting their cameras on a tripod and allowing lengthy exposure times.

Curtis had begun her photography while in her mid-forties and did all of her own developing and printing. She continued for at least ten years, and, when her enthusiasm abated, one of her daughters assumed the role of family photographer.[35] Curtis also photographed

the Atlantic coast near Sharksmouth and the interior of the Boston home. While these images are noteworthy, it is the images of children at home going about normal activities that are exceptional. These are documents of Victorian childhood and young adulthood without the mask of Sunday clothes in an impersonal, formal studio setting.

The images Alice Austen made of her home are characteristic of the types of photographs young women took of their environment in the late nineteenth century. Encouraged first by her uncle, a Danish sea captain, when she was only ten years old, she was later aided by a younger uncle, a chemist at Rutgers. Alice was exceptionally talented, and she became a prolific photographer who kept meticulous records. Her family obviously took great delight in her humor and imagination and encouraged her photographic efforts. Never marrying, Alice continued her hobby of photography for about fifty years, making an estimated nine thousand images.[36]

Fig. 5    Mealtime for the Curtis family, mid-1880s. Photograph by Mrs. Greely S. (Harriot) Curtis (1841–1923). Curtis Collection, Society for the Preservation of New England Antiquities (neg. 12871-B).

The public and private spaces in the home that Austen recorded provide an intimate view of the family. The Austen household included Alice's mother, her grandfather and grandmother, and her aunt and uncle. They posed without hesitation for Alice, and the images are so vivid that her family members almost step off the print. There appears to have been very little staging in order to present the best domestic view of the Austen household. Objects do not seem to move from room to room—the type of arranging evident in some amateur collections.[37] Both the interiors and exteriors reflect the travels of her seafaring aunt and uncle: oriental vases and cachepots are strewn about the rooms and across the front lawn. No place was sacrosanct from Alice's camera in the Austen household—she not only recorded her room with all the adornments of a young girl's space, but also her aunt's sitting room with its immense collection of oriental travel mementos and her fine collection of bathroom humor—chamber

pots, ceramic figurines, and other bric-a-brac.[38]

Alice Austen was conceivably more uninhibited than most Victorian ladies whose lives have been chronicled. She lived what she termed the "larky life," and she took photographs of almost every sporting and leisurely activity imaginable in the 1880s and 1890s. She spent her entire life on Staten Island, a rural retreat from the teeming streets of New York. In the 1890s, Staten Island was a bucolic paradise with roads for biking and unspoiled private beaches.[39] Austen apparently photographed most all aspects of her life, and, when recording leisure activities, she usually posed in the picture also. Evidence of the shutter cord is noticeable in a large number of the pictures (fig. 6). Her friends are seen on the beach with the shutter cord trailing in the sand and Alice to the side, hastily crouched in the pose. She and her women friends dressed as men with cigars and looked boastfully into the camera (fig. 7). She recorded her trips, includ-

Fig. 6  A group of Austen's friends posed beside the family's tennis court on 5 August 1886. The photograph reveals not only the cumbersome and restrictive clothing that women wore to play tennis, but also the shutter cord—not quite concealed by tennis rackets on the ground—leading to Alice's camera. Courtesy Staten Island Historical Society.

ing a visual diary of a week-long house party in Pennsylvania and a sailing trip from New York to the Chesapeake. She documented the Staten Island Cricket Club, the setting for the first lawn tennis games in the United States.[40] Alice and her friends were soon playing, and she preserved scenes of the courts, the game, and the after-game celebrations. From these pictures we learn what the women wore— dresses that seem impossible to play in—how the courts were laid out, the position of the players, and other aspects of the occasion. She appears in these images, looking straight into the camera with an indisputable degree of confidence. Alice challenged the bounds of acceptable behavior.

Alice made many of her photographs purely for amusement, but they were made with great attention to detail and exacting quality. She and Trude, the daughter of the local Episcopalian minister, posed in her room at the rectory late one night in what would have been considered scant clothing (fig. 8). Wearing only their short petticoats and hose and shoes, with their hair hanging down past their waists, the girls each have a cigarette posed in their mouths. Alice noted on the negative envelope: "Trude and I masked: short skirts, 11 p.m., Thursday, Aug. 6th, 1891. Gas on. Flash. Stanley 35, Waterbury lens, 11 ft." Only the most adventurous amateurs were photographing with flash in 1891.

The appropriate subjects suggested in photography journals may have been in keeping with the domestic ideology, but once women experimented, what they actually *continued* to

Fig. 7 "Julia Martin, Julia Bredt, and self dressed up as men," photograph by Alice Austen, 15 October 1891. Alice stands at the left. Courtesy Staten Island Historical Society.

photograph was seldom inside their homes. A review of the surviving collections by women photographers reveals that there are few straight shots made of interiors to savor the past arrangement of things, as articles in *American Amateur Photographer* advocated. Photographing leisure and sporting events, gardening, and travel was still viewed as an acceptable extension of domestic space. Adventurous women photographers, however, journeyed from their sheltered environment into the nearby public environment, and they took their cameras with them. Rowdy street scenes in large cities and the workaday world of trains and barnyards were areas seldom seen by "ladies" but familiar to men and working-class women. With camera in hand, upper-class women slipped into this different world and interacted with people unlike themselves.

Alice Austen crossed the harbor by ferry to New York and photographed street vendors on the Lower East Side and bewildered immigrants in Battery Park. She recorded the ferry, people shopping, postmen, bootblacks, street sweepers and snow cleaners, rag pickers and peddlers, and little children selling newspapers—the city scenes and the "ubiquitous small boy[s]" that Catharine Barnes felt unsuitable for ladies' work.[41] Even though she was carrying fifty pounds of equipment, the quality of these photographs, like those of her friends at play, is exceptional. She privately published some of these images in a small booklet entitled *Street Types of New York*. The

Fig. 8 "Trude and I masked: short skirts," photograph by Alice Austen, Staten Island, New York, 6 August 1891. Courtesy Staten Island Historical Society.

young girl at the Sixth Avenue El station, "Newsgirl, 23rd Street," 1896, looks at Alice's camera with much self-confidence (fig. 9). In making these photos of street people, Alice would have interacted with them—she caused them in most cases to stop their work and look directly at the camera. These folks would never see their image, and this lack of sharing with the subject changes the composition of the photograph. Had the picture been made *for* the young girl, the background and content would have been different. Here we see her in everyday surroundings with no attempt to exclude the poster, stairs, or miscellaneous people. The newsgirl is not photographed close

up—Austen's objective seems to have been to record the scenes, not merely to take portraits. Austen's photographs of the street types are perhaps a truer document of the city than the better-known published images.[42] Cameras allowed such women as Alice Austen entrance, not necessarily unobtrusively, into heretofore forbidden areas.

Family and travel photos, everyday scenes from the city or country, gardens and boot-blacks are all fairly straight images of the real world. Photographers were not completely objective, but little manipulation, if any, occurred as amateur photographers used the medium to record their domestic and leisure

Fig. 9   "Newsgirl, 23rd Street and 6th Avenue El Station," photograph by Alice Austen, New York City, 1896. This photograph was part of a large collection of "street types" that Austen copyrighted at the Library of Congress. Courtesy Staten Island Historical Society.

activities. The women who concentrated on the world around them, however, also occasionally arranged and created "artistic images." A passing fancy among some women photographers, they were the core of the photographic work of many others. An artistic approach was their primary objective. They spent considerable time producing photographs that were in many ways reminiscent of fine art or used detailed costumes and backdrops in order to illustrate poems and stories. In *American Amateur Photographer*, Catharine Barnes recommended "a variety of rugs, furniture, and bric-a-brac" as invaluable for help in the studio, and she wrote an article on "Illustration of Poems by Photography."[43] This

second dimension of amateur photography—posed genre scenes and soft-focus pictorial "painting"—was an extension of the socially acceptable skills of sketching and painting that women had long pursued. Pictures could be accomplished without "knowledge of pen and brush," but artistic skills were definitely an asset.[44] Art training was a normal part of female education in the late nineteenth century to which many women photographers had been exposed. Their subjects often began as stylized portraits—people in costume posed as characters from the past or in regular dress in an intimate or romantic setting—or as straightforward bucolic genre scenes. Scenes became more posed and more artificial; portraits bore less and less likeness to the sitter. Finally, photographers created rooms, staged events, and illustrated Bible verses and fiction in much the same way Catharine Weed Barnes had arranged a Victorian parlor in her studio.

Photographic journals encouraged staged illustrations and each month chose the best to share with other interested "camerists." In the fall of 1890 *American Amateur Photographer* featured for three consecutive months a series of images by Barnes, among them her photographs to illustrate "Enoch Arden" (figs. 10 and 11).[45] Barnes had illustrated this poem by Tennyson for a national competition and had placed second out of fifty entries. An editorial comment (presumably by her co-editor, F.C. Beach) accompanied the first portrayal: "Such work is excellent practice for amateurs. . . . [We] hope more will undertake it—they more than the professional have the needful leisure for careful and thoughtful work."[46] In her monthly column, Barnes recalled how she posed and executed the three images. Using a carpenter to build the frame like a cottage in her studio, she created a very elaborate setting. Both the interior and the exterior of the cottage were represented. A sailor's costume for Enoch was easy, but Annie's dress "needed the soft clingy material of one hundred years ago."[47] The length to which Barnes choreographed her images was exceptional, but illustrating stories or poems by attempting to tell a story with the picture was quite commonplace.

Kate Matthews, a photographer working in the 1890s in Kentucky, is best remembered for her illustrations in *The Little Colonel*, by Annie Fellows Johnston. Johnston lived near Matthews in the small town of Pewee Valley, a genteel suburb outside Louisville. The town was a summering place for the wealthy from Louisville, and, with its large white pillared houses flanked by tree-lined entrances, it was the perfect setting for a book focusing on the sentiment of the antebellum South. Matthews did the original frontispiece of the "Little Colonel," posing a neighbor child, Hattie Cochran, as the model. She later illustrated the story

with a complete series of pictures showing Hattie, as the Colonel Lloyd Sherman, in various poses with other characters from the story. Elizabeth Matthews, her niece, was the physical prototype for "Betty" in Johnston's text, and she posed on the Matthews's veranda with her feet on a bearskin rug (fig. 12). To Johnston, Matthews's portrayal of Betty was the "most real in [all] the books."[48]

The Matthews photographic collection is relatively small and contains few straight documentary or portrait views. As one biographer has noted, Matthews seemed to see people in terms of roles. She used props even when the models were not posing as book characters. She photographed local workers, black men and women working in fields, in characteristic poses with farm tools, surrounded by abundant vegetables. She gave the photographs titles. Although they represent a very small portion of her work, they are artistic illustrations of the way Kate viewed southern culture. She seldom ventured beyond the confines of her home—the overwhelming majority of her work is of her friends and family. Most of Matthews's photographs seem to portray traditional feminine concerns.[49] Women and children are seen in the home, often in costumes, with only a few male family members occasionally posing for her camera. She captured Mary Johnston in "Miss Mary in the Garden" in a becoming arrangement (fig. 13). This is a popular pose of the time and most likely was copied from photographic journals featuring ideal poses.

Matthews entered some competitions, and several magazines featured her images. Her photographs from *The Little Colonel* were also made into postcards, possibly used by Annie Fellows Johnston to respond to fan mail.[50] Although she was not particularly talented, her photography seemed to give her a great deal of pleasure and a degree of prominence within the community. She apparently never did much else with her time except sporadic painting and occasional work for the church.

Both books on amateur photography and those on ladies' art recreations praised pho-

Figs. 10 and 11   "Enoch Arden [1] and [2]," photographs by Catharine Weed Barnes, Albany, New York, 1890. Courtesy International Museum of Photography at George Eastman House.

tography as "educating, refining and health-giving" and a certain "cure for mental weariness."[51] Photography carried an aura of the outdoors. Advertising showed women with cameras outside, on flowered winding paths and in the mountains whose scenic vistas waited to be recorded. A century later, it is difficult to imagine that photography could have been promoted as physical exercise, but, compared to the physical activity available to housebound ladies or white-collar gentlemen, tramping about the woods and along river-

banks carrying clumsy cameras and heavy glass negatives was an improved form of exercise. Publications compared photography to other forms of recreation and claimed nothing else could serve such multiple needs and interests. It combined science and art while allowing for both mental and physical exercise. Those who suffered ill health shed their Victorian pallor as, without a doubt, the exertion of photography put color in their cheeks.

Kate Matthews was a sheltered child, educated at home after suffering a bout of whoop-

ing cough at an early age. She apparently never attended public school nor received any higher education because of her frail condition—she was excused from the family chores expected of her eight siblings. Kate was in her teens when her brother-in-law introduced her to photography on a vacation trip, and her father soon purchased camera equipment for her. Although she took photographs for possibly as long as fifty years, the bulk of her surviving collection indicates that she did most of her photography when she first began in the 1890s. We cannot know the extent of Kate's illnesses, real or imagined, but photography got her out of her bed and into her garden (see fig. 13),

and, despite her early delicate health, she lived until the age of eighty-six.

Catharine Weed Barnes also took up photography after suffering health problems. Unlike Matthews, however, she used photography as a vehicle to expand not only her skills but also her way of life. Barnes attended the Albany Female Academy and the Friends' School of Providence, Rhode Island. She dropped out of Vassar College after two years because of "ill health" and the following year traveled abroad with her parents.[52] She then cared for her mother, who was sickly, for twelve years. It was at the suggestion of her mother in 1886 that she took up photography.[53] An acquaintance

Fig. 12  "Betty," photograph by Kate Matthews, Pewee Valley, Kentucky, 1890s. Courtesy Kate Matthews Collection, Photographic Archives, University of Louisville.

gave Barnes, then age thirty-seven, "critical advice," and within a year she was mentioned in the local paper as a successful amateur photographer and soon won a competition in Boston.[54] Whatever her earlier illness, Barnes went on to become internationally known as a talented amateur photographer and fine lecturer. In her monthly column, "Woman's Work," in *American Amateur Photographer,* she urged women to become involved in photography for its benefits, noting in an article in 1896 that photography had "challenged [her] mind" and she recommended it as a "real mental and moral tonic."[55]

In 1892 Catharine Barnes moved beyond taking pictures of domestic interiors and staged illustrations to travel photography.[56] In May, she began an extended trip to England, sending articles and photographs back to the journal. While there, she spoke extensively on the responsibilities of an amateur photographer and the role of women in the field and appeared on a panel with Henry Peach Robinson, an internationally recognized leader in artistic photography. The following summer Barnes, then forty-two, married H. Snowden Ward, editor of a British photography publication, and moved permanently to England. She continued as "English correspondent" to *American Amateur Photographer* and was soon replaced as editor by Alfred Stieglitz. In March 1896, still championing the cause of women in photography, she recalled how happy she was to have her collection of photographs with her "to recall those no longer here" and to be able to see her homeland.[57] Barnes played a multifaceted public role in promoting women in photography. For her, however, the medium still fulfilled the most fundamental private need—it was the visual report of people separated over time and space.

When Catharine Barnes appealed to women to stop seeking the "so-called 'fads' devised to kill time" and to take up the challenging and rewarding work of photography, she spoke from experience. Through her columns, she became exemplary of the new roles open to women. Photography provided the means for women to expand their lives and associate with people beyond their immediate surroundings. Like women writers of the nineteenth century, however, their new energies were still bound up with the celebration of the home. Domesticity was the dominant theme of their images.

What began as an amusement often became profitable, but there is evidence that these women continued to think of themselves as amateurs. They began photography as a pastime, as ladies' fancy work, and the pay they received was not the major source of their income. Indeed, those with the most recognizable names during their lifetimes called themselves "amateur."[58] Catharine Weed Barnes

Fig. 13   "Miss Mary in the Garden," photograph by Kate Matthews, Pewee Valley, Kentucky, 1890s. Courtesy Kate Matthews Collection, Photographic Archives, University of Louisville.

considered herself amateur "in the sense of being a lover of photography" and repeatedly referred to herself as "amateur," even as she served as editor of a major journal for five years, became an accomplished speaker on the subject, and owned one of the largest collection of lenses in America.[59]

Ambiguity is often found in the lives of women achievers—while breaking beyond domestic bounds themselves, they still adhere to and promote accepted traditional roles. "Literary domestics" in the early nineteenth century found that their financial success was an embarrassment and considered unfeminine.[60] The same appears true of these amateur photographers. Many were capable of professional employment after the first blush of amusement wore away, but they remained "amateurs" to protect the social status of the families.[61]

Domestic photography was a form of domestic feminism—traits usually found in the home environment were extended into the public sphere. Domestic photography also did

not challenge woman's accepted role: it was all right to be entertained by a hobby but not to labor at a profession or craft. While remaining an amateur photographer allowed women to avoid conflict, it also permitted them to move beyond their traditional sphere. Those who remained "private," seeking only to preserve special memories, nonetheless had skills of which the other family members could be proud. Those who carried a camera on city streets and into barnyards, posing children and friends with spinning wheels and farm animals and recording sports events and private gardens, were not radical in so doing. But as they gained entrance into photographic competitions and camera clubs, published their work and won awards, they achieved a status that challenged accepted cultural standards about gender.

## Notes

1. Catharine Weed Barnes, "Photography from a Woman's Standpoint," *American Amateur Photogra-*

pher, January 1890, 10; "Women in Photography," *American Amateur Photographer,* January 1896, 97.

2. Historian Alan Trachtenberg has noted that the "historical and documentary value of . . . photographs does not lie wholly in the visual subject matter . . . but also in the buried and hidden social uses they originally performed." See Trachtenberg, *The American Image: Photographs from the National Archives, 1860–1960* (New York: Pantheon Books, 1979), xxvi. On looking at photographs as documentary evidence, see also Thomas Schlereth, *Material Culture Studies in America* (Nashville: The American Association of State and Local History, 1982); Alan Trachtenberg, ed., *Classic Essays on Photography* (New Haven: Leete's Island Books, 1980); Marsha Peters and Bernard Mergen, "Doing the Rest: The Uses of Photographs in American Studies," *American Quarterly,* Bibliography Issue (1977): 280–303; and Thomas Schlereth, "Graphics as Artifacts," in *Artifacts and the American Past* (Nashville: The American Association for State and Local History, 1980), 31–43. Peters and Mergen explain that photography has had three distinct roles: "a medium of entertainment, a means of communication, and a record of physical and social landscape."

3. Barnes, "Photography from a Woman's Standpoint," 11.

4. "Photography for Girls," in Nugent Robinson, comp., *Collier's Cyclopedia of Commercial and Social Information, and Treasury of Useful and Entertaining Knowledge* (New York: Collier, 1882), 731–36.

5. Frederick Felix, "Young Women and Photography," *American Amateur Photographer,* January 1896, 4.

6. This project initially began as an overview of amateur photography with consideration of the variety of subjects amateurs chose to record once the camera left the studio for the outdoors. I was struck by the number of collections attributed to women that immediately surfaced. Women were pictured extensively in advertising, and the leading magazine for amateurs of the period, *American Amateur Photographer,* gave considerable recognition to the female audience beginning with its first issue. Other general statements in this paper are drawn from my research in preparation for "Ladies of Leisure: Domestic Photography in the Nineteenth Century" (M.A. thesis, University of Delaware, 1989).

7. Reese V. Jenkins, "Technology and the Market: George Eastman and the Origins of Mass Amateur Photography," *Technology and Culture* (January 1975): 13.

8. For a general history of photography, see Beaumont Newhall, *The History of Photography* (New York: The Museum of Modern Art, 1964). For the development of photography with emphasis on America, see Robert Taft, *Photography and the*

*American Scene* (1938; reprint, New York: Dover Publications, 1964); and William Welling, *Photography in America: The Formative Years, 1839–1900* (New York: Thomas Y. Crowell Company, 1978).

9. See Grace Seiberling, *Amateurs, Photography, and the Mid-Victorian Imagination* (Chicago: University of Chicago Press, 1986). Seiberling's informative work on the role of the amateur in Great Britain provides an excellent comparison to the development in America.

10. Scovill Manufacturing Company began publishing a yearly photographic manual in 1886, and its advertising frequently featured women. See Walter E. Woodbury, ed., *The American Annual of Photography and Photographic Times for 1900* (New York: The Scovill Company, 1899).

11. See William F. Robinson, *A Certain Slant of Light* (Boston: The New York Graphic Society, 1980).

12. See Marion Kemble, ed., *Art Recreations: A Guide to Decorative Art* (Boston: S. W. Tilton and Company, 1884), 327.

13. Welling, *Photography in America,* 189, states that *American Amateur Photographer* was the most popular of the three photography magazines then published. Women were not unknown in the field of photography before the 1870s and 1880s. They seem to have been particularly active in this sideline business in small rural towns. "In artistic taste, the woman photographer of the country village is usually superior to the man," an article in 1896 stated. "It is also to be noted that in many villages the woman photographer can live where her male competitor fails." *The House and Home: A Practical Book,* vol. 1 (New York: Charles Scribner's Sons, 1896), 70–71. See also Barnes, "Photography from a Woman's Standpoint," 10–13; and *American Amateur Photographer,* November 1891, 415.

14. "Photography for Girls," *Collier's Cyclopedia,* 731–36.

15. Catherine Clinton, *The Other Civil War* (New York: Hill and Wang, 1984), 49.

16. Welling, *Photography in America,* 297.

17. Catharine Weed Barnes, "Why Ladies Should Be Admitted to Membership of Photographic Societies," *American Amateur Photographer,* December 1889, 223–24; "Photography from a Woman's Standpoint," 13; and "Women in Photography," 95.

18. Barnes, "Why Ladies Should Be Admitted," 224. When Barnes's portrait appeared as the frontispiece of the November 1891 issue of *American Amateur Photographer* (p. 415), the accompanying caption praised her efforts: "Probably no other woman has done as much in promoting a general interest in photography."

19. Barnes, "Why Ladies Should Be Admitted," 224.

20. Frederick K. Morrill, "The Ladies of the Chicago Camera Club," *American Amateur Photographer,*

November 1891, 415–17.

21. Mrs. C. S. Jones and Henry T. Williams, *Ladies' Fancy Work, Hints and Helps to Home Taste and Recreations* (New York: Henry T. Williams, 1876).

22. Abba Goold Woolson, *Woman in American Society* (Boston: Roberts Brothers, 1873), 35, 39, 45, 59–60.

23. D. J. Tapley, *The New Recreation, Amateur Photography: A Practical Instructor* (New York: Hurst and Co., 1884), 9.

24. Harvey Green, *The Light of the Home: An Intimate View of the Lives of Women in Victorian America* (New York: Pantheon Books, 1983), 145.

25. Almon C. Varney, *Our Homes and Their Adornments* (Chicago: People's Publishing Company, 1885), vi.

26. Catharine Weed Barnes, "Woman to Women," *American Amateur Photographer,* May 1890, 185–88.

27. *American Amateur Photographer,* September 1889, 108.

28. Catharine Weed Barnes, "The Study of Interiors," *American Amateur Photographer,* September 1889, 91–93.

29. Editorial in *American Amateur Photographer,* September 1889, 108.

30. Barnes, "Photography from a Woman's Standpoint," 10–13.

31. For additional information on family photograph albums, see Alan Thomas, *Time in a Frame* (New York: Schocken Books, 1977); Christopher Mussello, "Family Photography," in Jon Wagner, *Images of Information: Still Photography in the Social Sciences* (Beverly Hills: Sage Publications, 1979); and Barbara Norfleet, "America Sits for Its Portrait," *Esquire,* 24 April 1979, 91–97.

32. The Harriot Curtis Collection is located at the Society for the Preservation of New England Antiquities in Boston, Massachusetts (hereafter cited as SPNEA).

33. Curtis's personal statistics were atypical. Of the fourteen women originally considered in this study, six never married and three married too late to bear children. Two were widowed early with one child. Three were married with families.

34. In the early years of amateur photography, a flash would have been a problem for most amateurs. Flash using magnesium was invented in Germany in 1887 and soon used by Jacob Riis for his documentation of the New York poor. See Welling, *Photography in America,* 309.

35. All information on Mrs. Greeley (Harriot) Curtis is in the files at the SPNEA and was compiled by archivist Ellie Reichlin. Much of the information came from Mrs. Curtis's granddaughter, Mrs. Isabella Halsted. Mrs. Halsted did not recall how her grandmother learned her photographic skills.

36. The Alice Austen Collection is located at the

Staten Island Historical Society, Staten Island, New York. Information on Austen comes from personal conversations with Charles Sachs, chief curator at the Staten Island Historical Society, and from Anne Novotony, *Alice's World: The Life and Photography of an American Original, Alice Austen, 1866–1952* (Old Greenwich, CT: The Chatham Press, 1976).

37. In the Howard Griswold Collection at the University of Louisville Photographic Archives, it is evident that the family moved favorite belongings about to set the stage for an image. A fine pair of oriental vases appear all over the house, giving the illusion that the house was decorated in the finest style throughout.

38. The Austen home was a late eighteenth-century house that had been modernized by Alice's grandfather with Victorian gingerbread and white paint into a charming "cottage" overlooking the New York harbor at the Verrazano-Narrows. The pictures Alice made in the 1890s of the interiors, the gardens, and the shoreline are presently being used to restore this historic site. The Alice Austen House Museum on Staten Island is the only house museum honoring an American woman photographer.

39. Photographic journals encouraged photographers to take the ferry over and to tour the island on their bicycles. Only an hour and a half from City Hall they could find subjects in the woodlands or photograph the "houses of historic interest." See Woodbury, ed., *American Annual of Photography,* 30–31.

40. John Richard Betts, *America's Sporting Heritage: 1850–1950* (Reading, MA: Addison-Wesley, 1974), 156. Mary Outerbridge purchased a net, rackets, and balls from regimental stores in Bermuda and returned with them to her home on Staten Island.

41. Alice Austen's social documentary shots were taken a decade before the better-known work of Lewis Hine and shortly after those made by Jacob Riis. Riis published *How the Other Half Lives* in 1890. Although he photographed the poor in New York, the publication used illustrations with drawings made from his photographs and halftone photographs of poor quality. Whether or not Riis's work influenced Austen is not known, but she provided her own extraordinary documentary record of New York in the 1890s. For information on Riis, see Newhall, *History of Photography,* 139.

42. Because the images of street scenes made by Austen were not made to instigate social reform, they may be a truer view than those made by the reformers. Edward Steichen felt that street scenes made by amateurs were "without opinion, slant, comment, or emotion." (See Welling, *Photography in America,* 379.) F. Jack Hurley, a photographic historian, concurs with this and suggests that the images made at the local level, not intentionally as so-

cial documents, may be the more realistic of the two. "Local 'straight' photographs are often truer documents of a time and place than the socially didactic work of many 'documentary' photographers." See F. Jack Hurley, "There's More Than Meets the Eye: Looking at Photographs Historically," in *The Center for Southern Folklore Magazine* 3, 3 (Winter 1981): 6.

43. Catharine Weed Barnes, "Illustration of Poems by Photography," *American Amateur Photographer,* April 1890, 126–29, and August 1891, 300–305.

44. Barnes, "Women in Photography," 98.

45. The message written on the back of one of the Enoch Arden images notes that she "illustrated poems with pictures from life, of her friends–posed in her fine studio–with scenery and 'knick-knacks' to suit any theme." This is probably not Barnes's writing. The photograph is in the collections of the Albany Institute of History and Art.

46. *American Amateur Photographer,* September 1890, 10–13.

47. Catharine Weed Barnes, "Woman's Work," *American Amateur Photographer,* October 1890, 347.

48. Margaret M. Bridwell, *Kate Matthews and the Little Colonel* (Louisville, KY: University of Louisville, 1963), unpaginated. The Kate Matthews Collection is located at the University of Louisville Photographic Archives, Louisville, Kentucky.

49. Norma Predergast Campbell, "Kate Matthews, Photographer" (M.A. thesis, University of Kentucky, 1975), 25–30. Information on Matthews comes from Campbell's thesis and discussion with David Horvath, curator at the University of Louisville Photographic Archives.

50. Campbell, "Kate Matthews," 7, 23–24. Unfortunately, Matthews's images failed to work at least as often as they succeeded. In January 1896, *American Amateur Photographer* observed that she needed to improve her skills.

51. Kemble, *Art Recreations,* 326. In the 1880s, Herbert Spencer toured America and encouraged exercise as a cure for physical and mental ailments. Both books on photography and ladies' art recreations quickly picked up on Spencer's admonition. See Kemble's *Art Recreations* and Tapley, *The New Recreation,* 9. Ellie Reichlin, director of archives at SPNEA, is currently working on the concept of using photography as a mental health therapy and shared her ideas with me. Much of the material I used does advocate the use of photography for mental health.

52. *The National Cyclopedia of American Biography* (New York: James T. White and Company, 1898), s.v. "Barnes, Catharine Weed."

53. Elizabeth Poulson, "Catharine Weed Barnes Ward, Another Forgotten Victorian Photographer,"

The History of Photography Monograph Series, 8, Arizona State University (May 1984), unpaginated. Quoted from Richard Hines, Jr., "Women and Photography," *The Photographic Times,* May 1899, 242.

54. Barnes, "Photography from a Woman's Standpoint," 11; and Poulson, quoted from Hines, "Women and Photography," 242.

55. Barnes, "Women in Photography," 98.

56. Photographs served as a travel diary for many photographers. In 1888 hotels in America began providing darkrooms for guests. Travelers could develop and print their photographs in transit—the primary reason was to check for any technical problems with the camera or film that would spoil the memories of the entire trip if left undetected. See Welling, *Photography in America,* 318; "The Old Witch House Dark Room," *American Amateur Photographer,* February 1892, 85; and Jeanette M. Appleton, "The Pleasures of Photography," *American Amateur Photographer,* February 1891, 79–80.

57. Barnes, "Women in Photography," 97. I was unable to locate the bulk of Catharine Weed Barnes's work. A few images of "Enoch Arden" are at the Albany Institute of History and Art. Presumably, as she indicated in her column, she took them to England.

58. Mary and Frances Allen published successful little catalogs of Deerfield images and participated in the active artisan community there for twenty years. They worked out of their home, and their work was accepted as part of the local arts and crafts movement. Both their obituaries confirm their status in the community as "artistic amateur photographers." See Ed Polk Douglas, "Frances and Mary Allen, A Biography" at the Henry N. Flynt Library, Historic Deerfield, Inc. (typescript, 1969), 31. Mabel Osgood Wright, author of twenty-five books on nature and fiction for children, whose photographs illustrated her books and appeared in those by others, referred to herself as an amateur photographer in an interview shortly before her death. See the Mabel Osgood Wright Collection, Fairfield Historical Society, Fairfield, Connecticut.

59. Dawbarn and Ward, eds., *The Photogram,* January 1894, unpaginated. In 1906, the journal's title was changed to the *Photographic Monthly;* it continued under that name until 1920. Holdings from January 1894 to December 1907 are located at the George Eastman House/International Museum of Photography, Rochester, New York.

60. See Mary Kelley, *Private Woman, Public Stage* (New York: Oxford University Press, 1984).

61. With the exception of Kate Matthews, all the women in the study achieved other notable accomplishments.

# Children's Play in American Autobiographies, 1820–1914

BERNARD MERGEN

The history of children's play presents some unique challenges of method and definition. If our goal is to understand the significance of play to children and from that to discover links between childhood play and adult behavior, then we need records that allow us to see play from a child's perspective. What is a child? What is play? Definitions of these deceptively simple terms vary according to the purpose of one's research. For the historian, the popular definition of childhood as the period of life between infancy and adolescence, roughly from age two to twelve, is adequate. Play is a more difficult term to define, but there is general agreement that play is behavior that involves a degree of self-awareness, is more or less voluntary, and mostly pleasurable. With this in mind, some experts argue that children do not play much until after the age of two.[1] Playfulness may define the beginnings of childhood, but not everything a child does is play.

The inner history of childhood—history from the diaper up—requires the methods of the literary critic and the ethnographer, as well as those of the historian. Because few children learn to write before the age of seven, and because only fragments of children's writing have been preserved, childhood is similar to a nonliterate, oral culture.[2] Our chief sources for the study of this culture are descriptions of children by adults, artifacts such as playthings, and recollections of childhood. Descriptions of children by adults take many forms, from casual comment to extensive scientific study. Most of the latter have been written since the 1880s, following the emergence of psychology, pedagogy, and folklore as professions.[3] Until recently, the purpose of most child study was less to understand the child's point of view than to change it. The artifactual record is also dependent on adult definitions of childhood, play, and playthings. The preservation of objects is usually left to parents, then curators, not children themselves.[4] Recollections of childhood are essentially of two kinds, oral histories recorded by an interviewer and autobiographies written in later life. Oral testimony is largely limited to the past eighty years and falls outside the time period of my analysis.[5] To learn about children and their play in the nineteenth century, we must turn to the written autobiographies of the men and women who describe their childhoods in that period.

This paper examines seventy-eight autobiographies written by Americans who were born between 1822 and 1913. This is about 15 percent of the total number of autobiographies containing some reference to childhood between the years 1820 and 1914 listed in the standard bibliographies.[6] These books were selected from a larger number available in the Library of Congress because they contain a significant amount of material on childhood. As the accompanying table indicates, my selection is somewhat skewed toward male writers of the late nineteenth century who grew up in New England and the Middle West, but this bias characterizes the universe of autobiographies from which this sample was drawn (see table). The childhoods depicted in these books may not be typical—they are the childhoods of boys and girls who grew up to become writers—but there is enough variety in the sample to show a range of play and to make some tentative generalizations about the nature and meanings of children's play in the nineteenth century.

The use of autobiographies in historical research requires consideration of two potential limitations—literary conventions and memory.[7] Even autobiographies that are little more than sketchy reminiscences published by vanity presses are written by literate individuals with some awareness of the traditional forms of the autobiography. The more skillful the author, the more literary conventions must be taken into account. Motivation is an important point. Some of the authors used in this study were motivated to write about their childhoods by a need to understand themselves, some by pure vanity, others by nostalgia. Some wrote with an awareness of Freudian theories of child development; others merely chronicle their happy memories. Nevertheless, each author had to make hard choices about what to include and how to organize the material. It is safe to assume that what they included was important to them. The process of

recall and writing forced them to complete what was previously inchoate. Some of the autobiographers are themselves good ethnographers, explicit in their assumptions and systematic in their descriptions. Many attempt a definition of childhood by describing its beginning and end. A few are aware of the problem of memory.

Autobiographical memory is not well understood. Experiments by psychologists suggest that we are better able to remember unique, important, unexpected, and emotional experiences than repeated and trivial events. Memories of childhood may be vague because the names of things and their meanings may not be known at the time they happen.[8] The authors of the books considered here, however, have been able to cue their memories, to reconstruct, if not to reproduce, the events and emotions of the past. Many of the autobiographers began with their earliest memories, which usually date from their third or fourth year and involve feelings of joy and fun. As children grow in self-awareness, so do their appreciation of the nature of play. They learn that play—purposeless, frivolous, and limited in time—is opposed by work—purposeful, serious, and ongoing. Yet play is tolerated, even demanded, by parents and other adults. Children discover that their own definition of play, the activities that make them happy, may be challenged by adults and playmates. Paradoxically, what begins as fun may end in combat. James Langdon Hill, who grew up in Grinnell, Iowa, in the 1850s, remembered that a game of marbles was often disrupted with cries of

"Don't fudge." "Stand back on the line." "Knuckle down tight." "Get back to taw." "Here, don't you work your marble forward." But in spite of all warning, the marble is fired and out of the ring goes the other boy's best China. Will he stand for it? Not on your life! He is defrauded. Then comes the altercation, "You did," "I didn't," the language in which most quarrels begin. Words can no further go. One of the boys, in his quick rage, would mount a chip upon his shoulder, and openly dare the other to knock it off. Off

## Table: Kinds of play in autobiographies*

| | TOTAL N = 78 | M (54) | F (24) | YEARS OF CHILDHOOD | | | REGIONS | | | | |
| --- | --- | --- | --- | --- | --- | --- | --- | --- | --- | --- | --- |
| | | | | 1820–1850 (16) | 1850–1880 (21) | 1880–1914 (41) | NE (21) | NY/PA (11) | S (14) | MW (24) | W (8) |
| Food | 42% | 40% | 48% | 38% | 48% | 41% | 43 | 45 | 36 | 46 | 38 |
| Pets | 23 | 26 | 13 | 19 | 14 | 29 | 29 | — | 36 | 21 | 25 |
| Violence | 45 | 53 | 19 | 38 | 62 | 39 | 29 | 55 | 50 | 50 | 50 |
| Make-believe | 55 | 48 | 71 | 44 | 71 | 56 | 62 | 55 | 50 | 67 | 38 |
| Imaginary other | 4 | 2 | 10 | 6 | 5 | 2 | 5 | — | — | 8 | — |
| Vertigo | 13 | 5 | 33 | 6 | 24 | 10 | 10 | 9 | 21 | 21 | — |
| Mimicry | 12 | 5 | 29 | 12 | 14 | 10 | 10 | 9 | 29 | 8 | — |
| Skill | 55 | 60 | 38 | 63 | 57 | 51 | 48 | 45 | 57 | 58 | 75 |
| Strategy | 42 | 41 | 38 | 50 | 48 | 37 | 24 | 45 | 71 | 46 | 25 |
| Chance | 6 | 7 | 5 | 6 | 10 | 5 | 5 | 18 | 7 | 4 | 13 |
| Board games | 10 | 9 | 14 | 12 | 19 | 5 | 10 | 18 | 7 | 8 | 13 |
| Handmade toys | 37 | 32 | 57 | 38 | 62 | 24 | 57 | 18 | 29 | 46 | — |
| Manufactured toys | 35 | 30 | 48 | 12 | 67 | 27 | 29 | 27 | 50 | 42 | 13 |
| Books | 46 | 46 | 48 | 50 | 57 | 39 | 48 | 36 | 50 | 54 | 25 |

*Percentage of mentions

goes the chip. They would try conclusions with their fists.[9]

Hill's autobiography, *My First Years as a Boy,* is one of the most detailed records of children's play, but it is not exceptional in its vivid detail. In this short passage, we learn not only about a game of marbles and its specialized vocabulary, but about the rituals of fighting as well. Typically, the author described an episode of childhood and commented on it at the same time. As in life, more than one thing happens at a time. I will discuss fourteen items (see table) representing broad categories of play or activities that may be playful and offer some hypotheses to explain the variations in their frequency over time, among regions, and between the sexes. These items are drawn from several earlier studies of play and my own research.[10] The frequency with which the items are mentioned in the autobiographies is summarized in the table, although the raw data have obvious limits. First, the numbers are not large, and my judgment as to whether an activity was one kind of play or another is subjective. Many games combine physical skill and mental strategy, so they are counted in both categories. Most board games have an element of chance, but I restricted the latter category to play in which luck was mentioned specifically. The statistical part of this paper is only meant to show some broad outlines and to raise questions more than to answer them. My primary purpose is to illustrate the rich variety of children's play in the nineteenth century, to provide historians of childhood and play with fresh information that will free them from the constraints of earlier, narrower, views of children's play. Toward that end, I want to begin with a brief consideration of the ways in which the authors have dealt with their earliest memories, their sense of place, and the significance of adults in their early lives.

## First Memories

First memories in these autobiographies are usually of physical sensations—sights, sounds, tastes, smells, and textures. Henry Adams described himself at age two or three sitting on the kitchen floor in a bright pool of yellow light. Irving Bacheller recalled singing as he rocked in a little rocking chair while his mother and grandmother looked on. James Baldwin wrote, "Of all my earliest and pleasantest memories, by far the greatest number are in some way connected with books and reading. . . . The very feel of the paper, its smoothness, its thinness, the cabalistic marks which it bore, had a magical influence no less potent than mysterious."[11] Others remembered trees, the color of clothes and ribbons, fireworks displays, or the arrival of a parent. Some believed their earliest memories were of journeys by boat or wagon, while a few began with memories of fires and rock fights. The variety is intriguing. Some are happy memories, some sad, all intensely personal.

In several cases, the earliest memory was not of a single event, but of a composite. "When I look back at my beginnings," wrote Janet Gillespie, "it is always a sunny morning at Snowden, our summer house, and people are laughing and running up and down stairs with their arms full of clean sheets and diapers."[12] Implicit in all of the mentions of earliest memories is the belief that memory is stored somewhere and discovered through recollection. Two writers had a more complex view, however. Theodore Dreiser, wracking his brain for glimpses of his past that would explain his career, concluded a paragraph of bittersweet memories with, "Again I recall one of the children falling into a well—I cannot recall which of us." This remarkable lapse was surpassed by S. N. Behrman, who told a long story about eating a double scoop of chocolate ice cream at Emma Goldman's ice cream parlor in Worcester, Massachusetts, before revealing that Goldman left the city a year before his birth. The memory, he realized, was his brother's, appropriated by other family members after innumerable retellings.[13]

## Space and Place

Almost all of the autobiographers mentioned special features of their homes, yards, and neighborhoods, but, again, the contexts of the remembered experiences are disparate. Emily Wilson and her sister, growing up in New England in the 1840s, discovered that the kitchen stove "had a rotary top turned by a crank at the side, thus obviating the necessity of changing the pots and kettles from the front to the back. We soon recognized the possibility of using it for our own amusement and one, seated on top, rode around and around while the other operated the crank." Although the kitchen was frequently mentioned, especially as the warmest room in the house in winter, it does not seem to have held as central a place in the life of children in the nineteenth century as it does today. Dorothy Howard, whose detailed account of childhood in east Texas between 1902 and 1910 is in a class by itself as autobiography of children's play, described the kitchen as a haven from darkness as well as cold.[14]

Howard remembered her attic as being too hot in the summer, but Thomas Ripley played in his mother's attic, a space that contained everything that generations of thrifty New Englanders could not throw away. After pretending to be a bird inside a cage made from a discarded skirt hoop, Ripley mailed letters to Santa Claus and God through a knothole on one of the stairs. "Like an attic," wrote Flannery Lewis, "a basement is a secret place, slightly removed from the world, but still within sight of it; and the time that you spend there is your own and of no relation to your everyday life on the surface, for it is a secret retreat, and that is why you feel guilty when you return to the world."[15]

Meta Stern Lilienthal, who lived in a seventeen-room house on the Lower East Side of Manhattan in the 1870s, described each room, including the mysterious attic and the second-floor bedroom where she pushed up an eiderdown quilt to make an igloo. "But dearest to memory," she wrote, "is the old rocking chair. In it my mother rocked me to sleep while she sang German and English songs. . . . When you turned that chair upside

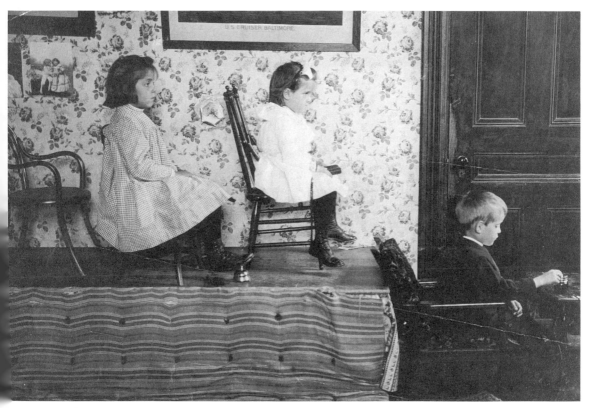

Fig. 1 "Playing streetcar in the nursery." The photograph's original caption identifies the children as, left to right, the conductor, the passenger, and the motorman. Photograph by Charles Hart Spencer, Pittsburgh, Pennsylvania, June 1902. Courtesy Elizabeth Ranney.

down, the crossbars of wood that held the rockers together served admirably as a coachman's seat. Then it became a wagon, a carriage, a sleigh, and later a Roman chariot."[16] A decade earlier, Lincoln Steffens had taken "three or four big chairs and all the small chairs in the house and made a mountain train of wagons and mules; a clothesline tied to the leader and strung through the other chairs was a rein which I could jerk as the black-bearded teamsters did." Across the continent, Walter Brooks played horses and coaches with turned-over chairs, adding a Scotch shawl to turn them into Bedouin tents.[17] These accounts are confirmation, if any is needed, of the importance of furniture in children's lives, though the meaning of chairs, tables, and beds may differ considerably between children and parents (fig. 1).[18]

Many of the autobiographers described the liberation they felt when they were old enough to leave the house alone, to play in the yard or on the street. John Albee, William Dean Howells, H. L. Mencken, and others recalled the exhilaration they felt exploring their neighborhoods, communities, and countryside. Like Albee and Howells, Harriette Arnow had vivid memories of nearby rivers. Lucy Larcom, Marie Jastrow, and Mencken all enjoyed watching shopkeepers and visiting stores. Edward Everett Hale and Mencken, growing up sixty years apart, were both passionate advocates of their local fire companies.[19] Whether on farms or in towns, children play with as well as in their physical environments. Anchored in the specific, familiar setting of their homes, they often make some object the center of their personal universe. For Dorothy Howard, it was a fence post at the corner of her yard, her "Thinking Post," from which she surveyed the surrounding countryside; for Edwin Way Teale, it was the roof of his grandparents' house, from which he could see the Indiana dunes on Lake Michigan.[20]

## Families and Strangers

As they explore space and place, children discover their families, neighbors, and strangers. Everyone is a potential playmate. Irving Bacheller, who grew up on a farm in a valley of the St. Lawrence River north of the Adirondacks in the 1860s, remembered the French Canadian woman who helped his mother, the hired man who told stories and jokes, an uncle who went to California and never returned, the pretty daughter of the richest man in Pierpont Center with whom he played croquet, and many others. Absent relatives were a topic of conversation and a source of fantasy. Albert Halper, born to immigrant parents in Chicago in 1904, began his autobiography with an account of an exchange of letters with an uncle who lived in New Zealand. City kids met a wider variety of individuals than rural, but the variety in both locales was great. Dorothy Howard encountered gypsies, peddlers, cowboys, teamsters, and hired men near her Texas farm in the first decade of the twentieth century. Wagon trains of emigrants from Arkansas, Alabama, and Mississippi sometimes camped across from the farm, allowing time for games of Wolf Over the River and Mumblety-peg (or Mumblepeg, or Mumble-the-peg).[21]

Boys often formed gangs, and girls sometimes organized clubs (fig. 2). Emily Kimbrough belonged to the Anti-Gun and Literary Society when she was growing up in Muncie, Indiana, between 1899 and 1910. No one mentioned organized sports in the years before 1914, because there were few school or playground competitions before World War I, but informal games of baseball or one of its variants, such as One Old Cat, One-Eyed Cat, and town ball, were mentioned by both girls and boys. Games in the street sometimes brought children into contact with the police. Mencken described his encounters with a cop he called "Cookie" and the use of a lookout to warn of his approach.[22] There are numerous mentions of Fourth of July parades, circuses, and other entertainment that brought children into contact with a wider world.

Several of the books contain descriptions of strangers who inspired fear. For William Dean Howells in Hamilton, Ohio, in the 1840s, the part was played by "the crazy man . . . a hapless, harmless creature, whom the boys knew as Solomon Whistler, perhaps because his name was Whistler, perhaps because he whistled." For James Baldwin, growing up in a Quaker community on the Indiana frontier in the same decade, it was a fugitive slave, the first black person he had ever seen. For Una Hunt in Washington, D.C., in the 1880s, it was both a family friend who frightened her when he was drunk and the "Night Doctors" who were said to steal bodies from the cemetery. Mencken too remembered that blacks in Baltimore told stories about body snatchers, but his great fear was "a half-grown yahoo who hunted small boys."[23] Although the authors recalled feeling real fear, there is also a sense that their fright was, like that induced by ghost stories and horror movies, a kind of thrilling play, the momentary, terror-induced heightened sensibility.

Much more could be written about the playful interaction between children and those around them. Zona Gale's description of one encounter in Wisconsin in the 1880s may serve as a conclusion to this topic:

> It was one of the wonders of my days: the utterly absurd questions that grown-up people could ask.
>
> For example: "How do you do to-day?" What had any reasonable child to answer to that? Of course one was well. If one wasn't, one wasn't going to tell anyway. Or, "What's she been doing lately?" Well! Was one likely to reply: "Burying snow. Hunting pignuts. Digging up pebbles from under the leaves. Making a secret play-house in the currant bushes that nobody knows about?" And unless one did thus tell one's inmost secrets, what was there left to say? And if one kept a dignified silence, one was sulky![24]

Memories of childhood encounters with

Fig. 2    Some Rochester, New York, boys formed the Clifton Athletic Club in the summer of 1909. They are pictured in front of their "private club house" with Indian clubs, dumbbells, and shirts bearing their own insignia. Courtesy Edwin Spelman.

adults, whether parents, neighbors, or strangers, are compounded of a mixture of scorn and fear. Grownups are powerful but easily avoided outside the home. Younger children especially are buffered from the adult world by older siblings. Children, it seems, admit adults to their world, especially their play time, on their own terms.

## Food

One of the central activities involving children and adults is eating. Thirty-three of the seventy-eight autobiographies, or 42 percent, mention food, usually in the context of family meals but often as part of the work and play of berry picking, nut gathering, and general for-

aging. "To hide and play games was one means of escape from the fatigue of the slow filling berry pails," wrote John Albee of 1830s New England, and he added that he and his companions also painted each other with berry juice (fig. 3).[25] Many of the writers named dozens of kinds of apples and seemed to remember the names of every tree and flower of their childhoods. All of the writers except the abused, neglected Richard Wright remembered being well fed. Three of the writers devoted lengthy sections of their books to descriptions of food consumption, preparation, and recipes.

*Home Grown,* the title of Della Thompson Lutes's autobiography of her childhood in rural Michigan at the end of the nineteenth

Fig. 3    "Gathering Berries," by Winslow Homer, *Harper's Weekly*, 11 July 1874.

century, suggests the centrality of food. Her preoccupation with eating is partly explained by her later career in home economics, but her loving attention to detail and her penchant for describing such things as hog boiling in terms of play imply a deeper pleasure. For her, the seasons were marked by changes in diet—dandelion greens in the spring, sweet corn in the summer, spareribs with the first freeze. School for Della meant trading lunches; June meant the strawberry festival.[26]

Mencken too became ecstatic over the picnics and banquets of his youth. While only 40 percent of the male autobiographers, compared to 48 percent of the female, mentioned food, Robert P. Tristram Coffin went into almost as much detail as Della Lutes. Describing the suppers his older sister prepared while they attended school in a small Maine town in the first decade of the twentieth century, Coffin recalled that Tuesday was fried sweet potato

day, Wednesday was liver and onions, and porridge with beans meant Sunday night.[27] Most of those who mentioned food confined themselves to a few lines about fruit and candy at Christmas, although some mentioned special foods for election day and the Fourth of July. As would be expected, regional differences do not seem pronounced. Food was mentioned by 45 percent of the writers who grew up in New York, Pennsylvania, and New Jersey, 43 percent of the New England autobiographies, 38 percent of the western states writers' work, 46 percent of the midwesterners', and 36 of the southerners'.

## Pets

Only 23 percent of the autobiographies mention pets, although it is curious that men mentioned them twice as often as women. None of the autobiographers except Nan Hayden Agle mentioned pets in any detail. Her brief account of her childhood in suburban Baltimore between 1905 and 1913 is organized around her donkey, cows, dog, and lamb. Hal Borland and Lincoln Steffens described their horses in detail, and Borland recounted his adventures with his dog, but play with animals is not an important element in any of the books. A few recalled the unhappiness they felt at the death of a pet, and Coffin ended his memoir and his childhood with the death of his dog.[28]

## Violence

By contrast, violence is a category of activity that received frequent mention in autobiographies. Forty-five percent of the total mentioned fighting, beatings, or the severe threat of bodily harm. Fifty-three percent of the men and 20 percent of the women described such scenes. The most violent of the autobiographies is Richard Wright's, but Woody Guthrie's childhood was hardly less brutal, and even gentle New Englanders such as Henry Adams, Thomas Bailey Aldrich, and Walter Brooks recalled fights and mobs. Ulysses Prentiss Hedrick, who grew up on the northern peninsula of Michigan in the 1870s, played lickety-cut, known as "rap jacket" in the South, in which two boys stand face to face and hit each other with beech poles or switches until one gives up.[29] Boys north, south, east, and west, city boys and country boys, described fights between ethnic groups.

Robert Lawson near New York City, Estilline Bennett in Montana, and John Taylor Waldorf in Nevada all referred to anti-Chinese activity.[30] Wright and Taylor Gordon experienced racism in Mississippi and Montana; Jimmy Savo participated in rock fights between Italian and Irish kids in New York City.[31] Girls recalled raids by boys that ended with broken dolls and chase-and-capture games. The line between play-fighting and serious warfare was often thin. Boys fought for respect and recognition on the playground, they defended territory, and in winter they built elaborate snow forts for ritualized combat. In most cases, the fights were recognized as part of the cycle of play activities. Disputes were expected to be settled by fists.

## Make-believe

The remaining twelve activities mentioned in or absent from the autobiographies are more conventionally defined as play than food, pets, or fighting. These are make-believe, a related category that I have termed the imaginary other, vertigo, mimicry, skill, strategy, chance, board games, handmade playthings and toys, manufactured toys, and books. As the table shows, make-believe and play involving physical skill were the most frequently mentioned activities of children. Forty-three of the seventy-eight autobiographies mention some kind of fantasy play and some games of skill. I counted as make-believe any activity that involved pretending—playing kings and queens, Indians, soldier, putting on shows—or that made reference to the imagination and pretending. Zona Gale gave a nice example of the latter:

"What'll we play?" I was pursuing politely. "Pretend?" I intimated. Because of course there is nothing that is quite so much fun as pretend. "Or real?" I considered the alternative, its second place.
"Pretend what?" Betty wanted to know.
"Well, what difference does that make?" I inquired scornfully. "We can decide that after."
However, we duly weighed the respective merits of Lost-in-the-Woods, Cave-in-the-Middle-of-the-World, and Invisible, a selection always involving ceremony.[32]

If "real" is the opposite of "pretend," it corresponds to my mimicry category, of which I found surprisingly few examples. To be classified as mimicry, the activity had to imitate something in the real world such as playing store, school, or house, or it had to be one of Newell's "playing at work" singing games such as "Virginia Reel," "Oats, Pease, Beans, and Barley Grows," "Here I Brew and Here I Bake," and "Threading the Needle" (fig. 4). Because few of the autobiographies referred to singing

Fig. 4  "A game of horse and buggy." Photograph by Charles Hart Spencer, Pittsburgh, Pennsylvania, July 1900. Courtesy Elizabeth Ranney.

games by title, it was usually impossible to know if these specific games were being played. An argument could be made for placing the game of soldier in the mimicry category, too, because many children grew up during and immediately after the Civil War when imitating the actions of the Grand Army of the Republic sometimes meant involving a local veteran in the play. And where should we place "dead man in the leaves" as described by Harriette Arnow, who, about 1914 in Burnside, Kentucky, played a game in which a child pretended to die and the others buried her in leaves and preached a sermon, but the dead man could become a ghost and play a more active role in the game.[33]

Toward 1914 make-believe play became influenced by technological innovations. Frederic Birmingham, recalling his childhood in Harlem in the years 1911 to 1920, gave prominence to the motion pictures he saw at the Re-

gent on 116th Street and the Orient on 125th Street and Lenox Avenue. He pretended to be what he saw in the movies and especially liked battle scenes. Edwin Way Teale, inspired by an air race around Lake Michigan in 1909, tried to build his own airplane. Prophetically, young Amelia Earhart played her own favorite make-believe game in her grandmother's barn in Atchison, Kansas, taking imaginary journeys in an old abandoned carriage. The future aviator and her friends pretended to get lost and have frightening adventures.[34]

Statistically, my sample shows that children in the Middle West and New England had a slightly higher incidence of make-believe play than those in the South, New York / Pennsylvania, and West, but, except for the small sample in the West, the differences are not significant. There is a considerable rise in the incidence of make-believe play from the period 1820–1850 to 1850–1880 and then a decline in the 1880–

1914 period. This corresponds with a slight drop in the mentions of games of skill and strategy across the three periods. The decline of percentages in all categories except pets from the period 1850–1880 to 1880–1914 may be explained in three ways. The larger sample of autobiographies in the later period (forty-one as compared to twenty-one) includes more of poorer quality, lacking the thoroughness and detail of earlier books, the result of the expansion of publishing in the twentieth century. Another possibility is that childhood itself changed. Children growing up in the late nineteenth and early twentieth centuries were subjected to more outside influences—schools, motion pictures, urbanization—than their parents and grandparents had been. In this period, children's play began to shift from traditional games to more activities supervised by adults. These activities may have seemed less memorable to the autobiographers. Finally, and most probably, the definition of childhood and play may have changed sufficiently that the later autobiographers were less nostalgic, less inclined to dwell on the everyday pleasures of tag, snowball fights, or even reading. There also seems to be a correlation between the popularity of make-believe and play and reading, leading to a hypothesis that the increased availability of books and magazines, greater leisure time, and parental encouragement of quiet, imaginative play contributed to this shift. References to make-believe play are more frequent among the books written by women than by men, probably because they were not allowed to go far from home to meet friends for play.

## Imaginary Playmates

Three of the autobiographers mentioned having imaginary playmates, or imaginary others, as they are sometimes called in the psychological literature. James Baldwin, a prolific author of popular history and author of *In My Youth: From the Posthumous Papers of Robert Dudley [Pseud.]*, seems to have been almost as obsessed by disguise and dual identities as Mark Twain. Addressing his imaginary descendants "in the fourth degree" late in the twentieth century, the pseudonymous Robert Dudley described his childhood in a frontier Quaker community in Indiana in the years 1841 to 1855. He depicted himself as a bookish boy who was in frequent conflict with neighbor children. He called his imaginary companion Inviz, short for invisible, and had long conversations with him throughout the book. A little more than halfway through the narrative, Inviz stopped using Quaker plain speech, but Dudley did not comment other than to note the change. The book ended with Dudley's death and noted that Inviz returned to him after fifty years to assure him that he is immortal through his books![35] Baldwin/Dudley is clearly concerned with something more than childhood reminiscences in this strange book, but it is rich in detail, and his use of conversations with Inviz to reveal a boy's feelings about the world around him rings true, in a way similar to the motif of the current comic strip "Calvin and Hobbes."

The most thorough depiction of an imaginary other is Una Hunt's *Una Mary: The Inner Life of a Child,* published in 1914, the same year as Baldwin's book. Una Atherton Clarke was born in Cincinnati in 1876 and lived there until 1885 when her father, a chemistry professor, became a chemist for the U.S. Geological Survey and the Smithsonian Institution and her family moved to Washington. After a preface in which she discussed the need of a sensitive and imaginative child for answers about the unknown, the author began a straightforward account of her first fourteen years. She remembered that she created her companion, Una Mary, at about age three-and-a-half to differentiate herself "from the Una who was just a member of a family, so different from the me our friends saw and talked to, who played with toys, sat on people's laps, and 'took walks,' dragged about the streets by the nurse who wheeled my sister's carriage; and, above all, who wore clothes I hated of dark blue or brown, because they 'did not show the soot like white.' "[36]

Una and Una Mary had an active play life with neighboring children, but her parents were Bostonians who believed in "plain living and high thinking," so she was envious of other girls who were allowed to wear fancy dresses, long curls, and shiny kid button shoes and kid gloves. In her imagination, Una Mary wore rings and bracelets. Walks with her father led Una to create a second companion, Edward, a young man in his late teens, and a wooded land she called "My Country." Playing by herself on a Persian rug, she used the patterns to imagine rivers and countries with an ocean surrounding the edges of the carpet. Later she invented the "Land of Little People" that could only be discovered by accident, where the inhabitants wore hats like those worn by Chinese coolies because she had been told that if she dug straight down she would come to China. One especially poignant passage is worth quoting in full:

> Whenever I had a bad day, because I was ill or in disgrace, I consoled myself with the thought that it did not really matter as the Una in the ordinary world was not the real Una at all, that I only really lived as Una Mary, in My Country, so I had merely to endure until night, when, as soon as I was in bed, a little door in my chest seemed to open and out came Una Mary and my real life began.
>
> I made myself a gold paper crown to wear in bed, for I did want to make even Una look worthy of these marvellous night adventures; but the paper tore to bits before morning, so in its place I painted points of gold on a black ribbon, the point in front ending in a star. This I used to wear all night, tied so it hid my two tight pigtails of hair that were fastened with dreadful rubber bands.
>
> Una Mary always came very quickly, and her adventures were especially exciting when the wind blew at night.
>
> When I was twelve years old I wrote this poem about her:
>
> "The far-off wind is calling me.
> Una Mary, shake yourself free,
> Tuck up your skirts and run away
> To the Land where the story people play.
>
> "Call to Edward to come with you

> Where clouds are floating in skies of blue,
> Where clothes are made of velvet and gold,
> And Knights are noble, gentle, and bold.
>
> "We'll run away from the outside Me,
> And from the Imp be wholly free.
> My flowing hair in ringlets dressed
> We'll only do what we like best."[37]

In Washington she shared some of her fantasy life with two friends from school, and they printed a magazine called the *Ghosts' Companion*, illustrated with labyrinths. They also invented words for feelings they were unable to express in English, such as the fear of children alone at night, which they called "pliditrants," or the half-exhilarated, half-giddy feeling of swinging, called "mingy." The book ended when her friends moved away and Una Mary was merged with Una who, at age thirteen, accepted herself as real. Although there are similarities between this book and Zona Gale's and Dorothy Howard's, it stands alone in its focus on the imaginary other and its power to evoke the make-believe play of children.[38] Janet Gillespie and her brother, growing up in Holyoke, Massachusetts, in the second decade of the twentieth century, invented a witch, Exzizzable, who lived in a closet, other characters with such names as "Lady Blue," who never had to go to the bathroom, and the "Whirly Grunt Man," who presumably did nothing else.[39]

A recent study of imaginary playmates has established that 25 percent of Americans have created an imaginary other at some time in their childhood.[40] The fact that only three autobiographers write about such playmates may indicate several things. First, some of the authors may have been reluctant to reveal very personal experiences. Some may have forgotten what they later considered a trivial episode of their childhoods. Others may have tacitly included imaginary companions in general references to playing house, Indians, or war. Finally, the creation of imaginary others, which was first studied by psychologists in the 1890s, may be a more recent phenomenon, the product of increased leisure time and smaller families. It may also be significant that, as the study of imaginary playmates argued, belief in the reality of common imaginary figures such as Santa Claus, the Bogy Man, the Sandman, the Easter Bunny, and the Tooth Fairy is stronger than in imaginary others. Santa is the only one of these figures mentioned frequently in the seventy-eight autobiographies used in this paper. The Bogy Man appears a few times, the Easter Bunny once (Birmingham), but the Sandman and Tooth Fairy appear to be of recent vintage, the creations of numerous children's authors.

As indicated earlier, play involving mimicry, imitation of the adult world—"real," to use Zona Gale's term—was not often mentioned by autobiographers. Girls and southerners played this way more than boys and children from other regions, but the differences are probably not significant. Dorothy Howard described playing school in two ways. One involved a child playing teacher while the others pretended to be students; the other "was an imitation of a Friday afternoon 'program' where the teacher called on individual children to stand before the class and recite a verse or sing a song." If there were no adults within hearing distance, some of the recitations were mildly vulgar parodies:

> The boy stood on the burning deck
> His feet were full of blisters
> The flames flew up and burnt his pants
> So he had to wear his sister's.

Howard also played "Needle and I," a singing game similar to "Threading the Needle" mentioned in Newell's *Games and Songs of American Children*. Although the action was similar to "London Bridge," the ultimate purpose of the game was to pair off boys and girls at community gatherings for kissing. Emily Kimbrough, who also grew up in the first decade of the twentieth century, played school on Sunday because other forms of play were forbidden by her parents.[41]

Another kind of imitative play involved making things such as baskets and dolls' hats from pine needles and leaves. Katherine Krebs mentioned such play as part of her Pennsylvania childhood in the 1870s. David Ward, who grew up in the 1820s in Michigan, built little mills and forges where he dammed streams. Several writers recalled printing newspapers for the amusement of their friends and parents. H. L. Mencken provided a lengthy description of his Baltimore No. 10 Self-Inker Printing Press and his publications.[42]

## Vertigo

Play involving vertigo, the enjoyment of motion and temporary loss of consciousness, ranks very low among the fourteen items counted, probably because this kind of play is so spontaneous, momentary, and simple. The most frequently cited examples are swinging on swings or from the branches of trees. Emily Wilson wrote of her New England girlhood in the 1840s: "There was the never-failing swing, in which one sat clutching the ropes on each side while, with her heart in her mouth, she was pushed up and up into the high branches of the big elm tree, to float back ready for another ascent skyward." Twenty years later, another New Englander, Thomas Ripley, recalled that there was a trapeze and rings for boys on one side of the house and swings for the girls on the other. Orra Phelps, Ripley's contemporary, wrote that when she was tired of swinging she would stop pumping and "let the old cat die," an expression with which Emily Kimbrough ended her book. For Kimbrough, the dying motion, the loss of her front teeth, and the birth of her brother symbolized the end of childhood.[43]

## Physical Skill

It is, of course, not surprising that games requiring physical skill should equal make-believe in being the most popular. Most of the play we associate with childhood—running, swimming, ball games—involves physical skill. Nevertheless, the category is not without its ambiguities, and there is an obvious overlap

Fig. 5   Children playing "Charlie Over the Water" in a Washington, D.C., schoolroom in 1899. Not only are the words to the singing tag game written on the blackboard, but an American flag is posed behind the group to signal that the purpose of the exercise is to Americanize the children through traditional Anglo-American play. Courtesy Frances B. Johnston Collection, Library of Congress.

between games involving skill and those involving strategy. Thus I counted some tag, chasing, and seeking games as both (figs. 5 and 6). All ball games, sledding, and skating I counted as games of skill. Kites, marbles, and Mumblety-peg are also included in this category, as are hopscotch, jump rope, tops, croquet, and leapfrog.

Typically, authors simply listed the names of games they remembered—ice-skating, crack-the-whip, tag, ice boats, Duck on the Rock, One Old Cat, Anti-Anti-I-Over (Georgia Hufford, Northern Michigan, 1880s), pom-pom-pull-away, Van Dieman's land, snap the whip (Orra Phelps, Connecticut, 1870s), Anty Over, Black Man, Crack the Whip, Red Rover, Skin the Cat, Top Spinning (Dorothy Howard,

Texas, 1910), Two-Old-Cat, Duck on the Rock, Anti-Anti-I-Over (Ulysses Hedrick, Northern Michigan, 1870s), ice-skating, snap the whip, (Walter Brooks, New England, 1860s), baseball, nicky-nicky-nee, and sailing (Edwin Beitzell, Maryland, 1915). Howard described each game briefly, so we know that Anty Over, Anti-Anti-I-Over, and nicky-nicky-nee are the same ball-and-chase game and that Black Man was a chase-and-capture game similar to Prisoner's Base. A few authors commented at length on the meanings of these games and play. James Langdon Hill found top spinning a little boring and invented ways to make it more interesting such as seeing how many times he could run around the house before his top "went to sleep" and making his top

Fig. 6    A game of leapfrog, Washington, D.C., public school, 1899. Courtesy Frances B. Johnston Collection, Library of Congress.

spin into another to see which would "conquer." Albert Halper, in Chicago in 1914, joined a group of boys who dove for pennies in a lagoon in Union Park. His account included a description of how the boys used younger boys as "bankers" to hold their money while they continued to dive, how a young girl successfully challenged the male domination of the game, and how a boy drowned during the excitement of the competition.[44]

Girls and boys in nineteenth-century America had ample opportunity to develop physical skills in the course of a day's work and play routines. Until the introduction of the bicycle and roller skates in the 1880s, walking, running, and an occasional wagon ride or railroad trip were the only ways to move about on land.

Ice skates and sleds made winter appealing to most children because they were essentially recreational, not part of everyday travel (fig. 7). Many skills, such as shooting, trapping, and boating, were both work and play. Hamlin Garland turned his plowing into play, as did Max Miller. Garland, whose father made him plow the Iowa prairie ten hours a day when he was only ten years old, amused himself by whistling, singing, studying the clouds, and stopping occasionally to torment the lizards whose nests he disturbed. Mixed with toil, Garland recalled, were the joys of the changing landscape, the songs of birds, and the play of small animals in the fields. Miller, who grew up in eastern Washington and Montana, pretended his plow was a cannon and played soldier to relieve the tedium.[45]

Fig. 7    Ice skates, Vulcan Skate Co., Philadelphia, Pennsylvania, about 1900.

Several authors provided detailed descriptions of games that combined physical skill with strategy, such as I Spy, Fox and Geese, and Hare and Hounds. All three games involve chase and capture, sometimes with a vigorous struggle at the end. James Hill described playing I Spy in the 1850s in Iowa:

> The bright moon, the crisp frosty air, and the keen rivalry among us all, combined to enhance our joy in the game of I Spy. The boys gave the rough breathing to the vowel and called the game High-Spy. It was played about the barn, and about the stacks, into which the cattle in feeding, had made deep lurking holes, and corners where everyone could secrete himself. We would lean a long pole against the stack, and blindfold one of our number, who was to count aloud one hundred, while others ran away and hid. Then he would look about and seek to find the boys. On sighting one, he would shout I spy John Doe who if he could first get to the goal, gould we called it, threw down the pole.[46]

This pronunciation of goal probably accounts for the mentions of games of "gool" by David Ward and Hamlin Garland. William Carlos Williams's description of Hare and Hounds as played in New Jersey in the 1890s provides a vivid sense of the game and its meaning:

> After giving the hares ten minutes start with their bags of torn newspapers on their shoulders, we set out after them. We knew they'd cheat, not drop any tracers at important places, but that was part of it. Two of the hares were the toughest fighters in the neighborhood and those were the ones we knew we'd be stuck with in the end.
>
> I thought I could run, though none of the others considered me especially good. We ran all Saturday morning until, the easy ones having been picked up and all traces of those last two lost, a few of us decided, or maybe some of their own side told us, that Dago and Jo had last been seen headed for the Cedar Swamps beyond the copper mines. What a spot! It was already past noon but that's where we headed and sure enough, as we got to the top of the hill overlooking the mines, we saw them, out along the old wood road into the marshes between the cedars and swamp maples. Those are the days and the excitement that I remember! How we went after them, and how they eluded us. . . . And when it was over, even to a fist fight during which they were overpowered—one even climbed a tree—we all walked out together, talking and laughing, delighted with ourselves, bruised, scratched and mudcaked. That was fun.[47]

Taylor Gordon, one of the few blacks in White Sulphur Springs, Montana, in the early 1900s, played a variation of Hare and Hounds called Stray Goose. The winner of a block race was given a half-mile head start; then the other children pursued him. Every time he turned or changed direction he had to stop and yell "stray goose." If caught, the gang was allowed to do anything short of killing him. One night—the game was always played from 9:00 p.m. to midnight—the goose fought back so violently that he was tied to a cart and pushed down a steep hill. The resulting crash destroyed the cart and frightened the boys into quieter play for a while.[48]

Fox and Geese is a game of tag played around a circle marked on the ground and involving several strategies for avoiding capture. Because it requires a marked track, it is a popular winter game; accordingly, it was only mentioned by those who grew up in regions where the snowfall was heavy. Albert Britt recalled that in Illinois in the 1870s, "Winter discouraged organized games, but a deep snow was hailed with delight. Then we built snow forts and fought fierce battles with the melting snow on milder days. Deep drifts gave opportunity for digging tunnels and making houses in the depths. Fox and Geese was another snow game, a variant of tag." Robert Lawson played yet another version of Prisoner's Base near New York City in 1900, called Head Off and Head On. In this game, two teams led by the two largest and toughest boys raced from one base to another trying to avoid capture. The capturer had to hold them long enough to shout, "Five and five are ten; you're one of my men." In the meantime, captured boys could be freed by being slapped on the hand by an uncaptured member of their team. Dorothy Howard played Run, Sheep, Run, a somewhat gentler hiding, chase, and capture game.[49]

Children engage in a great deal of negotiation before, during, and after games and play. Choosing sides, agreeing to rules, tolerating violations of those rules, and punishing flagrant offenses are all part of the play and fun. Strategy within and around the game is ubiquitous. Board games usually combine strategy and chance and may illustrate these categories better than any others, although autobiographers also mentioned playing cards, dice, and making wagers on other kinds of contests.

## Board Games and Chance

Only eight writers mentioned board games, and only five mentioned play involving chance or luck. Clearly the impact of manufactured board games, other than chess and checkers, occurred later than the period discussed or was more limited than catalogs and advertising suggest (fig. 8). Yet board games and games of chance are among the earliest games mentioned in the autobiographies. Edward Everett Hale played checkers and "Goose: The New Game of Human Life" in Boston in the 1830s, and he gambled with "props" on the mud flats of Back Bay. Props is a game in which the tops are sliced off small sea shells and then filled with red sealing wax. Players bet that they can throw odd or even numbers of red "spots." Jimmy Savo, playing in the streets of New York seventy years later, played checkers with girls but shot dice with boys for marbles and baseball cards. John Taylor Waldorf played poker and faro for matches and participated in speculation in mining stocks as he grew up in

Fig. 8  A game of checkers, *Youth's Companion*, 20 February 1896.

Virginia City, Nevada. None of the autobiographies mention the kind of penny- and picture-card-pitching described by Stewart Culin in "Street Games of Boys in Brooklyn, N.Y." in 1891. Dorothy Howard played guessing games such as Hul Gul, and other girls reported playing Authors and Twenty Questions. MacKinlay Kantor played Old Maid and Lotto.[50]

## Handmade Toys

Handmade toys were mentioned by 37 percent of the autobiographers, manufactured toys by 35 percent. Girls mentioned handmade and manufactured toys more often than boys, because girls almost always mentioned dolls (fig. 9). Writers from New England and the Midwest mentioned handmade toys more often than those of other regions, while southerners and midwesterners mentioned manufactured toys more frequently than New Englanders, westerners, or those from New York and Pennsylvania. Once more the statistics belie the importance of objects for children. Objects within the home and yard take on personal importance for children before they are aware of special objects made for their exclusive use.

Fig. 9 This paper doll and clothes are part of a large set handmade by a girl in Rochester, New York, about 1910. Some dolls in her set were hand drawn; others were made from magazine and/or catalog advertisements. The clothes are pen-and-ink or pencil drawings and watercolors. Although the clothing has no tabs, it was attached to the doll with tiny clothes clips made of bent wire covered with thread.

As Dorothy Howard pointed out, "The word 'toy' was not in the vocabulary of the Mills children. They had 'playthings' and 'play pritties.'"

> Manufactured (store-bought) toys were rare among the children in Sabine Bottom except in the fairy-tale pages of the Sears, Roebuck catalogue. Play tools included sticks, stones, dirt, water, wind, sky and clouds, leaves, flowers, vines, tree limbs, rope, string, spools from sewing thread, corncobs, cane joints, broken dishes, discarded coffee grounds, burnt matches, match boxes, shoe boxes, cigar boxes, scraps of cloth, leftovers from dressmaking, rags from the ragbag and any needed things or object borrowed or appropriated from farm and household equipment.[51]

Mencken described "Playing Sebastapool," a game that combined handmade and manufactured toys. Young Henry and his friends took sand from construction sites and built ramparts in a gutter, decorated them with tissue paper flags, and defended them with tin soldiers and Indians. The sand castle remained in place until the rain washed it away. Robert P. Tristram Coffin learned to make perfect little Oldtown canoes from peapods and little bits of matches. Sticks made into horses and guns were mentioned by Hamlin Garland, Woody Guthrie, and others.[52] Dorothy Howard clarified the significance of these objects:

> A "plaything"—a stick, for example—was not a stick but (metaphorically) a horse to ride, a thermometer for playing doctor, a writing or drawing tool for marking on the ground, a log for building log cabins, a boat to float down a rivulet from a spring shower, play candy, a shotgun for hunting, or another person. A "plaything" could be and was anything the mind willed—for a moment, an hour, for months or years. The definition, unarticulated, was communicated by action in a context common to and understood by all players. Play was metaphoric action.[53]

As early as the 1830s boys were making toy railroads, and they remained popular through the century. Edward Everett Hale made toy locomotives and boats, some merely planks on rollers propelled across the attic floor with shingles for paddles. He also had a variety of store-bought toys including magnets, springs, pulleys, and a burning glass. Fifty years later, John Bowman celebrated his fourth birthday with a present from his older brother who had made him a train of cars and an engine all painted red. "The engine had a string tied to it. I took the string and pulled. The train roared across the pine boards of the kitchen floor." At about the same time, Theodore Dreiser played with a train he had created from cigar boxes, moving it back and forth across the yard or floor past stations he had built of twigs.[54]

### Manufactured Toys

The manufactured, often imported, store-bought toy does not appear prominently in the autobiographies except in the period 1850–1880, an anomaly I cannot explain except to point out that mentions of all kinds of play seem to increase in the books describing this period and then to decline in the period 1880–1914. It is possible that the novelty of manufactured toys between 1850 and 1880 caused them to be remembered, while children growing up in the later period took them more for granted (fig. 10). Although the American toy industry grew steadily during this time, it did not really emerge as a major influence on consumers until the 1890s. The appearance in 1903 of *Playthings,* a journal for the toy industry, is an indication of the growth of the manufacturing and retailing business, but the disruption of the German toy industry in 1914 did the most to boost American toy manufacturing.

A good measure of the changes from 1860 to 1914 in children's attitudes toward manufactured toys can be seen in the autobiographies of Walter Brooks, William Allen White, Jim Washburn, MacKinlay Kantor, Eda Lord, and Flannery Lewis. Writing in 1915 of his childhood in the 1860s, Brooks lamented the loss of a simpler time: "the rag doll and the monkey on the stick were its emblems—not yet replaced by the dressy little princess from the Parisian atelier or the mechanical toy from a German workshop." Yet Brooks also gave an evocative account of his Noah's Ark set:

What child of half a century ago was not the proud possessor of a Noah's Ark, that requisite of every well-organized nursery. I have of late years failed to find one in any shop window and fear like most old-fashioned toys it has had to stand out of the way of progress. In my own case the Noah's Ark helped me pass many a tedious day when minor floods were abroad and its hoards of paired inhabitants were an endless source of diversion and speculation.

The ark itself was a flat-bottom boat on which was constructed a house with peaked roof. I can not now recall the color of either the boat or the house, but the roof, I know was painted red, for the paint would sometimes come off on my fingers, moistened as they would be by the nervous tension of play. I also know the taste of the paint for childlike I used my tongue for cleaning purposes, since life was entirely too short to provide any interim for the ordinary process of washing in a basin. I generally had to undergo that trial, however, sooner or later accompanied by reproof

Masthead text in image: "Vol. VIII.—No. 418.] NEW YORK, SATURDAY, DECEMBER 31, 1864."

Fig. 10   Thomas Nast's "Christmas Morning" depicts an idealized holiday, where children receive manufactured playthings in an era when such toys were still a novelty. *Harper's Weekly,* 31 December 1864.

as the red in the corners of my mouth was sure to betray me. . . .

The dove had a green leaf in its mouth which I assumed to be part of a hasty meal taken just before embarking. I did not at the time recognize him as the pioneer bearer of news at sea.

My mind even now presents the picture of a double row of animals winding across the nursery floor, with Noah, his wife and their descendants leading the troop and just nearing the ark. The camels and the giraffes had a place of prominence in the van, the humps of the former and the long necks of the latter making them conspicuous among their fellows.

An open door would create a draught, an unfriendly skirt would sweep through the room so that constant vigilance was necessary to keep the procession in martial order.

Gone now is Noah! gone his wife and children! and gone are all the animals! but what is still sadder, gone is not only their ability to amuse me, but the very belief in their existence![55] (Fig. 11)

Fig. 11 "Noah's Ark" toy, carved wood, leather, and paper, American, 1880–1920.

William Allen White linked the passing of homemade toys to the arrival of the railroad in Kansas and listed among his possessions a cast-iron bank in the shape of a fat Tammany politician in a yellow vest, a scroll saw, skates, musical instruments, bats and balls, masks, books of games and magic, dumbbells, and boxing gloves, everything except the bank acquired by selling subscriptions to the *Youth's Companion*.[56] Washburn, describing Christmas gifts about 1910, mentioned candy, oranges, nuts, raisins, firecrackers, baseballs, a baseball mitt, and an air rifle. Kantor was given an Indian costume but confessed to being envious of the toys of wealthier children and to stealing a red, white, and blue eraser from a store and money for toys from his mother's purse. His father's friend, the entertainer Sophie Tucker, gave him a toy revolver in a leather holster that could be used as a watch fob, and later he got a glass pistol filled with candies and a papier-mâché cornet with real keys and a kazoo in the mouthpiece.[57]

As the First World War approached, manufactured toys appear to have become increasingly abundant. Eda Lord provided an inventory of her things at the time of one of her family's frequent moves:

Some objects we could never leave behind: the electric train and all the tracks (the curved tracks took up a terrible amount of space), Meccano sets, dynamos, telegraph sets, water pistols, airguns, and our fleets. Deflated footballs, boxing gloves, baseball bats. We had to abandon all of Jimmy's stores: old bicycle wheels, pulleys, coils of wire and rope, chains, and a number of dry batteries. We left behind all childish things like Teddy Bears, the plush monkey, and building blocks; useless things like clockwork toys which had broken down or no longer had a key.[58]

Earlier in her book, Lord described some play with toys:

Our most pressing concern was what we were going to make with the Meccano sets. With the sheets of metal and the girders we could build almost anything but we wanted to make something which needed some of our pulleys. We were limited by not having traction wheels. No matter what shape our construction took, it turned out to be a lifting crane. It would lift objects large in comparison to its size but never so large that we couldn't lift them ourselves with one hand. Finally we left it as a dock crane to supply the fleet with ammunition. For a short time we changed over from a war footing to a merchant fleet but the continuous loading and unloading was dull. We tried freighters-attacked-by-pirates but the booty and excitement went to whoever was pirate, and that wasn't fun.[59]

Flannery Lewis recalled a visit to a store at Christmas during World War I:

And of course upstairs in that store there were tables of toys; one table alone of cowboy suits and cap pistols, and another with soldier suits and of machine guns that fired wooden bullets, a dozen bullets to a belt. There were new boots for boys just his size, and raincoats with oilskin helmets the shape of firemen's hats, alongside of baseball suits with heavy red sweaters. Mechanical sets with real screw drivers and metal braces were everywhere, in a wonderful confusion of bolts and screws and designs for bridges. But best of all was a brown truck-line machine, a miniature army tank on real rubber wheels.[60]

The favorite toys of boys and girls in Worcester, Massachusetts, in the 1890s, a list compiled by T. R. Croswell, provides an effective comparison:

Boys: top, ball, marbles, express wagon, football, bicycle, drum, skates, checkers, gun, car, engine (fig. 12), sled, tool chest, tools, bat, boats, horses, books, cards, blocks, kite, house, dominoes, dog, puzzles.
Girls: dolls (including paper dolls) (fig. 13), tea set, doll carriage, books, top, ball, bicycle, sled, jump rope, skates, piano, checkers, hoop, stove, paint, blackboard, dominoes, doll's bed, doll's table, doll's chairs, doll's cradle, blocks, cards, play school, play house.[61]

The prominence of tops, balls, marbles, express wagons, and football for boys and dolls, tea sets, doll carriages, books, and tops for girls is only partly corroborated by the autobiographies, which do mention balls, marbles, dolls, and books frequently. Playthings and toys have many meanings and functions to the children who play with them and to the adults who give them. Clearly a major change took place in children's lives in the first decades of the twentieth century as manufactured toys became available and affordable. Moreover, as Brian Sutton-Smith has argued, the child with an expanding number of toys is increasingly defined by what he or she has. Toys encourage solitary or small-group play rather than large-group play; they promote consumerism, even driving some children to theft as they did MacKinlay Kantor; they stimulate make-believe play; and in some cases they promote the mastery of simple technologies. Finally, the toy becomes an identity around which the child organizes his actions.[62]

## Books

Books and reading were mentioned by 46 percent of the autobiographers, the third most frequently mentioned item. Men and women mentioned books with about the same frequency. Western children had less access to books and mentioned them less, but they were significant in all regions. The importance of books to men and women who grew up to be writers is not surprising. What is more interesting is the range of books they read and the personal meanings the books had for them (fig. 14).

The titles James Baldwin lists are revealing of the eclectic nature of children's reading. In his Quaker father's library he read George Fox's *Journal*, the Bible, William Penn's *No Cross, No Crown*, John Woolman's *Journal*, Noah Webster's blue-backed spelling book, *McGuffey's First Reader*, and other books. During his childhood, he was given a *Boy's First Book of Animals*, Jesse Olney's *The Little Reader; or, The Child's First Book*, Charles Dickens's *A Child's History of England* (1852–54), and Defoe's *Robinson Crusoe*. He traded a handmade toy windmill for a copy of *Parley's Geography* and earned money to buy John A.

Fig. 12    "The 999" toy locomotive, cast iron, American, about 1910.

McClung's *Sketches of Western Adventure* (1832). He also mentioned reading *The Youth's Cabinet* (Boston, 1858) and *Uncle Tom's Cabin* serialized in the *National Era*. At school, he read Shakespeare and looked at copies of the *London Art Journal*. The variety seems remarkable considering the conditions of the Indiana frontier in the 1840s and 1850s, and Baldwin's reading also confirms that children read adventure stories with the same intensity as religious tracts. As Lucy Larcom observed twenty years earlier of her library that contained works by John Calvin and Lord Byron, it was "a rather peculiar combination . . . but I was not aware of any unfitness or incompatibility. To me they were two brother-books, like each other in their refusal to wear limp covers. It is amusing to recall the rapid succession of contrasts in one child's tastes. I felt no incongruity between Dr. Watts and Mother Goose."[63]

Ulysses Hedrick referred to his "wallpaper education," the result of his mother papering the house with *Harper's Weekly*. Hedrick also read *Ivanhoe*, but he found the rest of Scott too difficult as a boy. McGuffey's *Fourth, Fifth,* and *Sixth Eclectic Readers* were more to his liking. He described at length the Friday afternoon school programs that included spelling bees, debates, and speaking pieces. "My taste," he wrote, "ran to the lachrymose; and I spoke

with much pathos parts of 'Enoch Arden,' 'Curfew Must Not Ring Tonight,' and 'The Dead Child's Ford.' " His prizes for winning spelling contests were *The Works of Robert Burns,* Moore's *Irish Melodies,* and Whittier's *Songs of Three Centuries,* although he did not state that he read them. The township library was well stocked with Scott, Dickens, Thackeray, Hawthorne, Irving, Emerson, Parkman, Prescott, and Cooper, but no Melville. Disavowing that he had high-brow tastes, he wrote, "A printed page was to me a printed page. I read avidly dime novels, the love stories of Mary J. Holmes, E. P. Roe, and Augusta M. Evans; seed catalogues and Patent Office Reports; magazines and newspapers of any kind that came to hand; almanacs; Sunday-school books; and I never went to town on a Saturday afternoon without visiting Lem White's Barber shop to have a peek at the *Police Gazette* (very disreputable in that day and age)." He and his brother and sister subscribed to the *Youth's Companion, Harper's Young People,* and *St. Nicholas* magazines.[64]

Across the continent in Nevada, Hedrick's contemporary John Taylor Waldorf read dime-novel detective stories about "Old Neversleep" and "Old Sleuth" and imagined himself a boy-hero in their mold. In Baltimore, H. L. Mencken was already a more discriminating reader, but "the first long story [he] ever read was 'The Moose Hunters,' a tale of the adventures of four half-grown boys in the woods of Maine, published in *Chatterbox* for 1887." Like Baldwin, Mencken read through his father's library before he could understand half the words. Again the list is eclectic, but at the age of eight he discovered *Huckleberry Finn*, which led him to read all the available works of Mark Twain, though *Huck* remained his favorite all his life. Mencken's second favorite book in childhood was Prof. Robert Griffith's *Boys' Useful Pastimes,* which led to failed attempts to make a steam engine, a whatnot, a rabbit trap, and a table.[65]

Less choice of reading material existed for children growing up in the West and the South, relatively poorer and more remote sections of the country. Hal Borland felt lucky to receive old copies of *Adventure, Top-Notch, Argosy,* and *Bluebook,* and Richard Wright attributed his early interest in writing to reading Zane Grey's *Riders of the Purple Sage,* serialized in a newspaper. He too read *Argosy, Flynn's Detective Weekly,* and *All-Story Magazine.*[66] Because most of the autobiographers became more serious when they discussed their reading, it is difficult to determine the extent to which reading was play (fig. 15). Yet the voluntary nature of reading and the liberating effect it had on children indicate that it should be included in any inventory of children's playfulness. Even more than toys, books encourage solitariness. As with toys, my statistics show a declining percentage of references to books and reading in the period 1880–1914, the result perhaps of a narrowing definition of play and the competition from motion pictures and other public entertainment. The increasing importance of the schools and the tendency to associate reading with classroom assignments may play a role, too.[67]

## End of Childhood

The end of childhood is symbolized and commemorated in several ways in these autobiographies. Significantly, for most of the writers,

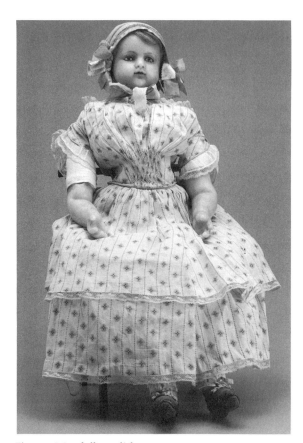

Fig. 13    Wax doll, English, 1870.

childhood ended at thirteen or fourteen years of age, often with the death of a parent, the birth or death of a sibling, or the departure from home to work or attend school. The role of schools in defining and teaching play is another large topic to which the writers only alluded. Some, like Una Hunt, came to a resolution of psychological tensions that allowed them to become "grown up"; others, such as Harriette Arnow, suffered a physical illness from which they recovered to behave in a new way. Edwin Way Teale used the burning of his house to symbolize childhood's end. Robert Lawson felt his childhood ended when his mother forbade him to remain friends with a young woman in her twenties who was ten years older than he was. For Hamlin Garland, the symbolic break with childhood was his defiance of his father over the choice of a new hat.

Fig. 14   "The Wonderful Story," Currier and Ives lithograph, about 1860.

Both the bewildering variety and the apparent patterns of play behavior offer the historian and the curator opportunities to present the history of play and playthings in the context of larger historical events, such as the Civil War and the coming of the railroad, and in the context of gender and class identity. Most clearly, this study indicates that play is intimately linked to the ways in which the individual thinks about himself and his world. The play of others inevitably leads us to reflect on our own play and its meanings.

Between the act of play and the act of remembering play lie many experiences, each adding to the context in which the playful moment finds its place. In telling the story of that moment, the autobiographer reveals how deeply embedded play is in the memory of childhood. The autobiographies indicate strongly that play is a way to create and to control a small part of the world in which children live. As they grow older and assume adult re-

sponsibilities, the importance of childish play declines, though not the need for fun and recreation. Skills learned in play in childhood, especially verbal skills involving manipulation and negotiation, serve the adult well. The pleasure the author experiences in sharing his memories of play is the ultimate proof of its power.

## Notes

1. Brian Sutton-Smith, *Toys as Culture* (New York: Gardner Press, 1986), 154.

2. Paula Petrik, professor of history at the University of Maine, Orono, is completing a study of childhood that includes an analysis of the role of the Novelty Toy Printing Press in creating a nationwide network of adolescent writers in the 1860s and 1870s.

3. Bernard Mergen, *Play and Playthings: A Reference Guide* (Westport, CT: Greenwood Press, 1982), 57–80.

4. Thomas J. Schlereth, "The Material Culture of Childhood: Problems and Potential in Historical

Fig. 15 "Mary, Elizabeth, and Why-Why in the sick chair." Photograph by Charles Hart Spencer, Pittsburgh, Pennsylvania, May 1906. Courtesy Elizabeth Ranney.

Explanation," *Material History Bulletin* 21 (Spring 1985): 1–14.

5. Jay Mechling, "Oral Evidence and the History of American Children's Lives," *Journal of American History* 74, 2 (September 1987): 579–86.

6. Louis Kaplan, *A Bibliography of American Autobiographies* (Madison: University of Wisconsin Press, 1961); Mary Louise Briscoe, *American Autobiography, 1945–1980* (Madison: University of Wisconsin Press, 1982); and Edith Cobb, *The Ecology of Imagination in Childhood* (New York: Columbia University Press, 1977).

7. Thomas Cooley, *Educated Lives: The Rise of Modern Autobiography in America* (Columbus: Ohio State University Press, 1976); and James Olney, *Metaphors of Self: The Meaning of Autobiography* (Princeton: Princeton University Press, 1972).

8. David C. Rubin, ed., *Autobiographical Memory* (New York: Cambridge University Press, 1986); and Marcia K. Johnson and Mary Ann Foley, "Differen-

tiating Fact from Fancy: The Reliability of Children's Memory," *Journal of Social Issues* 40, 2 (1984): 33–50.

9. James Langdon Hill, *My First Years as a Boy* (Andover, MA: Andover Press, 1928), 168–69.

10. John M. Roberts, M. J. Arth, and R. R. Bush, "Games in Culture," *American Anthropologist* 61 (1959): 597–605; Roger Caillois, *Man, Play, and Games* (New York: The Free Press, 1961); and Mergen, *Play and Playthings*.

11. *The Education of Henry Adams* (1906; reprint, New York: Modern Library, 1931), 5; Irving Bacheller, *Coming Up the Road: Memories of a North Country Boyhood* (Indianapolis: Bobbs-Merrill, 1928), 13; James Baldwin, *In My Youth: From the Posthumous Papers of Robert Dudley [Pseud.]* (Indianapolis: Bobbs-Merrill, 1914), 12.

12. Janet Gillespie, *With a Merry Heart* (New York: Harper & Row, 1976), 1.

13. Theodore Dreiser, *Dawn* (New York: Liveright,

1931), 16; Samuel Nathaniel Behrman, *Worcester Account* (New York: Random House, 1954), 189.

14. Emily Wilson, *The Forgotten Girl* (New York: The Alphabet Press, 1937), 13; Dorothy Howard, *Dorothy's World: Childhood in Sabine Bottom, 1902–1910* (New York: Prentice Hall, 1977), 141–42.

15. Thomas Ripley, *A Vermont Boyhood* (New York: Appleton-Century, 1937), 81; Flannery Lewis, *Brooks Too Broad for Leaping: A Chronicle from Childhood* (New York: Macmillan, 1938), 121–22.

16. Meta Stern Lilienthal, *Dear Remembered World: Childhood Memories of an Old New Yorker* (New York: Richard Smith, 1947), 13.

17. *The Autobiography of Lincoln Steffens,* vol. 1 (New York: Harcourt, Brace & World, 1931), 9; Walter Brooks, *A Child and a Boy* (New York: Brentano's, 1915), 62–63.

18. Mihaly Csikzentmihalyi and Eugene Rochberg-Halton, *The Meaning of Things: Domestic Symbols and the Self* (New York: Cambridge University Press, 1981).

19. John Albee, *Confessions of a Boyhood* (Boston: Badger, 1910), 39; William Dean Howells, *A Boy's Town* (New York: Harper and Brothers, 1890), 32; H. L. Mencken, *Happy Days, 1880–1892* (New York: Knopf, 1940), 50; Harriette Simpson Arnow, *Old Burnside* (Lexington: University Press of Kentucky, 1977), 1–50; Lucy Larcom, *A New England Girlhood* (Boston: Houghton Mifflin, 1889), 29; Marie Jastrow, *A Time to Remember: Growing Up in New York before the Great War* (New York: Norton, 1979), 30; Edward Everett Hale, *A New England Boyhood* (Boston: Little, Brown, 1964), 133.

20. Howard, *Dorothy's World,* 2; Edwin Way Teale, *Dune Boy: The Early Years of a Naturalist* (New York: Dodd, Mead, 1943), 3.

21. Bacheller, *Coming Up the Road,* 14–24; Albert Halper, *On the Shore: Young Writer Remembering Chicago* (New York: Viking, 1934), 3–9; Howard, *Dorothy's World,* 6–8.

22. Emily Kimbrough, *How Dear to My Heart* (New York: Dodd, Mead, 1944), 41; Mencken, *Happy Days,* 143.

23. Howells, *A Boy's Town,* 25–26; Baldwin, *In My Youth,* 123; Una Atherton Hunt, *Una Mary: The Inner Life of a Child* (New York: Scribner's, 1914), 145–50; Mencken, *Happy Days,* 82, 294.

24. Zona Gale, *When I Was a Little Girl* (New York: Macmillan, 1925), 40.

25. Albee, *Confessions of a Boyhood,* 136.

26. Della Lutes, *Home Grown* (Boston: Little, Brown, 1937), 167–73.

27. Mencken, *Happy Days,* 54–63; Robert P. Tristram Coffin, *Lost Paradise: A Boyhood on a Maine Coast Farm* (New York: Macmillan, 1934), 13–15, 135–55.

28. Nan Hayden Agle, *My Animals and Me: An Autobiographical Story* (New York: Seabury Press, 1970); Hal Borland, *High, Wide and Lonesome* (Philadelphia: Lippincott, 1956); *Autobiography of Lincoln Steffens;* Coffin, *Lost Paradise.*

29. Richard Wright, *Black Boy: A Record of Childhood and Youth* (New York: Harper and Brothers, 1945); Woody Guthrie, *Bound for Glory* (New York: E. P. Dutton, 1943); *Education of Henry Adams,* 42; Thomas Bailey Aldrich, *The Story of a Bad Boy* (Boston: Houghton Mifflin, 1911), 110–21; Brooks, *A Child and a Boy,* 108–13; Ulysses Prentiss Hedrick, *Land of the Crooked Tree* (New York: Oxford University Press, 1948), 20.

30. Robert Lawson, *At That Time* (New York: Viking, 1947), 48; Estilline Bennett, *Old Deadwood Days* (New York: J. H. Sears, 1928), 20–30; John Taylor Waldorf, *A Kid on the Comstock: Reminiscences of a Virginia City Childhood* (Palo Alto, CA: American West Publishing Co., 1970), 25–50.

31. Wright, *Black Boy;* Taylor Gordon, *Born to Be* (New York: Covici Friede, 1929); Jimmy Savo, *I Bow to the Stones: Memories of a New York Childhood* (New York: Howard Frisch, 1963), 18.

32. Gale, *When I Was a Little Girl,* 151–52.

33. William Wells Newell, *Games and Songs of American Children* (1883; reprint, New York: Dover Books, 1963); Arnow, *Old Burnside,* 55.

34. Frederic A. Birmingham, *It Was Fun While It Lasted* (Philadelphia: Lippincott, 1960), 46; Teale, *Dune Boy,* 150; Amelia Earhart, *The Fun of It* (New York: Harcourt Brace, 1932), 15.

35. Baldwin, *In My Youth.*

36. Hunt, *Una Mary,* 6.

37. Ibid., 82–83.

38. Hunt, *Una Mary.*

39. Gillespie, *With a Merry Heart,* 7, 42.

40. Ernestine H. Thompson and Tanya F. Johnson, "The Imaginary Playmate and Other Imaginary Figures of Childhood," in *Studies in the Anthropology of Play,* ed. Phillips Stevens, Jr. (West Point, NY: Leisure Press, 1977), 210–22.

41. Howard, *Dorothy's World,* 196, 198; Kimbrough, *How Dear to My Heart,* 173.

42. Katherine Stauffer Krebs, *Back Home in Pennsylvania* (Philadelphia: Dorrance, 1937), 10; *The Autobiography of David Ward* (New York: n.p., 1912), 14; Mencken, *Happy Days,* 202–17.

43. Wilson, *The Forgotten Girl,* 13; Ripley, *A Vermont Boyhood,* 104; Orra Phelps, *When I Was a Girl in the Martin Box* (New York: Island Press, 1949), 35; Kimbrough, *How Dear to My Heart,* 244–67.

44. Hill, *My First Years as a Boy,* 171; Halper, *On the Shore,* 68–85.

45. Hamlin Garland, *A Son of the Middle Border* (New York: Macmillan, 1917), 87; Max Miller, *Begin-*

*nings of a Mortal* (New York: E. P. Dutton, 1933), 192.

46. Hill, *My First Years as a Boy,* 174.

47. William Carlos Williams, *Autobiography* (New York: Random House, 1951), 12–13.

48. Gordon, *Born to Be,* 38–40.

49. Albert Britt, *An America That Was: What Life Was Like on an Illinois Farm Seventy Years Ago* (Barre, MA: Barre Publications, 1964), 72; Lawson, *At That Time,* 56–70; Howard, *Dorothy's World,* 233–34.

50. Hale, *A New England Boyhood,* 70; Savo, *I Bow to the Stones,* 61; Waldorf, *A Kid on the Comstock,* 114; Stewart Culin, "Street Games of Boys in Brooklyn, N.Y.," *Journal of American Folklore* 4, 14 (July– September 1891): 221–37; Howard, *Dorothy's World,* 211; MacKinlay Kantor, *But Look the Morn: The Story of a Childhood* (London: The Falcon Press, 1950), 64. For an extensive list of indoor and outdoor games of skill, strategy, chance, and make-believe, see John D. Champlin and Arthur E. Bostwick, *The Young Folks' Cyclopaedia of Games and Sports* (New York: Holt, 1890).

51. Howard, *Dorothy's World,* 180–81.

52. Mencken, *Happy Days,* 17; Coffin, *Lost Paradise,* 173; Garland, *A Son of the Middle Border,* 11; Guthrie, *Bound for Glory,* 104–6.

53. Howard, *Dorothy's World,* 181.

54. Hale, *A New England Boyhood,* 56–57; John Gabbart Bowman, *The World That Was* (New Brunswick, NJ: Rutgers University Press, 1947), 8; Dreiser, *Dawn,* 81–82.

55. Brooks, *A Child and a Boy,* 17–18, 48.

56. *The Autobiography of William Allen White* (New York: Macmillan, 1946), 80.

57. Jim Washburn, *Jim, the Boy: Autobiographical Sketches of the Author's First Eighteen Years* (Lake Lure, NC: n.p., 1952), 15; Kantor, *But Look the Morn,* 125–26.

58. Eda Lord, *Childsplay* (New York: Simon and Schuster, 1961), 111.

59. Ibid., 27.

60. Lewis, *Brooks Too Broad for Leaping,* 257.

61. T. R. Croswell, "Amusements of Worcester School Children," *Pedagogical Seminary* 6, 3 (September 1899): 314–71. See also Miriam Formanek-Brunell, "Guise & Dolls: The Rise of the Doll Industry and the Construction of Girlhood, 1870–1930" (Ph.D. diss., Rutgers University, 1989).

62. Sutton-Smith, *Toys as Culture,* 207.

63. The titles in *In My Youth* are as Baldwin remembered them. See Baldwin, *In My Youth,* 43–73, 121, 158, 205, 214, 286, 389  400; Larcom, *A New England Girlhood,* 100, 130. For an autobiography focused entirely on reading, see Caroline M. Hewins, *A Mid-Century Child and Her Books* (New York: Macmillan, 1926).

64. Hedrick, *Land of the Crooked Tree,* 271, 285.

65. Waldorf, *A Kid on the Comstock,* 154–57; Mencken, *Happy Days,* 161–73.

66. Borland, *High, Wide and Lonesome,* 89; Wright, *Black Boy,* 144–47.

67. See two good regional studies of play: Valerie Quinney, "Childhood in a Southern Mill Village," *International Journal of Oral History* 3, 3 (November 1982): 167–92; and Elliott West, "Heathens and Angels: Childhood in the Rocky Mountain Mining Towns," *The Western Historical Quarterly* 14, 2 (April 1983): 145–64.

# Fox and Geese in the School Yard

Play and America's Country Schools, 1870–1940

ANDREW GULLIFORD

As late as 1914, more than 212,000 one-room country schools served America's rural youth. On vast stretches of the Great Plains, on islands off the coast of Maine, in lumber communities in Oregon, in mining communities in West Virginia, and in Hispanic villages in New Mexico, country school teachers struggled with meager budgets, outdated textbooks, and inadequate facilities to teach thousands of youngsters the elements of reading, writing, and arithmetic. In the 1870s, one-room schools were being built in Nebraska at the rate of one per day. A quarter century later, pioneer Nebraskans were still erecting a new schoolhouse every two days.[1]

For years critics have argued that these simple country schools, taught by teachers often only slightly older than their eighth-grade students, were inadequate to serve the needs of a growing industrial nation. Yet a new generation of educational historians is revising earlier thinking and conventional wisdom about country school teaching techniques, because they are realizing that despite the odds, country school teachers indeed succeeded in educating America's rural populace.[2] In 1890, half a century after major educational reforms had

been initiated in Massachusetts by Horace Mann, the states with the highest literacy rates—Nebraska, Iowa, and Kansas—also had the highest number of one-room schools.[3]

Tangible qualities of a country school education included community support, active parental involvement, the opportunity for younger children to learn from older children, a thorough grounding in the fundamentals, an introduction to what is now called "cultural literacy," and freedom to play.[4] Understanding play in America's country schools is vital to understanding the entire milieu of nineteenth-century rural education, because the playground had several functions, not the least of which was the assimilation and Americanization of myriad ethnic and cultural groups including Native Americans, Hispanics, blacks, Greeks, German Russians, Swedes, Italians, Norwegians, and others. In schools where stern teachers demanded that every word spoken be in English regardless of a child's native tongue, playgrounds offered both physical and psychological refuge. The freedom to explore, to share, to dramatize, to fantasize, and even to engage in dangerous elements of what anthropologists have termed "deep play" all existed on or within the acre that primarily made up the country school playground.

During the fifteen to thirty minutes of morning and afternoon recess, and especially during the noon lunch hour, nineteenth-century rural schoolchildren could explore to their heart's content all the brooks, creeks, trees, hills, ditches, fields, and forests adjacent to the school. By tradition, country schools were set on their own acre, which was usually donated by a landowner who was willing to give land for a school so that his own children would not have far to walk.[5] Often the donated land was marginal for cultivation or was on a corner of the farmer's property and accessible to a county road. Because the land was not useful for farming, it frequently had excellent habitat for wildlife. Rural schoolchildren could wander across open meadows, pet horses housed in the school stables, dig holes in the dirt, chase butterflies, lizards, and snakes, and play a wide variety of folk games, many of which had been passed down by oral tradition from generation to generation.[6] Such games included rhyming motifs, such singing games as London Bridge, eye-hand coordination games such as hopscotch, ethnic games with ethnic rhyme schemes and ethnic language patterns, and all manner of make-believe that was learned on the playground from older children and not from books or by specific formalized teaching.

At country school playgrounds there existed no rigid lines of demarcation. Where school yards were fenced, the purpose was to keep the smaller children in and the cattle out. In Jiggs, Nevada, a craftsman made for the school yard a finely wrought turnstile gate without any latches.[7] Children could freely come and go, but livestock feared the iron turnstile. In the mountainous country of Appalachia, Harriette Simpson Arnow wrote, "School playground was an elastic term, embracing as it did half the lower end of the valley and the slopes of the hills on all sides."[8]

The boundaries of country school playgrounds were auditory, not physical, and children chose where they went during recess and which games they played. Their only requirement was to heed the sound of the teacher's hand bell and to come quickly when recess was over. Inside the one-room school, children opened their minds to books; outside the classroom, they explored the natural environment. Writing about the rolling prairie and high plains of eastern Colorado where he attended a country school, Hal Borland stated: "The boundaries of boyhood as I knew them for a time were that thin distant line of horizon; and even that did not bound the dreams and the imagination. . . . Those who live with a far horizon in their boyhood are never again bound to a narrow area of life. They may bind themselves, but that is a different matter."[9]

The same can be said of play at America's country schools. The only limitations placed upon children were self-limitations. Play was creative, unrestrictive, and usually harmonious because of the community atmosphere that existed at one-room schools. Children created their own play by improvising with the materials they had in full consort with the natural landscape and environment. Trees became tree forts. Brushy areas near the school could become make-believe houses. A small creek running with water could become the Mississippi River with steamboats on it. Children's play was unrestricted, and the teacher usually stayed inside (fig. 1). Family members supported their brothers and sisters when occasional arguments among students were settled with fists and wrestling matches.

It is no accident that country schools were called school*houses,* because they were about the size of a homesteader's house at the end of the nineteenth century, and, by moving the school desks around, the buildings could house the members of local communities in a single structure. Nor was play at country schools limited to children: adults attended pageants and holiday-centered special programs in them. Adults also came to country schools for adult literacy programs, meetings of literary societies, box socials, debates, and dances.[10]

The physical condition of the buildings var-

Fig. 1   Teachers usually stayed indoors during recess, giving children the freedom to play without supervision. "The Noon Recess," by Winslow Homer, *Harper's Weekly,* 28 June 1873.

ied from tight, well-built, white clapboard structures with three windows on a side and Gothic-style bell towers, to vernacular frame, log, adobe, stone, and sod structures.[11] Fred E. H. Schroeder describes one Vermont school in which an exterior schoolhouse wall even "served as one wall to a putrid swine pen, where unwanted calves were thrown to be torn and devoured by the hogs."[12] Such indecencies were far from the norm, and the buildings themselves were often part and parcel of children's play. At the Disappointment Creek Valley Schoolhouse in southwestern Colorado in 1897, teacher Nellie Carnahan Robinson wrote of the school's sod and timber roof:

> On some days we had occasional showers of dirt when a wood rat would be prowling up there. The floor was of unfinished boards, and if a child dropped a pencil he learned to be quick to retrieve it or it rolled through the cracks under the floor. At times we would have a general upheaval

at the noon hour when the boys would take up the floorboards and reclaim the erasers, pencils, chalk and various other articles the wood rat had hidden under there.[13]

Farm children familiar with a rugged outdoor life defined the nature of country school play. They were the predominant group of children in America's country schools, and they either walked the proverbial five miles to school (through snow falling deeper every time the story is told) or they came on horseback. Rural children were familiar with the natural world, and, weather permitting, they played almost exclusively outdoors. In the Midwest, and specifically in the Wheat Belt states of North and South Dakota, Montana, Kansas, Nebraska, Oklahoma, Texas, and eastern Colorado, most country school pupils were the children of immigrants. Generally parents permitted their children to attend country schools unless farm chores needed to be done, but the immigrant families had barely enough ready money, or "spot cash," for subsistence and for school desks and books. Thus, prior to 1910, formal playground equipment at country schools rarely existed.[14]

Children made their own toys and games, and those games reflected their parents' cultural heritage. The folklorist Dorothy Howard in her autobiographical book *Dorothy's World* described childhood from 1902 to 1910 in the east Texas community of Sabine Bottom:

> Manufactured (store-bought) toys were rare. . . . Play tools included sticks, stones, dirt, water, wind, sky, and clouds, leaves, flowers, vines, tree limbs, rope, string, spools from sewing thread, corncobs, cane joints, broken dishes, discarded coffee grounds, burnt matches, match boxes, shoe boxes, cigar boxes, scraps of cloth leftovers from dressmaking, rags from the ragbag and any needed thing or object borrowed or appropriated.[15]

Improvisation was not unique to the children of subsistence farmers in east Texas. In the Swiss-Mennonite schools near Bluffton, Ohio, children made jacks from grains of corn which they soaked and tightly strung together with needle and thread. For the game Rounders, they used a ball made from tight, raveled old wool socks with round sticks for bats or bats made from boards with whittled-down handholds.[16]

Studying play at one-room schools can tell us a great deal about implicit and explicit cultural values from the mid-nineteenth to the early twentieth century. A brief review of the literature on play in the United States focuses almost exclusively on "the play movement" as an urban phenomenon.[17] Just as country schools have not received proper credit for their major role in assimilating thousands of immigrant children, so have country school play motifs been ignored by researchers and theoreticians who have primarily studied play in America's turn-of-the-century cities.

Country schools were community schools in the truest sense of the term. Various age groups studied in one-room school buildings, which were governed by locally elected school boards. One-room schools differed from region to region, but as a rule they had children in attendance from all grade levels drawn from a half-dozen farm families who lived nearby. Given the large rural family size in the nineteenth century, it was not uncommon to have more than thirty children squeezed into a twenty-by-thirty-foot one-room building. Children's ages varied from a surprisingly young four or five up to sixteen and even eighteen for farm boys returning to learn their lessons before or after harvest season (fig. 2).

By the antebellum period, in response to Catharine Beecher's book *The Duty of American Women to Their Country* (1845) and her assertion that women made the best teachers because of their innate maternal instincts, more than two-thirds of the teachers in most western states were women.[18] The schoolmarm replaced the schoolmaster as men found better jobs at higher pay (fig. 3). Because little cash flowed through frontier farming areas, many country school districts were abysmally poor, so in the West and Midwest school boards hired female teachers who were considerably cheaper than their male counterparts. Women enjoyed teaching careers in the late nineteenth century because teaching offered opportunities for travel, personal advancement, and marriage. If women teachers came from a lower middle-class background in the East, they could marry well in the West and have considerable social and financial influence. Albany County, Wyoming, became known as a "mating ground" because of all the young teachers who married into farm and ranch families. Educated and attractive female schoolteachers, though often without dowries, were also highly sought in Utah and Colorado.[19]

Country schoolmarms understood play in only one context—as the release of surplus energy.[20] School, by contrast, was work intended to exercise the brain. Turn-of-the-century theorists reasoned that the brain acted like a muscle. If not continually flexed, it might atrophy and lose all its knowledge; therefore, country

Fig. 2    Country school class sizes varied during the harvest season when older farm boys worked instead of attending school. These pupils posed outside their Kansas sod school in 1907. Courtesy Library of Congress.

schoolteaching exercises concentrated on memory, recitation, and other rote techniques. Such techniques built upon oral tradition, which in the nineteenth century was one of the standard modes for transmitting folk culture. The lack of paper, pencils, and other school supplies at one-room schools also necessitated a reliance on oral lessons. Though playground activities outdoors offered a release for the children and relief for the teacher, the best teachers combined verbal play with schoolwork.

Because students of diverse ages attended, country schoolmarms had to have various study groups going on in the same room while they taught at the head of the class. Like a circus master in a three-ring circus, if the teacher was drilling her fourth graders, she also had to keep her first, second, and third graders occupied. The older sixth, seventh, and eighth graders would help out. Verbal play and rote lessons became essential not only to maintain classroom decorum but also to keep all the children involved. The result was often twofold: younger children learned from older children who were often less threatening and less formal than the teacher, and older children

mastered their lessons in order to teach their younger peers. Consequently verbal lessons learned in a one-room schoolhouse were repeated several times. The names and boundaries of states were learned in rhyming patterns, as were other historic and political facts.[21] Teachers daily used mnemonic devices as learning aids. For instance, teachers would say, "When two vowels go walking the first one does the talking." Children also learned their ABCs in a singsong fashion. The lack of school supplies required imagination and innovation from exasperated teachers who had few teaching aids or resources. Harriette Simpson Arnow, at a one-room log school in the heart of Appalachia, taught her children about the products of Kentucky by having them bring a collection of "corn, beans, cow peas, garden plant seeds, shells, and periwinkles from the river, a piece of wool, a fox tail, a strip of ground hog hide, feathers of birds and domesticated fowls . . . and a host of wild fruits, nuts, and berries from the wood."[22]

Because her mountain children had never been out of their hollow, which was accessible only by mule, Arnow had difficulty teaching them the abstract concepts of geography.

Then, in a pure gestalt learning experience, one of her students, Rie, had a flash of inspiration—she suggested creating their own globe by drawing on the potbelly of the stove. The children delighted in cleaning and burnishing the old stove and in outlining the continents and oceans with colored chalk, but Rie was not content with the improvised globe. The country schoolteacher recounted Rie's additional contribution:

> Next day she and Mable were gone a remarkably long time to the spring, leaving shortly after morning recess and returning at well nigh dinner time, covered with Spanish needles, corn pollen, and chigger bites but without water or the bucket and dipper they started with. Instead Rie carried clasped to her stomach a large, round, bright orange pumpkin which they had "packed clean frum Pop's lower corn field." . . . She patted it affectionately. "This yer, Teacher, is th' sun. She's round an' she's yaller, an' she kin come up an' go down."[23]

The teacher then had to take three lessons to explain that the stove should go around the pumpkin, not the pumpkin around the stove.

Country school lessons easily merged with country school play. Play merged with schoolwork in a country school curriculum of both indoor and outdoor activity that utilized the natural environment to the fullest. Arnow's impromptu geography lesson perfectly illustrates contemporary play theory and the significance of spontaneity. The eminent psychologist Jean Piaget has written about the importance of sensory motor activity and movement patterns as the basis for future mental growth.[24] Piaget sees play as the primary mode of learning in young children, and certainly diverse play activities were encouraged at America's country schools, where it did not matter if games went unfinished during recess. Unstructured play would simply resume during the next recess. There were not enough children for competitive sports activities, not enough for "a real rootin' game" of baseball or football, so children played together freely and easily.[25]

Solitary play, parallel play, and group play

Fig. 3   "The District School Teacher," by A. R. Ward, in *Harper's Weekly*, 9 November 1867. Society began encouraging women to become teachers in the mid-nineteenth century.

depended upon the seasons. Spring and summer games included versions of baseball (fig. 4) and the popular Anty Over, in which a ball was thrown over the schoolhouse roof and team members who caught the ball raced around the building to tag opposing players. In addition to ball games of various types, there were innumerable chase and tag games such as Rover Red Rover, Black Man, Pom Pom Pullaway, Capture the Flag, Duck on the Rock, and I Am the Cheese. Circle and handholding games included London Bridge, Farmer in the Dell, Ring Around the Rosey, Three Deep, and Crack the Whip, also known as Sling the Biscuit (fig. 5). Winter games included the solitary play of making angels in the snow and the group play of Fox and Geese, in which the spokes of a wheel were tramped into the snow. Children who were the geese had to stay on set paths while being pursued by another child who was the fox.

Fig. 4    Baseball in the school yard, about 1900. Courtesy City of Greeley Museums, permanent collection.

Country school games were essentially folk games, and each playground reflected the cultural patterns and ethnicity of the community. As Johan Huizinga wrote in his seminal work *Homo Ludens*, "Inside the playground an absolute and peculiar order reigns. Here we come across another, very positive feature of play: it creates order, is order. Into an imperfect world and into the confusion of life it brings a temporary, a limited perfection."[26] Huizinga believed in play as a cultural, not a biological, phenomenon, and it is this cultural aspect of play that stood out at country school yards as America sought to assimilate hundreds of thousands of immigrant children between the Civil War and World War I.

Historian Marcus Lee Hansen has stated that the nineteenth century characterized the greatest migration of all time.[27] From the Columbian Exposition in 1893 to the beginning of World War I in 1914, fifteen million immigrants came to America, and many of them rode west in immigrant cars on the new steel rails of the Atchison, Topeka and Santa Fe, the Great Northern, and the Northern Pacific. They came to homestead and farm, and their children attended one-room schools. In 1900 immigrants made up 47.6 percent of the population of eleven western states. In Utah, Montana, California, and Nevada, they were in the majority, and they composed a full 77.5 percent of the population of North Dakota, 74.9 percent in Minnesota, and 61.1 percent in South Dakota.[28]

The languages spoken at country school playgrounds on the Great Plains included German, Russian, Swedish, Finnish, Hungarian, and regional dialects such as Slovak. With few newspapers in the new farming communities and few other media influences, many country schools helped to retain old-world culture for the children of immigrants whose fathers served on local school boards. For twenty years, from the 1870s to the 1890s, country school boards in the West and Midwest could determine most aspects of rural education. With the influx of millions of immigrants in the early 1890s, and jingoism brought about by World War I, the issues of Americanization and the mandatory teaching of English became important legislative concerns. Ethnic language and history lessons had been offered first thing in the morning in the native tongue of the immigrants whose children attended school. But because of World War I, teachers hired locally now had to adhere to state statutes and state standards of instruction only in English no matter how isolated the country schools. For instance, at the Huber School near the Swiss-Mennonite community of Bluffton, Ohio, all classroom instruction was in English, but all playground conversation was in German and included numerous rhymes, riddles, and puns. Similar folk play occurred at the Mennonite settlement near Berne, Indiana.

Most country school classrooms were extremely uncomfortable for children whose parents' native tongue was not English. The children respected and revered their teachers, but they often could not communicate with them. Teachers in turn thought their immigrant children were ignorant or slow without realizing the extreme difficulty inherent in trying to learn school lessons in a foreign tongue, especially for children whose parents had the

Fig. 5 "Snap the Whip," by Winslow Homer, *Harper's Weekly,* 20 September 1873.

same language difficulties. For those children caught between the obligatory world of English at school and their own cultural traditions and language patterns at home, only the playground offered a neutral zone. Children were motivated to learn English not so much for educational success, but to communicate with their playground peers.

Accompanying the babble of children at lunch, often in several languages, was a brisk trade in foodstuffs brought to school in half-gallon buckets or recycled syrup pails. Exotic homemade dishes of lutefisk (a Norwegian baked whitefish dish cured in lye), stuffed spicy meatballs, tortillas, or Danish rolls were traded for peanut butter sandwiches. In a school yard near Sweet Grass, Montana, close to the Canadian border, slabs of bear meat on homemade brown bread were no match for the luxuries of bologna on store-bought bread.[29] Once the food was quickly consumed,

the lunch buckets could be used for capturing insects, collecting stones, or rolling down hills.

Dramatic school yard play hastened the children's assimilation and acculturation. Because of new state laws requiring instruction in English, many immigrants who wanted their children to retain their old-world cultural heritage utilized one-room schools during vacation periods for training in European language, culture, and history. These ethnic language and history sessions became known as vacation schools. Writing in *Life in an American Denmark,* Alfred C. Nielsen explained:

> For a thousand years my people had lived among the lakes and hills of Jutland, Denmark. Some of the well-meaning if misguided, teachers of the vacation school had told us that we owed our first allegiance to Denmark. We did not argue with them . . . but when we children played war on the playgrounds we were not divided between

Danes and Germans. . . . No! We fought the battles of Lexington, Bunker Hill, Gettysburg and San Juan Hill all over again.[30]

For Native American children, country school attendance was often sporadic because of the need to maintain family ties with distant relatives. Attendance also waned during different seasons because of the importance of travel to tribal rituals such as ceremonial dances and annual festivals. The Bureau of Indian Affairs routinely selected teachers with little regard to their racial sensitivity. These teachers often did not understand or appreciate the play activities of Indian children, particularly dancing, which mimicked their parents' movements during sacred ceremonies. By trying to bring tribal traditions into the secular schoolhouse, teachers angered Indian parents. One teacher attempted to solve the problem of absenteeism for the practice of ritualistic dancing by having the children "dance Indian" at school. He immediately provoked the ire of mothers who insisted that the schoolhouse was the place to learn from books. Dancing was to be the exclusive province of parents.[31]

In Hispanic communities throughout the Southwest, no such cultural conflicts occurred because local school boards chose their own teachers from community members. Country school play utilized homemade objects of wood, clay, stone, or animal hides in simple games for the younger children. Older siblings generally herded cattle and sheep and did not attend school.[32] Outdoor games included *Los Aguantes* (Endurance), *La Cazoleja* (The Saucepan), *Las Iglesias* (The Churches), and the popular *Chueco* known as Shinny or Indian hockey. Indoor games included *Pitarrilla* (New Mexico checkers) and *El Coyote y Las Gallinas* (Coyote and Hens).[33] Traditional singing games were *La Naranja Dulce* (The Sweet Orange), *La Vibora del Mar* (The Sea Serpent), *La Rueda de San Miguel* (St. Michael's Wheel), *Doña Ana No Esta Aqui* (Lady Anne Isn't Here), and *Juan Molinero* (John the Miller), thought to be one of the first and last

of the play-party games from the Texas panhandle. Adults in the Baptist Bible Belt, who could not condone dancing, sponsored play-party games as a safe, chaperoned activity for their teen-age children.[34]

In addition to the play motifs unique to specific cultures, under wide-open skies children also played with a variety of animate objects because of the richness of the natural environment. Creative play in the Southwest included chasing lizards and chameleons with sticks to capture them as lunch-bucket pets. On the Great Plains where fall annually brought out rattlesnakes, the deadliest of regional reptiles, children would hunt them down and kill them during the noon recess. With country schools isolated by miles of open prairie and physicians few and far between, this dangerous type of play epitomizes what anthropologist Clifford Geertz terms "deep play" after the work of Jeremy Bentham, who described it in the eighteenth century as "play in which the stakes are so high that it is . . . irrational for men to engage in it at all."[35] At one eastern Colorado school yard, older schoolboys coming upon an especially active snake den casually killed sixteen rattlers during a single lunch recess.[36] Such obvious expressions of "deep play" were rare, but fairly common was the pursuit and capture of gophers which children flushed from their holes with pails of water. Too young to help their fathers place hot brands on squirming cattle, country schoolchildren could imitate their parents by playing at branding. Gophers, the reluctant victims of such dramatic play, were branded by children in both Wyoming and Canada. They used tiny branding irons made from a length of hay wire.[37]

Schoolchildren built forts of wood and snow from available materials. They hid in creeks and ravines and incorporated into their play brush piles, fence lines, and dead trees. Things to throw on the country school playground included mud balls, snowballs, rocks, sticks, and even flowers. Play theorists have argued that "play is to the child what verbalization is to the adult. It is a medium for expressing feelings, exploring relationships, describing experiences, disclosing wishes, and self-fulfillment."[38]

Another play medium unique to country schools was the ubiquitous outhouse. These outdoor rest rooms not only served as places to hide, safe bases for games of tag, and outbuildings where students could gossip about the teacher, but were also, because most outhouses were at the rear of country schools, the preferred places to learn to smoke. Students started off smoking rolled corn silk or lengths of vine. Elderberry stems made hastily improvised pipes when filled with wild grass.[39] Tobacco, however, was a scarce commodity. Because male students played at smoking in imitation of their fathers, Laura Eisenhuth, the state superintendent of public instruction for North Dakota, in 1894 called the condition of outhouses in the state "the greatest moral question affecting schools." She urged school boards to provide healthy outhouses "free of all kinds of drawings and writing, immoral influences that burn and blacken the pure young souls of innocent children, and perpetuate and strengthen evil."[40] Obviously she felt that children's play in and around outhouses could not be condoned. She probably was not keen on having children jump off the roofs of outhouses and stables, either, but they did that, too.

Barns were equally integral to the country school playground. C. Ross Bloomquist, who attended The Birtsell School, District No. 3, in Foster Country, North Dakota, remembered, "We played in the barn occasionally on rainy days, but its main use was as a place to hide behind during recess and noontime hide-and-go-seek games." He added, "The schoolhouse yard of somewhat more than an acre was virgin prairie. . . . During vacation time many species of prairie flowers managed to grow and bloom in spite of the children's efforts to wear out the grasses and plants during playtime."[41] Country school children engaged in active play using their imaginations, rather than recapitulating stereotypes from electronic media as children often do today. A favorite

game played in the schoolhouse barn was horse and rider, where the small pupils played horses who trotted around and whinnied at the command of the older students. On the country school playground children became rodeo cowboys by riding a bucking barrel suspended by ropes tied to a fence post and a few trees.

In the high Rocky Mountains where deep snows prohibited school in winter, summer schools were popular. A schoolmarm who began her career teaching in a one-room log school in a wide alpine meadow near Steamboat Springs, Colorado, told about convening school after the lunch recess, but finding that her children would not sit at their seats. Instead, they stood at attention near their desks. After a moment of awkward silence and muffled giggles, they opened their shirts and jackets and pelted her with wildflowers they had spent their noon hour gathering. She did not know whether to laugh or cry, so she did both! Though she was delighted with the flowers, she was not sure her pupils were showing proper respect for her as an authority figure.[42]

Indeed, on many occasions country school play and roughhousing took on a much deeper meaning as play events rapidly escalated into serious confrontations. Frank Grady, who attended a one-room school in Nebraska in the early 1900s, stated, "The first teacher in Raymond School was run out by the boys, who used stones as weapons of assault."[43] Schoolmarms were frequently intimidated by the brash and brawling farm boys who returned to school after harvest and painfully stuffed themselves into small wooden desks, which soon bore scars from sharpened barlow knives.[44] In schools with young female teachers and rowdy older male students, the playground generally became the students' domain. Teachers fought long and hard for their right to authority in the classroom, but they often relinquished any such rights outside the building.

Even brawny male teachers faced personal confrontations in the name of play. In his autobiography *All Is but a Beginning: Youth Re-*

*membered, 1881–1901*, Native American scholar John G. Neihardt wrote about a snowball fight at the one-room school where he taught in Nebraska:

> Bill Kendrick loomed up before me out of the melee. I can see him yet as I saw him then in a vivid, timeless moment—a robust youth, perhaps a trifle overgrown for his years but amply shouldered and chested like a buffalo bull calf. I caught the triumphant grin upon his flushed face as he stooped in front of me, reaching with his right hand for a fistful of snow.[45]

Neihardt described a scene in which country school play became a test of manhood between a strapping adolescent and the recently hired male teacher. Fortunately for Neihardt, he had just learned a new wrestling technique, and "Bill had accidentally placed himself in the best possible position for my trick throw." Neihardt recalled with satisfaction, "Bill's size and weight were greatly in my favor now. He came down like a wagonload of brick."[46]

Accounts of such confrontations abound in the country school literature, and they vary from good-humored playful tussles in the snow to bare-knuckled fistfights between teacher and students. Jesse Stewart fought in order to keep teaching at the Lonesome Valley School in Kentucky. His student Guy Hawkins came "down the broad middle aisle, taking long steps and swinging his big arms."[47] Hawkins had driven Stewart's sister out of the school, and he was determined to do the same to Stewart himself. Stewart wrote that after several minutes of close punching,

> his [Hawkins's] fingernail took a streak of hide from my neck and left a red mark that smarted and the blood oozed through. I pounded his chin. I caught him on the beardy jaw. I reeled him back and followed up. I gave him a left to the short ribs while my right in a split second caught his mouth. Blood spurted again. Yet he was not through.[48]

Jesse Stewart finally whipped Guy Hawkins and continued teaching at the Lonesome Valley School in relative peace. Such serious confrontations were not unusual, however, and country school play could take on violent connotations as one-room school teachers struggled to maintain classroom control.

Because rural teachers were physically isolated, they had to be resourceful and quell student unrest lest in a time of danger their authority be questioned. In dangerous situations teachers often utilized play motifs to gain the cooperation of all their students regardless of age. Rather than alarm their children when tornadoes or blizzards threatened on the Great Plains, teachers would have their pupils join hands and sing as they moved quickly away from the school and toward the safety of an adjoining farmhouse. Teachers made a game of an emergency evacuation to keep the children from becoming fearful and panicked. These incidents were not rare. The spring blizzard that swept across the Great Plains in 1888 stranded so many pupils and teachers in one-room schools that it became known as the Schoolchildren's Blizzard (fig. 6).[49] Those teachers who fled with their children to safety utilized nursery rhymes and play motifs. The teachers who chose to wait in their schools for help and relief certainly used games and play to while away the time and to keep their children moving and their blood circulating lest they develop hypothermia and begin to freeze.

Because one-room schools were community schools, and because they were the main focus for both the play of children and adults in the decades before telephones, scheduled events were almost never called off because of the weather. At a 1914 Christmas program near Towner, North Dakota, every person in the community crowded into the school despite temperatures of forty degrees below zero and a wind-chill factor that lowered the mercury twenty more degrees. At another North Dakota Christmas program scheduled during a bitterly cold blizzard, pupils performed the pageant twice, then wrapped themselves in coats and slept on the floor while the adults conversed and played cards while they waited for daybreak and safe passage home.[50]

The success of programs and pageants at country schools could make or break a coun-

Fig. 6 Cover sheet for "Thirteen Were Saved," a song about a midwestern blizzard in 1888. It was known as the Schoolchildren's Blizzard because many schoolchildren were stranded in one-room schools. The song praises Minnie Freeman of the Myra School District in Nebraska, who led her students to safety. Courtesy Nebraska State Historical Society.

Fig. 7 Country school students celebrating a special occasion with a watermelon feast outdoors, about 1900. Courtesy Country School Legacy Collection, Western Historical Collections, University of Colorado Libraries.

try school teacher in the days before teachers' tenure (fig. 7). Dramatic play at America's country schools was vitally important because country schools served as community centers, and teachers knew quite well that the audience would include parents, grandparents, and all members of the local school board. Consequently, planning and preparations for Christmas programs began immediately after Thanksgiving. Teachers' contracts often stipulated that they present at least two programs per year. Schoolchildren performed in buildings so crowded that spectators stood along the edges of the schoolroom, in the entryway, and even at open windows outside the building, weather permitting. Lettie B. Zion described the enthusiasm of an eastern Colorado audience of farmers and homesteaders for such events:

> A flurry of excitement filled the place on these occasions, and the children usually found places to sit—but couldn't sit still—they twisted, turned, wiggled and squirmed, or had to get up and go outdoors often before it was time for the program to begin. Many people had to stand up as often there were not enough seats—even with wagon seats and planks laid across nail kegs.[51]

Significant seasonal programs and pageants included Presidents' Day in February, Arbor Day specifically in Nebraska and all across the Great Plains, May Day, and the various saints' days in the Hispanic Southwest (fig. 8). Comedies were quite popular, such as *Aaron Slick from Punkin' Crick, The Irish Detective, Robin Hood and His Merry Men,* and *Let Toby Do It.* In the early 1900s one production at a rural school district in Spirit Lake Township, Kings-

Fig. 8   Students and their teacher commemorating Arbor Day with a picnic, near Groton, New York, 1912. Courtesy Verne Morton Collection, DeWitt Historical Society of Tompkins County.

bury County, South Dakota, earned enough money in admissions fees to pay for a new school floor![52]

Adult play and educational competition included ciphering and spelling matches. For the evening competitions, usually schoolchildren competed in the preliminary rounds, and then adults displayed their mental prowess. Spelling matches were keenly enjoyed on the frontier, and the colloquial phrase "toeing the line" refers to barefoot children placing their toes on wooden floorboards in country schools while they lined up for spelling matches. Squire Hawkins, one of the main characters in Edward Eggleston's 1871 novel *The Hoosier Schoolmaster,* explains the importance of spelling. He describes in the vernacular, "Spelling is the corner-stone, the grand underlying subterfuge, of a good eddication."[53] The significance of spelling matches as a form of verbal play for both children and adults cannot be underestimated. Noah Webster's *The Elementary Spelling Book,* first printed in 1855 and commonly known as the Blue-Back Speller, had a phenomenal printing of thirty-five million copies between 1855 and 1890. The 1866 edition alone sold 1.5 million copies, though ironically not a single definition was given for any of the words listed in its 174 pages.[54] Americans learned to spell, but they did not really know the meaning of the words they were studying. Verbal play was more important than useful knowledge.

Other forms of adult play at America's country schools featured very popular literary societies, box socials, and dances. In the early 1900s in Ford County, Kansas, fifty literary societies actively met in country schools. At the Yarnold School in Douglas County, Kansas, adults formed a society in 1902 "for our mu-

Fig. 9    President Theodore Roosevelt, who was on a hunting expedition in the area, addressed about 250 people at a church service held in Blue School, near Rifle, Colorado, 30 April 1905. Courtesy Rifle Creek Museum, Rifle, Colorado.

tual improvement, for the entertainment of our friends, and for the cultivation of the amenities of social life."[55] In these adult societies, face-to-face verbal exchange remained the key element in adult play.

Literary societies functioned not only to disseminate culture on the frontier, but also to sponsor lively debates on both trivial and crucial topics (fig. 9). Contemporary issues included the free coinage of silver, women's suffrage, the Spanish-American War, and the platforms of local political candidates. More philosophical issues were debated at the Hilty School in the Swiss-Mennonite area near Bluffton, Ohio. Skilled debaters discussed such aesthetic questions as "Resolved that art is more pleasing to the eye than nature," "Resolved that the love of fame is a more powerful motive in human affairs than the love of

money," "Resolved that love is a greater incentive to action than fear," and "Resolved that the field of oratory affords a greater opportunity to influence human action than the editor."[56] Political resolutions debated at the school in 1898 included, "Resolved that the American eagle will outlive the British lion" and "Resolved that the President of the United States should be elected directly by the people for a term of 6 years and should not be elected for a second term."[57]

Box socials were a highlight of adult play both in terms of the intense competition among country women to produce the best cold dinner and also in the creation of elaborate decorations for the exterior of the box. These boxes were auctioned off and the proceeds donated to needed one-room school projects such as the piano or book fund (fig.

Fig. 10    Globes and dictionaries, such as the ones shown in this North Dakota school about 1910, were frequently purchased with money earned at box socials. Courtesy State Historical Society of North Dakota.

10). As part of paying for the tasty meal—which included homemade pies, jellies, cakes, and huge chunks of beef or pork sandwiched between rolls spread thickly with butter—the highest bidder also earned the right to sit next to the woman who had prepared the dinner. Most dinner boxes were sold for between fifty cents and a dollar, but, on the western frontier where males outnumbered females by as much as seven to one, the opportunity to sit next to an eligible single woman, particularly the schoolmarm, could result in furious bidding. More than one cowboy spent half a month's wages on a cold biscuit sandwich just to sit next to the schoolteacher.[58]

If box socials synthesized adult country school play and fund-raising events, dances at one-room schools exemplified the role of country schools as community centers. Everyone attended, both young and old. Those too small to dance played outside until it got dark and then played hide-and-seek games underneath the school desks while their parents practiced the schottische, the butterfly, the polka, and the waltz. Because of the distances people traveled, dances were often all-night affairs. A supper was served at midnight; then, after an hour's respite, the weary musicians again picked up their fiddles and bows and made music until dawn. Describing country schools in central California at the turn of the century, John Steinbeck wrote in *East of Eden:* "The schoolhouse was the meeting place for music, for debate. The polls were set in the schoolhouse for elections. Social life, whether it was the crowning of a May queen, the eulogy to a dead president, or an all-night dance, could be held nowhere else."[59]

Yet with the advent of World War I, American education and America's country schools began to change irrevocably. National organizations such as Theodore Roosevelt's Country Life Commission argued for a higher quality of life, a concept that included consolidated schools. As women became more and more dominant in their new roles as local and state school superintendents, they also argued for school consolidation in such influential books as Mabel Carney's *Country Life and the Country School* (1912).[60] Consolidation arguments focused on poor curriculum, inadequately trained rural teachers, shoddy buildings, and the unnecessary duplication of services.

The first Model-T Fords that coughed and wheezed across the Midwest spelled the end for one-room schools. In the states of Iowa, Indiana, Illinois, and throughout New England, school buses could quickly pick up farm children and transport them to larger, centralized schools where rural children supposedly received a better educational background with specialized instruction in art, science, and language. But what of the free-flowing play that had characterized the country school? What about the interaction among all age groups on the country school playground and the importance of adult play at those vital community centers?

Certainly play at one-room schools had shaped the lives of America's youth as decisively as any lessons they had learned, particularly immigrant children whose only refuge was the country school playground. In the schools, the children were frequently the object of criticism and ridicule because they could not speak English. On the playground, they could speak the language of their parents, gather in cliques to discuss their exasperated teacher, and offer each other essential support as they made the difficult transition from the sons and daughters of immigrants to full-fledged young American men and women. Despite initial differences of language and culture, the country school and the country school playground created a common background for America's rural youth. The late psychologist Bruno Bettelheim, former head of the University of Chicago's School for Disturbed Children, stated,

> Children in the one-room school had a common background; they would normally have played together, too. So, without any effort, the teacher could understand what life was like in their families. In addition, a one-room school can't func-

tion unless the older children help teach the younger ones. The one-room school was the best school we ever had.[61]

Other experts agree with Bettelheim about the importance of group play at country schools. In her book *No Easy Answers: The Learning Disabled Child* (1981), Sally L. Smith described how a learning-disabled child functioned in a country school classroom. She wrote, "The one-room schoolhouse of yesteryear allowed for slow maturing. The heterogeneous groupings allowed a child to proceed at his own pace."[62] If country school play benefited disabled children, for other students country school play helped to establish personal independence and individual, creative thinking. Children who participated in various rural play activities may have grown up with strong egos and a heightened sense of their own individuality, because from the first day at a country school their participation was needed and wanted.[63] School consolidation eliminated this consensual play in which children chose their teammates and made up their own rules. Consolidation also resulted in increased competition in athletics and sports. The larger the number of children, the fewer the opportunities to participate in such structured outdoor games as baseball. By 1914, when country schools still thrived in remote areas of the West, formal playground equipment began to be installed in the more prosperous school districts (fig. 11). Standardized schools even had movable sandboxes for the younger children. Soon the war would bring even more drastic changes to American rural schools.

As World War I intensified, communities settled by German immigrants changed their names, and the names of country schools were changed, too. Last-day programs for eighth-grade graduation became even more significant as rites of passage, and rural school pageants more than ever before featured patriotic themes with the proliferation of stars, stripes, and red, white, and blue bunting (fig. 12). After Armistice Day, prices for farm crops plum-

Fig. 11 This homemade giant stride in a Los Angeles playground shows the movement toward more formal school yard play. Arthur Leland and Lorna Higby Leland, *Playground Technique and Playcraft* (1910).

meted. Just as many homesteaders abandoning their failed dryland farms meant the end of the last wave of frontier settlement, the consolidation of country schools into graded schools marked the end of an era in American education that is still poorly understood.

America's rural schools had provided for cultural assimilation as well as for cultural pluralism. Children who had not been ruled by the clock and had played at their leisure now were segregated by age in classrooms that stressed competition. Buses brought country children into town schools, and after World War II, children's folk play was replaced by organized sports. An entirely different ethos reigned in which individualism was sacrificed

to conformity. Yet child's play is serious business. Children today need the opportunity to invent their own games, to fail and to succeed with their friends, and to experience the natural world as previous generations did with such unbounded enthusiasm on the playgrounds of America's country schools.

### Notes

The author owes an intellectual debt to folklorist Dorothy Howard for reading an earlier draft of this paper, to archivist Anna Selfridge of the Allen County, Ohio, Historical Society for helping to locate Ohio country school play sources, and to American studies professor Bernie Mergen of

Fig. 12   Students from a rural school in Fowler, Colorado, about 1918, participating in a patriotic program. Courtesy Pueblo Library District.

George Washington University for his suggestions and advice.

1. Barc Bayley and Beth S. Bohling, eds., *And Cattle Ate the School* (Lincoln: Nebraska State Education Association, 1967), 8. Many references in this article refer to country schools in the Midwest and in the Rocky Mountains, but in fact the entire nation is covered by these general themes and citations. Examples come from the Midwest and West because of the author's familiarity with those schools and sources.

2. Recent scholarship on the significance of country schools in American education includes Wayne E. Fuller, *The Old Country School* (Chicago: University of Chicago Press, 1982); Ellis Ford Hartford, *The Little White Schoolhouse* (Lexington: University Press of Kentucky, 1977); Carl F. Kaestle, *Pillars of the Republic: Common Schools and American Society, 1780–1860* (New York: Hill and Wang, 1983); William Link, *A Hard and Lonely Place* (Chapel Hill: University of North Carolina Press, 1986); Diane Manning, ed., *Hill Country Teacher* (Boston: Twayne Publishing, 1990); Jonathan P. Sher, ed., *Education in Rural America: A Reassessment of Conventional Wisdom* (Boulder, CO: Westview Press, 1977);

Thad Sitton and Milam C. Rowold, *Ringing the Children In* (College Station: Texas A & M University Press, 1987); and Donna M. Stephens, *One-Room Schools: Teaching in 1930s Western Oklahoma* (Norman: University of Oklahoma Press, 1990).

3. Wayne E. Fuller, "Country Schoolteaching on the Sod-House Frontier," *Arizona and the West* (Summer 1975): 121. See also Lee Soltow and Edward Stevens, *The Rise of Literacy and the Common School in the United States* (Chicago: University of Chicago Press, 1983).

4. E. D. Hirsch in *Cultural Literacy: What Every American Needs to Know* (Boston: Houghton Mifflin, 1987) stresses establishing a common cultural framework of shared historical knowledge for American students. In fact, eighth-grade examinations for country school graduates required similar types and categories of essential information.

5. Andrew Gulliford, *America's Country Schools* (Washington, DC: The Preservation Press of the National Trust for Historic Preservation, 1991), 162.

6. Folk games are "part of our culture which display a measure of traditional stability balanced by dynamic change and informal transmission from person to person." Though there are innumerable

definitions possible for "folk" and "folklore," this one comes from Jan Harold Brunvand, "The Study of American Folklore," in Brunvand, ed., *Readings in American Folklore* (New York: Norton, 1979), 425.

7. Gulliford, *America's Country Schools*, 176.

8. Harriette Simpson Arnow, *Mountain Path* (1936; reprint, Lexington, KY: University Press of Kentucky, 1985), 167. This book is one of many autobiographical firsthand accounts of country school teaching. See also Marshall A. Barber, *The Schoolhouse at Prairie View* (Lawrence, KS: University of Kansas Press, 1953); Eulalia Bourne, *Nine Months Is a Year* (Tucson: University of Arizona Press, 1968); Mary Ley and Mike Bryan, eds., *Journey from Ignorant Ridge* (Austin, TX: Texas Congress of Parents and Teachers, 1976); and Della Lutes, *Country Schoolma'am* (Boston: Little, Brown, 1941).

9. Hal Borland, *High, Wide and Lonesome* (1956; reprint, New York: G. K. Hall, 1984), 27.

10. The best introduction to early twentieth-century adult literacy programs in one-room schools can be found in Cora Wilson Stewart, *Moonlight Schools for the Emancipation of Adult Illiterates* (New York: E. P. Dutton, 1922). For sources on country schools as community centers, see Gulliford, *America's Country Schools,* and the biographical or fictional accounts by Bess Streeter Aldrich, *A Lantern in Her Hand* (New York: Grosset & Dunlap, 1928); Alberta Wilson Constant, *Miss Charity Comes to Stay* (New York: Crowell, 1959); Hamlin Garland, *A Son of the Middle Border* (New York: Macmillan, 1917); and Owen Wister, *The Virginian* (1902; reprint, New York: Signet Books, 1979).

11. For an introduction to the topic, see William A. Alcott, *Essay on the Construction of School-Houses* (Boston: Hilliard, Gray, Little, Wilkinson, and Richardson, Lord, Holbrook, 1832); Henry Barnard, *School Architecture; or, Contributions to the Improvement of School-Houses in the United States,* vol. 42 in *Classics in Education,* ed. Jean and Robert McClintock (1848; reprint, New York: Teacher's College Press, Columbia University, 1970); Thomas Henry Burrows, ed., *Pennsylvania School Architecture* (Harrisburg, PA: A. B. Hamilton, 1855); Fletcher B. Dresslar, *American Schoolhouses* (Washington, DC: Government Printing Office, 1911); Gulliford, *America's Country Schools;* Kingston Heath, "A Dying Heritage: One-Room Schools of Gallatin County, Montana," in Camille Wells, ed., *Perspectives on Vernacular Architecture* (Annapolis, MD: Vernacular Architecture Forum, 1982); Fred E. H. Schroeder, "Educational Legacy: Rural One-Room Schoolhouses," *Historic Preservation,* July–September 1977, 4–9; Eric Sloane, *The Little Red Schoolhouse* (Garden City, NY: Doubleday, 1972); and Gordon Wil-

son, "Traditional Aspects of the One-Roomed School," *Kentucky Folklore Record* 13 (January–March 1967): 14–19, 43–49.

12. Fred E. H. Schroeder, "The Little Red Schoolhouse," in Ray B. Browne and Marshall Fishwick, eds., *Icons of America* (Bowling Green, OH: Popular Press, Bowling Green State University, 1978), 145.

13. Michael L. Husband, "The Recollections of a Schoolteacher in Disappointment Creek Valley," *Colorado Magazine* 51, 2 (Spring 1974): 150. For additional references to country schools in the West, see Charles E. Rankin, "Teaching: Opportunity and Limitation for Wyoming Women," *Western Historical Quarterly* 21, 2 (May 1990): 147–70; Donna M. Stephens, *One-Room School: Teaching in 1930s Oklahoma* (Norman: University of Oklahoma Press, 1990); Diane Manning, *Hill Country Teacher* (Boston: Twayne Publishing, 1990); and Thad Sitton and Milam C. Rowold, *Ringing the Children In* (College Station: Texas A & M University Press, 1987).

14. Playground equipment at one-room schools came about as a result of books such as R. L. Parker, *Rural Schoolhouses and Their Equipment* (Fort Hays, KS: Fort Hays Normal School Bulletin, June 1916); S. A. Challman, *The Rural School Plant for Rural Teachers and School Boards, Normal Schools, Teachers' Training Classes, Rural Extension Bureaus* (Milwaukee: WI: Bruce Publishing Company, 1917); and Fletcher B. Dresslar and Pruett Haskell, *Rural Schoolhouses, School Grounds and Their Equipment,* Bulletin No. 21, U.S. Office of Education (Washington, DC: Government Printing Office, 1930).

15. Dorothy Howard, *Dorothy's World: Childhood in Sabine Bottom, 1902–1910* (Englewood Cliffs, NJ: Prentice Hall, 1977), 180. From pages 180 to 257, Howard presents an excellent catalog on rural play. To put that play into cultural perspective, see Bernard Mergen, *Play and Playthings: A Reference Guide* (Westport, CT: Greenwood Press, 1982).

16. Mary L. Sheeley, ed., *Putnam County, Ohio, One-Room Schools* (Evansville, IN: Whippoorwill Publications for the Putnam County Historical Society, Kalida, OH, 1985), 549. Also see Levina Gratz Zimmerly (b. 1896), manuscript on Ohio schools donated to the Allen County Historical Society, Allen County Museum, Lima, OH, 1986.

17. See Clarence E. Rainwater, *The Play Movement in the United States* (Chicago: University of Chicago Press, 1922); Elmer D. Mitchell and Bernard S. Mason, *The Theory of Play* (New York: A. S. Barnes, 1937); Peggy L. Miller, *Creative Outdoor Play Areas* (Englewood Cliffs, NJ: Prentice Hall, 1972); and Doris Sponseller, ed., *Play as a Learning Medium* (Washington, DC: National Association for Education of Young Children, 1976). For an urban com-

parison with country schools, see Amanda Dargan and Steven Zeitlin, *City Play* (New Brunswick, NJ: Rutgers University Press, 1990).

18. Catharine Beecher, *The Duty of American Women to Their Country* (New York: Harper and Brothers, 1845); see also Redding S. Sugg, *Mother-teacher: The Feminization of American Education* (Charlottesville: University Press of Virginia, 1978); and Kaestle, *Pillars of the Republic.*

19. For information on wages, see Gulliford, *America's Country Schools,* 69. The "mating ground" reference is from Gulliford, 67. See also Charles E. Rankin, "Teaching: Opportunity and Limitation for Wyoming Women," *Western Historical Quarterly* 21, 2 (May 1990): 147–70; Polly Welts Kaufman, "A Wider Field of Usefulness: Pioneer Women Teachers in the West, 1848–1854," *Journal of the West* 21 (April 1982): 16–25; Kaufman, *Women Teachers on the Frontier* (New Haven, CT: Yale University Press, 1984); Kenneth Wiggins Porter, "Catharine Emma Wiggins: Pupil and Teacher in Northwest Kansas, 1888–1895," *Kansas History* 1, 1 (Spring 1978): 16–38; Lila Gravatt Schrimsher, ed., "The Diary of Anna Webber, May–June 1881," *Kansas Historical Quarterly* 38, 3 (Autumn 1972): 320–37; and Jessie Embry, "Schoolmarms of Utah: Separate and Unequal" (manuscript in the Country School Legacy Collection of the Utah State Historical Society, Salt Lake City, UT, 1980).

20. For a brief description of theories of play, see the chapter "The Nature of Play" in Joe L. Frost and Barry L. Klein, *Children's Play and Playgrounds* (Boston: Allyn and Bacon, 1979).

21. A contemporary version of this type of cultural knowledge is described in the previously cited Hirsch, *Cultural Literacy.*

22. Arnow, *Mountain Path,* 100.

23. Ibid., 102.

24. See Jean Piaget's classic works *The Language and Thought of the Child* (London: Kegan Paul, 1926) and *Play, Dreams, and Imitation in Childhood* (New York: Norton, 1962).

25. Play at country schools today in the wide-open spaces of the American West replicates play at one-room schools in the nineteenth century. See Andrew Gulliford, "Not Enough for a Real Rootin' Game—Riding the Blackboard in Rural Wyoming," *Christian Science Monitor,* 26 January 1981.

26. Johan Huizinga, *Homo Ludens: A Study of the Play-Element in Culture* (Boston: Beacon Press, 1950), 10.

27. Marcus Lee Hansen, *The Immigrant in American History* (New York: Harper & Row, 1940), 15.

28. Gulliford, *America's Country Schools,* 91.

29. Professor Bonnie Maldonado, Chairman, De-partment of Education, Western New Mexico University, interview with author, 22 September 1987. Maldonado attended a country school near Sweet Grass, Montana.

30. Alfred C. Nielsen, *Life in an American Denmark* (Des Moines, IA: Grand View College, 1962). For additional sources on one-room schools and Americanization, see Nora Mohberg, *A Home for Agate* (Grafton, ND: Record Printer Publishers, 1966); Mohberg, *The Straddlebug* (Grafton, ND: Record Printer Publishers, 1977); Robert A. Carlson, *The Quest for Conformity: Americanization through Education* (New York: John Wiley and Sons, 1975); Playford V. Thorson and William C. Sherman, "Education and Ethnicity: A Study of German-Russians and Norwegians in North Dakota" (manuscript in the Country School Legacy Collection, University of North Dakota Archives, 1981); and Randall Teeuwen, "Frontier Education and the Americanization of Germans from Russia" (manuscript in the Country School Legacy Collection, Western Historical Collections, University Libraries, University of Colorado, Boulder, 1981). For a sensitive fictionalized account, see O. E. Rolvaag, *Peder Victorius: A Tale of the Pioneers Twenty Years Later* (1928; reprint, Lincoln: University of Nebraska Press, 1981).

31. Gulliford, *America's Country Schools,* 100.

32. Hispanic Cultural Heritage Project, Education Division, Museum of New Mexico, *Juegos y Juguetes de Nuevo Mexico* (Toys and Games of New Mexico) exhibit catalog (1974), 1. See also Costales Dioniso, "Spanish Games in New Mexico" (M.A. thesis, University of New Mexico, 1937); and Federal Writer's Project, *The Spanish-American Song and Game Book* (New York: A. S. Barnes, 1942).

33. Hispanic Cultural Heritage Project, *Juegos y Juguetes de Nuevo Mexico,* 4. Also see Gulliford, "Hispanic Americans," in *America's Country Schools,* 106–8. To put Hispanic culture in New Mexico into context, see the section on "Spanish New Mexico" in the chapter "Regional Cultures" in Richard M. Dorson, *American Folklore* (Chicago: University of Chicago Press, 1977), 101–12.

34. John Q. Anderson, "Miller Boy: One of the First and Last of the Play-Party Games," in Brunvand, *Readings in American Folklore,* 319–23.

35. Jeremy Bentham quoted in Mihaly Csikszentmihalyi, *Beyond Boredom and Anxiety* (San Francisco: Jossey-Bass, 1975), 74.

36. Gulliford, *America's Country Schools,* 75.

37. Milton Riske, "Country School Legacy in Wyoming," (manuscript in the Country School Legacy Collection, Wyoming State Museum, Cheyenne, WY, 1981). For Canadian gopher branding, see John C. Charyk, *The Little White Schoolhouse,* vol. 1

(Saskatoon, Saskatchewan: Western Producer Prairie Books, 1977), 175.

38. Gary L. Landreth, ed., *Play Therapy: Dynamics in the Process of Counseling with Children* (Springfield, IL: Charles C. Thomas, 1982), ix. For additional references to play therapy, see Virginia Mae Axline, *Play Therapy: The Inner Dynamics of Childhood* (Boston: Houghton Mifflin, 1947); and Clark Moustakas, *Children in Play Therapy* (New York: Jason, Aranson, Inc., 1973).

39. E. J. Kirchoff, "Letter to the Editor on Country Schooling," *Oregon Historical Quarterly* 87, 1 (Spring 1986): 93.

40. Laura Eisenhuth quoted in Gulliford, *America's Country Schools*, 175. The matter of rural school outhouses received an entire chapter in Challman, *The Rural School Plant*.

41. C. Ross Bloomquist, manuscript in Country School Legacy Collection, University of North Dakota Archives, 1980. Also quoted in Gulliford, *America's Country Schools*, 197.

42. Pat O'Neill, "The Country School and the Community" (paper presented at the Colorado Heritage Center, 13 June 1981, at the film première of *Country School Legacy*). Original manuscript in the Country School Legacy Collection, Western Historical Collections, University Libraries, University of Colorado, Boulder.

43. Gulliford, *America's Country Schools*, 64.

44. For good descriptions of carving on school desks, see Jonathan S. Minard, "The Frontier Schoolhouse," *York State Tradition* (Winter 1974): 11–14; and Barber, *The Schoolhouse at Prairie View*. Barber states that because immigrant children sat at the same desks day in and day out, they came to understand the writing on their school desks long before they learned to read from their texts.

45. John G. Neihardt, *All Is but a Beginning: Youth Remembered, 1881–1901* (New York: Harcourt, Brace, Jovanovich, 1972), 162.

46. Ibid., 163.

47. Jesse Stewart, *The Thread That Runs So True* (New York: Charles Scribner's Sons, 1958), 12. Also see William Link, *A Hard and Lonely Place* (Chapel Hill: University of North Carolina Press, 1986).

48. Stewart, *The Thread That Runs So True*, 13. For another vivid description of a country school fight, see the chapter "A Schoolroom Battle" in Carol Ryrie Brink, *Caddie Woodlawn* (New York: Macmillan, 1935), 59–70.

49. Lyon and Healy in Chicago even published "Song of the Great Blizzard: Thirteen Were Saved" in 1888. Original sheet music is in the collections of the Nebraska State Historical Society. The song extols Minnie Freeman of the Myra School District in Nebraska. That same blizzard cost North Dakota teacher Hazel Miner her life when she lay down on top of her brother and her sister when the three of them lost their way home. In remembrance of her bravery, the citizens of North Dakota erected a bronze statue in her honor in front of the state capitol at Bismarck.

50. Gulliford, *America's Country Schools*, 80.

51. Lettie B. Zion, *Fairview: True Tales of a Country Schoolhouse* (Oceano, CA: Tower Press, 1981), 46.

52. Gulliford, *America's Country Schools*, 85.

53. Edward Eggleston, *The Hoosier Schoolmaster* (1871; reprint, New York: Regents Publisher, 1974).

54. Gulliford, *America's Country Schools*, 52.

55. Goldie Piper Daniels, *Rural Schools and Schoolhouses of Douglas County, Kansas* (Baldwin City, KS: Telegraphics, 1978).

56. Anna B. Selfridge, transcriber, *Allen County (Ohio) Country Schools* (Lima, OH: Allen County Historical Society, Summer 1987), 11. These are transcriptions of meetings of the Swiss Historical Society membership discussing the one-room schools of Richland and Monroe Townships in Allen County, Orange Township in Hardin County, and Riley Township in Putnam County.

57. Selfridge, *Allen County Country Schools*, 9.

58. Gulliford, *America's Country Schools*, 84. For a great fictional account of a box social, see Constant, *Miss Charity Comes to Stay*.

59. John Steinbeck, *East of Eden* (New York: Bantam Books, 1955), 147. For a midwestern reference to country schools as community centers, see Helen Peterson-Wood, "Uncle Johnnie, Honey Creek Correspondent, 1895–1903," *Kansas History* 3 (Summer 1980): 112–36.

60. Mabel Carney, *Country Life and the Country School* (Chicago: Row, Peterson, and Company, 1912).

61. Bruno Bettelheim and Elizabeth Hall, "Our Children Are Treated Like Idiots," *Psychology Today*, July 1981, 28–32.

62. Sally L. Smith, *No Easy Answers: The Learning Disabled Child* (New York: Bantam Books, 1981). A strength of country schools has been the mix of a variety of children with different backgrounds. For the effects of mixing boys and girls together, see David Tyack and Elisabeth Hansot, *Learning Together: A History of Coeducation in American Public Schools* (New Haven: Yale University Press, 1990). Also see Charles Leslie Glenn, Jr., *The Myth of the Common School* (Amherst: University of Massachusetts Press, 1988).

63. Though this is a difficult topic to assess, current work on one-room schools seems to link ego strength of students with the school's isolation. I

first became aware of this link while discussing one-room schools with Dr. Ivan Muse of Brigham Young University. See Ivan Muse, Ralph B. Smith, and Bruce Barker, *The One-Teacher School in the 1980s* (Las Cruces, NM: ERIC Clearinghouse on Rural Education and Small Schools and the National Rural Education Association, Fort Collins, CO, 1987). Also see Educational Networks Division, Office of Educational Research and Improvement, *Rural Education: A Changing Landscape* (Washington, DC: U.S. Department of Education, May 1989).

# The Natural Limits of Unstructured Play, 1880–1914

DONALD J. MROZEK

In studying play I have come to believe that it affords the best and most profitable way of studying humankind itself, both individuals and races. Play consists of that which people do when they have food, shelter, and clothing, are rested and free from worry, when the physical compulsions of life are removed temporarily and the spirit is free to search for its own satisfactions. Then man is at his best. The pursuit of food, shelter, clothing, and safety is in the main the means to life; but these things are not the end for which life seems to exist. For this reason I believe that man is better revealed by his play, or by the use he makes of his leisure time, than by any other one index.[1]

These were the thoughts of Luther Halsey Gulick, head of the Physical Training Department at the YMCA's Training School at Springfield, Massachusetts, founder and promoter of the New York Public Schools Athletic League, a guiding spirit of the Camp Fire Girls, a leading force in the Playground and Recreation Association of America, and clearly a giant in the history of American play and recreation (fig. 1).[2] Gulick's words do more than summarize the conventional distinction between "work" and "play." They do more than just extend a rhetoric rich in cliché, nostalgia, and romantic escape from the burdens of the workaday world. Gulick reveals the underlying and pervasive predisposition to view play as natural and work as artificial—to see the origins of play as rooted in human nature and the origins of work as grounded in social necessity—to see the proper bounds of work as set by practical material need and the rightful limits of play as determined not by human society but by nature itself. In this predisposition to see play as the "default condition" to which humankind returns when freed of arbitrary external social pressure, Gulick was not unique. Though more visible and articulate than most, he was only one among many spokespersons for a basic rationale reconciling work and play and, on another level, reconciling nurture and nature, which "work" and "play" roughly paralleled.

Gulick saw intellect as "a tool to accomplish ends" but not as a guide to determining them. It was in play where "the great desires" showed themselves, operating with "indifference to consciousness or intelligence."[3] According to this logic, a society might be pieced together mechanically, but its motive force grew naturally. The tension between mechanistic and organic or natural models, then, roughly conformed to the distinction between work and play. So, too, it paralleled the tension between social demands as expressed in morals and individual rights. Yet to speak of "individual rights" was not to endorse a person's radical autonomy. Gulick said that his years of observation had led him to conclude that "the individual is more an agent in life than a directing force."[4] The individual was swept over by what Gulick—recalling the recapitulation theory of psychologist G. Stanley Hall—called "great waves or tides of desire," roughly conforming to "successive periods of progress of prehistoric man."[5] Gulick spoke of a "play progression,"[6] marking the growth of the child through a succession of play forms; and, although these play forms shaped and strengthened the social identity of the child, the society was not entitled to choose the play forms arbitrarily. Unstructured play might have only limited effects on people, yet it was also true that the very structure of nature itself, as through evolutionary processes, put limits—controls—on the effectiveness of social intervention.

Gulick and Hall were not identical in their concerns or views, yet they shared a fundamental sense that play was a necessary part of early human development precisely because they also saw it as natural—inherent in humans as a species. Far from seeking to suppress what was natural, they thought they could optimize it and put it to society's advantage. For G. Stanley Hall, this meant guiding the young in those forms of play, as well as other activities, that suited particular stages in their physical development and psychological growth. The key to Hall's scheme of personal development was his theory of "recapitulation," according to which each human being repeated rapidly the entire biological evolution of the race. Thus each young human passed through "culture phases" that reflected the biological heritage of the race as it passed through seaborne, amphibian, mammalian, and primate forms. In itself, play did not need

Fig. 1    Luther H. Gulick was a YMCA educator, the first president of the Playground Association of America, and a leading figure in the history of American play and recreation. Courtesy Library of Congress.

to be suppressed—or, rather, it *must* not be suppressed. Yet it was important that each individual pass from phase to phase at the right time, using the activities appropriate to each stage of development to confirm those traits being acquired and to grow ready to acquire those of the next. Simple, unstructured "child's play," then, was not the enemy of society—so long as its practice was properly timed. Society had no need to discourage children from casual, unstructured play that had not been directed by social workers, provided that these children had not passed to the cultural stage where social integration and teamwork were the hallmark features. In the end, then, the most effective "social control" was really self-control ingrained in the individual. At more advanced stages, such as adolescence, the young individual might better get these newly important attributes such as self-control and the spirit of cooperation by engaging in supervised structured play—that is, organized sport. Meanwhile, the much younger child could play, as in a sandbox, with a minimum of direct intervention by adults, even when the young were being observed constantly (fig. 2).

Fig. 2 A playground in St. Paul, Minnesota, provided sandboxes and blocks for young children at the turn of the century, allowing them to play with adult supervision but without intervention. Arthur Leland and Lorna Higby Leland, *Playground Technique and Playcraft* (1910).

But the inexorable physical growth of every human being, recapitulating the history of the biological development of the race as a whole, required that his play shift from unstructured to structured forms. In the view of such men as Gulick and Hall, society facilitated this kind of shift in a conscious act of scientific management. Yet they did not see it as "social control" nearly so much as the will of nature itself. If in any sense "anatomy was destiny," then the physical recapitulation of biological evolution was destiny of the surest sort. Play, too, was a part of that destiny, and the theorists of play who sought to read the runes of nature knew

that they were kept within the deceptively simple lives of children.[7]

For Gulick as for many of his contemporaries, human beings seemed to possess a certain fundamental shared inheritance, and this in turn governed the range of human play. "The whole human race," Gulick asserted, "has had feelings regarding the significance of fire." It is hardly surprising that a founding force of the Camp Fire Girls should rhapsodize the mastery of fire, which he named as a basic part of the "racial inheritance." And not only mastery—it was mystery as well. Playing with fire was, in Gulick's words, "one of the great means for the realization of mystery, in its good sense."[8] Gulick wanted this access to mystery protected, so that a sense of what he called "the great beyond" would be preserved. Thus, human needs beyond the intellectual and calculating part set limits on the degree and nature of intervention into play. What he believed in was a kind of forbearance, restraining one's capacity for social control out of concern to save the mysterious and instinctual dimension. In a way, the Camp Fire Girls epitomized the use of social organization by adults who already possessed it to foster in the young what Gulick called "the instinct feelings of the past," thus drawing forth the natural power that gave energy to the social relationships that young people were only beginning to form. Drawing on the recently coined lore of the Camp Fire Girls, Gulick quoted from "The Ode to the Fire" to express these values:

> O Fire!
> Long years ago, when our fathers fought with
>     animals, you were their protection.
> From the cruel cold of winter, you saved them.
> When they needed food you changed the flesh of
>     beasts into savory meat for them.
> During all the ages your mysterious flame has
>     been a symbol to them for Spirit.
> So (to-night) we light our fire in remembrance
>     of the Great Spirit who gave you to us.[9]

In their need to go beyond the purely rational, calculating, intellect-driven part of life, all human beings were united.

Yet Gulick did not think people were all the same or that their specific behavior was predetermined by genetic inheritance. Nature established basic limits and proclivities. But each culture set its own agenda, socializing its offspring with its own idiosyncratic practices. Although he believed that some forms of play were universal and generic—characterizing them in such terms as "shelter plays," "hunting and fighting plays," "fire play," "playing with toys," "doll play," and "plays with ownership"—Gulick recognized that every culture shaped its own version of each and the balance among them.[10] Thus play became an expres-

sion of identity and a means of confirming it within future generations. To set the limits of play for each culture was to establish the limits of its identity.

This was not some simplistic "social control," yet it was not exactly a matter of free choice, either. One way of understanding this is to realize that Gulick did not equate play with fun. Whether play was perceived as fun was secondary. The primary importance of play was that it reflected a biological requirement to develop, largely in conformity with the "culture phases" matching the stages of recapitulation of the race's evolution. Once again, the pressures came from nature more than from society, although this did nothing to lessen them. Gulick suggested that play should not just be distinguished from work and warned that it not be confused with recreation. It was no less serious than work, even though it did not depend on "external compulsions" such as the specific needs for food and shelter in a particular environment. Since play was "an expression of the self" and "the result of desire" that welled up as instinctual forces, it was a matter of *inner* compulsion.[11] Play was thus a matter of necessity, whether it was fun or not. To the present age, which has redefined the notion of a "natural act" to almost anything that a human can physically manage to perform, it is especially useful to remember that things were different a century ago. Then, a "natural act" was one conforming to a schedule of appropriate behavior set by one's membership in the species. The physical capacity to deviate from play that was deemed appropriate to one's species—or to one's society—was not the same as the freedom and right to do so.

For those familiar with the historical discussion of organized play and sport, there may be something fairly "off-key" about the foregoing thoughts—something out of phase with the general stream of ideas. The mechanisms of "social control" were applied to play and sport with skill and purpose a few generations ago. But the question is why—that is, was it really a matter of suppressing the radically individualistic and animal element so that society would be aided rather than injured? Such an approach would have assumed that the animal element was both radically individualistic and destructive. But the underlying tone of such thoughts as Gulick's was that the visceral, vital, animal component of the human being was to be prized, saved, and used. As G. K. Chesterton once noted, a paradox is truth standing on its head to gain attention. Here, the paradox of organized play is that play may have been more important than organization. The energy and vitality that welled up spontaneously in child's play was never inherently bad, even though there were stages of personal and social development at which these energies might be put to supposedly higher social purposes by being carefully managed and channeled. The animal element in man had an ever-present potential for social benefit, provided that informed adults guided the young through each successive phase of development so as to match methods with timing. The chance to benefit society by exploiting the play instinct was in this sense a matter of good timing.[12]

The kind of intervention that would be needed to win maximum social benefit from the way young people experienced their biological and psychological growth, then, varied according to the changing age and "culture stage" that the young people had attained. In this regard, organized sport conformed better to the situations and needs of older children, and notably adolescents, than to younger ones. Sport was "superior" to unstructured play in the sense that it came at a later and "higher" state in the development of the young. Yet it was only comparable in importance with play in the sense that structured and unstructured play both had continuing usefulness to humans as individuals and in society. The issue was when that usefulness could be realized. The character and the pace of intervention had to be adjusted according to the demands of nature. Luther Gulick thought it undesirable to gather very small children together in large groups, as organized games would inevitably

do. Hence, their dispersal exempted them from close governance. But when children played in large groups, expert leaders became crucial to prevent what Gulick called the "more disorderly boys" from becoming intolerable and menacing.[13] In such a formula, however, one may recognize the limits of human social order as well as the limits of natural character formation. The expert was an asset in organized play. But too much expertise and intervention struck Gulick not only as unsuitable but even as downright harmful to the very young. As Gulick suggested, "The role of the teacher appears to come in when the child has exhausted his own ability to invent."[14]

The emphasis on the proper timing of intervention also suggests the respect widely accorded to each component element of the play instinct. Arthur Leland and Lorna Higbee Leland, for example, drew upon the writings of psychologist William James to emphasize the need for prompt action at every stage in the development of instinct. The Lelands saw instinct as transitory, as James did, and they all concluded, as a matter of logic, that the only purpose evolutionary selectivity would allow transitory instinct was the "giving rise to habits."[15] The moment at which a specific instinct emerged forcefully, then, was not only a threat if abused. It was a loss if ignored.

Decades of historical analysis have tended to emphasize the societal effort to create order, discipline, regularity, and predictability while tending to understate the degree to which orderly processes were perceived as inherent and natural. Gulick's discussion of differences in the play of males and females underscores the ineluctable power of nature to determine the range within which individual and social choices were seen as suitable. Gulick believed that different subgroups of instinct resided within males and females. He thought the instinct to fight and hunt stronger in the man, as an expression of the principle of tribal loyalty even more than of familiar association. The interest in dolls and in "playing house" seemed to Gulick to prove the primacy of loyalty to the home among females. It is especially important to understand that he considered this quality innate rather than socially dictated.

Although present-day historians tend to see such distinctions as a confusion of socially established tradition with the dictates of instinct and nature, Gulick recognized the risk of making this mistake and specifically denied that he had made it. He believed that a people could make conscious efforts to deviate from their instinctual predispositions, but he questioned the sense of doing so. The choice of play appropriate to each gender and to each age thus called upon society to stay in conformity with its own natural impulses. For example, Gulick argued that the question "whether young women shall play competitive games hinges on the question of what woman is going to be. If the states of mind involved in basket-ball are related to the states of mind desirable for women," he continued, "then basket-ball is good. Indiscriminate basket-ball is certainly bad." Careful selection of behavior for men and women could allow enough change to foster "the new woman," but too much engineering seemed poor policy to Gulick. Males and females remained so different in primary instincts that they would always incline toward a common good by differing, distinctive methods. The greater interests of the society as a whole would be fostered by the most efficient melding of instinct and training—such as in cultivating "power and the barbaric virtues of manhood" in the boy and "the gentler virtues of the love of home, kindness, sympathy, and forbearance" in the girl.[16] By such standards, the real test of "social efficiency" lay not in the unrestricted application of Taylorism and scientific management but in the reasoned correlation of what was perceived to be instinct with the means most useful to cultivating it. Instinct and impulse were not reasoned out of social mechanisms but reasoned *into* them. As Gulick believed that "instinct developed through imitation," efficiency meant not only proper governance of the process of imitation but deference to instinct in the first place.[17]

Gulick himself was well acquainted with much of the growing literature on instinct and its role in human society. He drew on such works as C. Lloyd Morgan's *Habit and Instinct* and Wesley Mills's *The Nature and Development of Animal Intelligence,* as well as on works explicitly dealing with instinct among the "lower" animals, such as Ernest Thompson Seton's *Wild Animals I Have Known* and W. H. Hudson's *The Naturalist in La Plata.*[18] Drawing on their observations, Gulick concluded that play, as that set of "actions done instinctively with no immediate purpose," was a "direct measure of the intelligence of the species as a whole and the individual in particular."[19] The findings of naturalists strengthened Gulick's notion that conscious human intervention to use tradition and example to mold the values and behavior of the young must be governed by the current racial inheritance. Human consciousness, itself a consequence of evolutionary processes, thus became a shaping and limiting factor in the furtherance of the species and the upbringing of the young. Humans erred perhaps most often because of what Gulick called "our inexcusable way of letting things take care of themselves."[20] It took conscious effort to stay in tune with the proper limits of nature.

Perhaps such an approach seems more clear and less idiosyncratic if one views it as a counterpart to the emergence of a rudimentary form of ecological thinking, such as in the work of Aldo Leopold. If Leopold urged "thinking like a deer" to do what was needed for their preservation, so Gulick and others urged "thinking like a human"—or thinking one's way back to the most basic and primal human needs and impulses. In asserting that there were "pulses of play" that naturally set a "rotation" of play and games over years and seasons, Gulick also affirmed the need to conform to natural drives even when one might have the narrow power to defy them.[21]

Determining the limits of and the proper ways of structuring play, then, depended largely on what one meant by "nature." Gulick addressed this issue directly. He warned that if one used too narrow a sense of the word, "the best possessions of human kind are unnatural." In a wider sense, however, it was better to "consider natural those things which have survived and approved themselves in the course of evolution." As Gulick saw it, human control had become a natural component of the race.[22] In this sense, unstructured—or, at least, ill-timed—play could slip outside the newly defined bounds of "nature" and itself become "unnatural."

To G. Stanley Hall, setting out the limits of "human nature" and determining human motivation were tasks of compelling interest.[23] As a pioneering psychologist and father of the concept of adolescence, Hall relied on the evolutionary thought so prominent in his day, seeing individual character as a fusion of personal will and natural constraints. In such works as *Adolescence,* he developed the view that personal growth "recapitulated" the evolutionary experience of the species. But Hall did not subscribe to a mechanistic explanation of human action or to a rigid and doctrinaire application of his own notions about human nature. He accepted the view that civilization was marked by regularity, while the more instinctual and primitive vital functions were marked by a periodic quality bred into the species eons ago, as Darwin suggested.[24] Yet he perceived that one needed to deal with people as they were and as they chose to be. Even if nature offered an ideal pattern for living, Hall did not expect that fallible humans would consistently comply.

Hall concluded that humans tended to play in ways that "filled in" spaces left open for play by social structure, in one sense plugging up the holes in the dike of social order, yet also permitting individuals to feel that they were escaping from society's rigors. It was a marriage of the greatest social convenience, using the personal instinct for freedom in ways that strengthened social order by avoiding conflicts with it. Hall's extended essay "The Story of a Sand Pile" outlines the way children playing on their own largely reconstituted the world they saw around them.[25] They developed a rudimentary legislative body, a jail, farms, a tavern, and much else. Thus, even in play not directly guided by adults, Hall thought children naturally tended to follow rules—indeed, to seek out rules and structures to which they might conform. He specifically observed that this "recapitulated" the movement into "primitive society" such as had occurred in prehistoric times, as if there were an innate compulsion toward order.[26] On the other hand, the children at the sand pile did not establish a church or a school. When quizzed about these omissions, the children explained that they had no church because "we are not allowed to play in the 'sand pile' on Sunday, but have to go to church." There was no school, they noted, because "it is vacation, and we don't have to go to school."[27] Imagination and reality were both at work, then; but each found its own special place. The natural impulse to play needed expression, but it did not need to break the boundaries of highly evolved forms of social order. The tendency to seek rules and order itself seemed natural.

In the progression of forms of play and games, Hall found a framework of human growth—in motor function, mental grasp, social involvement, and imaginative power. His ideas provided a clear example of an accommodating disposition, for while he set out an ideal norm, which he believed was determined by nature, he sought ways of dealing creatively with individual deviation from the norm. Tellingly, Hall was even willing to tolerate some socially distasteful behavior in order to protect the underlying vital force without which he was sure society must fail.

Hall acknowledged a "bestial" side to many human instinctual drives, and he affirmed that it often showed itself in boyhood. He spoke of fights fought with "desperate abandon," in which "noses are bitten, ears torn, sensitive places kicked, hair pulled, arms twisted, the head stamped on and pounded on stones, fingers twisted." Hall went on: "In unrestrained anger, man becomes a demon in love with the blood of his victim. The face is distorted, and there are yells, oaths, animal grunts, cries, and then exultant laughter at pain."[28] Hall allowed that the "grosser and animal manifestations of anger" were offensive, terming them "repulsive." But it was the love of such spectacle that offended him more than the fact of physical conflict, even when undertaken with great intensity. He considered righteous anger an essential element in "moral education," and he dismissed "non-resistance" (or pacifism) as "unmanly, craven, and cowardly."[29] Sounding remarkably like the Theodore Roosevelt of *American Ideals* and *Applied Ethics,* [30] Hall said that an able-bodied man who would not fight physically was "generally a milksop, a lady-boy, or a sneak" who could "hardly have a high and true sense of honor."[31] The physical fight was not the problem. It was the perverted attitude that troubled Hall—it was quite all right to crush one's enemy, but it was deplorable taste to exult too much while doing so.

In a sense, the "limits" of natural impulses were licensing as much as restrictive. Hall's thoughts about boxing suggest this, precisely because he thought boxing had been badly corrupted in his own day but insisted on preserving it nonetheless. He called prizefighting "degrading and brutal," but he still approved it as a corrective for defects in character. At first, he recommended it for "a certain class of boys," although it soon became clear that he meant it for practically all of them. While condemning "overpugnacity," Hall thought "a scrapping boy" was "better than one who funks a fight." He continued, "I have no patience with the sentimentality that would here pour out the child with the bath, but would have every healthy boy taught boxing at adolescence if not before." What is particularly interesting here is not Hall's notion that play, games, and sport might be used to mold character—a notion so common as to become nearly trivial to repeat. It is rather that Hall thought the *innate* worth of this specific physical activity was so great that even "evil associations" should not be allowed to displace it.[32] The needs of each person grew from nature itself, and the means to meet those needs also grew from nature rather than from society. Hall focused his impatience on ephemeral aspects of society—on its seeming errors—but not on the underlying animal forces, which he clearly wished to keep. His aim was not to replace or suppress primal natural forces but to fulfill them.

Play, games, and sport, then, were admittedly used as tools for social control—ways of manipulating common folk to adapt to the mores of their self-styled betters. But men such as Hall and Gulick were scarcely bound to such paternalistic and condescending purposes. For them, play and games were not tools for social control, as a wrench relates to a machine; they were integral elements within human life, like genes on a string of DNA. True enough, order and regularity were imposed by a kind of "carrot and stick" method—sport as carrot and discipline as the stick. But to say only this is to slight their desperate desire to preserve the vital, wild, animal side of the human being.

This expansive love of the more visceral side of humanity deserves special emphasis in that it helps us understand the permissive, legitimating quality of the concept of "natural limits" in play. A century ago many Americans were virtually obsessed with the question of personal as well as social energy. Vital force, *élan vital,* spermatic economy, the "body electric"—a host of terms serve as reminders.[33] As Henry Adams observed, the dynamo was a force with nearly mystical attractiveness to his contemporaries. Looking back at the America of one hundred years ago, historians have focused on the imposition of order, discipline, system, and regularity in part because there was so much of it. Yet perhaps creating order was easier than creating energy; imposing discipline was easier than generating vital force. As the concept of spermatic economy suggests, it was energy—not order—that many Americans feared was in short supply. In some respects, of course, the truism that play, games, and sport were vehicles of order is exactly that—a truism because the statement is true. But at least as much and perhaps even more, they were means of conveying energy, dynamism, vitality, and the deepest of natural and animal force.

Fig. 3    A class photograph from about 1880 of young women posed with dumbbells and other exercise materials.

The prescriptions of play for women illustrate the importance attached to enhancing social energy by enhancing individual vitality. In this respect, the conventional interpretation that play, games, and sport for women were grotesquely constrained needs adjustment. Clearly, the range of activities recommended for females and the manner in which females were expected to play differed from those for males. Yet here, too, the limits for females interpreted (or misinterpreted) from nature were permissive ones, enlarging the options open to them beyond what had been accepted for some time.[34] Nor did males suppress some widespread female urge to engage in play in exact equality with males. First, such a supposition of replicative equality was virtually nonexistent. Even more, such controls as did exist commonly came from women themselves, notably from women who could scarcely be regarded as stooges of the men and who often showed a measure of contempt for what and how males played. Among those eager to mark off distinctions between men's and women's

sport were talented and skilled educators such as Gertrude Dudley of the Women's Department of Physical Education at the University of Chicago and the widely published sociologist Frances A. Kellor.[35] The noted educator Amy Morris Homans also regarded the differences between men and women as sufficient to justify separate professional tracks for male and female physical educators (fig. 3). Other female advocates of play, exercise, and games deliberately focused on the special features of the anatomy of the human female, seeing this not as a source of restriction but as an argument for expanding and enriching their lives far beyond present custom and behavior.[36]

In promoting play and games for females, even apart from whether their play forms had to be made different from those of males, the idea of natural instinct held great force. Take the example of Joseph Lee, a leading philanthropist and social reformer from Boston.[37] Lee advocated dancing for males and females as combining the aesthetic and motor benefits of music with the muscular and coordinative benefits of gymnastics. But Lee's special approval of folk dancing, as distinct from the formal social forms called "aesthetic dancing," is significant and revealing—folk dances were superior, Lee said, largely because "they are more firmly planted upon instinct."[38] Any distinction to be made between male and female must stem from the same logic as the distinction among forms of dancing—that is, from one's understanding of natural drive rather than social preference. Lee saw himself as widening the participation of females in play, games, and sport, as well as giving their participation greater intensity and staying power. He urged that girls get some experience in various forms of play before the end of each crucial stage, lest they lose forever the powers of play that nature had intended for them. Like a good many others, Lee was positive and boosterish, noting that "some girls can beat most boys" in sports such as tennis, golf, and baseball.[39] The goal was to have women enjoy their capacities to the fullest, but the trick was to determine just what those capacities were. And even though the answer was rooted in nature, its specifics were not self-evident, precisely because each human being was shaped in a long developmental process.

Learning to play—or at least learning how to play in satisfying ways—meant discovering one's own self as a part of nature's broad scheme. Implicitly it meant learning about nature itself. In one sense, this was inevitable, since the prescriptions of the recapitulation theory hinged on an underlying interpretation of nature. But some play activities suggested the extent to which nature was both the goal and the means of the play enterprise. If it was natural to play, it was also "natural" to study nature. In *Playground Technique and Playcraft* (1910), for example, Arthur and Lorna Leland portrayed the playground as an especially suitable place for children to come in contact with the natural environment of which cities too often deprived them.[40] A small fish pond provided the chance for "nature study," even if later sensibilities might dismiss the pond as a pathetic little confinement, deplorably inade-

Fig. 4   Nature study around a fish pond in a Los Angeles playground. Arthur Leland and Lorna Higby Leland, *Playground Technique and Playcraft* (1910).

quate to the needs of aquatic life forms (fig. 4).[41] So, too, the effort to beautify parks, according to leaders of the playground movement, resulted in a variety of benefits. Writers such as Henry S. Curtis pointed out that parks were not only a means of placating neighboring property owners who might worry over the effect of an unsightly playground on the market value of their real estate. They also provided a "mediated landscape" which let the young city-dweller slip out into the anteroom of nature, if not into its most sweeping spaces (fig. 5).[42] The value of play for the city-dweller came, at least in part, from knowing through experience that the city was not the whole of reality. Excursions to outlying forest preserves (such as those that inspired the founding of the playground system in Rochester in 1903), camping trips, promotion of Boy Scout encampments—in all of these the aim was not

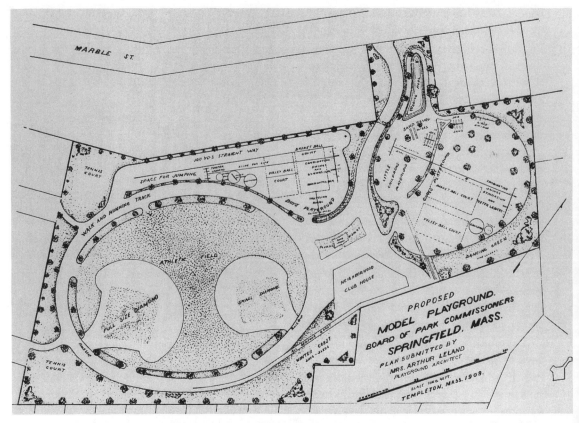

Fig. 5   This playground model, developed by architect Lorna Leland in 1909, demonstrates the effort of the playground movement to create a "mediated landscape" between nature and the city. The schematic includes not only landscaping, a wading pool, and a floral display, but also separate playgrounds for boys and girls. Arthur Leland and Lorna Higby Leland, *Playground Technique and Playcraft* (1910).

imposition of social order but a refreshing and enlivening of the animal side of the human spirit in the very best sense of the terms "animal," "human," and "spirit."[43]

The logic for play that had been drawn from an appraisal of nature by such persons as G. Stanley Hall persisted in the minds of American physical educators and social reformers even toward midcentury. In *Play in Education,* for example, published in 1917 and republished in 1942 for the National Recreation Association, Joseph Lee pressed a modified version of Hall's recapitulation theory, observing a progression in the forms of play through four ages of childhood: babyhood (from one to three years); the dramatic age (from three to six); the "Big Injun" age (from six to eleven); and the age of loyalty (from eleven years on). Lee emphasized the need for

creativity in the teacher, to guide the young through the stages of play without being shackled to a rigid and archaic framework. Put simply, children at play might recapitulate the long history of the species, but there was no need for them to do so in proportion to the length of each stage in evolutionary development.[44] Of course, Hall himself would have agreed.

For Lee, as for Hall decades earlier, "child's play" was serious business. Lee continued the traditions that saw play as actualizing the energy and potential within the individual child. Play, Lee affirmed, "is the letting loose of what is in him, the active projection of the force he is, the becoming of what he is to be." By "making an infinite and insatiable demand for power and courage," play did not exhaust energy; it stimulated it, rather as if energy were the product of exercising the play instincts and the physical organism in which they resided.[45] Again, the notion of "natural limits" seemed less a restrictive cap than a potential whose fullness had yet to be touched.

At times, Lee wrote as if reason needed defense at least as much as animal vitality did. Lee emphasized, "I do not set up instinct against reason either as a rival or as a substitute. Their functions are different and supplementary."[46] Reason was central to thought, but it did not reign sole and supreme over life. Nor did Lee wish it to do so. Reason served the instincts, "discovering practical methods for their satisfaction." It permitted the imaginative projection of the consequences of actions set in motion by instinct. But instinct was more basic. As Lee observed, "A compass cannot point north unless there is a north, nor unless it has in itself some relation to it."[47] Reason served as a compass, but instinct was the north itself.

If there was a "modern tone" in the language of play advocates of the turn of the century, perhaps it lay in the celebration of life as valuable in itself. As Luther Gulick put it, "Life, self-activity, is an end in itself."[48] It lay in the view—again from Gulick—that "desire is a greater word than duty," because what was done for duty's sake would never be done with absolute commitment.[49] In this way, the society benefited most when the individual enjoyed the greatest self-expression and most fully gratified personal drives. Indeed, Gulick chose to pair the individual's sense of joy in following instincts and drives with what he termed "the growth of personality."[50] To the extent that a turn from character to personality marked the "modern tone," such men as Gulick took the step.

Perhaps even G. Stanley Hall also pointed toward the coming primacy of personality, feeling, and self-gratification. He remained committed to the goal of shaping character, which was a highly traditional concern in the nineteenth century. But his agreement that character could be shaped by a secular process that governed natural physical development,

rather than by some form of "spiritual" guidance, had a distinctly modern tone. What determined personal behavior in society was thus society itself, interacting with properly perceived natural impulses, and not some transcendent or "spiritual" moral scheme. But this rather self-referential dependence of society on a "bootstraps" approach to its own development was not what mainstream nineteenth-century thought recognized as "character" at all. Experts such as Hall were preparing the way for the modern temperament.

Buster Keaton's film *College* (1927) suggests the ambivalence of Americans toward play in the early decades of this century. In episodic fashion, *College* follows Keaton's fumbling and sometimes pathetic efforts to achieve success as an athlete, all to win the affections of the coed he loves. Especially when compared with the talented athletic star who is his rival, Keaton marks the limits of formalized play—he knows the structures of a game but has no true feel for its "innards," its gut, its spirit. And so these formalistic efforts yield only more frustration. Toward the end of the film, however, when the girl he loves is menaced by the star athlete and manages to telephone a plea for help, Keaton takes his character over a virtual obstacle course to rescue her. Each obstacle conforms to some sporting event, mostly from track and field competition. He runs, jumps, vaults—all efforts at which he has failed when the circumstances of competition were artificial. Now, however, the efforts serve a deeply instinctual purpose—saving someone from harm and pursuing a mate. Evidently, the instinctual drives prove more compelling and even more effectual.

The instincts were no enemy, then, and so it is easy to comprehend that passion for "teaching people to play" in the 1930s, which may have been even more representative of the era than training them to be orderly.[51] Play itself became more important in the 1930s, yet not because of rules and orderliness which might become beneficial when turned to work and the business of society—it was important as an end in itself. In this way, personal fulfillment

Fig. 6    Children enjoying a boxing lesson in a Visalia, California, camp for migrant workers, March 1940. Farm Security Administration photograph by Arthur Rothstein, courtesy Library of Congress.

was not to be achieved in work—surely not in work alone—even if it was fulfilled in a social context. If the context was social, however, it was as likely as not to be in the realm of group play and sport rather than in work and supposedly "higher" ventures. To the extent that fulfillment came from feeling tied in with one's peers in a net of associations, then the feeling was more important than its specific source. And to this end, play was at least as useful as anything else. To learn to play was to learn a mode of self-expression—that is, a new vocabulary of behavior through which one defined as well as expressed what one's self entailed. As psychiatrist Martha Wolfenstein has noted, play "tends to be measured by standards of achievement previously applicable only to work. . . . And at play, no less than at work, one asks: Am I doing as well as I should?" The pursuits of the adult are, Wolfenstein cautioned, "haunted by self-doubts about his capacity for having as much fun as he should."[52]

According to play theorists, if there was a special learning to be done, it may well have been in regaining the unrestrained joy of play

in childhood—what Wolfenstein called the "fierce pleasures of autoeroticism and . . . dangerous titillations."[53] The great photographic inventories of American life in the 1930s, such as the landmark work of the Farm Security Administration, leave us with the signs of ease and acceptance enjoyed in play activities. If it was an era prizing the idea of personal and group relationship—an "Adlerian" age, as Warren Susman has suggested—then the easy manners of the people at play in the 1930s may have served a social goal by feeding people's sense of their instinctual, cohering, tribal, folk side.[54] If there was effort to train children in organized sport such as boxing, going far beyond unstructured play, there was also a simple and natural joy that survived among many of the children (fig. 6). If there was organization in the athletic competition of the young such as in schoolboy basketball, there was also an uncommon ease allowed in their manners on the court (fig. 7). If there was emphasis on group experience and loyalty to a team, as so often shone through at college football games, the goal was also to enliven a forgotten spirit of natural and spontaneous elation (fig. 8). The love of the group, after all, was no special property of the exponents of "social control." The prelogical dimension within human beings included such unprogrammed affections.

Perhaps even the seemingly rationalistic bent of Freudian analysis in the 1920s did less to foist mechanisms of social control upon a victimized mass than to release their inner urges from the taint of sin and the constraints of arbitrary social rules. And by the 1930s, perhaps it was as great a task to refresh the instinctual side—to restore nature, to teach people how to play—as it was to restrain them (fig. 9). Ironically, "nature" did not come naturally. Or it seemed, at least, that nature could not preserve itself without outside help. Given the conscious effort to foster play and a more instinctual spirit that emerged in the 1930s, it may be necessary to rethink the whole purpose of the structures that were imposed on play in

Fig. 7   Basketball players between periods of a game at Eufaula, Oklahoma, February 1940. Even at the high-school level, their easygoing manners would seem unusual today. Farm Security Administration photograph by Russell Lee, courtesy Library of Congress.

the preceding generations. Even if nature first came naturally, it was bolstered socially. If it served social purpose, it did so when the instinctual drives were fulfilled in timely fashion and not shackled or suppressed. It was less that unstructured play had limited social application than that play, like nature, set out a vast potential which society's structures had as yet only begun to tap.

## Notes

1. Luther Halsey Gulick, *A Philosophy of Play* (New York: Charles Scribner's Sons, 1920), xii.

2. See Gulick, *Philosophy of Play;* also Gulick, *Mor-* als and Morale (New York: Association Press, 1919); Gulick, *The Dynamics of Manhood* (New York: Association Press, 1917). For general background, see Ethel Dorgan, *Luther Halsey Gulick* (New York: Teachers College, Columbia University, 1934). For Gulick's role in the YMCA, see C. Howard Hopkins, *History of the Y.M.C.A. in America* (New York: Association Press, 1951).

3. Gulick, *Philosophy of Play,* xii.

4. Ibid., xv.

5. Ibid. The recapitulation theory was widely accepted by play theorists. See also Cephas Guillet, "Recapitulation and Education," *Pedagogical Seminary* 7 (October 1900): 397–445. Arthur and Lorna Higbee Leland relied on the recapitulation theory in explaining the importance of play in the development of children as social beings. See Leland and

Fig. 8   The duty to loyally support the home team combines with a more natural enthusiasm as popular bandleader Kay Kyser joins a University of North Carolina cheerleader in a football game with Duke University, November 1939. Farm Security Administration photograph by Marion Post Wolcott, courtesy Library of Congress.

Leland, eds., *Playground Technique and Playcraft* (New York: Baker & Taylor Company, 1910), 19.

6. Gulick, *Philosophy of Play,* 147.

7. See G. Stanley Hall, *Aspects of Child Life and Education* (1907; reprint, New York: Arno Press, 1975), 142–56; and *Adolescence* (1904; reprint, New York: Arno Press, 1969).

8. Gulick, *Philosophy of Play,* 59, 65.

9. Ibid., 64.

10. Ibid., 10.

11. Ibid., 126.

12. A conventional and insightful study of the application of mechanisms of social control to play in America is Dominick Cavallo, *Muscles and Morals: Organized Playgrounds and Urban Reform, 1880–1920* (Philadelphia: University of Pennsylvania Press, 1981). From various perspectives, other works treat the effort to develop the young so that they would fit the expectations of the society into which they would emerge. See Joseph Kett, *Rites of Passage: Adolescence in America, 1790 to the Present* (New York: Basic Books, 1977); Michael Katz, *Class, Bureaucracy and Schools* (New York: Praeger, 1975); and Joel Spring, *Education and the Rise of the Corporate State* (Boston: Beacon Press, 1972).

13. Gulick, *Philosophy of Play,* 12.

14. Ibid., 71.

15. Leland and Leland, *Playground Technique and Playcraft,* 21.

16. Gulick, *Philosophy of Play,* 97, 98.

17. Ibid., 200. Frederick Winslow Taylor pioneered in the systematic study of work and human movement, applying what he considered to be scientific principles of organizational efficiency to social situations and human performance. See Taylor, *Scientific Management* (New York: Harper, 1947).

18. C. Lloyd Morgan, *Habit and Instinct* (London: Edward Arnold, 1986); Wesley Mills, *The Nature and Development of Animal Intelligence* (New York: Macmillan, 1908); Ernest Thompson Seton, *Wild Animals I Have Known* (New York: Charles Scribner's Sons, 1900); W. H. Hudson, *The Naturalist in La Plata* (London: Chapman & Hall, Ltd., 1892).

19. Gulick, *Philosophy of Play,* 99, 105–6.

20. Ibid., 116.

21. Ibid., 162.

22. Ibid., 210.

23. See G. Stanley Hall, *Life and Confessions of a Psychologist* (New York: Appleton, 1923); Dorothy Ross, *G. Stanley Hall: The Psychologist as Prophet* (Chicago: University of Chicago Press, 1972). A concise summary of Hall's views on child development appears in Cavallo, *Muscles and Morals,* 55–60.

24. Hall, *Adolescence,* 215.

25. Hall, "The Story of a Sand Pile," in *Aspects of Child Life and Education,* 142–56.

26. Hall, *Aspects of Child Life and Education,* vi.

27. Ibid., 151.

28. Hall, *Adolescence,* 217.

29. Ibid., 216–17. Hall thought that the intensity of the fight actually had a positive, creative effect on the individual. He believed that it was especially important for an adolescent to range widely across intense experience, thus to be stretched and pulled "to expand in all directions its possibilities of the body and soul in this plastic period when without this occasional excess powers would atrophy or suffer arrest for want of use" (216).

30. Theodore Roosevelt, *American Ideals* (New York: Putnam's, 1897); and Roosevelt, *Applied Ethics* (Cambridge, MA: Harvard University Press, 1911).

31. Hall, *Adolescence,* 217.

32. Ibid., 218.

33. An insightful assessment of "the body electric" and the focus on human energy appears in Stephen Kern, *Anatomy and Destiny: A Cultural History of the Body* (Indianapolis: Bobbs-Merrill, 1975). Concerning "spermatic economy," see G. J. Barker-Benfield, *The Horrors of the Half-Known Life: Male Attitudes Toward Women and Sexuality in Nineteenth-Century America* (New York: Harper, 1976).

34. A good example is Luther Halsey Gulick, "The Camp Fire Girls and the New Relation of Women to the World," *Proceedings of the National Education Association* 15 (1912): 322–27.

Fig. 9  Juanita Coleman, left, helps adults learn how to play by leading a recreation class in the "fundamentals of education," Gee's Bend, Alabama, 1939. Farm Security Administration photograph by Marion Post Wolcott, courtesy Library of Congress.

35. Gertrude Dudley and Frances A. Kellor, *Athletic Games in the Education of Women* (New York: Henry Holt, 1909).

36. See, for example, Mary Taylor Bissell, *Physical Development and Exercise for Women* (New York: Dodd, Mead, 1890). Bissell was a medical doctor.

37. See Joseph Lee, *Constructive and Preventive Philanthropy* (New York: Macmillan, 1902); and Lee, *Play in Education* (New York: Macmillan, 1917).

38. Lee, *Play in Education*, 398.

39. Ibid., 392–402, 414.

40. Leland and Leland, *Playground Technique and Playcraft*.

41. Ibid., frontispiece.

42. Henry S. Curtis, *The Practical Conduct of Play* (New York: Macmillan, 1915).

43. See various suggestions for excursions as well as photographs illustrating examples in Leland and

Leland, eds., *Playground Technique and Playcraft*. See also Curtis, *Practical Conduct of Play*.

44. Joseph Lee, *Play in Education* (New York: National Recreation Association, 1942), 62–69. In several of his own works, in fact, G. Stanley Hall explicitly referred to some of Lee's writings.

45. Lee, *Play in Education*, viii.

46. Ibid., ix.

47. Ibid., x.

48. Gulick, *Philosophy of Play*, 277.

49. Ibid., 280.

50. Ibid.

51. This emphasis on the critical importance of play to Americans in the 1930s is clear in Warren I. Susman, ed., *Culture and Commitment* (New York: George Braziller, 1973). As he points out, games such as Monopoly, created in the period, stress order. Susman notes that the literature dealing with

leisure and play as a "problem" sharply increased in volume after World War I and especially in the 1930s. Bibliographic entries for 1900–1909 numbered 20; for 1910–1919 nearly 50; between 1920 and 1929 about 200; and in 1930–1939 some 450. The issue was not how to use leisure and play in service of work so much as how to deal with the abundance of leisure in itself and with the need to find ways for fulfilling the self in a world where work seemed in increasingly short supply.

52. Martha Wolfenstein, "Fun Morality: An Analysis of Recent American Child-Training Literature," reprinted in Susman, *Culture and Commitment*, 91.

53. Ibid.

54. The notion that a succession of psychological and psychoanalytical theories might conform to periods in the development of twentieth-century America appears in Warren I. Susman, " 'Personality' and the Making of Twentieth Century Culture," in Susman, *Culture as History* (New York: Pantheon Books, 1984), 271–85.

# A Glossary of Outdoor Games

JAMES WILDER AND ROBYN HANSEN, COMPILERS

Because many outdoor games of the preceding century and the first several decades of this one are now obscure, this glossary provides rules and definitions for forms of outdoor play mentioned by the authors in this volume. The game rules and definitions that appear here are quoted from three types of nineteenth- and early twentieth-century sources—books that illustrated contemporary activities for young boys and girls, books intended for teachers or parents listing suitable recreations for children, and books compiling children's games and songs as a form of folklore. These sources are cited fully in the bibliography and by authors, short titles, and years of publication within the glossary itself. Some games mentioned in the essays (for example, Cave-in-the-Middle-of-the-World) were evidently unique to a small group of individuals, and rules for them were probably never codified and published. Other games (such as Crack the Whip) were played for more than a century before their rules began to appear in games instruction books. Some popular games like baseball or Prisoner's Base have variations for which no rules can be found.

The games in the glossary are in alphabetical order. Initial spellings are taken from the source cited; variant spellings and other names for the game are shown in parentheses immediately afterward.

**Ante Over** (also Andy I Over; Andy Over; Annie, Annie Over the Shanty; Anti-Anti-I-Over; Nicky-Nicky-Nee).

This old and popular boys' game requires a building over which the ball is thrown. In the gymnasium a curtain is often stretched across the center.

The two teams take their places on opposite sides of the building. A player of Team A calls "Ante Over" and throws a softball over the building. The Team B players attempt to catch it. If someone succeeds, he and his team mates dash around the building and the player holding the ball attempts to hit one of the Team A players, who may take refuge by running around the building. If he succeeds, the hit player joins Team B and the ball goes to Team A. If no one catches the ball when it is thrown over the building, the side doing the catching calls "Ante Over" and the ball is thrown back. The side wins which has the most players when play ceases.

In some sections the boys call "Pigs tail" if the ball hits the building and bounds back. It is then thrown over again.

Mason and Mitchell, *Active Games and Contests* (1935)

## Base-ball

It is only within a few years that Base-ball has become the "national sport" of America. The present scientific game, which we naturally do not intend to describe, was known in Massachusetts, twenty years ago, as the "New York game." A ruder form of Base-ball has been played in some Massachusetts towns for a century; while in other parts of New England no game with a ball was formerly known except "Hockey." There was great local variety in these sports.

We may refer to some features of the old-fashioned game which possess interest. The first duty, in games with the bat, is "to choose up." The two best players, or any two selected, toss the bat from one to another; the tosser places his right hand above the hand of the catcher, who in turn follows with his own left, and so on. He who can get the last hold has first choice; but the hold must be proved by ability to whirl the bat three times round the head, and throw it. Another test of a sufficient grasp is for a player to hammer with a second bat on the hand which is uppermost. In this last case, therefore, the grasp must be low enough for the wood of the bat to be struck by the blow.

In this game there were three "bases" besides the "home" base, at about the same distance as at present; but the number of players was indeterminate. The pitcher threw the ball, and the catcher stood close behind the striker. When the batsman struck the ball, a run must be made; and the ball was not, as at present, thrown *to* the base, but *at* the runner, usually with all the force possible. If he was hit, he was out; and each member of the side had to be put out separately. There were, moreover, ways in which a side could recover its lost players. When all were out but one, who was on one of the bases, the pitcher and catcher, approaching to within some thirty feet, tossed the ball to and fro, and the runner must "steal" his next base, while the two former watched his movements, ready to throw to the nearest fielder of their side, who in turn would hurl the ball at the remaining player. If under these circumstances he could reach home untouched, he might "put in" any player of his side.

As there was never any umpire in these games, the field for controversy was unlimited. One way, as we recollect, of settling disputes was as follows: All proceeding to the spot of the doubtful catch, the best player on one side hurled the ball with all his force upwards; if it was caught by the designated player of the other party, the point was given in the latter's favor, and *vice versâ*.

We need only mention the game of "Old Cat," in which there are two goals—the striker's and the pitcher's—and the run is made from the former to the latter and return. The game is then named from the number of batters, "One Old Cat," or "Two Old Cat."

Newell, *Games and Songs of American Children* (1883)

## Black Tom (also Black Man)

The boy who is "it" stands in the middle of the street, and the others on the pavement on one side. When "it" cries, "Black Tom" three times, the other players run across, and may be caught, in which case they must join the one who is "it" in capturing their comrades. "It" may call "Yellow Tom" or "Blue Tom," or whatever he chooses; but if any one makes a false start, he is considered caught, or if one of the captured should cry, "Black Tom" three times, and any player of the other side should start, he is considered caught. The first one caught is "it" for the next game.

Culin, "Street Games of Boys in Brooklyn, New York" (1891)

## Capture the Flag

[Arkansas]

The playing space for this game should measure one hundred by five hundred yards and should be wooded or hilly or both. There are two teams of from fifteen to twenty players each and a referee. The object of the game is to get the opponents' flag and bring it back to the home base without being tagged by those of the other side. Each flag is concealed behind a bush, a stone, a tree, or a small hill. A narrow strip (about ten yards in width) in the center of the playing area is "No Man's Land." If a player is caught inside it, he must join the team of the captor. The game may be won either by capturing the flag of the other team or by capturing all the players on the opposing team.

Brewster, *American Nonsinging Games* (1953)

## Crack the Whip (also Sling the Biscuit; Snap the Whip)

*Open Ice*
*Elementary to Senior High School*

The players on skates join hands forming a line. The player at the left end is the snapper, and the player at the right end the cracker.

The snapper skates forward with the others following with joined hands. The line goes faster and faster, then suddenly the snapper cracks the whip by turning and skating back in the opposite direction with the rest of the line following. The object is to snap the cracker off the end of the whip. If the cracker parts hands with the line, he becomes the snapper, and the next to the last player becomes the cracker. If the cracker is not snapped off, he stays in that position until he is snapped off.

Mason and Mitchell, *Active Games and Contests* (1935)

## Croquet

This game (pronounced cro-kay') is of French origin, and has been only recently introduced into this country. As it is an out-door game,

requiring some skill, and giving a variety of exercise, without being too fatiguing, it is likely to become popular; and we will give its details in full.

Croquet can be played only on a level piece of ground; but a good Croquet-ground should be close turf—the grass cut short, the moss killed out, and the ground well rolled. The area required is not large—about sixty by ninety feet. If it be for a permanent Croquet-ground, there should be a shallow ditch around it, to prevent the balls from straying. Of this rectangle laid out for the course of the ball, the lower part is the base, or foot, the opposite end the head, while the sides are respectively the right and left flanks. In the centre of the foot is the spot from whence the play begins, and here the starting-stake is set; and in the centre of the head is the turning-stake. There are ten bridges, with a span of twelve inches, made of iron wire, and stuck in the ground, leaving six to eight inches above ground. The stakes are of wood, two feet in length, and having eight rings of different colors, running down in this way: black, yellow, red, white, blue, orange, brown, green. It is from the starting-stake, through the bridges, touching the turning-stake, and from the other flank, back to the spot, that the balls are driven, by a mallet in the hands of the player. The course of the ball will be seen by an examination of the diagram.

The balls are made of wood, are turned to be ten inches in circumference, of beech, willow, or plane tree, eight in number, and painted to correspond to the rings on the starting-stake. This allows one to each player, though when four play they can either use four, or play two each. The mallet has a head with a diameter of two and one-third inches, and a length of four, a cylinder, slightly hollow in the middle, and having the ends slightly convex. The shank of the mallet is slender, tapering toward the head, about nine-tenths of an inch in diameter at the butt, and two feet and a half long. The shank should be of well-seasoned hickory—the head of dogwood, heart-hickory, or box—the latter preferable.

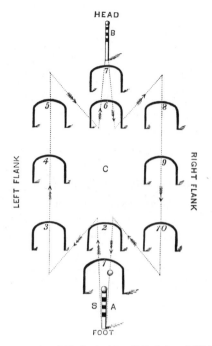

HEAD

LEFT FLANK

RIGHT FLANK

FOOT

A, The Starting-stake.　B, The Turning-stake.　C, The Centre.　S, The Spot.
1, 2, Lower Central Bridges.　　　3, 4, 5, Left Flank Bridges.
6, 7, Upper Central Bridges.　　　8, 9, 10, Right Flank Bridges.
The dotted lines and arrows indicate the course of a ball in making the grand round of the game.

Fig. 1　Diagram of croquet court, in *American Boy's Book of Sports and Games* (1864).

*American Boy's Book of Sports and Games* (1864)
(Fig. 1)

Scientific croquet originated in New-England about 1880, and so greatly was the interest of the players increased by the changes that the new game grew into popular favor rapidly. The uneven surfaces of the natural lawn at home gave way to an absolutely level, smooth and sanded court of stated dimensions, with a boundary board which checked the rolling of the ball just at the edge of the field of play. Wooden balls and long-handled mallets were succeeded by spheres of hard rubber and mallets with short handles and long rubber-tipped heads. The wide arches of the common game, which were suitable for the grassy lawn, were replaced in the sanded court by narrow wickets of wire, through which the balls could just be driven without much room to spare. Good playing then be-

came possible, and the new game now excites the ardent attachment of its votaries.

Croquet is not an athletic game, nor could it become one unless balls and mallets should become gigantic in size and ponderous in weight. But the fact that croquet as an open-air pastime depends for its interest on the exercise of skill alone, does not diminish its value. On the contrary, the absence of the necessity for great physical exertion makes it an admirable amusement for people of mature years, who may derive from it delightful and gentle occupation in the open air, and the zest which comes from a competition of skill.

Hall, *The Tribune Book of Open-Air Sports* (1880)
(Fig. 2)

### ¿Cuantas Naranjas? (also *La Naranjas Dulce* or *The Sweet Orange*)

This is a Spanish counting game for a group of small children sitting around in a circle, who are about to go to the market for oranges when the orange seller arrives. The fun of the game is in the fast counting backwards without tripping over words.

A player is chosen to start the game, and begins this way:

First player:　*Amigos, vamos a naranjas.*　(Friends, let's go for oranges.)

Others:　*¿Cuántas vamos a traer?*　(How many shall we get?)

First player:　*Una para mi y una para usted.*　(One for me and one for you.)

Others:　*¡Mira! ¡El naranjero está aquí!* (Look! The orange seller is here!)　*¿Cuántas naranjas queremos?*　(How many oranges do we want?)

First player:　*Una para mi y una para usted.*　(One for me and one for you.)　*¿Cuántas naranjas hay aqui?*　(How many oranges are there here?)

Then first player continues as fast as possible, the others counting with him. Any slip of the tongue and a player must drop out of the game.

First player and the others [*all together, and*

Fig. 2  Croquet players, in R. Valentine, ed., *The Home Book of Pleasure and Instruction* (1868).

*very fast*]: *De quince, catorce* (from fifteen, fourteen); *de catorce, trece* (from fourteen thirteen); *de trece, doce* (from thirteen, twelve); *de doce, once* (from twelve, eleven); *de once, diez* (from eleven, ten); *de diez, nueve* (from ten, nine); *de nueve, ocho* (from nine, eight); *de ocho, siete* (from eight, seven); *de siete, seis* (from seven, six); *de seis, cinco* (from six, five); *de cinco, cuatro* (from five, four); *de cuatro, tres* (from four, three); *de tres, dos* (from three, two); *de dos, una* (from two, one); *de una y nada mas* (from one and nothing more).

Brewster, *American Nonsinging Games* (1953)

## Duck on a Rock

We will suppose a party of boys to be debating what game to play. "What shall we play?" "Duck on a Rock," suggests one. The idea is instantly taken up. "My one duck," cries some boy. "My duck," shouts a second, seizing a stone. The last to "speak" gets no duck, and has to guard the "drake." The drake is a good-sized stone, which is placed on an elevated position, or boulder, if such be at hand. The "ducks" are stones about the size of the fist. The object is to knock the drake off the rock. After each player has thrown his duck, and missed, he must recover it. The guardian stands by the "rock," but cannot tag a player until the latter has touched his own duck, when he must replace the keeper. Meanwhile, if the drake is knocked off the rock, the keeper must replace it before he can tag any one, and this is therefore the signal for a rush to recover the thrown ducks. The game is not without a spice of danger from these missiles.

Newell, *Games and Songs of American Children* (1883)
(Fig. 3)

## The Farmer in the Dell

The children join hands and walk round in a ring. The farmer stands in the center during the first verse and chooses a wife during the

Fig. 3   Duck on a Rock, in Frank M. Chapman, "A City Playground," *St. Nicholas,* June 1891.

second. During the third verse the wife chooses a child, during the fourth the child chooses the nurse, and so on. During the ninth verse all crowd round the cheese and clap their hands. The cheese becomes the farmer and the game is repeated.

1. The farmer in the dell, the farmer in the dell, Heigh-o, my dearie O, the farmer in the dell.
2. The farmer takes a wife, the farmer takes a wife, Heigh-o! my dearie O, the farmer takes a wife.
3. The wife takes the child, etc.
4. The child takes the nurse, etc.
5. The nurse takes the dog, etc.
6. The dog takes the cat, etc.
7. The cat takes the rat, etc.
8. The rat takes the cheese, etc.
9. The cheese stands alone, etc.

This game is also played as follows: After all are chosen, the children sing:

The cheese goes away,
The cheese goes away,
Heigho! my dearie O,
The cheese goes away.

The cheese joins the ring.

The rat goes away, etc.

The rat joins the ring.

Repeat until all have joined the ring.

Brown and Boyd, *Old English and American Games* (1915)

### Foot-Ball

The players are divided into two parties, equal in number, and each party has to defend one of two goals, or homes (see diagram), into which the other tries to kick the foot-ball. The party who gains two out of three "goals" is generally considered to have won the game. The lines CD, drawn at right angles to the goal lines A B, are called "touch-lines;" when the ball is kicked behind these, it is said to be "in touch," and a player brings it forward to the line, flinging it to his players, who wait at the edge for it. "Place-kick" is when the ball is put on the ground and kicked from where it lies. "Punting" is when the ball is dropped from the hands and kicked before it reaches the ground. In a *drop,* the ball is dropped and kicked at the moment it touches the ground. A *free kick,* is the privilege of kicking the ball, without obstruction, in such manner as the kicker may think fit. A *fair catch,* is when the ball is caught, after it has touched the person of an

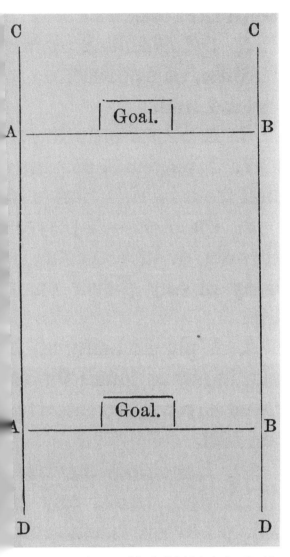

Fig. 4    Diagram of football field, in Arthur David Hosterman, *In Door and Out* (1882).

FOOTBALL—THE DROP KICK.

Fig. 5    Football—the drop kick, in Albert Ellery Berg, ed., *The Universal Self-Instructor and Manual of General Reference* (1882).

adversary, or has been kicked, knocked on, or thrown by an adversary, and before it has touched the ground, or one of the side catching it; but if the ball is kicked from out of touch, or from behind goal-line, a fair catch cannot be made. *Hacking*, is kicking an adversary on the front of the leg, below the knee. *Charging*, is attacking an adversary with the shoulder, chest, or body, without using the hands or legs. *Knocking on*, is when a player strikes or propels the ball with hands, arms, or body, without kicking or throwing it. *Holding* includes the obstruction of a player by the

hand or any part of the arm below the elbow. The goals are placed eighty or one hundred yards apart, and are generally marked by stakes being driven in the ground.

The ball should be an ox-bladder, inflated with air and covered with leather. In order to dispose of the players to the best advantage, the best man should stand in front; and goal-keepers should remain at their stations, to prevent the ball passing through, and not leave them, except when their assistance seems absolutely necessary. After each game, the players change sides: by which means any advantages of wind, sun, or sloping ground are neutralized.

[Hosterman], *In Door and Out* (1882) (Figs. 4 and 5)

## Fox and Geese
*Winter Playground, Camp, Yard*
*Elementary and Junior High Schools*

For this old favorite of the winter days, tramp down in the snow the design shown. . . . Select a fox and station him at the hub of the wheel.

Figs. 6 and 7   Diagrams of Fox and Geese circles, in Bernard S. Mason and Elmer D. Mitchell, *Active Games and Contests* (1935).

The geese scatter along the rivers (trodden paths of the wheel). The game is played as in ordinary tag except that the runners cannot leave the rivers. A goose who is tagged by the fox becomes the fox, and tagging back immediately is permitted. The intersections of the spokes with the outer circle constitute safety zones—the geese cannot be tagged while standing on them.

(Fig. 6)

**Variation:** The intersection of the cross lines is known as the goose shed. The outer circle is known as the goose ring, and the inner circle as the fox ring. The object of the geese is to reach the goose shed without being caught. The geese roam about the rivers at will and risk capture only on the cross lines between the fox ring and the goose shed.

The more noise a goose makes in dashing for the goose shed the greater the honor of the achievement.

Should the game continue too long without a goose being captured, the farmer (leader) begins to cluck, calling the geese to the goose shed immediately, for since it is now night the fox may roam at will around the rivers and capture a goose any place.

A goose who is tagged immediately becomes the fox.

**Variation:** Tramp down a single circle. . . . The game is played as before except that there are no safety zones.

Mason and Mitchell, *Active Games and Contests* (1935)
(Fig. 7)

### Hare and Hounds

This favorite sport is almost too well known to require a description. The hares (there are generally two) are supplied with small sacks full of colored paper torn up very small. As they run they throw out handfuls, and so show the "scent." The hares get ten minutes to a quarter of an hour's law. They generally try to baffle the field by adopting a course of considerable difficulty, but they are "on honor" to fairly scatter the paper. At every gap, at every turn, and at every few yards in fact, out goes a handful. The hounds wait the required time, and then start off in full cry. There are huntsmen and whippers-in duly provided with horns. The runs are from eight to fifteen miles, and generally wind up with a good dinner. This pastime is a favorite during the winter and early spring. The party generally rendezvous at some hotel, from which they start, and to which they return to change clothes and dine.

Berg, *The Universal Self-Instructor* (1882) (Fig. 8)

The city boys have a substitute for this game known as "Chalk Chase" or "City Hare and Hound." Two hares are chosen, as in the country game, but instead of the paper scent, chalk arrows are used, on the ground, walks or walls, the arrow pointing in the direction they are running. If they wish to hide they must chalk a large capital H in the center of a circle, and hide within twenty paces of it. The hounds must cross out every arrow as they pass, or the hares are not fairly caught.

Mustain, *Popular Amusements for In-doors and Out of Doors* (1902)

HARE AND HOUNDS.

FIVES

Is probably the oldest game o[f] with the palm of the hand ag[ainst] the base of the wall a wooden

Fig. 8   Hare and Hounds, in Albert Ellery Berg, ed., *The Universal Self-Instructor and Manual of General Reference* (1882).

## Here I Bake, Here I Brew

The players form a circle by joining hands, and shut one of their number into the middle of it. The captive touches one pair of joined hands, and says, "Here I bake;" then passing on to two others (generally on the opposite side of the circle), she says, "Here I brew." Then she touches two others, saying, "Here I make my wedding-cake." Then suddenly she springs on two of the clasped hands which appear least to expect her, and breaks through the circle if she can. But her effort is strongly resisted by the players, who keep her prisoner as long as they can. If she tries three times in vain to escape from the circle, she pays a forfeit. If she breaks through it, the pair whose hands were not strong enough to hold her pay a forfeit each, and another player becomes captive. If this game is played out of doors, or in a large hall, when the captive breaks through she runs around the lawn or hall, until one of the players can catch her. Then the circle forms again, and the one who caught the captive becomes captive. This game continues in the same way until a change is desired.

Smith, *American Home Book of Indoor Games, Amusements, and Occupations* (1873)

## Hop-Scotch

A figure of about twelve feet in length . . . is described on the ground, and selection made of a small flat stone, having sharp edges. From a line drawn at a distance of a few paces, a stone is tossed into No. 1, after which the boy or girl hops on one foot into No. 1, and kicks out the stone, which is then thrown into No. 2. The player now hops into No. 1, and jumps into No. 2, in such a way that one foot is in the division 2, and one foot in 1. The stone is kicked into 1, and then out, and so on. In passing through divisions 1 and 2, 4 and 5, 8 and 9, a straddle must be made, one foot being placed in each; in the others a hop only must be taken. A failure to throw the stone into the right place, or to kick it into the right division, or leaving it on any line, or touching the raised foot, or stepping on a line, puts out, and the next takes his or her turn.

In other localities, no straddling step is taken, but the player, in certain divisions, is allowed to place the stone on his foot, and so expel it from the figure at a single kick; the compartments also vary in number and arrangement.

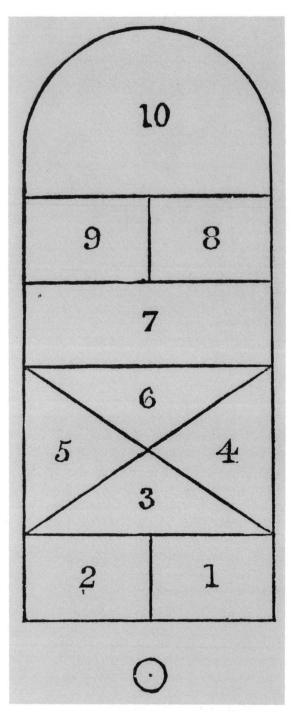

Fig. 9 Diagram for hopscotch, in William W. Newell, *Games and Songs of American Children* (1883).

Newell, *Games and Songs of American Children* (1883)
(Fig. 9)

## Hul Gul

This game is played by three, four, or more, who stand in a circle. A child then addresses his left-hand neighbor, and the dialogue is:

"Hul Gul."
"Hands full."
"Parcel how many?"

The second player then guesses the number, two guesses being sometimes allowed. If, for example, the guess is five, and the real number seven, the first responds, "Give me two to make it seven," and so on until all the counters have been gained by one player. The number allowed to be taken is often limited, by agreement, to six or ten.

The counters are beans, grains of corn, marbles, nuts, and, in the South, *chinquapins.*\*

A childish trick is to expand the hand as if unable to hold the number of counters, when in fact they are but one or two.

Newell, *Games and Songs of American Children* (1883)

## I Spy (also Hide and Seek)

A boundary of a block is agreed upon, within which the players may hide, and then they count out to determine who shall be "it" for the first game. A lamp-post or tree is taken as the "home" or "hunk;" the one who is "it" must stand there with his eyes closed, and count five hundred by fives, crying out each hundred in a loud voice, while the others go hide. At the end of the five hundred, "it" cries:—

One, two, three!
Look out for me,
For my eyes are open,
And I can see!

and goes in search of those in hiding. They may hide behind stoops, in areas, etc., but are not permitted to go in houses. When "it" dis-

\*"*Chinquapin (Castanea primula)*, an ovoid, pointed, sweet nut, half the size of a common chestnut."

covers a player in hiding, he cries out, "I spy so and so," calling the person by name, and runs to "hunk," for if the one spied should get in to "hunk" first, he would relieve himself. The players run in to the "hunk" when they have a good chance, and cry *relievo!* and if they get in first, they are free. Sometimes the game is also played so that, if a boy runs in and relieves himself in this way, he also relieves all the others, and the same one is "it" for the next game. Two players will frequently change hats in hiding, so as to disguise themselves, for if the one who is "it" mistakes one player for another, as often happens through this change of hats, and calls out the wrong name, both boys cry, "False alarm!" and are permitted, according to custom, to come in free. The game is continued until all the players come in, and the first caught becomes "it" for the next game. In "I spy," the one who is "it" is sometimes called the "old man."

Culin, "Street Games of Boys in Brooklyn, New York" (1891)

## Jack-Stones (also Jacks)

A game played by one or more persons with five small pebbles, or little pieces of iron. . . . These are thrown up and caught in various ways, and if more than one plays, he wins who first succeeds in going through in order with a certain number of exercises. These exercises differ in kind and number in different places; but some of them are given below.

1. The five Jack-stones are thrown into the air and caught all together on the back of the hand.
2. One of the Stones is tossed up and caught in the hand and on its back alternately. At the successive catches the player calls out "Five!" "Ten!" "Fifteen!" "Twenty!" and so on by fives up to One Hundred.
3. *Ones.* The Jack-stones are held in the hand, and one, called the "Jack," is thrown into the air, while the four others are laid on the floor or table in time to catch the Jack as he comes down. These are then picked up, one by one, each one while the Jack is thrown into the air. When all

have been taken into the hand they must be laid down as before, ready for *Two's.* Only one hand must be used.
4. *Two's, Three's,* and *Four's.* The same as ones, except that the Stones are picked up first two at a time; then three and one at a time; and then all four at a time.
5. The Stones are all taken in the hand and laid down, first one at a time, then two at a time, and so on, always while the Jack is in the air. Each time after all are laid down, they are picked up all at once.

Champlin and Bostwick, *Young Folks' Cyclopaedia of Games and Sports* (1890)

## Jumping Rope

This play should likewise be used with caution. It is a healthy exercise, and tends to make the form graceful; but it should be used with moderation. I have known instances of blood vessels burst by young ladies, who in a silly attempt to jump a certain number of hundred times, have persevered in jumping after their strength was exhausted. There are several ways of jumping rope:

1. Simply springing and passing the rope under the feet with rapidity.
2. Crossing arms at the moment of throwing the rope.
3. Passing the rope under the feet of two or three, who jump at once, standing close, and laying hands on each other's shoulders.
4. The rope held by two little girls, one at each end, and thrown over a third, who jumps in the middle.

The more difficult feats should not be attempted, until the simpler ones are perfectly learned. A smooth hard surface should be chosen to jump upon, where there is nothing to entangle or obstruct the feet.

[Child], *The Little Girl's Own Book* (1831)

## Leapfrog
*2 to 100 players.*
*Playground; gymnasium.*

The first player makes a back, standing either

Fig. 10    Leapfrog, in William Clarke, *Boys' Own Book* (1885).

with his back or his side toward the one who is to leap over. The next player runs, leaps over the back, runs a few steps forward so as to allow space for a run between himself and the first player, and in his turn stoops over and makes a back. This makes two backs. The third player leaps over the first back, runs and leaps over the second, runs a short distance and makes a third back, etc., until all the players are making backs, when the first one down takes his turn at leaping, and so on indefinitely.

**Variation:** This may be made much more difficult by each player moving only a few feet in advance of the back over which he has leaped, as this will then leave no room for a run be-

tween the backs, but means a continuous succession of leaps by the succeeding players.

Bancroft, *Games for the Playground, Home, School and Gymnasium* (1915) (Fig. 10)

**London Bridge** (also Oranges and Lemons)

No game has been more popular with children than this, and any summer evening, in the poorer quarters of the cities, it may still be seen how six years instructs three years in the proper way of conducting it. Two players, by their uplifted hands, form an arch, representing the bridge, under which passes the train of children, each clinging to the garments of the predecessor, and hurrying to get safely by. The last of the train is caught by the lowered arms of the guardians of the bridge, and asked, "Will you have a diamond necklace or a gold pin?" "a rose or a cabbage?" or some equivalent question. The keepers have already privately agreed which of the two each of these objects shall represent, and, according to the prisoner's choice, he is placed behind one or the other. When all are caught, the game ends with a "Tug of War," the two sides pulling against each other; and the child who lets go, and breaks the line, is pointed at and derided. The words of the rhyme sung while the row passes under the bridge are now reduced to two lines,

> London Bridge is falling down,
>    My fair lady!

Newell, *Games and Songs of American Children* (1883)

This pleasant old game begins by two of the older or taller players . . . taking places opposite each other and joining their hands high, thus making an arch for the rest to pass under in a long line. . . . As the procession moves along, the two players forming the arch repeat or chant these lines:—

> "Oranges and lemons,"
> Say the bells of St. Clement's.
> "You owe me five farthings,"

Fig. 11   London Bridge, in R. Valentine, ed., *The Home Book of Pleasure and Instruction* (1868).

Say the bells of St. Martin's.
"When will you pay me?"
Say the bells of Old Bailey.
"When I grow rich,"
Say the bells of Shoreditch.
"When will that be?"
Say the bells of Stepney.
"I do not know,"
Says the great bell of Bow.
Here comes a candle to light you to bed,
And here comes a chopper to chop off the last
    man's head.

With these final words the arch-players lower their arms and catch the head of the last of the procession. In order that the arrival of the end of the procession and the end of the verses shall come together, the last line can be lengthened like this—

> And here comes a chopper to chop off the last—
> last—last—last man's head.

Fisher, *What Shall We Do Now?* (1907)
(Fig. 11)

## Marbles

The old-fashioned marbles were made by the attrition of pieces of stone against each other in a kind of mill, and were far better than many of those now in use, which are made of porcelain. When we were young the painted marbles, now a deal in vogue, were called "Chinese," and were not valued so much as others. They are generally too smooth to shoot well. Marbles then, and still are wherever marbles is much played, divided into common marbles and "alleys." Of these last, a "red alley" is equal to two common marbles, a "black alley" equal to three, and a "white alley" to four. Very large marbles called "tom-trollers" are sometimes, but not often, used—never in

Fig. 12    Marbles, in Frank M. Chapman, "A City Playground," *St. Nicholas*, June 1891.

the ring games; and the very small marbles, called "peewees," are only fit for children with very small hands.

There are three ways of shooting a marble. 1. *Trolling*, which consists in projecting the marble so that it rolls along the ground, until it strikes the marble at which it is aimed. 2. *Hoisting*, where the marble is shot from at or above the level of the knee, while the party stands; and *Knuckling down*, where the player shoots with the middle knuckle of his fore-finger touching the ground, but makes his marble describe a curve in the air on its way to the ring. A boy has to be a good player, "a dabster," as they say—to knuckle down well.

To shoot a marble properly, it must be held between the tip of the fore-finger and the first joint of the thumb, resting on the bend of the second finger, and propelled forward by suddenly forcing up the thumbnail. Some boys place it between the bend of the first finger and the thumb-joint. This is called "shooting cunnethumb," and not only subjects those who do it to the ridicule of their associates, but tires the thumb very much.

[Hosterman], *In Door and Out* (1882) (Fig. 12)

## Mumblety-peg (also Nimbley Pegs)

In this game of boys and girls, a knife is cast to the earth, on a piece of turf, with the point downwards, and must remain sticking there; there are several successive positions of throwing, as follows: (1) the knife is held in the palm, first of the right and afterwards of the left hand, point outward, and thrown so as to revolve towards the player; (2) it is rested successively on the right and left fist, with the point uppermost, and thrown sideways; (3) the knife is pressed with the point resting on each finger and thumb of both hands in succession, and cast outwards; after this it is held by the point, and *flipped;* (4) from the breast, nose, and each eye; (5) from each ear, crossing arms, and taking hold of the opposite ear with the free hand; (6) over the head backwards. If the knife does not "stick," the next player takes his turn; the first to conclude the series wins. The winner is allowed to drive a peg into the ground with three blows of the knife, which the other must extract with his teeth, whence the name "Mumblety-peg." Another title is "Stick-knife."

Newell, *Games and Songs of American Children* (1883)

## Oats, Pease, Beans

This game gives great pleasure to children on account of its different motions. One child stands in the center of the ring, which moves round, singing:

"Oats, pease, beans and barley grows,
Oats, pease, beans and barley grows;
You, nor I, nor nobody knows
How oats, pease, beans and barley grows. . . ."

The children pause, while they sing—

"Thus the farmer sows his seed,

[Swing arms back and forth.]

Thus he stands and takes his ease;

[Stand erect with hands on hips.]

Stamps his foot and claps his hands,
And turns around to view his lands."

Fig. 13   Oats, Pease, Beans, in Josephine Pollard, comp., *Plays and Games for Little Folks* (1889).

Stamp, clap, and turn, then join hands again and go round, singing:

"A-waiting for a partner,
A-waiting for a partner,
Open the ring and choose one in,
And kiss her when you get her in."

The boy chooses a girl, and the two kneel in the ring:

"Now you're married, you must obey,
You must be true to all you say;
Live together all your life,
And I'll pronounce you man and wife!"

Or this stanza:

"Now you're married, you must obey,
You must be true to all you say;
You must be kind, you must be good,
And keep your wife in kindling-wood."

Pollard, *Plays and Games for Little Folks* (1889) (Fig. 13)

### One Old Cat

A kind of base ball played by any number of persons. The Home base is the only base, and the positions of the players are Batsman, Catcher, Pitcher, and any number of fielders, called First Field, Second Field, and so on. The striker keeps his place till he is put out. He is out only if a fair fly or a foul bound is caught, all balls being fair that strike in front of the base, or if the Catcher catch[es] the ball after his third strike. If the ball is not caught at the third strike he has three more, and no strikes are counted except those actually made. When the striker is put out he takes the place of the lowest fielder. Each fielder then rises one step in rank, and First Field becomes Pitcher, while Pitcher takes the Catcher's place, and Catcher goes to the bat. Sometimes, when a fair ball is caught, the fielder who makes the catch is allowed to go to the bat at once. The Batsman takes the lowest place as before, but only those lower than the successful fielder rise in rank.

One Old Cat is sometimes varied by having two bases, Home and First Base, and making the Batsman run to the latter and back when he strikes a fair ball. If he does so without being put out at Home, he scores a run. There is no First Baseman.

Champlin and Bostwick, *Young Folks'*
*Cyclopaedia of Games and Sports* (1890)

## Picture-Card Pitching

This game is a recent invention, and is played with the small picture cards which the manufacturers of cigarettes have distributed with their wares for some years past. These pictures, which are nearly uniform in size and embrace a great variety of subjects, are eagerly collected by boys in Brooklyn and the near-by cities, and form an article of traffic among them.

Bounds are marked of about twelve by eight feet, with a wall or stoop at the back. The players stand at the longer distance, and each in turn shoots a card with his fingers, as he would a marble, against the wall or stoop. The one whose card goes nearest that object collects all the cards that have been thrown, and twirls them either singly or together into the air. Those that fall with the picture up belong to him, according to the rules; while those that fall with the reverse side uppermost are handed to the player whose card came next nearest to the wall, and he in turn twirls them, and receives those that fall with the picture side up. The remainder, if any, are taken by the next nearest player, and the game continues until all the cards thrown are divided.

Culin, "Street Games of Boys in Brooklyn, New York" (1891)

## Pom-Pom-Pull-Away (also Pull Away; Rushing Bases)
*Playground, Street*
*Elementary and Junior High Schools*

Establish a goal line at each end of the playing space. The one who is "it" stands in the middle ground and calls,

"Pom-Pom-Pull-Away
Come away or I'll fetch you away."

At this all of the players, who have taken places behind one of the goals, must run across to the other goal. All those tagged join the original tagger and help to tag the rest, who must run across again when the call is repeated. All the taggers yell the call in unison under the leadership of the original "it." The game continues till all are caught. The first one tagged is "it" for the next game.

**Hill Dill:** This game is played exactly like Pom-Pom-Pull-Away, except for the call:

"Hill Dill, come over the hill
Or else I'll catch you standing still."

Mason and Mitchell, *Active Games and Contests* (1935)

## Prisoner's Base (also Dare Base)

Prisoner's Base used to be considered a game for boys only; but the hardier education of the young ladies of the present day has caused it to become a game for both brothers and sisters. The exercise and animation of this pastime will render it delightful on a cold winter afternoon.

It is played thus: A long straight line is marked out on the ground parallel with a wall, hedge, laurel fence, &c., but at about two or three yards distance from it; and this space is divided into two equal portions. These are called bases. One belongs to the first of the two parties or sides into which the players are divided, the other to their antagonists. At some tolerable distance from the bases, two prisons are marked out parallel with each other, with a good space between them; each prison must be opposite to its own party's base.

The players should consist of an even number, and should have two leaders or chiefs, under whom they must be equally divided.

They range themselves in a long row, just behind the front line of their respective bases, and the game begins by one player (called "the Stag") running from her own base in the direction of the prisons. When she has run a few paces she shouts "Chevy," at which signal, one from the opposite party rushes out and tries to touch her.

Instantly another player from the stag's party darts off to intercept the pursuer, whom she endeavours to touch before she can reach the one who began the game, and who, of course, makes for her own base again.

Player after player follows, each trying to "touch" an enemy or to avoid being touched by one.

Those who are touched on either side have to go to prison.

The leaders on both sides endeavour to rescue the prisoners from their adversaries, which they may do if they can reach the prison, and *touch* their captive followers, without being touched by the enemy themselves; but it is very difficult to achieve this, as a good look-out is kept over the prisons.

The game is ended when *all* the players on one side are in prison, with the leader, who alone can rescue them.

If the prisoners on both sides are all released, it is a drawn game, and they must begin again.

Valentine, *The Home Book of Pleasure and Instruction* (1868)

## Red Rover

The boy who is "it" is called the "Red Rover," and stands in the middle of the street, while the others form a line on the pavement on one side. The Red Rover calls any boy he wants by name, and that boy must then run to the opposite sidewalk. If he is caught as he runs across, he must help the Red Rover to catch the others. When the Red Rover catches a prisoner, he must cry, "Red Rover" three times, or he cannot hold his captive. Only the Red Rover has authority to call out for the others by name, and if any of the boys start when one of the captives who is aiding the Red Rover calls him, that boy is considered caught. The game is continued until all are caught, and the one who is first caught is Red Rover for the next game.

Culin, "Street Games of Boys in Brooklyn, New York" (1891)

## Ring a Ring a Rosie (also Ring Round Rosy)

Children go round, singing,

Ring a ring a rosie,
Pocket full of posie,
All the girls in our town,
Cry for little Josie.

At the last word all squat down. The one who is down the last is out of the game.

Pollard, *Plays and Games for Little Folks* (1889)

The children form a circle, taking hold of one another's hands, and circle around, singing:

"Ring round Rosy,
Pots filled with posies,
The one that stoops last
Has to catch."

At the last word all stoop; the slowest child or the one who "stoops last" must stand in the center of the ring and count ten. As the word ten drops from her lips all other children must rise and run in any direction, the "catcher" trying to touch some one or more of them; all thus caught must in turn help touch the remainder. The children who are being caught are at liberty to stoop at any time or place, and remain thus until the leader again counts ten, when all rise and run again. The game continues until all are caught.

Mustain, *Popular Amusements for In-doors and Out of Doors* (1902)
(Fig. 14)

## Rounders

This game is played with a ball and bats, or sticks something in the form of a policeman's truncheon. A hole is first made about a foot across and a half foot deep. Four other stations are marked with pegs stuck into the ground, topped with a piece of paper so as readily to be seen. Sides are then chosen, one of which goes in. There may be five or more players on each side. Suppose that there are five. One player on the side that is out stands in the middle of the five-sided space and pitches the ball toward the hole. He is called the feeder. The batsman hits it off, if he can; in which case he drops the stick and runs to the nearest station, thence to the third and all around if the hit has been a

Fig. 14.   Ring a Ring a Rosie, in Josephine Pollard, comp., *Plays and Games for Little Folks* (1889).

far one. The other side are scouting and trying to put him out, either by hitting the batsman (or runner) as he is running, or by sending the ball into the hole, which is called grounding. The player at the hole may decline to strike the ball, but if he hits at it and misses twice running he is out. When a player makes the round of the station back to the hole his side counts one toward the game. When all the players are out, either by being hit or the ball being grounded, the other side gets their inning. When there are only two players left a chance is given of prolonging the inning by one of them getting three balls from the feeder; and if he can give a hit such as to enable him to run the whole round all his side comes in again and the counting is resumed. The feeder is generally the best player on his side, much depending on his skill and art. The scouts should seldom aim at a runner from a distance, but throw the ball up to the feeder or to some one near, who will try to hit or to ground, as seems the most advisable. A caught ball will put the striker out.

This was a simple game, easily learned, designed simply for relaxation. Young boys and even girls could play it during their inter-vals from study in the schools. It is almost entirely devoid of the features that characterize baseball as now played in all our cities. Still "Rounders" or "Sockey," as it was sometimes called in portions of the States, was a popular game in its time and had many followers. It is still played in some of the Western and Southern States. The ball used is of course soft, and the sting when hit with it is slight. Sockey played with the hard regulation ball of the League or American Association would soon send half the players to the hospital.

Hall, *The Tribune Book of Open-Air Sports* (1887)

### Run, Sheep, Run
*Playground, Woodland*
*Late Elementary and Junior High Schools*

This is a team game of hide and seek. Two teams are chosen, one hiding and the other blinding. The captain of each team is the shepherd and does not hide, but he hides the others. When the captain of the hiding team has his players hidden he returns to the goal and accompanies the searching team. He calls warning to the sheep as the others search, either directly or through the use of code words, previously agreed upon. When a member of the searching team sees one of the hiding team he tells his captain, who calls "Run, sheep, run," whereupon all players of both teams run for the goal.

If the hiding players are not detected and the captain of the hiding team thinks the searchers are far enough away from the goal to enable his team to reach the goal first, he calls "Run, sheep, run." The player reaching the goal first wins the game for his side. Then the other side hides, and so on.

Mason and Mitchell, *Active Games and Contests* (1935)

## Sack Race (also *Sackhüpfen*)
*Playground, Picnic*
*Late Elementary School to Adult*

The contestants stand in burlap sacks which are long enough to reach to the hips. Holding the sacks hip high, they jump or run to the finish line. If they fall down, they are permitted to regain their feet and continue. A distance of twenty-five yards is far enough.

Mason and Mitchell, *Active Games and Contests* (1935)

## School-Keeping

This is likewise a favourite amusement with little children. One acts the part of the school-mistress, and all the others must obey her. They read, say lessons, bring their work to be fitted, are ordered to stand in the corner of the room for whispering, &c. Sometimes they vary this play, in the following manner: The school-mistress says, "Ah, Mary, you are a naughty little girl, you tell tales out of school." The one addressed says, "Who told you so, ma'am?" If the school mistress says, "My thumb told me," Mary must answer, "She knows nothing at all about it;" if she say[s], "My fore-finger told me," Mary replies, "Do not believe her;" if she says, "My middle finger told me," Mary says, "Let her prove it;" if the fourth finger, the an-swer is, "She is an idle gossip;" if the little finger, the whole school must exclaim, "Ah, that lying little finger!" If any one makes a mistake in these replies, the school-mistress orders some droll punishment, that will make the others laugh. Care must be taken to order and do every thing with good-nature and propriety.

[Child], *The Little Girl's Own Book* (1831)

## Shinny (also *Chueco;* Indian Hockey)

This is called "Hockey" in England, "Shinty" in Scotland, and "Bandy" or "Harley" in Ireland. It is played with a stout leather-covered ball, of the same size as that used for cricket, and sticks, shaped like a Golf-stick, but not so heavy at the turn. There are two sets of players, each of which have their own base. One on each side is selected as a "mounter." He places the ball at his base, and "mounts" it by driving it as far as he can with a blow of his shinny-stick toward the opposite base. Those on his side strive to help it along; those on the opposite side, to beat it back. If it be sent "home" to the opposite side, it counts one to the mount-er's party. If it be driven back it counts one to the others. Every man must "shinny on his own side;" that is, must drive the ball forward toward the opposite home. The party who drive it toward their opponents' home get the next mount.

The distance between the two bases—the "home" of one party is the base of the other—is two hundred and twenty feet; and the distance between the stations, from the base to the first station, and from the last station to the home, is twenty feet. The play should be for the best two in three games, or three in five.

The best ball with which to play is made of yarn, tightly wound upon an inch thickness of rubber, covered with well-sewed calfskin. Wooden balls and blocks are also played with, but these are objectionable, being very dangerous.

Shinny is one of the best of ball-games, and should not be marred by any unnecessary

Fig. 15  Street game of Shinny, in Frank M. Chapman, "A City Playground," *St. Nicholas,* June 1891.

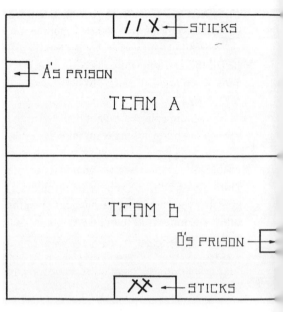

Fig. 16  Diagram of Stealing Sticks playing area, in Bernard S. Mason and Elmer D. Mitchell, *Active Games and Contests* (1935).

roughness on the part of the players. Our young friends should remember that the absence of good-nature and fairness will spoil any game, however good it may be.

[Hosterman], *In Door and Out* (1882)

(Fig. 15)

### Stealing Sticks

*Playground, Gymnasium*
*Late Elementary and Junior High Schools*

This is a game similar to Prisoner's Base, requiring team work, strategy, daring, chase, and capture.

Arrange the play area . . . and place three or four sticks in each stick base. The game proceeds just as in Prisoner's Base with all the rules of Prisoner's Base applying in regard to capturing and freeing prisoners. It presents the additional objective of stealing the opponents' stick. When a player succeeds in reaching the enemy's stick base and touching a stick without being tagged, he is permitted to take one stick back to his own territory without being tagged. Teams should organize and elect a captain and a stick guard. The stick guard stands

in front of the stick base but cannot enter it until an opponent enters it. The winner is determined by the number of sticks stolen.

Mason and Mitchell, *Active Games and Contests* (1935)

(Fig. 16)

### Tag

In its simplest form, one player, who is "it," attempts to tag, or touch, one of the other players, and when successful runs away, so as to not be tagged in his turn. The game is sometimes rendered more complicated by certain places which are called "hunks" or "homes" being agreed upon, where the players may find refuge when closely pursued.

Culin, "Street Games of Boys in Brooklyn, New York" (1891)

### Thread the Needle (also How Many Miles to Babylon?)

Thread the needle may be played by a considerable number of boys, who all join hands, and the game commences with the following dialogue between the two outside players at each end of the line: "How many miles to Babylon?" "Threescore and ten." "Can I get there by candlelight?" "Yes, and back again." "Then open the gates without more ado, and let the king and his men pass through." In obedience to this mandate, the player who stands at the opposite end of the line and the one next him, lift their joined hands as high as possible; the other outside player then approaches, runs under the hands thus elevated, and the whole line follows him, if possible, without disuniting. This is threading the needle. The same dialogue is repeated, the respondent now becoming the inquirer, and running between the two players at the other end, with the whole line after him. The first then has his turn again.

[Clarke], *Boys' Own Book* (1885)

## Threading the Needle

A boy and a girl, standing each on a stool, make an arch of their hands, under which an endless chain passes, until the hands are dropped, and one of the players is enclosed.

> The needle's eye
>     That doth supply
> The thread that runs so true;
>     Ah! many a lass
>     Have I let pass
> Because I wanted you.

Or—

> The needle's eye
>     You can't pass by,
> The thread it runs so true;
>   It has caught many a seemly lass,
> And now it has caught you.
>               *Massachusetts.*

In the following more complicated form of the game, in use half a century ago, both a boy and a girl were caught by the players who raised their arms:

> The needle's eye
> None can surpass

> But those who travel through;
>     It hath caught many a smiling lass,
> But now it hath caught you.
> There's none so sweet
> That is dressed so neat;*
>     I do intend,
>     Before I end,
> To make this couple meet.

The pair then kissed, and the game proceeded as in "London Bridge," ending with a tug-of-war.

Newell, *Games and Songs of American Children* (1883)

## Three-Deep
*Playground, Gymnasium*
*Late Elementary School to Adults*

Three-Deep is probably the best known and most commonly played circle game. Its popularity is doubtless deserved but some of its variations described below possess greater playing values.

First choose a player for chaser ("it") and another for a runner. Arrange the remaining players in a circle, count off by twos and have each number one step behind the player at his right. This quickly gives a double circle.

"It" chases the runner and attempts to tag him. The runner may become safe by going in front of one group of two and remaining there, thus forming one group that is "three deep." The chaser can tag the rear one of any group that is three deep. The player who finds himself at the rear of a group of three, should hasten to go in front of a group before the chaser can tag him. One who is tagged at once becomes chaser, and should tag the one who caught him if possible.

The rules for chasing vary as follows:

(1) Neither runner nor chaser is permitted to cut across the circle.

(2) The runner may cut across the circle at will but the chaser is not permitted to do so.

---

*"We considered this a personal compliment. I remember we used to feel very much pleased—children are so sensitive!"—*Informant.*

(3) Both runner and chaser may cut across the circle at will.

Nothing is gained by the first method. The second method places the odds in favor of the runner and slows up the game. A much faster and more satisfying game with more frequent changes, is achieved by using the third method and permitting both to run across the circle as they choose. Running away from the circle should be prohibited by restricting the play to a zone close up to the sides of the circle.

By frequent suggestions, the leader can discourage long runs and encourage frequent changes.

Mason and Mitchell, *Active Games and Contests* (1935)

## Tops

Tops are very good toys—that is to say, the peg-top and whip-top. The humming-top we have always looked upon rather slightingly, as unfit for any but very little boys; for there is no skill required in its use, nor does it afford healthy exercise, or teach a boy that lesson which even in the play-ground he may always be advantageously learning—namely, the right way of using his wits. Peg-tops are made of various kinds of wood, beech and box being the chief. Tops of box-wood, or "boxers," as they are usually called are much the best for all purposes, from their superior strength; and, as they are more expensive than tops made of other woods, they are generally provided with the best pegs. Every boy knows that there are two ways of spinning a peg-top—namely, *underhand* and *overhand*. The former method consists in holding the top, with the string wound round it, in the hand, with the peg downwards; and it is spun by suddenly dropping the top, and drawing away the string with a jerk, or snatch, as it falls. This is undoubtedly the easiest way of spinning; but it is justly decried by school-boys as a girlish and shuffling proceeding, and totally inferior in every way to the honest *overhanded* method of holding the top tightly in the hand with the peg upward, the end of the string being secured by a loop

round the little finger, or a button between the third and fourth fingers, and then bringing the top down, by a bold circular movement of the arm over the head, with a force which will make it spin three times as long as by the *underhand* method. We should advise our friends in this, as in every other more important affair in life, to eschew all underhand proceedings.

[Hosterman], *In Door and Out* (1882)

## Town-Ball

This is the game called "Rounders," in England, and is undoubtedly the origin of the popular game of Base-ball. It is played as follows: The players divide into two sides—about eight on each side is the best number. One side has first innings, and must assemble in the circle called "home," while the players on the *out* side are distributed over the ground to watch for the ball, or "fag out," with the exception of one, who acts as feeder, and whose position is indicated in the diagram. The first player on the *in* side takes up a little hand-bat, and the feeder pitches the ball toward him. The batsman strikes at the ball. If he misses it, or tips it behind the home, or if it is caught off his bat by any of the scouts, he is out, and the next player takes his place. If he succeeds in hitting the ball he at once flings down his bat, and runs off toward base No. 1, while the outsiders try to pick up the ball, and hit him with it, before he can get to the shelter of the base. If he can manage it, he may run to the second, or even the third base: and sometimes such a good hit is given to the ball, that he is enabled to run all round, from one base to another, and get home, before it is flung at him; and this feat is called a rounder, and counts one. However, suppose him only to have got to base No. 1, when the ball is thrown up, he must stay there until the feeder has it in his hands again to feed for the second player, who has now taken up the bat in the home. As soon as the feeder begins to feed, the player at any base may make a bolt for the next. The feeder knows this, and therefore sometimes makes a feint of throwing the ball to the batsman, while he really retains it in his hand, to have a shy at the incautious player, who leaves his ground; for when a base is once quitted, there is no returning thither. The player must run on to the next, and stand his chance of getting put *out* by the way. . . .

When all the players on one side, excepting two, have been put out, it is competent for the best player of the two, with his friend's leave, to demand *two fair balls for the rounder*. This arrangement is carried out in the following way: The less skillful player retiring altogether, the other stations himself in the "home," bat in hand, and the feeder begins feeding him. The batsman need not strike at any feed unless he likes, as he is to have two "fair" or favorable balls; but if he strikes at the ball, and misses, or does not send it far enough to warrant him in running, this counts as one of his two balls. At the second hit, he must, *nolens volens*, drop the bat, and start off at full speed; for his task is to accomplish a "rounder," and get home again, without being hit by the ball. If he accomplish[es] this, his whole side goes in again; if he fails, they are out. When some of the players on one side are out, and the remainder in different bases, so that the home is left empty, if even for a moment, the feeder, or any scout who can get the ball, may run into the home with it, or pitch it in, and then the other side is out; but if the ball misses the home, it counts one against the side who throws it. The side that counts most in rounders wins the match.

*American Boy's Book of Sports and Games* (1864)
(Fig. 17)

## Two-Deep

This is similar to Three-Deep except that players are in a single circle. When the runner steps in front of a player, that player becomes the runner.

This is a better game than Three-Deep in that the latter game keeps too many players inactive. When there are enough players for Three-Deep it is usually better to start two games of Two-Deep.

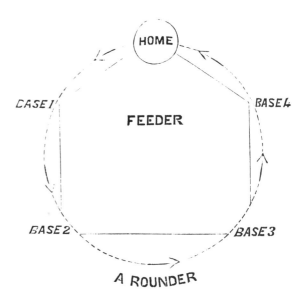

Fig. 17    Diagram of town-ball field, in *American Boy's Book of Sports and Games* (1864).

Mason and Mitchell, *Active Games and Contests* (1935)

## Two Old Cat

This differs from One Old Cat only in having two Batsmen, to whom the ball is pitched alternately, the Catcher for one acting as Pitcher for the other. The fielders are partly behind one Batsman and partly behind the other.

Champlin and Bostwick, *Young Folks' Cyclopaedia of Games and Sports* (1890)

## Bibliography

*American Boy's Book of Sports and Games: A Repository of In-and-Out-Door Amusements for Boys and Youth*. New York: Dick and Fitzgerald, [1864].

Bancroft, Jessie H. *Games for the Playground, Home, School and Gymnasium*. 1909. Reprint. New York: Macmillan, 1915.

Beard, Daniel C. *The American Boys' Handy Book*. New ed. New York: Charles Scribner's Sons, 1905.

Beard, Lina, and Adelia A. Beard. *The American Girls' Handy Book*. New York: Charles Scribner's Sons, 1887.

Berg, Albert Ellery, ed. *The Universal Self-Instructor and Manual of General Reference.* New York: Thomas Kelly, 1882.

Brewster, Paul. *American Nonsinging Games.* Norman: University of Oklahoma Press, 1953.

Brown, Florence W., and Neva L. Boyd. *Old English and American Games for School and Playground.* Chicago: Saul Brothers, 1915.

Champlin, John D., and Arthur E. Bostwick, eds. *The Young Folks' Cyclopaedia of Games and Sports.* New York: H. Holt and Company, 1890.

Chapman, Frank M. "A City Playground." *St. Nicholas,* June 1891, 609–16.

[Child, Lydia Maria Francis.] *The Little Girl's Own Book.* Boston: Carter, Hendee, [1831].

[Clarke, William?] *Boys' Own Book: A Complete Encyclopedia of Athletic, Scientific, Outdoor and Indoor Sports.* New York: T. R. Knox, [1885?].

Culin, Stewart. "Street Games of Boys in Brooklyn, New York." *Journal of American Folklore* 4 (July–September 1891): 221–37.

Fisher, Dorothy Canfield, et al. *What Shall We Do Now? 500 Children's Games and Pastimes: A Book of Suggestions for Children's Games and Employments.* New York: F. A. Stokes Co., [1907].

Hall, Henry, ed. *The Tribune Book of Open-Air Sports.* New York: New York Tribune Association, 1887.

[Hosterman, Arthur David.] *In Door and Out: A Book of Amusements for the Play Ground and Parlor.* Springfield, OH: Mast, Crowell and Kirkpatrick, [1882].

Mason, Bernard S., and Elmer D. Mitchell. *Active Games and Contests.* New York: A. S. Barnes and Co., 1935.

Mustain, Nelle M. *Popular Amusements for In-doors and Out of Doors.* [Chicago?, 1902].

Newell, William W., comp. *Games and Songs of American Children.* New York: Harper and Brothers, 1883.

Pollard, Josephine, comp. *Plays and Games for Little Folks: Sports of All Sorts, Fireside Fun, and Singing Games.* New York: McLoughlin Brothers, [1889].

Smith, Caroline L. *The American Home Book of Indoor Games, Amusements, and Occupations.* Boston: Lee and Shepard; New York: Lee, Shepard and Dillingham, 1873.

Valentine, R., ed. *The Home Book of Pleasure and Instruction.* Rev. ed. London: F. Warne; New York: Scribner, Welford, [1868?].

# Contributors

**David A. Gerber** is professor of history at SUNY-Buffalo and author of *Black Ohio and the Color Line, 1860–1915* (University of Illinois Press, 1976) and *The Making of an American Pluralism: Buffalo, New York, 1825–1860* (1989) and editor of *Anti-Semitism in American History* (1986).

**Russell S. Gilmore,** director of the Harbor Defense Museum in Fort Hamilton, Brooklyn, New York, is the author of *Guarding America's Front Door: Harbor Forts in the Defense of New York City* (Publishing Center for Cultural Resources, 1983). He holds a doctorate in American history from the University of Wisconsin and is a fellow of the Company of Military Historians.

**Katherine C. Grier** is a visiting scholar at the Humanities Center, University of Utah, and a former historian at the Strong Museum. Grier has a doctorate in the history of American civilization from the University of Delaware and is the author of *Culture and Comfort: People, Parlors, and Upholstery, 1850–1930* (1988). She is currently at work on a book about popular thought about animals and animal-human interaction in nineteenth-century America.

**Kathryn Grover** is an independent researcher, writer, and editor and former editor and director of publications at the Strong Museum. She holds masters degrees in journalism from the University of Michigan and in American history from Boston University. She has edited several books in American social and cultural history, including *Dining in America* (1987) and *Fitness in American Culture,* published by the University of Massachusetts Press in conjunction with the Strong Museum.

**Andrew Gulliford** directs the Public History and Historic Preservation Program at Middle Tennessee State University in Murfreesboro, Tennessee. He holds a doctorate in American culture from Bowling Green State University in Bowling Green, Ohio. He is the author of *America's Country Schools* (The Preservation Press, 1984) and *Boomtown Blues: Colorado Oil Shale, 1885–1985* (University Press of Colorado, 1989). For UMI Research Press he is editing *Museums and Material Culture in the American West.*

**Dwight W. Hoover** is a former professor of history and director, Center for Middletown Studies, at Ball State University and author of

*Magic Middletown* (Indiana University Press, 1986). He was also coeditor of *Sports and Society*, a 1983 volume in the *Conspectus of History* series.

**Bernard Mergen** is professor of American civilization at George Washington University and author of *Play and Playthings* (Greenwood Press, 1982).

**Madelyn Moeller** is former assistant director at Lockwood-Mathews Mansion Museum, Norwalk, Connecticut. She is currently the director of the Museum of Early Southern Decorative Art in Winston-Salem, North Carolina.

**Donald J. Mrozek** is professor of history at Kansas State University, where he has taught since 1972. He is the author of *Sport and American Mentality, 1880–1910* (University of Ten-

nessee Press, 1983) and received his doctorate from Rutgers University.

**Colleen J. Sheehy** is assistant director at the University of Minnesota Art Museum and recently received her doctorate in American studies at the University of Minnesota.

**Glenn Uminowicz** is director of the Berrien County Historical Association in Berrien Springs, Michigan, and serves as the chief historical consultant for a documentary film on Ocean Grove being produced for public television.

**Shirley Wajda,** bon vivant, recently received her doctorate in American civilization from the University of Pennsylvania and is an assistant professor of American studies and history at Boston University.

# Index

*Italicized* page numbers denote illustrations.

Temperance movement: antiforeign nativism and, 41; selective enforcement of antialcohol laws, 53

Temptations. *See* Backsliding

TenBroeck, Frank L., 30

Theater: at Asbury Park, 27; contributions of German community, 55

Thornley Chapel (Ocean Grove), 17, *18*

Threading the Needle (game), 247

Thread the Needle (game), 246–47

Three-Deep (game), 247–48

*Times* (London, England), 103

Timon, John (Bishop), 50

Top-spinning: childhood recollections, 174–75; methods, 248

*Torn Hat, The* (painting), 86–87

Town-Ball (game), 248–49

Toys: effect on children's lives, 181; favorite kinds (circa 1890s), 181; handmade, 177–78, *178*; improvised, in country schools, 191; manufactured, 178–81, *179*, *180*, *182*, *183*

Train service: to Asbury Park, 30; OGA preserving ban on, 30

Travel: as middle-class characteristic, 114; as recreational activity, 49–50; via stereographic images, 116–17

Trick shooting, 108

*Trout Fisherman* (painting), 81

*Trout Stream, The* (lithograph), 81, *82*

Turner associations, 40–41; festival participation, 52, *53*

Turnerfeste, 52

Twain, Mark, 88–89

Two-Deep (game), 249

Two Old Cat (game), 249

*Universal Traveller*, 114

Unstructured play: in country school playground, 189, *190*; intervention in, 214; social control and, 211–12; sport versus, 214

Urban culture: Alice Austen documenting, 150–51, *152*; angling as escape from, 77–78; effect on recreation, 42–50; play movement in, 191; value of play in, 219–20

Urban work, farm work versus, 44–45

Vacation, as retreat, 133–34

Vacation communities: Christian, *see* Religious resorts; "middle landscape" concept, 13

Vacation schools, 195–96

Van Dyke, Henry, 83

Variety shows. *See* Mass culture

Verbal play, in country school, 192

Vereine, 39, 51, 52; crowd control by, 53; Schützenbünde, 94–96, *96*

Vertigo, childhood play and, 173

Victorian house, physical layout meeting social needs, 123; disintegration of, 133, *134*

Victorianism, in America, 19; portrayed in stereographs, 132

Violations, camp regulations, 20; reporting of, OGA encouraging, 21

Violence, childhood play and, 169

Visiting, as recreational activity, 49

Visual literacy, 114–15, *115*

Voluntary associations, 47

Volunteer militia units, marksmen forming, 94

Wachtells Royals roller polo team, 72, *73*

*Waiting for a Bite* (engraving), 88

Waldorf, John Taylor, childhood memories, 177; books read, 182–83

Walling's Hall, 64

Walton, Isaak, 83

Ward, David, childhood memories, 173

Ward, H. Snowden, 156

Washburn, Jim, childhood memories, 180

*Weltbürger* (Buffalo, N.Y.), 51

Western culture, Catholic church as link to, 50

*Western Field and Stream*, 82

Westphal's Garden, 52–53

West Seneca (New York), as popular destination, 49

White, William Allen, childhood memories, 180

Wilderness, fishing in, 85–86; recapturing boyhood image, 86

Wild West shows, targetry in, 108

Williams, William Carlos, childhood memories, 176

Wilson, Emily, childhood memories, 164

Wingate, George Wood, 97; creating NRA, 97; organizing Amateur Rifle Club, 97; organizing American challenge team, 97–98; training New York Guardsmen, 103. *See also* International Rifle Match (1874)

Winter sports, 49

Wolfenstein, Martha, 222

Women: acceptable leisure activities for, 143–44; as amateur photographers, *see* Domestic photography; as country school teachers, 191–92; fishing and, 86, *87*, *88*; friendships, 49; participation in Schützenfest, 95; participation in sports, 66, *67*; participation in sports, Gulick's views on, 215; play prescriptions for, *218*, 218–19; rifle shooting practice, 105; in stereographs, non-traditional versus traditional roles, *130*, 130, *131*

Women's Christian Temperance Union, 18, 63

Women's Home and Foreign Missionary Societies, 18

Work: evaluating, standards for, 222; and overwork, 23; as play, children and, 175; as play, Gulick's views on, 213; rural versus urban, amusement possibilities and, 44–45; and use of time in middle class, 44–45

Work ethic, 23

World War I (1914–1918): effect on country schools, 202–4, *205*; effect on German community, 203

Worship pattern, at Ocean Grove, 16–18

Wurstschnappen (game), 52

Wysor, Jacob H., 64, 70

Young People's Temple (Ocean Grove, N.J.), 17

Zettler's Gallery, 106